VIOLENCE AND NAMING

BORDER HISPANISMS

Jon Beasley-Murray, Alberto Moreiras, and Gareth Williams, series editors

VIOLENCE AND NAMING

On Mexico and the Promise of Literature

DAVID E. JOHNSON

University of Texas Press
AUSTIN

Printed in the United States of America
First edition, 2019

Requests for permission to reproduce material from this work should be sent to:

Permissions
University of Texas Press
P.O. Box 7819
Austin, TX 78713-7819
utpress.utexas.edu/rp-form

♾ The paper used in this book meets the minimum requirements of ANSI/NISO Z39.48-1992 (R1997) (Permanence of Paper).

LIBRARY OF CONGRESS CATALOGING-IN-PUBLICATION DATA

Names: Johnson, David E., 1959– author.
Title: Violence and naming : on Mexico and the promise of literature / David E. Johnson.
Other titles: Border Hispanisms.
Description: First edition. | Austin : University of Texas Press, 2019. | Series: Border Hispanisms | Includes bibliographical references and index.
Identifiers: LCCN 2018025277 | ISBN 978-1-4773-1796-9 (cloth : alk. paper) | ISBN 978-1-4773-1798-3 (library e-book) | ISBN 978-1-4773-1799-0 (nonlibrary e-book)
Subjects: LCSH: Mexican literature—History and criticism. | Women—Crimes against—Mexico. | Women's rights—Mexico. | Violence—Mexico. | Violence in literature. | Literature and society—Mexico.
Classification: LCC PQ7118 .J64 2019 | DDC 860.9/972--dc23
LC record available at https://lccn.loc.gov/2018025277

doi:10.7560/317969

For Pauline and Elena

Cuando cuentes cuentos,
Cuenta cuántos cuentos cuentas
Porque si no cuentas cuantos cuentos cuentas,
Nunca sabrás cuántos cuentos cuentas tú.

SPANISH TONGUE TWISTER

CONTENTS

ACKNOWLEDGMENTS

Were it not for Margarita Vargas, in all likelihood I would never have fallen in love with Mexico. I owe her a tremendous debt of gratitude for this immense gift. Bronia Karst was vital for the completion of this book. More than anyone else, Bronia reminded me that it was time—*il est temps*, she would say—to get it done, and she was right. Once the manuscript was more or less finished, Bronia was its first reader. The text is better for her comments and questions. I thank her for this.

Although this book concerns Mexico, the writing of it took place in Santiago de Chile; Buffalo, New York; and Paris, France. The book began as a lecture and a three-part seminar given at the Instituto de Humanidades at the Universidad Diego Portales in Santiago, where I am lucky to count Andrés Claro, Juan Manuel Garrido, Aïcha Liviana Messina, Pablo Oyarzún, and Andrea Potestà among my friends. I owe the book's title to conversations with Juan and Andrés.

Several friends in Buffalo read and commented on parts of the manuscript: Galen Brokaw, Donald Cross, Paula Cucurella, Rodolphe Gasché, Shaun Irlam, Steven Miller, and Tyler Williams. I thank them for their comments and encouragement, but also for their good company, which has made Buffalo's too-long winters and too-short springs bearable. Stephen Gingerich and Martin Hägglund read the entire manuscript. Stephen's reading of my work is always challenging; his friendship, delightfully, is not. At just the right moment and in just the right way, Martin made just the right comment. I have come to expect this from him, and to depend on it.

Francesco Vitale of the Università di Salerno, Robbie Schwartzwald of the Université de Montréal, and the faculty of what is now the Department of Comparative Humanities at the University of Louisville invited me to read parts of the book at their respective universities. I thank them for these opportunities.

I drafted chapter 3 in Paris—in 2013–2014—while living in Andrés Claro and Miriam Heard's apartment, which they opened to me again in three successive Januarys (2016, 2017, 2018) while I continued working on the manuscript. The depth of my gratitude for their unstinting generosity, while surely finite, would be difficult to fathom.

Countless times over a period of some thirty-six months (beginning in January 2016), whenever I was in Paris during the writing and rewriting of this book, Andrea Garrido kept me company, often interrupting her hectic life to join me for lunch, dinner, or drinks, or to accompany me to the movies or to a museum. Andrea's conversation, laughter, and brilliant smile made Paris a brighter and warmer place during the three dark Januarys I spent there revising. No doubt I could have written this book without her support and the joyful distraction she provides, but both the book and my life would be poorer for having done so. I thank her for the gift of her time, but I also thank her brother, Juan, for having introduced us and for giving me her phone number—not without some hesitation—when I asked for it.

This book is dedicated to two women who, in singular ways, have left indelible marks on me. My mother, Pauline, is one-half (my father would say she's the better half, and he wouldn't be kidding) of a great American love story. The most enduring memory of my family life—with my two parents, seven siblings, multiple (and occasionally changing) in-laws, my parents' twenty-nine grandchildren (including James, who survives in all of us) and ten great-grandchildren (and still counting)—is of laughter, of wonderfully spontaneous yet nearly constant eruptions of laughter in all the kitchens and dining rooms and backyards of all the houses in which we have lived and in all the restaurants and hotels and sports arenas and on the sidewalks of the various cities we've visited together in the United States, Europe, Canada, and Mexico. Pauline was always at the center of it. She is the heart and soul of my family, the axis around which all our lives turn. And if the world grows increasingly dark for her, the memory of her light, like that of the sun, still shines in me. My daughter, Elena, reminds me of Pauline in the strength of her character, her love of laughter, and in her inexhaustible joy for sharing life. Simply put, Elena makes me laugh.

Parts of this book have been published elsewhere and in somewhat different form. Chapter 1 first appeared as "Dar(se) cuenta: La lógica del secreto," in *Modern Language Notes* 127, no. 2 (2012): 208–226 (copyright © Johns Hopkins University Press; reprinted with permission). Chapter 2 was first published as "Asesinato y símbolo: El resto del femicidio," in *Fenomenología, firma, traducción: En torno a Jacques Derrida*, edited by Zeto Bórquez, 407–436 (Santiago, Chile: Pólvora Editorial, 2015); ISBN 978-956-9441-02-8. A large part of chapter 3 first appeared as "As If, As Such: On Derrida, Husserl, and Literature," in *Research in Phenomenology* 45 (2015): 386–411. Finally, a portion of chapter 5 was published as "Rendir(se)," in *Revista pensamiento político* 2 (2012): 62–84. I thank Johns Hopkins University Press, Pólvora Editorial, Brill, and the Universidad Diego Portales for the right to reuse this material—revised and translated—here.

VIOLENCE AND NAMING

INTRODUCTION

Accounting for the Name

The Ciudad Juárez/northern Mexico feminicide and Felipe Calderón's "war" on organized crime; the massacre at Iguala; unremitting violence; dead bodies, corpses, cadavers, body parts, ashes—haunted by all the dead, by all the murdered and the disappeared, Sergio González Rodríguez notes, "For the legal system, the victim is usually one of the agents who are present or converge in an act of violence. Its existence is included in a juridical-police narrative that will determine the act of violence as conflict and will measure its injury" (2014, 63).[1] As the quantum of injury, the "victim" is a necessary figure in the juridical narrative. But "victim" is not only the unit of measure necessary for counting and calculating injury. The designation is itself a form of violence; it violates the injured by situating her within a discursive frame that accounts for her, as if she were nothing other, nothing more, than the injured, the victim; nothing more than that homogeneous unit of measure without singularity, without history. González Rodríguez observes: "In the absence of justice, the conformation and conformity of the victim turn it into a mere cipher beside others in some official register" (2014, 64). This or that singular being becomes one more instance—the "victim"—in the official chronology of "events":

> The victim usually appears as part of a judicial investigation that confers on it (her, him) the identity that links its (her, his) experience to the limit between life and death and institutional review, subject to chance [*al accidente*] and the eventualities of the probable. Its happening is incorporated into the logic of the chronological and the urgency of going each time farther back (to the antecedents) in order to clarify the truth of what happened. And although the victim finds itself (herself, himself) outside the judicial order, its stay in the world embodies the potential of being incorporated into the logic of the document and the official investigation, where the human phenomenon can be the letter and perhaps the ulterior cipher that in its turn fills columns of data in disciplinary registers. (2014, 67)

There are victims and there is victimization, but to *be* a victim—that is, to be counted as (only) a victim—is to be identified in such a way that one is no longer who or what one was: no longer part of a community, no longer a citizen, no longer a person with rights and his or her own story (*historia*, *cuento*). Rather, to be a victim is to be a cipher in an official chronology, part of an official history (*historia*), an official account (*cuenta*). The victim is situated—found *as* "victim" and therefore lost *as* "person"—in a series that precedes it, anticipates it, not only to explain what will have happened but also to anticipate the victim(s) to come, to explain *our* potential victimization. In this account, which takes the form of a count, we are all victims.

González Rodríguez complicates this becoming-cipher, becoming-figure—a chalk outline of a body no longer "there," "present," no longer capable of accounting for itself, one more integer in a series that never adds up, which is nevertheless a *certain* narrative, a *certain* account, *una cuenta*—by supplementing another narrative, another account, *otra cuenta*. He trades one *cuenta* for another, one body (a cadaver) for another (a life fleshed out): "Cuerpo/persona de Adriana Ruiz . . . cuerpo/persona de Genaro Macías . . . cuerpo/persona de Daniel Arteaga . . . cuerpo/persona de Elías Castillo . . . cuerpo/persona de Jesús Torrijos . . . cuerpo/persona de Eliud Naranjo . . . cuerpo/persona de José Barrera . . . cuerpo/persona de Rodolfo Nájera . . . cuerpo/persona de José Antonio Elena" (2014, 67–77). In each case, González Rodríguez gives an account of the "body/person" (*cuerpo/persona*) and the circumstances of its/his/her victimization—which range from threats, to abduction, to abduction and murder—and the body's condition when discovered:

> She is decapitated. She presents traces of torture. . . . In brief, his body is found in a spot on the outskirts of the city, close to the highway to

> Guadalajara. . . . The victims show a naked torso and traces of torture. . . . They shot him in the head and he bore the letter Z scored into his forehead. . . . They shot at him with firearms. . . . Behind the wall that divides the border, in United States' territory, a Border Patrol agent shot at the victim eight times: two in the head, four in the chest, the other bullets were incrusted in the wall of a doctor's office close to where the body fell. (2014, 68, 69–70, 75, 77–78)

González Rodríguez makes an important gesture, one calculated to remember not only the process of victimization, but also the life of the person victimized. Everyone, he is saying, is more than his or her victimization. We may all be (actual, potential) victims, but that is not all we are. Yet if the gesture to account for the person as much as for the body is imperative, it is also fraught, troubled and troubling, because in order to identify the "body/person" it is necessary to traverse the name: It is always the "body/person of . . ." followed by a given name. The body/person makes no sense without its belonging to, being identified by and as a given name. The risk is visible, legible even in gestures of mourning and memorialization. A street-art painting in the Shoreditch district of London, depicting the forty-three students murdered in Iguala, Mexico, makes this clear (fig. I.1). The mural of mourning-memorial-protest consists of the forty-three names of the murdered and disappeared: the names are painted principally in red, but certain letters and even entire names are in black, such that a black "43" appears amid a field of red. The names—which indicate forty-three singular beings, shorthand for forty-three different identities, each name condensing a narrative, an account, of a life interrupted, violated—nonetheless spell out an anonymous calculus: the forty-three names of singular beings become 43, a count, a sum, the number of victims.[2] The artwork's last line of protest testifies to the complicated relation of the name to the necessity of narrative and the ineluctability of calculation (fig. I.2): "THE 43 STUDENTS DISAPPEARED IN AYOTZINAPA GUERRERO HAVE NOT BEEN FORGOTTEN AND WE WILL KEEP SHOUTING OUT THEIR NAMES UNTIL THEY ARE FOUND AYOTZINAPA MEXICO 43." The name makes all the difference, for better and for worse. Without the name there is no chance for the narrative necessary to remember a singular being, but with the name that singularity is already displaced within an accounting, a calculation.[3]

The slash (/) marks the place of the name that puts "body" and "person" in touch with one another and, at the same time, inscribes an unbridgeable gap between them. The name suspends relation, both making it possible (putting us in touch with one another) and impossible (separating us, dividing us).

FIGURE I.1. Anonymous street art naming the forty-three students murdered in Iguala, Mexico. Photograph by Andrea Garrido Wainer; used by permission.

The name is that to which both body and person "belong" (*cuerpo/persona*). Belonging is inscribed on the bias, along the "slash" that divides the body/person from the name that identifies it/her/him and to which it/she/he "belongs." The possibility of such "belonging," in other words, is *im*possible inasmuch as it depends on a name that is not properly one's own, that can become one's own only through an act of *ap*propriation that is no less an act of *ex*propriation. The name's ineluctable gesture of "propriation" instances originary violence.[4] This becomes obvious in a series of notes that accompany González Rodríguez's identification—as body and person, thus as victim and something other, something more, than victim—of those he names in *Campo de guerra*. Of the "bodies/persons" named above, four of the names (Genaro Macías, Daniel Arteaga, Elías Castillo, José Barrera) have been changed to protect the victims' identities: "The name of the victim is simulated to protect its [*su*: its, his, her] identity" (2014, 147nn102–104, 107). The point is not that these people had "proper" names that were then changed to protect their identities. Rather, the point is that the structure or logic of naming simultaneously protects (creates and conserves) identity and violates it. Put simply, the name makes it possible to identify the other (oneself, a loved one, an enemy) *as* a singular being even as it "murders" the singularity of the other. This is the double bind of the name: it is necessary in order to recognize the other *as* other, *as* singular; and it necessarily destroys that singularity insofar as it renders it repeatable, imitable, substitutable. We are capable of recognizing, of identifying, whatever is or appears before us only *as* what it is, what it appears to be. This "as" marks the name and instances the originary, nonderivative, and unrelievable fiction of the world. The irreducible violence of the name opens the singular world of every other. Yet the violence of opening, of naming, cannot be limited; it cannot be domesticated or pacified. The violence that opens the world also ineluctably promises the violation that closes it.

If the burden—the responsibility—of anyone writing on, thinking about, or responding to violence (here, violence in Mexico) is to flesh out the narrative of a body's victimization, thereby remembering that the victim is always a singular being, a person (hence more than a victim) who has been victimized, then this responsibility can be fulfilled only by *naming* the person, thus

FIGURE I.2. Anonymous street art naming the forty-three students murdered in Iguala, Mexico. Photograph by Andrea Garrido Wainer; used by permission.

identifying and thereby *protecting* the person *as* this singular being. This is the violence of the name, the violence that opens the singular world of this or that singular person, that makes it possible to recognize another *as* who or what he/she is. Yet sometimes, to protect the person as this singular being, to save his/her life, it is necessary to violate the person by *not* protecting its (his/her) identity: changing its (his/her) name thus violates that identity. In short, in order to protect the person—while still giving account of her story, her life—it is necessary to deny her "her" name and to call her by another or in an other's name. But in denying the person her name, one violates the person who will have been *forged* in an act of violence, in the certification of a singular birth, of a singular death both documented and identified. In every case, in every instance of the name, there is violence. The possibility of memory, of remembering, is violence.

To do justice to the victims—who are always victimized twice (first in the assault on their bodies, on their persons; second in the account of that victimization, their reduction to the status of "victim")—González Rodríguez substitutes one name (a "proper" name, a pseudonym) for another (a classification: victim, victim of threats, torture victim, rape victim, murder victim); he substitutes one account (*cuenta*, a narrative), for another (*cuenta*, a statistical report). It would be a mistake, however, to think that we could tell which *cuenta* does more or less violence to the other, because there is only violence and an account (*cuenta, cuento*) must be rendered. Because the name refers to and identifies both the body and the person, it occludes the gap or interval—the slash—that both separates them and joins them, that suspends them. The name is necessary to account for the irreducible division not only *between* body and person but also, and no less irremediably, *within* the "person"; that is, the name makes it possible to identify the person as such even though such figuration—such naming—in determining the "who" or the "what" of the person, in delimiting the person as such, suspends any chance of knowing the singular person, as if a singular being could ever be known as such. Indeed, a singular being can be known only as if it were as such, that is, in and through the name. The unrelievable division within the person is an effect of temporal finitude, of our mortality. The name, which is necessary only because the person is divided from the body and within itself, is necessary to account for death, to explain the delay that makes everything possible even as it ruins its being "as such." The name, then, is the sign of our constitutive indebtedness, of a bill that is, from the start, past due and impossible to pay in full.

Because a name can be proper only insofar as it is not one's own, one always dies in the name of another, in a name to which one belongs but which is not one's own. But if we always die in the name of the other, it is also the case that we are mourned and remembered and that we mourn and remember, that we survive, in the name of the other. The violent logic of the name means, in effect, that from the moment we enter the world we are all victim-survivors. The following pages track the play of nomination—which both hides and reveals the violent separation, the wound, at the heart of all identity—from scenes of the conquest of Mexico to the feminicide in northern Mexico, from Bolaño's *Savage Detectives* and *2666* to the Zapatista revolt in Chiapas. And if the autoimmunity of the name means that violence is irreducible, unrelievable, then it is even more urgent to testify to the effects of violence, to bear witness both to constitutive and hence irreducible violence and to empirical and thus in principle avoidable, unnecessary violation.

Who will ever be able to tell one name (a given name, a proper name) from another (a pseudonym)? What name does not—*simultaneously*—both protect and violate, both grant and deny, the identity of the named? The name instances the first fiction *in* the world and the first fiction *of* the world. What name is not necessarily marked by the *as*-structure, by the *as if* at the heart of every *as*-structure? This is the question: How is the phenomenological "as"—the "as" of essence, thus the "as" of truth and of being, the "as such"—an effect of the "as if," of that which is not, of the made-up or fictive? What account (*cuenta*) in and of the world is not a story, a fiction (*cuento*) of the world? Another name for the irreducible "as if," for the originary *cuento* in and of the world, is "literature." At issue is another account of literature and the world, of the place of literature *in* the world, and of the opening of the world *in* literature. To put this another way, the following chapters think together two enigmatic but compelling statements: on the one hand, Roberto Bolaño's claim in *2666*, with reference to the numerous murders of women in northern Mexico, that "no one pays [*presta*: lends] attention to these murders, but in them is hidden the secret of the world" (2004, 439/2008, 348); and, on the other hand, Derrida's remark that literature is "the most interesting thing in the world, maybe more interesting than the world" (1992, 47).

Although this work focuses almost exclusively on social-cultural phenomena—the northern Mexican feminicide, the twentieth-century philosophical determination of the place of *lo indio* in Mexican culture, the Ejército Zapatista de Liberación Nacional (EZLN) and the revolution in Chiapas—and only rarely takes up literary texts (principally Bolaño), its principal concern remains literature. Ultimately, this is a work of *literary* theory in that it articulates a thought of literature that cannot be reduced to any other discourse or discipline; it cannot be reduced to anthropology, history, philosophy (whether understood as epistemology, metaphysics, ontology, or political philosophy), psychology, or sociology. None of these disciplines can do justice to literature even if in most cases literature is read as if it did these disciplines' work, as if it were virtually identical to them.[5] No doubt it often does and often is. Literature, however, is not exhausted in or by—which means it cannot be limited to—any discipline, not even its own. To be sure, literature often represents empirical (thus anthropological, cultural, and historical, whether individual or systemic/institutional) violence.[6] The argument articulated in the following pages is that "literature" concerns—which does not mean either "represents" or "thematizes"—constitutive violence. Such violence does not merely manifest itself *in* the world; rather, it *opens* the world, makes the world as such possible. It is the violence of finitude, and it shows up *in* and *as* the world *in* and *as* language. In other words, "before" it is an instrument of the human, language instances the violence that co-implicates the human and the world. This is irreducible, constitutive violence, and it is this violence that can be read in the play of nomination and in all the scenes of "cultural"—thus, reducible, unnecessary—violence.

Chapter 1, "*Dar(se) cuenta*: The Logic of the Secret," explains the paradoxical logic or economy of the secret as that which can be kept only by being told, which means the possibility of keeping a secret is its constitutive openness to others, its structural secretion. A secret separates "us" from others, thereby constituting singularity, identity, and culture, but it does so only insofar as it is shared, insofar as it is codified. Such codification depends on structural iterability. In sum, to keep a secret among "us" means exposing it to others. As that which both separates (secrets) and exposes (secretes), the logic of the secret is legible in the first scenes of encounter as described in Columbus's diary of his first voyage.

From the beginning, the diary's scenes of encounter are scenes of exchange, but between Columbus and his Amerindian "interlocutors" pass *both* things of little value ("*cosas de poco valor*": glass beads, or *cuentas* or *cuenteçillas*) *and* self-consciousness: Columbus traces his path through the Caribbean archipelago from the movement of beads that Amerindians return to him. This "economy" is repeated in 1519 in an exchange of "virgins" (twenty Amerindian women for one icon of the Virgin Mary), one of whom would become Malinche/doña Marina, ultimately the most important figure in the conquest of Mexico. Indeed, conquest happens over and across women's bodies and in women's names. Everything turns on a secret that passes through women, when an Amerindian man tells his Amerindian wife a secret she then reveals to Malinche, who then passes it to Cortés. One catastrophe (the destruction of Cortés's expeditionary force) is averted, while another (the destruction of the Aztec empire) is enabled. The secret instances the promise of culture, both the chance of its preservation and the threat of its ruin and loss.

Chapter 1 thus establishes this book's principal concerns: the economies of consciousness (the secret, the symbol, and the name) and the (dis)placement of women and Amerindians in Mexican culture. In the broadest sense, this work outlines a certain Columbian legacy and its critical inheritance; in other words, it concerns the *cuenta* (the bead, the bill, the account) Columbus will have left "us."

Chapter 2, "Murder and Symbol: Feminicide's Remains," takes up the logic of the symbol—the relation of name to body and its incorporation in the signature—as it operates in the late twentieth- and early twenty-first-century feminicide in northern Mexico, mostly in and around Ciudad Juárez. The feminicide (which refers to the killing of women because they are women) is often dated from 1992, the five-hundredth anniversary of Columbus's arrival. At stake in this chapter is a non-anthropological, non-sociological attempt to think about *how* to think about the murder of women because they are women. What is ventured in the assassins' "play" with the victim's identities? What is the "message" the murders send? For whom is it intended? What does it mean to refer to the bodies of murdered women—to this singular body, to this singular woman—as a symbol? The chapter draws largely from accounts of events around El Paso, Texas: the journalist Diana Washington Valdez's book *The Killing Fields: Harvest of Women* (2006) and the Mexican journalist Sergio González Rodríguez's *Huesos en el desierto* (2006). It also explores anthropological and sociological attempts to think about feminicide, employing all these sources to highlight the logic of the name and the symbol and to look at the fight over the right to use the murdered women's names. This latter struggle—between the mothers and relatives of victims (who are themselves victims of these crimes) and both national and international NGOs—is ultimately a struggle over symbolic capital. "Murder and Symbol" asks, simply, how do we count and account for the dead? How can we do justice to the murdered women? How can we avoid violating them (again) in the necessary—but nonetheless violent—(re)counting and accounting for them? How do we mourn the dead without murdering them once more? In short, how can we take an *interest* in the dead that is not *usurious*? Because these questions are not thematized in the anthropological and sociological literature surrounding the feminicide, the chapter concludes with a turn toward literature, toward Roberto Bolaño's *2666* and Alicia Gaspar de Alba's *Desert Blood: The Juárez Murders.* A large "part" of Bolaño's *2666* is famously devoted to an accounting and recounting of the murders, giving each, singular murdered woman, each victim, a pseudonym, thus both naming and unnaming, mourning and violating, each one in the impossible task of doing justice to each *one* while also accounting for *all* of them. Although in *Desert Blood* Gaspar de Alba speculates that the murders will be solved only when someone without any interest in them arrives to investigate them, Bolaño famously claims, "No one *lends* attention to the murders, but they hide the secret of the world," which suggests that *interest* must be *paid.* Chapter 2 concludes on this note, in the tension between the call for a disinterested justice and the desire for more interest in order to uncover the secret of the world.

Chapter 3, "As If . . . Literature before the World," picks up the question of interest and literature—what interest literature can have in the world—by turning to the Mexican polymath Alfonso Reyes's prolegomenon to any literary theory, his *El deslinde,* which he describes as a *fenomenografía* of the literary object. Reyes defines literature as a specific interest and intention that must contain a "minimum of reality." His definition of literature as necessarily dependent on an already constituted reality, along with his peculiar rejection of Husserlian phenomenology, demands a patient account of the problem of literature and its "noematic structure," both in Husserl's phenomenological project and in Derrida's transformational reading of him. Accordingly, this chapter constitutes the book's philosophical-theoretical center, the thesis of which is, simply, that literature "grounds"—*virtualizes*—the world: there is no world without the "as if" structure constitutive of literature. Or, as Derrida puts it, "Fiction cannot be derived," which means literature does not come after the world; it does not follow from any experience of the world. On the contrary, if the "as if" grounds experience and the experience of the world, literature must come before the world, before any subject in and of the world. The point is not that literature does not refer to the world. Rather, the world has the structure of literature. The stakes of this argument are immense. The world "as such" is in play. Previously literature's dependence on and representation of a "minimum of reality" meant that it was subordinate to or derivative of the disciplines of anthropology, history, physics, sociology, and even philosophy. Once literature is rethought as what Derrida calls "the most interesting thing *in* the world, maybe more interesting *than* the world," its peculiar or "strange" status opens the world in which and upon which the other disciplines depend. "Literature," therefore, is not simply the effect of an intentional consciousness. The intentional structure of literature exceeds the subject; indeed, literature names a nonsubjective, transcendental "fiction" *before* consciousness and the world. At stake is the difference (and thus the delay or deferral) that makes all the difference in and of the world. And this difference—which is nothing in itself, which is nothing other than the "as if"—violates the world it makes possible.

Chapter 4, "Killing Time: Jet Lag, or the Anachronism of Life," returns to Alfonso Reyes and his preoccupation with telepathy. For Reyes, telepathy instances the chance of a world without constitutive difference, thus without constitutive violence. Because Reyes's understands time—difference, delay—as a threat to human understanding, he posits an ahistorical "divine" origin of communication mirrored in a future "transmission" not of signs (language) but of things themselves. Against Reyes's conception of telepathy and literature, Roberto Bolaño theorizes the delay that makes all the difference in the world. Bolaño's incessant return to the figure of "jet lag"—as the figure for the temporal disjunction that opens the world and the possibility of life—provides the key for reading across his work, much of which focuses on Mexico and the relation between literature and violence. Jet lag, which "kills time," allows Bolaño to fret the same problems (the name, the body, the signature, and their iterability) that anthropological and sociological discourses of feminicide have been unable to think.

Whereas chapter 4 concerns Bolaño's response to the feminicide and his theorization of jet lag, the name, and the signature, chapter 5, "Suspending Sur/render: Accounting for the Other," returns to the problem of Mexico's inheritance of Amerindia in Mexico's postrevolutionary philosophical and cultural determination of *lo indio*, of its place in Mexican culture. The chapter concludes with a reading of the Zapatista texts and an interrogation of their appropriation as instances of an "indigenous" response to this philosophical and cultural delimitation and its critical reception. In short, it tells the tale of two inheritances of Columbus's legacy. On the one hand, reading from José Vasconcelos to Octavio Paz, the chapter outlines the way in which Mexican philosophy and cultural criticism have situated indigenous cultures as both necessary and marginal to Mexican culture. Beginning with Vasconcelos's *The Cosmic Race* (1925) and continuing through Samuel Ramos's influential *El perfil del hombre y la cultura en México* (1934) and Octavio Paz's *El laberinto de la soledad* (1950, 1959) and *Posdata* (1971), the discourse of *lo mexicano* describes indigenous culture as the static, pure (and thus unchanging) repetition of a form of life.

In these accounts indigenous peoples lack imagination and vitality. They are *at once* the dead weight holding down Mexican culture and the sacrificial force repeating itself in scenes of violence. (Hence the massacre at Tlatelolco is seen as one in a series of violent events inspired by Mexico's indigenous spirit of sacrifice.) Accordingly, the burden of postrevolutionary Mexican culture is to overcome its relation to indigenous tradition. This is one way to inherit Columbus's legacy. On the other hand, on 1 January 1994, the same day the North American Free Trade Agreement (NAFTA) became effective, the EZLN revolted, announcing their concerns and interests in two documents, one of which—"Chiapas: El suroeste en dos vientos" (Chiapas: the southwest in two winds)—defined NAFTA (and the neoliberal globalization that supports it and that it supports) as one more instance of colonial exploitation and thus as part of the five-hundred-year expropriation of indigenous peoples. The Zapatista uprising is another way to inherit Columbus's *cuenta.*

Finally, the postscript, "Fear of Democracy," takes up a series of recent works speculating on Mexico's democracy and its "future" in the wake of the "transition" from the PRI (Institutional Revolutionary Party) toward a more democratic state. Taking points of departure from Elena Poniatowska's *La herida de Paulina* (Pauline's wound) and Mexico's democratic response to abortion and the right of women to their bodies, the postscript addresses three pre-2012 (the election that returned a PRI candidate to the presidency) analyses of Mexican democracy: Héctor Aguilar Camín and Jorge Castañeda's *Un futuro para México* (2009), Guillermo Hurtado's *México sin sentido* (2011), and Roger Bartra's *La sombra del futuro: Reflexiones sobre la transición mexicana* (2012). In each of these analyses the question centers on establishing a purer, more authentic democracy. Again, the question is of interest and of loss and gain: How, here and now, can democracy guarantee an inheritance that can only be promised?

Although this work develops out of an engagement with Mexican culture and its legacy of cultural violence, it nevertheless describes a universal structure of constitutive violence. At stake is an understanding of "literature" as the name for unrelievable, originary violence. Wherever there is the "as if"—and the "as if" is everywhere, before everything, as the condition of whatever is *as such*—there is violence. The importance of this cannot be overstated. This work does not describe some Mexican cultural essence. On the contrary, the structures identified and described herein—the logics of the secret, of the name, of literature, of jet lag, of surrender—are universal. They are legible in every culture. Yet it would be a mistake to think that in the pages that follow these structures or logics are simply applied to the Mexican case, as if there were universal structures, on the one hand, and empirical phenomena, on the other, as if structures and phenomena exist without relation. It would be a mistake to think that the distinction between thinking *from* a culture (as if there were an indigenous thought, a thought absolutely immanent to a culture) and thinking *with* or *about* a culture (as if this thought were not already marked, contaminated by the culture about which or with which it thinks) was defensible, was valid. This has never been the case. The freedom of thought makes it impossible for any thought, any thinking, ever to be either simply from (within) or about (outside) a culture.[7]

Insofar as this book is a work of theory, the structures or logics herein described are necessarily universal. They must be legible everywhere, in every instance, in every context. That said, they nonetheless appear in Mexico—in Mexican cultural products and formations, in Mexican cultural institutions—in singular ways, with singular effects, with a singular legacy and inheritance. And if what this book describes is, first and foremost, the irreducible—hence necessarily involuntary, universal—violence of the name, of the act of naming, it is no less concerned with the legacy of violation, with the voluntary acts of violence that mark Mexican culture and Mexican institutions. It is important to stress that the one (irreducible violence) neither justifies nor excuses the other (the legacy of violation). Neither should they be conflated: the irreducible violence of our subjection and interpellation (of our insertion into language, into culture) and the constitutive violence of naming are not the same as the violation of women and of Amerindians. And while constitutive violence is necessarily irreducible, the violation of women and Amerindians ought to be reducible, eliminable. But the reduction of the violation of and the violence against women and Amerindians, of and against any other, of and against ourselves, nonetheless entails constitutive violence. Consequently, the violence necessary for the elimination of the violation of others ineluctably opens the ongoing chance of the violation of others. There is no way around this dilemma, and because there is none, it is all the more urgent, more necessary, to remain vigilant and to mark the moments—the instances—of empirical violation.

CHAPTER 1

DAR(SE) CUENTA

The Logic of the Secret

La acción de los hombres en el tiempo es la historia. A condición de que alguien quede para darse cuenta de lo que ha pasado. Ese darse cuenta, por su parte, es precisamente la acción de la historia sobre los hombres. Por ese darse cuenta podemos ponernos en una actitud de recibir o rechazar el pasado.

ARTURO USLAR PIETRI, *LA INVENCIÓN DE AMÉRICA MESTIZA* (1996)

Le secret . . . brûle—les mains et la langue—on ne peut pas le garder, c.q.f.d. Il reste secret, ce qu'il est, mais doit aussitôt circuler, comme la plus hermétique et la plus fascinante des lettres anonymes—et ouvertes.

JACQUES DERRIDA, *LA CARTE POSTALE: DE SOCRATE À FREUD ET AU-DELÀ* (1980)

Edmundo O'Gorman's *La invención de América* (1958) establishes the philosophical and historical conditions for the discovery of "America." The act of discovering, he explains, depends on the consciousness of the discoverer and on the being (or meaning) of the discovered. O'Gorman proposes the following example: "Let us suppose that the night watchman of an archive finds an old papyrus in a storeroom. The next day he tells a university professor of classical literature who recognizes it as a lost text of Aristotle. The question is this: Who is the discoverer of this document, the night watchman who found it or the professor who identified it?" (22). O'Gorman argues that in this case there are two discoveries. If one speaks of the discovery of the papyrus itself—as a physical object lacking any meaning—the discoverer is the night watchman. But if one speaks of the discovery of Aristotle's lost text, then the discoverer is the university professor, because he "was conscious" (22) of the meaning of what was discovered. He thus concludes: "If someone knowledgeable of the event wished to maintain that the true discoverer of the Aristotle text was the archive's night watchman and that he deserved the scientific fame for the discovery, no one would be in agreement unless it was demonstrated that he was conscious of what he had found in that storeroom. This is precisely the situation in which one finds Oviedo and everyone who, after him, sustains that Columbus was the discoverer of America" (22).

At stake is the possibility of finding something without discovering it, of stumbling upon a terrestrial mass without recognizing it, without knowing what it "is." It is the chance of the event of discovery. There can be no doubt that Columbus arrived at a landmass, but insofar as he thought that he had arrived on the coasts of India, he never found himself in the New World *as such*. On the first voyage he never had consciousness of the event of his discovery of a landmass previously unknown to Europeans. He never realized what had happened, what it meant for him to be there. Or, more exactly, what Columbus took to be the meaning of the event, was not.

According to O'Gorman, the discovery of America depends on the difference between "existence" and "being." The distinction challenges what was, at the time O'Gorman was writing, the dominant interpretation of the twentieth century: Samuel Morison's understanding, promulgated in his *Admiral of the Ocean Sea* (1942), that Columbus had discovered America by accident. In other words, Columbus discovered America without having intended to do so, without realizing (*darse cuenta*) he had done so, hence without being conscious of the meaning—the *being*—of the landmass. In O'Gorman's argument, Columbus could have discovered America only if America were something in itself, if it were endowed with "a fixed, predetermined and inalterable being" (48). That is, "the being—not the existence, notice—of things would be, thus, something substantial, something mysteriously and intimately sheltered in the things; their nature itself, that is to say, that which makes things be what they are" (48). O'Gorman argues that were the being of things substantial, their meaning would be immutable and, therefore, the same for everyone. Such an understanding of the world implies that the meaning or sense of things is not the attribution or effect of the consciousness that finds or invents them. It is against this understanding that O'Gorman emphasizes that the discovery depends on a "being aware" or "having consciousness" ("*tener conciencia*") that attributes meaning and, along with it, being, to what is found. In this scientific and philosophical revolution, the secret, mystery, is lost. In the moment O'Gorman identifies being as *meaningful existence*, as sense, and determines phenomenologically that meaning results from intentionality or a certain "being aware," he excludes the possibility of the secret. Insofar as the being (meaning) of the thing does not exceed the intentionality of the subject, the being of the thing—whatever it might be, the sun, the moon, America, a glass bead—cannot remain secret. Things neither resist us nor reveal themselves to us. Rather, both resistance and revelation depend on intentionality and, as O'Gorman declares, "the American continent is not, obviously, something capable of having intentions" (46). Like any other thing, "America" is a cipher, and as a cipher, it only *corresponds* to "its" being, which means that its being—its meaning or value, its sense—is the effect of an economy. Consequently, the being (or meaning) of the thing is not its own, is not proper to it. There is always a distance, a difference, an interval or delay between existence and being, a difference that constitutes the thing *qua* thing, that is, *qua* meaningful, identifiable. This difference is ciphered in the thing *as* thing.

When Columbus found himself among the islands of the Caribbean thinking that he had arrived in the Asian archipelago, nothing revealed itself to him. He had not discovered anything: the American continent did not reveal its secret simply because it had no secret. Columbus's conviction that the islands in which the Spaniards found themselves corresponded to the Asian coast for a short time established the *being*—the meaningful existence—of the continent until others realized that the landmass represented, *for Europeans*, an unknown continent. For a short time, the being of the landmass upon which Columbus ran aground corresponded to the being of the Asian continent, simply because, on the one hand, no European knew the difference between the two and, on the other hand, as O'Gorman signaled, the continent itself was incapable of intentionality and therefore had no proper being. It had no proper meaning, no consciousness of itself: the landmass could not say what it was, what it meant. Being is granted to the continent: "The evil that is at the root of the entire historical process of the idea of the discovery of America consists in the supposition that this piece of cosmic material that we now know as the American continent has been that forever, when in reality it has been that only since the moment in which that meaning [*significación*] was conceded to it, and it will cease being it the day on which, through some change in the current conception of the world, we no longer concede it that meaning" (49).

On the one hand, consciousness renders the landmass meaningful, thereby giving it being and whatever meaning it has (first, on Columbus's account, Asia, later, the American continent, the New World). On the other hand, because the found object has no intentionality and thus no being or meaning of its own, it can never surrender itself to the consciousness that discovers it. Discovery is thus always an act of appropriation. Because the object cannot surrender itself, however, and only consciousness can render it meaningful, a gap remains between being and existence. This gap or interval marks the non-self-coincidence of both the object and the consciousness that intends it. In short, what remains is the gap or delay between the object that cannot surrender itself, insofar as it is incapable of giving account (*dar cuenta*), and a consciousness that in giving account of the other (*dar cuenta del otro*) ineluctably gives account of itself (*darse cuenta*). Between the object that cannot render itself and the consciousness that can render itself only in rendering the object, the trace of the other, the secret of the other, remains.

The pages that follow account for the secret that cannot (not) be told and that in being told cannot (not) be shared. At stake is a structural secret between existence and being, death and life, the body and the name. At stake is the secret of violence.

THE LOGIC OF THE SECRET

In the 1930s the French surrealist poet Antonin Artaud traveled to Mexico, Roger Bartra observed, "with the certainty that the Indians would reveal to him" the secret of the Mexican soul, which Artaud believed to be "capable of unchaining ancient natural forces that can regenerate modern man" (1987, 90). In "La cultura eterna de México," one of the lectures published in 1936 in *El Nacional*, Artaud writes, "Mexico possesses a secret of culture bequeathed by the ancient Mexicans" (176). Such a secret would govern the manifestation or appearance of distinct civilizations. Artaud affirms that there exists "an essential difference between civilization and culture" and that "the exterior forms of art can differentiate among themselves a multitude of civilizations, but their variety leaves intact the profound spirit of a culture. Beneath the diverse exterior appearances that only art differentiates, exists in Mexico a unique cultural aspiration" (179–180). According to Artaud, the appearing of different civilizations—which distinguish themselves through the forms of their art—suggests that there is a unique or single culture that organizes and unifies them. Civilizations, therefore, appear as empirical modifications of the underlying and foundational culture that becomes knowable only by means of civilizational phenomena.

In "Secretos eternos de la cultura," an essay that makes no distinction between one underlying and regulating culture and multiple, empirical civilizations, Artaud holds that "every authentic culture has its secrets" (192). What is the secret of authentic Mexican culture? Artaud answers that

Mexican culture is "the coppery culture of the sun" (180). For him it is not a question of elaborating the multiple figures or metaphors of the sun. Unlike what occurs in Europe, where "a state of decadence" reveals itself in "the confusion of words" because "words no longer mean anything" (135), in Mexico, in "the part of the Mexican soul that has remained pure of all influence of European spirit" (181), the secret means *only one thing*. It has only one meaning and is therefore not equivocal. The secret of Mexican culture, he writes, "is not a charlatan's secret" (180). On the contrary, "in the ground of the true solar culture" lies "a secret meaning" (183), what Artaud calls, "the true secret" (184). Although the sun appears to be "the maintainer of life" and "the fecund element, the provocative sovereign of germination," it "is a principle of death and not a principle of life" insofar as it "ripens what exists" (184). This is the secret of "authentic" Mexican culture: "The very ground of the ancient solar culture consists in having signaled the supremacy of death" (184).[1]

The eternal secret of Mexican culture is death, which "is transformational" (184). The sun "burns, consumes, calcinates, eliminates, but does not destroy all that it suppresses. It maintains the eternity of its forces by means of which life conserves itself beneath the pile of destruction and thanks to destruction itself" (184). Life nourishes itself from the finitude of death and the transformations that finitude implies: "Life maintains its continuity through the transformation of the appearances of being" (184). Culture is born of the universality and singularity of death. Life is death in that life manifests itself in the always conditioned appearing of life, such that life as such never is.

The inscription of death as the singularization of life, as its appearing, leaves a trace of the meaninglessness of death—its *sin sentido*—in life. Death names the absolute secret, as Derrida affirms in *Aporias*, "since it signs the irreplaceable singularity. It puts forth the public name, the common name of a secret, the common name of a proper name without name [*le nom commun d'un nom propre sans nom*]" (1996a, 130/1993a, 74). Insofar as it denominates the secret of the secret of culture, death marks the limit (the "*margen de vacío*," "margin of emptiness"), according to Artaud) in which—universally, without exception—all living beings exist. At the same time, however, the limit is that which no one can experience. Thus Derrida contends that "culture itself, culture in general, is essentially, before anything, even a priori, the culture of death" (83/43). Consequently, he asks: "Who will guarantee that the name, the ability to name death (like that of naming the other, and it is the same) does not participate as much in the dissimulation of the 'as such' of death as in its revelation, and that language is not precisely the origin of the nontruth of death, and of the other" (132–133/76). Derrida's question announces the principal concern of this book.

What does it *mean* to name death, to name the other? What violence is done to the "other" in such naming? But also, and no less important, what is the alternative? How *not* to call death, to call the other, by name? If there is meaning, if life makes any sense at all, has any value at all, it does so in relation to death, to finitude. And if this is so, how, then, to avoid naming death, naming the other? These are not idle questions. They go to the heart of all community, of all politics. We cannot not name death; we cannot not name the other. Yet naming death, naming the other, as Derrida suggests, dissimulates death and the other, does violence to them, erases them, murders them, in the moment that such naming makes life meaningful by exposing the living being to death and the other. In short, insofar as life "is" death and insofar as we can never (not) say either *what* or *that* death *is*, it is necessary finally—as Artaud put it—to recognize that "no one has ever been able to say what life is" (1984, 192). We name death and the other in order to say *what* life is and that life *is*, but in doing so we ineluctably ground life's meaning, hence its being, on a simulacrum, a fiction, *un cuento*. Which means, simply, life remains as secret to the living being as it is foreign to it.

Artaud's engagement with Mexican culture makes clear the limit of the anthropological interpretation of the secret of culture: namely, the desire to reveal a secret capable of "regenerating modern man" (Bartra 1987, 90). This desire reveals itself in Artaud's insistence that "every authentic culture has its secrets" (Artaud 1984, 192) and in his contention that the foundational secret of authentic culture is, at the same time, both meaningful and ineffable: "The true secret will not be revealed, because it forms part of the ineffable. At the foundation of every true culture exist . . . ineffable secrets, because they proceed from that margin of emptiness [*margen de vacío*] where our eternal ignorance obliges us to situate the origins of truth" (193). The logic of Artaud's understanding of the secret results in an unrelievable paradox. On the one hand, the secret must be meaningful, for if it were not, it would be impossible to distinguish authentic and inauthentic cultures. On the other hand, the secret must be ineffable, for if it were revealed (known, articulable), it would be repeatable, imitable, by everyone, which would ruin the distinction between authentic and inauthentic cultures. Therefore Artaud recognizes that were the secret known to those who belong to an authentic culture, it would already be revealed to too many. Accordingly, the secret of an authentic culture cannot be told *even to the members of that culture*. The secret must be kept from those who keep the secret of culture.

For a meaningful and ineffable secret to establish the limit between authentic and inauthentic cultures—to distinguish ourselves from others—the secret would have to be universal and immediately communicable to everyone (of us) without its running the risk of exteriorization, without its being mediated by any communicative technology (including language itself). It would have to be telepathic but restricted in its dissemination. It follows from these strictures, however, that Artaud's distinction between authentic and inauthentic cultures is untenable insofar as a meaningful and immediately communicable secret cannot describe the limit between us. Such a secret would not be a secret in that it would be open—exposed—to everyone.[2]

If it is true that death "names" the secret of culture, it can do so only because death "itself" or "as such" has no meaning—because we don't know what "death" names—and, at the same time, is universal and singular. From the moment in which a culture (and this is the moment of the possibility of culture) organizes its "relation" to death and gives it meaning—hence, from the moment we call death by its name, "death"—a secret determines the limits and thus the form of culture. But this secret (the secret that is the meaning or sense of death) is neither universal nor ineffable. It follows, then, that the necessity—the demand—for the secret is universal and unavoidable, while the secret is always singular. Indeed, the secret denotes the aporetic logic or structure that opens the possibility of relation and communication. The secret marks and at the same time trespasses the borders separating and identifying cultures and communities. The secret is defined in the paradoxical demand that it be *simultaneously* told and kept. Only in telling the secret is it kept, and only by keeping the secret is it told. This aporetic logic has two implications. First, the secret—and therefore culture—is essentially tied as much to narrative (whether understood as story/account or telling/recounting/accounting) as to calculation (as counting/accounting). In each case, it is a question of the relation of the Spanish verb *contar* (to tell, to count) to the substantives *cuento* (story) and *cuenta* (account), which are also the first- and third-person singular conjugations of *contar* in the present tense. There is no secret that is not realized and of which an account is not given, in every sense, then, of the Spanish idiom *dar(se) cuenta*, which means, in its reflexive form, "to realize" or "to be aware" of something (*darse cuenta*), and also, nonreflexively, "to give account" (*dar cuenta*). Second, that the secret is kept by being told and is told by being kept means that it is structurally incalculable and asymmetrical. On account of the secret's structural openness to the other, there is no secret that can be told among us and remain kept among us, that remains restricted to us, absolutely and without remainder. This is the law of the secret. By definition, there is no secret that is not exposed to the other. This exposure or openness is not an empirical modification—a corruption or violation—of a secret that ought to remain, in principle, closed off from others and kept only among us. On the contrary, the exposure to the other is the ultra-transcendental principle of the possibility of the secret, which means the possibility of such empirical exposure is inscribed within the transcendental rule of the secret: no secret without contamination and corruption, without the betrayal of the secret. In other words, the possibility of betrayal instances the historicity of the secret, its necessary historical inscription. The secret, then, is not an Idea in the Kantian sense, abstracted from the circumstances of space and time but nonetheless providing a rule or limit to the understanding; on the contrary, spatial-temporal circumstances—finitude—make the secret inevitable and impossible. The absolute and universal necessity for the secret instances the demand for the singular secret *here and now*, the secret between us that divides us and, at the same time, constitutes us—our identity—in that division. As Artaud understood, however, this demand ineluctably exposes us, opens us to the future, to the absolute other, to death. Each secret, *here and now*, immediately and without relief, opens us to death. The secret inscribes the other—the future, death—in us, *here and now*, as the condition of auto-affection and, therefore, of life. If the secret protects us from the other—secreting (hiding, occulting) us, dividing or separating us from the other—it also exposes us to the other, secreting (suppurating) us absolutely. The secret secretes.

SECRETS BETWEEN US

The secret articulates the limit of culture, of the possibility of culture, and thus determines the difference between cultures. In the encounter of cultures, at the border between cultures (and there is always more than one culture), the secret is always in play. The secret is the issue of the border. On the one hand, there are those who want to discover the secret, to extract or steal it; on the other hand, there are those who want to keep the secret, to protect and preserve it. The border traces the inscription of the economy or logic of the secret: the secret must be told in order to secrete it away (for "us") and to secrete it (to "others"). But if to secrete is to secrete, then the secret is always already a secretion shared between (at least) two.

We pass the secret, however, neither to "enemies" nor to "strangers." We keep it among us; we share it among "friends," between "brothers." But since the secret is that which determines friends and enemies, brothers and strangers, us and them, it is always possible that in passing the secret between "us," it slips away to "them." This limit of the secret is legible in the history of the conquest of Mexico, in the archive that anticipates the formation of modern anthropology some three centuries later, that is, in Bernardino de Sahagún's remarkable *Historia general de las cosas de Nueva España* (c. 1585).[3] The first sentences of Sahagún's prologue establish the horizon within which the *Historia* must be read: "The doctor cannot correctly apply medicines to the sick without first knowing from what humor, or from what cause the illness proceeds; so that the good doctor must be expert in the knowledge of medicines and of illnesses, in order to apply . . . to each sickness the contrary medicine" (17). For Sahagún, priests and confessors are "doctors . . . of souls" and in order "to cure spiritual sicknesses they should have experience of spiritual medicines and illnesses" (17). It is vital, then, for them to "know what is necessary to perform their duties" (17). But Sahagún suggests that not knowing the indigenous language makes it impossible for the priests and confessors to ask Amerindians about their idolatrous practices, and, were they able to ask, they would be incapable of understanding their responses. According to Sahagún, the *Historia* is "like a trawl to bring to light all the words of this language with their proper and metaphorical significations" (18), and he claims that the *Historia*'s twelve books will be "a treasure for finding out many things worthy of being known and for facilitating knowledge of this language with all its secrets" (21). Moreover, and not unimportantly, Sahagún confesses that it is out of love for the other that he wants to know the secrets of the Amerindian language: "It is very certain that all these peoples are our brothers, proceeding from the tree of Adam like us; they are our neighbors, whom we are obliged to love as ourselves" (20). We must learn their language as a gesture of love: for us to *save* our *brothers*, our *neighbors*, those who are *like us*, we must know their secrets. Their salvation requires us to learn their language, the technology that permits them to keep their secrets to themselves, thereby secreting—separating—themselves from us. Language is the mechanism, the operator of the secret, of secrecy and, inevitably and unwittingly, of secretion. The appearing of language inaugurates the secret. The possibility of communication—even with oneself, in oneself, thus in secret—depends on the necessary and yet impossible secret.

Because it marks or traces the limit between the two sides of encounter, and does so as the cipher of the difference between cultures, the secret implicates translation—among friends as much as among enemies, between "us" and "them." Perhaps nowhere and at no time in the history of the conquest of Mexico is the violence of the secret—its determination of friends and enemies and the ineluctable violence it does to "us"—more dramatically and economically exemplified than on Cortés's march from Veracruz to Tenochtitlán in 1519, on the road to Cholula, when Cortés realized that, on Moctezuma's orders, the Cholultecans were preparing an ambush. In his *Historia verdadera de la conquista de la Nueva España* (1576), Bernal Díaz del Castillo writes that the Spaniards were on high alert because they were certain—from information that they had forced out of Moctezuma's ambassadors—that the Mexicas as well as the Cholultecans were going to attack them. Although the Spaniards already knew of the threat, Bernal Díaz narrates or tells (*cuenta*) an account (*cuenta*) or story (*cuento*) that reveals the relation between the secret and intimacy or familiarity. He explains:

> An old Indian woman, the wife of a chief, since she knew of the agreement and plot that had been ordered, came secretly to Doña Marina, our translator [*nuestra lengua*], and as she saw that she was a beautiful and rich girl, she told and advised her to go with her to her house if she wanted to escape with her life, because certainly that night or another day they were going to kill us, because it had already been planned and ordered by the great Moctezuma. (Díaz del Castillo 1991, 219)

It is a question of proximity, of familiarity. The old woman sees in Marina a person like herself. She sees her as "family," as one of "us," insofar as she wanted to marry her to one of her sons. She thus sees Marina as belonging on "this side" of the border between "us" and "them." So she tells Marina the secret, because secrets are always kept among us. But to keep them among us, they must be told, shared, among us. And it is finally impossible to know if another is one of us or is one of them, one of the others. It is impossible, in the final accounting, to know if we are not to be counted among the others. According to Bernal Díaz, Marina—whom the old Amerindian woman undoubtedly identified as Malinche or Malintzín, that is, by her Amerindian name—played her part well: she "dissembled with the old woman" (220) in order afterwards to tell (*contar*) everything to Cortés.

It would be a mistake, however, to deduce from this anecdote that in Mexico, or anywhere, for that matter, the secret passes only between women or that only women betray the "fatherland," the "nation-state," or, more simply, that they betray "us." Culture is opened or opens itself to the other not simply through women. When Marina asks the Amerindian woman: "'How, this business being so secret [*siendo tan secreto ese negocio*], did you find out about it?'," according to Bernal Díaz, "she said that her husband, who is captain of a district of that city, told her" (219). The secret—in order that there be a secret—is betrayed, revealed, by whoever keeps it. The secret passes between us in order to identify us, in order to establish the line between those who "keep" the secret and those from whom it is kept. But the possibility of the secret depends on it passing between (at least) two, and for it to pass between (at least) two, it must be open, exposed to everyone. Legible in this scene is the impossible calculus of the secret: the structure of "$n + 1$" that defines the promise—both the chance and the threat—of the secret.[4]

Although the secret does not pass only between women—that is, although structurally the secret is open to everyone, without exception—historically, men have accused women of telling their secrets, which means, simply, that men have thought women incapable of *not* telling *their* secrets. For instance, in the *Secreto de los secretos*, a Spanish version of an Arabic text once mistakenly attributed to Aristotle and in which pseudo-Aristotle advises Alexander the Great, the introductory paragraph reads: "Never reveal your secrets to women or to children, because women and children hide what they do not know" (Jones 69). Women and children hide or keep only the secrets they do *not* know. Yet the logic of the secret demands that for a secret to be kept, it must be told. Consequently, for there to be secrets between men, such secrets must be open to women in that they must be structurally open *to any and every other*. Betrayal is inscribed not in women but in the logic of the secret.

In *El laberinto de la soledad*, Octavio Paz grants an important, albeit negative, place to Marina/Malinche (and by extension to women in general) during the Conquest and in the subsequent development of Mexican culture. He named her "la Chingada" and described her as "passive": "Her passivity is abject: she does not resist violence, but is an inert heap of bones, blood and dust. Her taint is constitutional and resides . . . in her sex. This passivity, open to the outside world, causes her to lose her identity. . . . She loses her name; she is no one; she disappears into nothingness; she is Nothingness. And yet she is the cruel incarnation of the feminine condition" (1999, 94/1985, 85–86). The determination of her passivity, however, is somewhat confused, for la Chingada—or the one whom Paz also calls "*la Madre violada*," incarnated by Malinche—does not merely resist her violation. Her opening to others is voluntary, in Paz's account, and thus constitutes a betrayal. Paz writes: "If the Chingada is a representation of the violated Mother, it is appropriate to associate her with the Conquest, which was also a violation, not only in the historical sense but also in the very flesh of Indian women. The symbol of this violation is doña Malinche, the mistress of Cortés. *It is true that she gave herself voluntarily to the conquistador*, but he forgot her as soon as her usefulness was over" (1999, 94/1985, 86; emphasis added). In saying that she gives herself voluntarily to Cortés, Paz himself violates

Malinche/Marina. The moment Paz defines Malinche as abject passivity, it becomes unreasonable to blame her for her "relation" to any other and thus for the violation of which she is the victim. To accuse or blame her, thereby making her responsible for the Conquest, one must attribute to her an agency, and thus a certain freedom. An abject, absolute passivity is not free. In any event, it is legitimate to ask (in the context of the Conquest but also in the context of an economy in which women pass between men) what it means for a woman to give herself *voluntarily*? What does it mean to be Cortés's "lover" (*amante*)?

More importantly, however, Paz appropriates Malinche as the *symbol* of betrayal. On Paz's account, Malinche not only betrays the Aztecs by opening herself to Cortés; she also symbolizes "*entrega*" (submission, handing over, or surrender). Consequently, Malinche not only surrenders herself to Cortés, but she also becomes the symbol of surrender. What does it mean to say that this singular woman not only surrendered herself to Cortés but is the symbol of surrender, of all women's surrender to men and all women's betrayal of their fathers, their culture, or their community? What does it mean that a singular woman becomes a symbol for us? What is a symbol and how does it pass between us?

THE SYMBOL OF COMMUNITY

What does it mean to speak of the symbol? What is lost, what is gained, and what *remains* when a symbol is constituted and passed between us?

According to Hegel, the symbol—like the sign—is composed of two parts: first, a meaning, an intelligible interiority; and second, the expression or the material support, that is, the sensible exteriority. Nevertheless, the relation between interiority and exteriority in principle distinguishes the sign from the symbol. Although "the symbol is *prima facie* a *sign* . . . in a *mere sign* the connection that meaning and its expression have with one another is only a purely arbitrary linkage." This means that the "expression"—the material exteriority of the sign—"far from presenting *itself*, brings before our minds a content foreign to it, one with which it does not need to stand in any proper affinity whatever" (1975, 1:304). Consequently, sensible materiality, the expression or body of the sign, *disappears* before the interiority, the meaning or the intention, of the sign. For Hegel, such arbitrariness constitutes the essence of the sign: "The predominant part of the sounds in a language is linked purely by chance with the ideas expressed thereby, so far as their content is concerned, even if it can be shown, by an historical development, that the original connection was of another character" (1:304). In the *Aesthetics*

Hegel is concerned only with the most spiritual form of the sign. In speech the material of the sign—its external expression—disappears in the sonorous articulation, leaving behind no material trace but only the intentional unity of the word in the voice.

The symbol, however, is both more and less than the sign.[5] Hegel claims, "The symbol is no purely arbitrary sign, but a sign which in its externality comprises in itself at the same time the content of the idea which it brings into appearance." In the symbol "the sensuously present things have already in their own existence that meaning, for the representation and expression of which they are used" (1:305). Although the material support of the symbol embodies or incarnates the idea, "nevertheless it is not to bring *itself* before our minds as this concrete individual thing but in itself only that universal quality of meaning" (1:305). In other words, whereas in the sign materiality or sensuousness is sublated—negated yet preserved—in the expression of the meaning, in the symbol the body is not relieved. Rather, it remains precisely in order to express "a wider and universal" meaning (1:304). The sign relieves space as time or, as Hegel puts it in *The Philosophy of Mind*, "The truer phase of the intuition used as a sign is existence in time (but its existence vanishes in the moment of being)" (1971, §459:213–214). The process of the symbol, however, is not an *Aufhebung*; that is, the symbol does not relieve itself of its sensuousness or materiality to do its work. The symbol's fundamental spatiality results in its irreducible polysemy and, consequently, its ambiguity. This becomes clear in Hegel's remarks on hieroglyphic writing. Whereas alphabetic writing "consists of signs of signs" (§459:215), hence it is temporally determined, hieroglyphic writing is fundamentally spatial. Consequently, hieroglyphic writing is composite, constituted of divisible elements, which means the idea expressed in hieroglyphs can be fragmented or dismembered. Hieroglyphic writing results in the mutilation of the word, that is, of the name, which Hegel insists is "the fundamental desideratum of language" (§459:217). Unlike in alphabetic writing, in which the name "is the simple sign for the exact idea" (§459:217) and is thus indivisible and univocal, "in hieroglyphics the relations of concrete mental ideas to one another must necessarily be tangled and perplexed," and "the analysis of these . . . appears to be possible in the most various and divergent ways. Every divergence in analysis would give rise to another formation of the written name" (§459:217). The polysemy of the symbol means it is always possible to take a symbol of something more universal, more abstract, for what it *appears* to be. It is always possible that we will not see the courage or magnanimity of the lion, but rather merely the lion itself. On Hegel's account, there is only one way to reduce the polysemy and ambiguity of the symbol: "Ambiguity is removed from the symbol, strictly so-called, if . . . the linkage of the sensuous picture with the meaning is made customary, and becomes more or less conventional—as is indispensably requisite in a mere sign" (1975, 1:307–308). For the symbol to be secured in its symbolic meaning, it must become a sign, which means it must be relieved of its spatial elements. In other words, for a symbol to be merely or only symbolic, it must no longer be a symbol. This is impossible for hieroglyphs, which are irreducibly corporeal.[6]

There is no symbol without the remainder of what cannot be relieved. In the symbol something remains that exceeds symbolic intention and comprehension. Hegel wants to make this excess disappear (murder) in his privileging not only of alphabetic writing but also of the language or speech that perfects itself in relation to alphabetic writing. According to Hegel, in perfect European speech there is no excess, not even an accent to indicate the materiality and therefore the locality, the being-situated, of the one who speaks. Comparing spoken Chinese to any spoken European idiom, Hegel suggests that the perfection of spoken Chinese "consists in the opposite of that *parler sans accent* which in Europe is justly required of an educated speaker" (1971, §459:216). Indeed, Hegel points out that the failure to reduce accent is a consequence of hieroglyphic writing: "The hieroglyphic mode of writing keeps the Chinese vocal language from reaching that objective precision which is gained in articulation by alphabetic writing" (§459:216). This is so because insofar as the hieroglyphic mode of writing represents not spoken Chinese, but the ideas themselves graphically, written and spoken Chinese are cut off from one another, absolutely separated. Hieroglyphic writing does not provide a support for spoken language, thereby denying it the chance to perfect itself. This is not the case with alphabetic writing, which represents not ideas but the sounds of spoken language. Hegel writes: "The progress of the language depends most closely on the habit of alphabetical writing; by means of which only does vocal language acquire the precision and purity of its articulation" (§459:216).

Yet despite what Hegel calls the "inestimable and not sufficiently appreciated" educational value of learning to read and write an alphabetic language, hieroglyphics—and thus the symbol—have their place in alphabetic writing. If learning to read and write an alphabetic character "leads the mind from the sensibly concrete to attend to the more formal structure of the vocal word and its abstract elements, and contributes much to give stability and independence to the inward realm of mental life," then it can do so only by way of the hieroglyphic character of alphabetic writing. "Acquired habit subsequently effaces the peculiarity by which alphabetic writing appears . . . as a roundabout way to ideas by means of audibility; it makes them a sort of hieroglyphic to us" (§459:218). In other words, by force of habit—through education, through repetition—spoken language perfects itself by means of *alphabetic* hieroglyphs. The sign realizes itself in and through the symbol. Although Hegel understands the sign as a great advance over and as more intelligent than the symbol, and although he seeks to reduce the polysemy of the symbol through its becoming a sign, the sign that Hegel praises becomes itself—realizes itself—through the symbol.

If the symbol is irreducible, and therefore necessary to the becoming-sign of the sign, then what remains of the symbol—and thus what makes the symbol symbolic without being *of* the symbol—is not the body, which is never present in itself except insofar as it is appropriated, *qua* expression, in the sign or the symbol. The body of the symbol does not remain *as such*. This is so because the symbolic *body* is necessarily identified as such; it is the body *of the symbol*. What remains as remainder—thus what exceeds and complicates the symbol by provoking its fundamental polysemy and ambiguity—is rather what Michael Naas calls "the ghost that *is* the body" (2008, 176). This remnant is a *revenant* that haunts the symbol, making it possible to see in it something other than the symbol. As Derrida observes in "Force of Law: The 'Mystical Foundation of Authority'": "Spectrality has to do with the fact that a body is never present for itself, for what it is. It appears by disappearing or by making disappear what it represents" (2002a, 102). What remains, then, is the trace of what will never have been present, whether as a life fully lived or an intention fully realized. The ghost—of the body that remains beyond its appropriation or relief in and as the symbol—haunts us, for it remains before us as the specter of what is no longer, not yet, and never was. What remains is the time of mourning, the delay that makes the name, the signature, and the symbol necessary and impossible.

The question, then, is not what *is* a symbol? The question is what is the relation between *us*, between those who pass or share the symbol among us, those who pass or share the body of a singular woman, of Malinche/Marina, for instance? A symbol always passes between at least two and is the "operator"—according to Edmond Ortigues in *Le discours et le symbole*—of communication and community. Accordingly, the symbol instances "a rule of exchange or of mutual obligations: Your law will be my law" (1962, 61). As Marcel Hénaff points out in *Le don des philosophes*, "All symbolism is implicitly a . . . pact" (2012, 290). Indeed, Ortigues suggests that the symbol instances the possibility of linguistic convention in the first place: "In a general way symbols are the material with which linguistic convention, a social pact, are constituted" (1962, 61). As symbol, then, the body of Malinche occasions the pact or convention of community and of communication; it instances the possibility of "talking to," which necessarily precedes the possibility of "talking about."[7] And this means that in passing Malinche between us—the one offering her to the other in a gesture of community and communication, the other receiving her and, in the economic gesture of reciprocity or of mutual obligation, accepting and affirming, thus countersigning, the pact or convention—we institute the possibility of community and communication. We come together over her body. If the body of Malinche is a symbol, if it symbolizes anything at all, it symbolizes "our" community and "our" communication. How not to accept—sign for, receive, countersign—this symbol? How not to affirm, countersign, the violence of community and communication?

IN THE NAME OF MALINCHE

Paz is not the first to accord such importance to Malinche. Bernal Díaz devotes a chapter to the fortuitous encounter that occurred in March 1519 when Cortés was given some twenty women, among whom was counted Malinche. At the time he was given Malinche, Cortés already had an "interpreter" or translator, another "tongue" (*lengua*), as Cortés himself most often referred to those who necessarily came between him and the Amerindians with whom he "spoke." His name was Gerónimo de Aguilar. A Spaniard who had been shipwrecked off the coast of Yucatán in 1511, Aguilar had spent eight years living among the Maya. When the Spaniards first saw him, but before he spoke, they did not recognize him as a Spaniard. Aguilar was the first translator—the first "tongue"—in whom Cortés was able to have confidence, no doubt because he spoke the same tongue (*lengua*) as Cortés: he was one of us. The appearance of Gerónimo de Aguilar notwithstanding, Bernal Díaz claims that the "gift" of Malinche "was the great beginning of our conquest" (1991, 87, 93). According to Bernal Díaz's account, undoubtedly a Christian story, Malinche was the daughter of "gentlemen and chiefs of a village that was called Painala" (91). In her infancy her father died, and her mother "married another young chief and they had a son" (91). Because Malinche's mother and her new husband wanted their son to be their heir, "in the night they gave the girl to some Indians from Xicalango, because they [Malinche's parents] were not seen, and they made it known that she had died, and at that time a daughter of one of her [the mother's] Indian slaves died, and they claimed that it was the heiress" (91). While ridding themselves of Malinche, her parents also deprived a recently deceased child the right to be mourned in her own name.[8] The fact that this child, this singular daughter, died in the name of Malinche—as if she were Malinche and thus was mourned and buried as Malinche—makes palpable the no less important truth that what is most properly her own (the singularity of her death) is nevertheless foreign to this dead girl. It is always possible—hence, necessary—that one's death will be appropriated in the name of another. In the name of the secret of the other, this girl without name, whose name will not have been recorded, will have died in secret.

In the *Historia de las Indias* (1561), Bartolomé de Las Casas recounts the same story (*cuento*), but somewhat differently:

> An Indian woman was found (who later was called Marina and the Indians called her Malinche),[9] of the twenty that they presented to Cortés in the province of Tabasco, who knew the Mexican language, because she had been, as she said, stolen from her land near Xalisco, from that part of Mexico that is to the west, and sold from hand to hand until Tabasco; she already knew the language of Tabasco, and although that language was different from that of Yucatán, where Aguilar had been, still she understood a few words. (1986, 3:224)

One could say, simply, that women do not count among men; or, rather, that they count only among men. They pass between men in order that things of greater value pass between and remain among men. Bernal Díaz notes, "The Indians from Xicalango gave her to the ones from Tabasco, who gave her to Cortés" (1991, 91). This exchange or transfer—this sex trafficking—does not end with Malinche's having been (re)gifted to Cortés. He passed her on ("*repartió*," Bernal Díaz says) to Alonso Hernández Puertocarrero (89), but Bernal Díaz adds, "as doña Marina, in all the wars of New Spain, Tlascala, and Mexico, was such an excellent woman and good translator . . . Cortés always brought her with him" (92). But Cortés was still not finished giving her away, even if he always had her with him. Las Casas observes, "Cortés . . . gave her to Aguilar, who communicated a lot with her . . . in order that they could understand each other and by means of this understand the secrets of the land" (1986, 3:245). Clearly, Malinche was vital to Cortés. She represented, according to Tzvetan Todorov, "an indispensable ally," whose importance to Cortés could be registered in "their physical intimacy" (1982, 106). She was easily the best tongue (*lengua*) Cortés ever had, but perhaps it is too romantic—that is, too sexist, too *machista*—to characterize the relations between them as "intimate" or to call Malinche Cortés's "lover" (as

Paz does) or his "mistress" (as Todorov does [106]). We know, however, that she had "a son by her lord and master Cortés" (Díaz 1991, 92).[10] And yet after the fall of Tenochtitlán and the Aztec empire, and for the third time, Cortés gave her away, passing her to Juan Jaramillo.

From the beginning, Malinche/Marina passes between men, but she also (tres)passes—crosses—cultural and linguistic borders.[11] Such displacement is one of the keys to the Conquest, because her movement across borders resulted in her becoming bilingual and later trilingual: "She knew the language of Coatzalcoalco, which is Mexico's own, and she knew that of Tabasco" (Díaz 1991, 92–93). What Todorov thus calls her "gifts for languages" (1982, 106) is less a "gift" than the effect of her being "gifted" between men; or, as Las Casas puts it, of being "stolen from her land" and "sold from hand to hand" (1986, 245). Because she had been gifted and regifted from one culture and one language to another, Malinche was able to communicate with Aguilar, who "knew the language of Yucatán, which is all one" (Díaz 1991, 93), although according to Las Casas's account, he understood this language "with many errors" (1986, 245), which is to say, not very well. Thus, in order for communication to take place, a word (*palabra* or *voz*) proceeding from Moctezuma, for example, or from one of his emissaries, would be passed to Malinche, who would then send it to Aguilar, who, in turn, "declared it in Spanish to Cortés" (Díaz 1991, 93). And when Cortés responded, the circuit would be reconstituted but in reverse, from Cortés to Aguilar to Malinche to Moctezuma. It would not take long, however, for Malinche to displace—to disappear—Aguilar, thereby making the economy of translation more efficient.[12] Marina/Malinche would take her place between Cortés and Moctezuma.

In doing so, in coming between Cortés and Moctezuma, she effectively displaced Cortés. And Cortés knew it. In his account—in the fifth letter he wrote to Carlos V—of the punitive expedition to Honduras (1524–1526), at the moment in which Cortés wants to prove his identity and assert himself as the same man who had passed through Tabasco some years before, he writes, "I responded to him that I was the captain who the Tabascans told him had passed through their land with whom they had fought, and in order that he believe that it was true, that he ask that translator with whom he was speaking—that is, Marina, who I always took with me—because there they had given her to me with another twenty women. And she told him and certified it for him" (1993, 574–575). Cortés's identity—and therefore his authority, his legitimacy—depends on Malinche's word and presence. Yet, in the public letters that Cortés sent to Carlos V, he not only resisted mentioning

Malinche/Marina by name but also customarily failed to recognize the place of the translator or interpreter as an unavoidable and necessary participant in all his communication with Amerindians.[13]

Malinche was, in fact, so necessary that it was impossible for the Amerindians who addressed themselves to Cortés not to address (him as) "Malinche."[14] Bernal Díaz explains:

> Before going any further I want to say how in all the villages through which we passed, or in others where they had news of us, they called Cortés Malinche; and like this I will call him from here forward Malinche in all the conversations that we had with the Indians . . . and I will not call him Cortés except where necessary; and the reason for having given him that name is that, as doña Marina, our translator, was always in his company, especially when ambassadors came or in conversations with chiefs, and she spoke for him in the Mexican language, for this reason they called him Cortés the captain of Marina, and more briefly they called him Malinche; and this name also was given to Juan Pérez de Arteaga . . . because he was always with doña Marina and with Jerónimo de Aguilar learning the language, and for this reason they called him Juan Pérez Malinche. . . . I have wanted to bring this to mind although there was no reason for it, in order to understand the name of Cortés from here on, that he is called Malinche. [He querido traer esto a la memoria aunque no había para qué, porque se entienda el nombre de Cortés de aquí adelante, que se dice Malinche.] (1991, 193–194)

In a sense, then, when talking to Cortés, which means talking to "Malinche," Amerindians cannot not talk among themselves. It is not simply that "Malinche" names Cortés: from the beginning the Aztecs recognize the central, mediate position and role of (*la*) Malinche, to whom both Bernal Díaz and Cortés himself always referred by her "given" name, as "Marina," in order rhetorically to underline her baptism. Calling her "Marina" identifies her as one of "us." But if in calling her "Marina" they were able—more or less "successfully"—to inscribe or to mark her as Christian, as one of us, it is no less the case that this same gesture of affiliation (naming) threatens the place and authority of Cortés: in the name of Malinche, Cortés passed to the "other" side of the border. He is both no longer one of "us" and one of "us." His authority derives from a name that is not his own. Only insofar as he sur/renders—both relinquishes and renders—himself in and to a name that dis/places him can he communicate with Amerindians, can he occupy any place among them and thus occupy *the* place among us.

Everything passes through Malinche, who will have already been passed between men (*"vendida de mano en mano"*). Her name—Malinali, Malinche, Malintzín, Marina—is the "proper" name of the secret. "Malinche" names not only both sides of the border between "us" and "them" but also the border itself, which is not one: a border is a border only if it divides, multiplying itself infinitely, crossing itself, trespassing itself in the instant of its nomination, of its inscription. "Malinche"—whether *la* or *el* Malinche—names the becoming-Spanish of the Amerindian and the becoming-Amerindian of the Spanish. "Malinche" names constitutive, originary contamination, inauthenticity, illegitimacy. It thus instances the homonymy of any identity, of any essence, of any culture.

Such homonymy is also Cortés's legacy. As is well known, Cortés had eleven children, five of whom were from extramarital relations. Two of the male offspring were given the same name, Martín Cortés, the name of Hernán Cortés's father. The firstborn Martín was the son of *la* Malinche and was legitimated by Pope Clement VII in a Papal Bull of 1529. The father-son, the son-father, Martín Cortés, is the offspring of two Malinches. How to think a certain "Spanish" legacy in Mexico, in the Americas? What does it mean that homonymy—which already divides the origin (*el/la* Malinche, "Martín" as both father and son to Hernán, Spanish and criollo and mestizo) from itself—structures the possibility of inheritance? Is this not the bastardization of all culture(s), of all identity? Is not every legacy compromised, usurped, illegitimate, as the condition of its legitimation? If "we"—whoever and wherever "we" are—are an effect of homonymy, what can be said of "our" belonging? In whose name do I speak when I speak in my name? In whose name do I sign when I sign in my name? The economy of homonymy determines, by undermining, all the relations between "us." Identity—my identity, our identity—passes between "us" as an absolute secret, a secret that "we" cannot *not* pronounce without knowing in whose name "we" speak and with what (af)filiation.

INHERITING THE SECRET

The secret passes between us, passes from hand to hand, like stories (*cuentos*), accounts (*cuentas*). The secret passes between us like the beads (*cuentas*), like the *chalchihuites*, that identified the Spaniards. Book 12 of Sahagún's *Historia general de las cosas de Nueva España* recounts (*cuenta*)—from the perspective, more or less, of Amerindians—contact with the Spaniards. Thus, it narrates as much the economy of the Conquest as the resistance to the Conquest. The first news of Spaniards that Moctezuma received testifies to the economy of encounter. It is worth noting what Moctezuma's captains brought him in order to *show* him the presence of Spaniards on the shores of the New World. They reported:

> You put us on guard at the edge of the sea; we saw some gods in the sea and we went to receive them, and we gave them several nice blankets, and you see here these beads [*cuentas*] that they gave us, and they told us, if it is true that you are Mexicans, *see here these beads*, give them to Moctezuma *in order that he knows us* [*para que nos conozca*], and tell him everything that happened when you were with them in the sea on the ships. (Sahagún 1999, 724–725; emphasis added)

Moctezuma responded: "I have received this in secret [*en secreto*], and I order you to say nothing of what has happened" (725). Beyond Moctezuma's desire to keep secret the arrival of others—who- or whatever they might be, gods or Spaniards—the most important element of this scene of exchange consists in what the captains say about the function or meaning of the beads (*cuentas*). The glass beads are intended to identify, to represent, Spaniards to Moctezuma. They are not given simply in exchange for the blankets that the captains had brought for that purpose but rather offered as signs of identity. The Europeans give account (*cuenta*) of themselves by giving beads (*cuentas*) to the Amerindians. Through the beads Amerindians realize (give account to themselves, *darse cuenta*) who the Spaniards are. The other knows us through the accounts/beads (*cuentas*) we give.

But the Spaniards did not give the beads to Amerindians only so that they could identify them. On the contrary, Spaniards recognize themselves by the beads they will have given the other. This is how it will have worked in the Americas from the first day of Columbus's arrival. Everyone knows that when he first encountered Amerindians, Columbus gave them glass beads, which, he remarked, were "of small value [*de poco valor*]" (Colón 1992, 110/1989, 65). On 15 October 1492, Amerindians gave them back. Between the islands of Santa María and Fernandina, Columbus encountered "a man who was passing alone in a dugout canoe." This man carried with him a little bread, a gourd for water, tobacco, and "a string of small glass beads [*un ramalejo de cuentezillas de vidrio*]" (115/85). The glass beads recount (*cuentan*) a story (*cuento*); they give an account (*cuenta*) such that Columbus could recognize or become aware of (*darse cuenta de*) the route this man had followed: "Because of [the beads] I recognized that he was coming from the island of San Salvador and had passed to that of Santa María and was passing to Fernandina" (115/85). This is not just the route the Amerindian had followed, however. The beads traced Columbus's itinerary in the New World. That is, in the encounter with the other, Columbus encounters or finds himself, determines where he will have been, whence he will have come. The events of 13–14 January 1493 make more transparent this economy of encounter. According to the diary of the first voyage, on 13 January Columbus gave to an Amerindian who had approached the ship "pieces of green and red cloth and glass beads [*pedaços de paño verde y colorado y cuentezuelas de vidrio*]" (195/331). The next day, on 14 January, several Native Americans approached the ship, including the one to whom Columbus had given "trinkets from the trade goods" (196/335) the day before. With him "came a king who had given some beads to the said Indian to give to the men in the launch as a sign of security and peace" (196/335). To this "king" who gave (returned) to Columbus the beads as a sign of peace and security, Columbus gave in turn, "a red cap and beads [*cuentas*] and a piece of red cloth" (196/337).

How to read this exchange of beads, of that which was worthless, of small value, as if it were of great value? After all, in addition to being the sign (to himself) of his presence in the New World, the beads are also the *sign* of peace and security, of Columbus's good intentions. But as the *sign* of peace and security and of self-presence, the beads also indicate their absence.

Beads (*cuentas*) pass between us; we share them among ourselves, giving them to the other giving them back, so that we may give account (*cuenta*) of ourselves. The economy of the *cuenta* (which is also a "bill," something to be paid, something that comes due, the sign of a debt) figures the secret of culture. Despite determining the limits of culture and of cultural identity, as well as defining the limit of consciousness in relation to the other, this secret—the *cuenta* (bead) and the *cuenta* (account) that it gives/is given—is of little value, *de poco valor*. It doesn't *count* (*no cuenta*); it is, finally, meaningless. Following O'Gorman's understanding of the relation between being and existence in *La invención de América*, the *cuenta* is not. It remains secret, in secret, secreting. It is precisely that which, without itself being of any value or worth, hence without being desired for itself, nevertheless marks—instances—the relation to the other, to ourselves. Columbus will have left this *cuenta* (bead, account, bill) to us. In the "Institución de Mayorazgo" dated and signed 22 February 1498, Columbus specified the order and conditions of inheritance: "First will concern Diego, my son, and all those who have from me succeeded or descended, and also my brothers Bartolomew and Diego, my arms that I will leave behind after my days, without reserving any of them, and will seal with their seal Diego, my son, and any other who inherits this Mayorazgo. And after having inherited and been in possession of it, sign with my signature" (Colón 1992, 356).

The signature looks like this:

.S.
.S.A.S.
X M Y
El Almirante

There were variations on this signature. For example, the "Memorial a los Reyes," which Columbus presented for the provisioning of his third voyage, was signed not by "El Almirante" but rather by ":Xpo FERENS./."[15] The variations, however, are of little importance. What is important is the following: *First*, the signature is a cipher, a secret. No one knows what it means.[16] *Second*, in what cannot have been a common gesture, Columbus wanted to leave his signature behind; he insisted that his son Diego—*or any other who inherited*—"sign in my signature [*firme de mi firma*]," therefore decreeing that all those who follow him counterfeit or falsify (dissemble, as Bernal Díaz said of Marina/Malinche) their identity *in his name*. Columbus demanded that his heirs sign in *his* name, in the name of the father, but in what was also the name of the other.

We are all Columbus's heirs.[17] Columbus stumbled upon modernity, thereby (perhaps accidentally) inventing us.[18] As heirs to Columbus, as moderns, the condition of our being is dissimulation, falsification, virtualization, which can neither be mitigated nor legitimated simply by giving (ourselves) an account (*cuenta*) of the fiction or artifice that constitutes us. Fiction is the secret of being. The secret of modernity—and not only of modernity—is the fiction of the meaning of being. It is a secret and a fiction that is revealed (both uncovered and re-veiled)—that is kept and told, that is promised—each time I sign (in) my *name*, as if I signed (in) *my* name. My proper name—the name singularly figured in my signature, in my hand (*letra*)—comes from the other. I sign always and only in another's hand (*letra*). In the name of the father and of the son and of the . . .

The signature—the cipher of my name—passes between others; it passes from hand to hand, as a *cuenta*, as a secret, as a thing of small value. And what is it that we cipher each time we sign? What does "our" signature reveal? No one will ever know. Our cipher remains (in) secret, a secret for/from us. We are secret to ourselves. Our signature—always already in the name of the other, in the name of Columbus, in the name of *el*/*la* Malinche, in the name of the father-son, Martín Cortés—reveals that we are secrets secreted absolutely to and from, for, ourselves.

ACCOUNTING FOR MEXICO

Why take seriously Columbus's legacy? Why take seriously the legacy of the *cuenta*, the *dar(se)* and *rendir cuenta* in Mexico? Why ask about the possibility of rendering account of oneself without surrendering (*rendirse*), without rendering oneself to another? Perhaps because the promise of democracy takes place within the horizon of the impossible demand to render oneself without surrendering. In the wake of the 2006 presidential election in Mexico, which was widely believed to have been fraudulently won by PAN candidate Felipe Calderón, supporters of Andrés Manuel López Obrador (AMLO) occupied the Zócalo (Plaza de la Constitución), the streets surrounding it, and the Paseo de la Reforma. In the name of democracy, López Obrador called for a complete recount of the votes. For fifty days, López Obrador and his supporters demanded *una rendición de cuentas*, a rendering of accounts. On Wednesday, 2 August 2006, López Obrador remarked:

> We are not going to enter into any negotiation that does not have as its point of departure the recount [*el recuento*] of the votes. They should not be thinking that they are going to coopt us; we are never going to betray the Mexican people.
>
> There is a number that I would like our adversaries to refute. You think it is normal that in an election in which there are 130 thousand ballot boxes, 130 thousand complaints are made, 72 thousand of which concerned mathematical errors, in 60 percent of all the complaints? Is that normal? (Poniatowska 2007, 88)

López Obrador suggested that such corruption derives from the simple fact that "the Mexican people don't count [el pueblo mexicano no cuenta]" (2007, 88). The failure to recount the votes amounted to the installation of "a simulated democracy, a democracy of lies" (2007, 88). Democracy counts. And because in Mexico the votes—and thus the people—do not count, López Obrador and his supporters, "in the name of democracy," refused to surrender: "Here no one surrenders [Aquí no se rinde nadie]" (2007, 58, 44). No surrender. The failure to render account of the votes, to recount the votes, results in the refusal to surrender. Yet, and this is the structural paradox, they—the Mexican people, *el pueblo mexicano*, in López Obrador's account—will already have surrendered themselves to López Obrador, who, Elena Poniatowska observes, is one of those who "provoke surrender [*provocan la rendición*]" (2007, 104). In the name of democracy, in the name of the recount, in the name of López Obrador, having surrendered to that name, no one surrenders.

How not to surrender surrendering? How (not) to give account (of oneself) without giving oneself away? Is this not the Columbian inheritance? But if so, is it not perhaps both before and after Columbus? Is it not the possibility (as the impossibility) of democracy, its promise? If, as Poniatowska suggests, democracy is freedom of expression, freedom of the word (2007, 118), then democracy is necessarily linked to the *darse cuenta*. Expression, insofar as it is always the expression of consciousness, is always self-expression; it is always *darse cuenta*. And the *cuenta* par excellence is the word, which is traded between us; and the word par excellence is the name in which we render and surrender ourselves, in which we give account of ourselves, giving ourselves away.

CHAPTER 2

MURDER AND SYMBOL

Feminicide's Remains

Son los restos de los restos.
PATRICIO GUZMÁN, *NOSTALGIA DE LA LUZ* (2010)

The only things that change are the names.
SERGIO GONZÁLEZ RODRÍGUEZ, *THE FEMICIDE MACHINE* (2012)

Mais on ne devrait jamais parler de l'assassinat d'un homme comme d'une figure, pas même une figure exemplaire dans une logique de l'emblème, une rhétorique du drapeau ou du martyre. La vie d'un homme, unique autant que sa mort, sera toujours plus qu'un paradigme et autre chose qu'un symbole. Et c'est cela même que devrait toujours nommer un nom propre.
JACQUES DERRIDA, *SPECTRES DE MARX* (1993)

In his account of the third voyage to the Americas, Columbus momentarily abandons his description of the Amerindians and the riches desired by Spain to speculate on the discovery of biblical Paradise, which he reasons is located near the equator in the mountainous region from which the Orinoco River springs. Columbus recalls that, according to Genesis, four rivers flowed from Paradise, and he thinks the Orinoco must be a branch of one of them for various reasons. First, following certain ancient texts, including Ptolemy, Columbus believed that Paradise lay at the earth's highest point, toward which he believed he was moving since the temperature steadily increased as they approached the equator. Second, from the distance that the Orinoco pushed fresh water out into the sea, Columbus understood that the river must have traveled a great distance, falling over time from a significant height. For these reasons Columbus offers a new geography of the world.

> I always read that the world . . . was spherical. . . . Now I saw so much deformity . . . and I found that it was not round in the form that they write, rather that it is the form of a pear that is all very round, save there where it has the nipple, there at the highest point, just like someone has a very round ball, and that in one area it was like a woman's breast was placed, and that this part of the nipple was the highest point and the closest to the sky. (Colón 1992, 376–377)

Columbus never set foot in Paradise, but it clearly concerned and fascinated him. No doubt this is one more instance of what Todorov understood as "Columbus's medieval mentality" (1982, 12), but his interest is not simply a symptom of a medieval illness that modernity cures. Columbus's interest and investment in Paradise coheres with his other primary activity in the Americas: that of taking possession of everything he saw by naming it.[1] Todorov writes, "The first gesture Columbus makes upon contact with the newly discovered lands . . . is an act of extended nomination" (28).[2] Naming, according to Todorov, "is equivalent to taking possession" (27).

There is a precedent for arriving in Paradise and naming things. In addition to reporting that four rivers flow from the Garden of Eden, Genesis also explains that although Adam lived there "to till it and keep it," God thought that it was "not good that man should be alone" (2:15) and thus determined to "make him a helper as his partner" (2:18). He thus brought forth from the ground "every animal of the field and every bird of the air and brought them to the man to see what he would call them; and whatever the man called every living creature, that was its name. The man gave names to all cattle, and to the birds of the air, and to every animal in the field; but for the man there was not found a helper as his partner" (2:19–20). Three things are evident from the start. First, Paradise leaves man wanting. He names every living creature but finds no companion. Literally, Adam is unable to name himself, to call himself or one like himself from among the animals. Second, God gives the power of naming to man. It is a gift, moreover, that cannot be returned or disavowed. There is man insofar as man names, and yet the power of naming is not proper to man; it comes from another. Third, God cannot name the living; He cannot name the animals. He cannot tell them apart. He cannot distinguish man (*'adam*) from the ground (*'adamah*), which perhaps explains why He does not know until after Adam names them that none of the animals or birds makes a suitable partner for His creation.[3] The animals come before Adam indifferently, and he gives to each the name that corresponds to it. The name puts each in its place, distinguishing one from another. But Adam is incapable of distinguishing himself: his is the one name he cannot say. Indeed, Adam calls himself "man" only after he is separated from himself. Though he names woman (*'ishah*) after himself (*'ish*), as derived from himself, he nonetheless names himself only after naming her. Adam's self-nomination, which is to say his self-symbolization or auto-affection and thus his survival, is possible only insofar as he is separated—secreted—from himself, only insofar as he comes after himself. The name designates this difference from the self that is constitutive of the self and of the desire for another. Plato tells a similar story in the *Symposium* when he has Aristophanes claim: "And so, Gentlemen, we are all like pieces of coin that children break in half for keepsakes—making two out of one, like the flatfish—and each of us is forever seeking the half that will tally with himself" (191d). We have the structure of the symbol; we are symbolic. We are separated from ourselves, and we desire to rejoin or reunite ourselves to ourselves, to make ourselves whole, such that we can recognize ourselves. We desire to become one. But such self-unity, such uniqueness, instances primordial violence, trauma, the first murder: "As soon as there is the One, there is murder, wounding, traumatism" (Derrida 1995, 124/1996c, 78).

Genesis, however, goes on to tell the story of God's "regret" for the world of desire: "When people began to multiply on the face of the ground, and daughters were born to them, the sons of God saw that they were fair [or good]; and they took wives for themselves of all that they chose" (6:1–2). Although it is the "sons of God" who trespass the border separating mortals from divine beings, only mortals are punished: "The Lord saw the wickedness of humankind was great on the earth, and that every inclination of the thoughts of their hearts was only evil continually. And the Lord was sorry he had made humankind on the earth and it grieved him to his heart" (6:5–6).

The violence of the name—and therefore of a certain interest in the other—also disturbs the New World paradise in which Columbus gives everything "a new name." Todorov rightly points out that Columbus recognized that everything he named already had a name, which suggests that although he appears to have thought that "things must have the names that correspond to them" (1982, 27), such correspondence is not simply natural. It is always possible for names to be changed, that one name take the place of another. Indeed, Columbus assumed that at the end of his life, his name would take the place of the name he gave to his son. In leaving his signature to his eldest son, by commanding him to sign in his name, Columbus commanded him to write over, to mark out, the name Columbus had already given him.

The question of how to understand the effects of such inheritance is especially pressing some five hundred years after Columbus's bequest, for the Latin Americas of the late twentieth and early twenty-first centuries have been marked by what have come to be called "feminicides" (in Mexico, Guatemala, El Salvador, Honduras, but also in Argentina and Chile).[4] Feminicide names the systematic and systemic (thus with impunity) murder of women because they are women, on account of their gender.[5] The ensuing analysis of the name, the body, and the signature—of the symbol, therefore—in the context of the appalling cultural phenomenon of feminicide (and of Mexican feminicide in particular), although necessary, is not sufficient.[6] A world of difference lies between the "symbolic" violence outlined in what follows and the "real"—historical and in each case singular—murder of women and girls. A world of difference lies between naming someone (a woman, a girl) and murdering her. Indeed, the difference between these two irreducibly violent acts is the world, for the *symbolic* murder of naming (symbolization) opens the possibility (as impossible) of the singular world, whereas the *murder* of another instances the end of the world insofar it destroys another's—a singular and irreplaceable being's—capacity for symbolization. Yet despite the difference between real and symbolic violence, there is no "real" or "historical" violence that is not, from the start, symbolic violence.[7] Consequently, the symbolic violence of naming is by no means innocent. On the contrary, it instances what Rossana Reguillo (2011, n.p.) calls "the ontological crime, that which erases singularity after its ciphered gain." "Ciphered" here translates *cifrada* (from *cifrar*), which means both "to calculate" and "to code" (hence "to secrete"). Naming thus destroys the singularity of the other not only to calculate—determine—but also to hide its interest and use. It subjects one to another. (It instances the first act of sovereignty; it is the first murder.) It opens a world of difference, of inequality. Yet it also constitutes the possibility of freedom. Symbolic violence is originary and necessary, hence unavoidable, which means the world begins and ends, opens and closes, in violence.

The final chapter of Sergio González Rodríguez's *Huesos en el desierto* (2006), titled "La vida inconclusa" (Unfinished life), counts and recounts the victims of feminicide. It begins with the "last" one, Erika Pérez, the one most recently discovered (before the book's publication) on 23 September 2002, and ends with the "first," Alma Chavira Farel, found 23 January 1993. It is a count and an account, however, as inconclusive as the lives of these murdered women, beginning and ending with ellipses (. . .) signaling that the list neither begins nor ends. The three dots, whether at the beginning or the end of the list, point out that to give an account of the dead is impossible, interminable, incalculable. And this is so despite the necessity of calculating, of counting and recounting, of giving an account, and thus of *repeating* the names of the victims. The impossible necessity of calculation, of counting and accounting, of re/counting, perhaps explains why every murder is always *both* the first and the last murder, absolutely singular, unrepeatable, *and*, at the same time, the symbol—thus the repetition—of every murder in and as the history of the world.

Although the list of murdered women begins and ends with named victims, of the 470 murdered women—at least 142 of whom were violated sexually before being murdered—the list includes at least 56 unidentified victims, the remains of women, both adults and children, *sin nombre*.[8] The delinking of name and body jeopardizes the *last right* of survival: namely, the right to the *last rites* of mourning. As Shaun Irlam points out, the denial of the right to last rites is perhaps the most intractable legacy of genocide.[9] The paradox of the name, or what Derrida calls its "double law" (1987b, 2:142/2008a, 139), complicates mourning. On the one hand, the name makes possible the determination of the other by constituting its singularity, for the name identifies as the same that which changes incessantly.[10] On the other hand, the name makes this determination impossible because no name ever unequivocally belongs to the "singular" being it designates. The name thus allows us to remember what it nonetheless forces us to forget. Consequently, I can love the other only in a name that does not belong to her. As Montaigne wrote in "Of Friendship," "We embraced each other by our names" (1:269). To embrace each other by name is to be estranged from the friend by the name that, at the same time, instances the only chance of intimacy, of friendship. The chance of friendship or love is its ruin, its impossibility, in that the name distances us infinitely from the singular being that it allows us to identify and to love.

The same impossibility is inscribed in the structure of mourning. We mourn the other by name, for in the name we remember the beloved. Yet, to mourn the name is to forget the other, the "singularity" of the irreplaceable being we mourn. The beloved survives in the name, but in living on in the name, the singularity of the loved one is abandoned, forgotten. It cannot be otherwise. In short, we live on in the name that outlives us; we are mourned and remembered in the name that consigns us to oblivion. Because no name belongs to or is proper to the being (living or dead) whose singularity is nonetheless constituted in and through it, names can be attached to anyone or anything, living or dead. One name can be substituted for another in the play of identification and misidentification. Names are infinitely repeatable; they are changed and exchanged among us. They are *usurious* in that they create interest and value. Names give meaning, sense, to the world even as they result in the loss of singularity.

The interest and value of the name explains the efforts by the mothers of feminicide victims to restrict the use of the victims' names by nongovernmental organizations (NGOs). In Ciudad Juárez mothers of victims have attempted, as Julia Monárrez has pointed out, "to categorically exclude and invalidate the voices of those women organizers and protesters who took their grievances before an international forum. In this discourse, the mothers wielded their maternity as a symbol of power and accreditation: if one is not a mother, one cannot feel how a mother feels" (2010a, 188).[11] On Monárrez's account,

> These mothers' hostile conduct and spiteful denunciations arise from . . . an abuse of power produced in the institutional sphere. Others' pain and grief have functioned as cultural capital that has been manipulated by those who need to provide justice and by those who represent the politics of human rights for Chihuahua women. In this way, legitimate pain has been transformed into the *painfulness* experienced by victims' families, and it has acquired a symbolic capital value that has come to be used by hegemonic groups against civil organizations that have protested against violence. (2010a, 189)

At issue is the distinction between *pain* (or "legitimate pain") and *painfulness*, which Monárrez defines "as the use and abuse of the family members' accumulated sorrow, anguish, suffering, and grief" (186). Painfulness thus describes the appropriation, *qua* symbol, of another's pain "in a dramatized and collective manner with the objective of generating pity for, and ruining the reputations of, those found in the sphere of violence" (186). Such appropriation—whether used for generating pity for the victim-survivors or for ruining their reputations—neither remedies nor vindicates the experience of the victim-survivors, the mothers, but represents them, Monárrez suggests, "as distorted figures, twisted and lacking logical reasoning beyond that of seeking to create a collective nuisance" (186). The mothers thus attempt to reclaim their pain from the others' appropriation of it as painfulness. Yet, Monárrez observes, "In refusing to acknowledge the activism of the women of these nongovernmental gender violence–fighting organizations, the mothers of Juárez's femicide victims resemble the Chihuahuan government, which denies the murder of their loved ones and the pursuit of justice" (189). In effect the mothers disappear the women who protest in their daughters' names, accusing them of capitalizing on their disappearance and death, on their names. The upshot is that both parties (the victim-survivors and the national and international NGOs) unwittingly and ineluctably reproduce the same violence that they accuse the state of participating in and ignoring.

The assertion of the difference between the mothers' "legitimate pain" and its appropriation by others as "painfulness" ignores the fact that the mothers' experience of pain is also an appropriation. There is no pain that is not, as a condition of its experience, mediated, denominated (or named), identified: it is always *my* pain or *her* pain. Strictly speaking, it can never be *our* pain, since in every case the loss and the mourning must be absolutely singular, which means it is incommunicable. To think otherwise is to deny the singularity of our passion and our suffering. Even so, the singularity of my pain must be communicable: I must be able to testify, if only to myself, to my pain. Otherwise there will be no chance for mourning. Temporal delay or disjunction, the fact that what happens always happens too soon and too late, means that mediation—hence the name—is constitutive of experience and that all experience has the structure of mourning. There is no pain that is not *in the name* of something, of someone, of some event; there is no pain that is not looking for a name. At stake, therefore, is a struggle not over an ostensibly immediate pain but over the right to the name in and by which one's pain is called and recalled, in which one *accounts for* and *recounts* one's pain. It is as impossible for one mother to feel the pain of another as it is for a nonmother to feel that of a mother. At the moment mothers claim the exclusive right to speak in the names of their daughters and in the name of their pain, their singular pain has already become symbolic or cultural capital. Because a name does not belong to any*one* or to any*body*, because a name can only ever be appropriated, the issue becomes who has the right to pronounce the name, to speak or protest *in the name* of the victims and the victim-survivors.[12]

The name haunts feminicide's victim-survivors (the families and friends, the loved ones left behind). That an irreducible difference separates bodies and names means that mourning is always ambiguous, uncertain, not only because it oscillates between the *who* (the name) and the *what* (the body), but also because one can never be sure that *this* name belongs to *this* body. Adding to this structural and transcendental impossibility of a name's "belonging" to a body, the bodies of murdered women in Ciudad Juárez have been misidentified so routinely that those who mourn the victims doubt that the bodies they bury belong to the names for which they suffer and weep.[13]

Olga Alicia Carrillo Pérez disappeared on 10 August 1995. Her body was found in Lote Bravo, a parcel of land on the south side of Ciudad Juárez; her "right breast was severed and her left breast was literally bitten off"

(Washington Valdez 2006, 8). According to the testimony of her mother, Irma Pérez, authorities established her daughter's identity through the reconstruction of the cranium, but she would not accept this conclusion, and she demanded DNA testing of the remains. The DNA test confirmed Olga's identity, but her mother "remained unconvinced" (8; see also Monárrez 2009, 172n69). "How can it be her, when all they gave me was a bag of bones? They told me, 'This is your daughter.' . . . She wasn't dead that long for her body to be so decomposed. To this day, I believe the authorities have hidden a lot of things from me about my daughter's death" (Washington Valdez 2006, 8).[14] And when asked why she will not accept the results of positive DNA tests, Irma responds, "Ah yes!, ay! . . . Would you accept it if they told you in a month that this was your child?" (Monárrez 2009, 172; Washington Valdez 2006, 8).

Brenda Esther Alfaro Luna's body—her DNA—was also tested, although Monárrez reports it took six years to confirm her identity (2009, 172). All the while, in the absence of an identifiable body, her mother continued to look for her. Her sister, Beatriz Lorena, testified that according to the Mexican authorities the tests—which were never shown to the family—"indicated that her sister was not the daughter of her father" (173). Tests meant to determine the identity of Brenda Esther became the occasion for interrogating her mother: "And they even said to my mother: 'Tell us the truth, okay? You're not going to keep anything from us. If she's only your daughter, if she's not his—.' My mom said: 'Of course I have to tell the truth, because it's urgent to find my daughter.' She said: 'Yes, she's his.' Then they said: 'Okay, we're going to do others because, well, they came out unclear," that's what they said" (173). Brenda Esther's father, Luis Alfaro Labrado, was told that the bone used in the DNA analysis had been lost and that they weren't able to do anything. Ultimately, he and Brenda Esther's mother, María Esther Luna Hernández, gave more blood and sent another bone to another DNA testing lab, this time in Houston, Texas, where the samples were lost once again. Eventually, positive DNA test results from Tamaulipas established that Brenda Esther was in fact the daughter of María Esther and Luis, but they did not put to rest Luis's doubts: "My daughter's already had her funeral, well, who knows if they were her bones, perhaps they were someone else's bones. . . . They told us: 'Don't think you're going to see her face, her body, no—.' Because I thought I was going to see the big box. And no, it was a little box for a baby that doesn't show the face or anything, everything's all covered, that is, as I think, they were just her bones" (Monárrez 2009, 174). The state's failure to handle victim identification professionally and compassionately has resulted in the loss of credibility and in the victim-survivors' uncertainty. But it also amounts to a criminal negligence that victimizes the victims again, violates them once more.

The violence done to the bodies of the victims is thus repeated. First, women and girls are disappeared, tortured, mutilated, raped, murdered. Later, the bodies—sometimes as cadavers, sometimes as skeletons—are found and the violence is repeated in scenes of identification and misidentification, but also through the state-sponsored disappearing of the remains, of both the body necessary for mourning and the evidence necessary for prosecution of the feminicides. González Rodríguez quotes attorney Irene Blanco, who claimed

> there was a forum in New Mexico, in Las Cruces, and they asked prosecutor Zully Ponce where the effects of the homicide victims were deposited, and she responded that there was no depository, "because there were superior orders that were indicated to me, that it no longer made sense to go on storing clothes and things like that." How is it possible that evidence was destroyed? This means that the crimes will remain unsolved, that all the evidence must be destroyed so that we will never get to the bottom of the truth. (2006, 193)

The State of Chihuahua penal code makes it a crime to destroy the "'instruments of the crime' and things implicated in it" (193). The state's disappearing of evidence repeats the murders' destruction of the victims' bodies. After five years of searching for her missing brother, Jorge, Patricia Garibay "is confident she knows what happened" to him "and why it will do no good to try to recover his body for burial." She claims, "'We won't be able to bury him, or find something that was left of him. . . . We were told . . . that acid was poured over him to dissolve his body'" (Washington Valdez 2006, 100). According to González Rodríguez, the murderers "employ a method that eliminates the bodies of the victims. They call it 'lechada': a mixture of lime and other chemical substances that they spread over the cadavers in the graves to disintegrate the organic tissues. *That no trace remains* . . . , that's the order, *that no trace remains*" (169–170). Whether they come from the state or the cartels or from other murderers, the orders are always the same: that no trace remains. Where there is no trace of the body, where nothing remains, where nothing survives, nothing can be said to have happened. It will be impossible to say that *there is*—that there will have been—anything at all. Mourning is deferred by the pain suffered in the absence, the disappearance, of the body, a pain that seems "sometimes worse than death."[15]

On the one hand, although they are necessary for mourning, the remains of the victims also complicate its possibility. On the other hand, justice demands that the remains remain and that they be identified not simply as remains but as victims. Yet, because identification is never immediately given, there must be a mechanism to authenticate or assure identity, that is, that this name belongs to this body. Because the signs of identity are transferrable, exchangeable, another—one authorized to do so—must identify me at the moment that I no longer can.[16] In every case—whether through DNA analysis, state-issued identity documents (identity cards, drivers licenses, passports), or eyewitness identification or testimony—such identification depends on some unique, distinguishing mark or "signature." This "singular" face or body and this nonunique name come together and thus become authorized, in and through the signature, which presents itself as the embodiment of the name. The signature instances the name's becoming-corporeal, singular, and the body's becoming-repeatable, identifiable.

In principle a signature is unique. One instances oneself in the signature that is uniquely one's own. Despite this necessary singularity, for the signature to be legal and therefore binding, which means in order for one to affirm oneself in the signature, the signature must be repeatable. That is, it must be recognizable as mine, as the articulation of my legal person. This recognition is possible only in and through repetition. I am legally present only in the infinitely repeatable signature that both constitutes and displaces my singularity. An unrepeatable signature, a signature that would be impossible to counterfeit, would not be a signature; but, at the same time, a repeatable (and therefore verifiable, authentic) signature also separates or segregates itself from the "I" that signs. This separation, which is the law of the signature, makes possible identity but also permits forgery, fraud, and counterfeit. As a consequence, I only ever sign in the name of another; I counterfeit my signature every time I sign in my own name. To identify oneself is to defraud oneself. To sign and to affirm oneself in one's own name is to betray oneself, to perjure oneself. There is no other possibility. The signature ciphers (secretes) identity.

The signature figures—is literally inscribed—in the murders; it marks the bodies, their interpretation and identification in Ciudad Juárez. From the beginning there is a conflict of interpretations that turns on the legibility, on the presence or absence, of the signature of the murderer(s). González Rodríguez cites Robert K. Ressler, the former FBI agent often acknowledged as having coined the term "serial killer," who points out that "aberrant conduct has no nationality. . . . Moreover, the serial murderer always leaves a personal mark on the surface, something that identifies him, for example, the shoes to the side of the victims could be a signature" (2006, 18). The serial murderer always signs. In September 1996 pathologist David Trejo Silecio argued against this reading of the signature of seriality. In addition to opposing the announcement of the sexual violation of decomposed bodies and noting the failure of authorities to follow procedures for the collection of evidence, including how bodies were removed from crime scenes, the pathologist "was also opposed to the idea that the murderer left idiosyncratic traces, something that the press had emphasized," at least in the case of "the shoes placed to the side of the [female] dead as a fetishistic gesture." He dismissed the consistent placement of the shoes as "an incidental fact [*un hecho incidental*]" (2006, 61). According to Trejo Silecio, then, the placement of the shoes is not a signature because it is not intentional. Because it is incidental, it is an accident, void of meaning.[17]

It is not so easy, however, to erase the signature from the surfaces, whether of the bodies themselves or the location of the body and the "intentional" and strategic organization of its surroundings. For example, a group of satanic drug traffickers "called themselves 'rayados,' because they customarily left ritual marks on the skin" (González Rodíguez 2006, 68). The serial murderer Henry Lee Lucas testified to making thirty-five trips to Mexico to transport children from the United States and turn them over to the bosses of a sect that occupied a ranch. "Lucas said he remembered that the sacrificed bodies bore a mark: 'Sometimes round, other times there were lines or a *z* engraved with the tip of a pen.' Or an upside-down cross in the center of the victims' breasts" (71). On 28 March 1996, Mexican authorities announced the identification of the body of María Guadalupe Del Río Vázquez. Hers was one of the many corpses that had a mutilated breast; in this case "the left nipple was mutilated" (75). In 1998 the detention of Daniel Arizmendi López resulted in the discovery of "the complex network of one of the country's cruelest bands of kidnappers: they usually mutilated one ear of their victims" (72). On 6 November 2001 two female corpses were discovered in cotton fields on the outskirts of Ciudad Juárez. "It seemed," writes González Rodríguez, "the women were murdered on different dates and during the previous six months. The bodies even had signs of having been in a refrigerated room. Someone had 'planted' them there" (2006, 232). The following day, 7 November, five more bodies were found in the same cotton fields, and again it was determined that they had been murdered several months before and kept in a refrigerated room. According to Washington Valdez, "Authorities could never explain the time gap" (2006, 54).

The cotton fields are (or at least were) the property of the Barrio family and form[ed] part of the ranch named for Jaime Bermúdez Cuarón, the so-called "father of the maquiladora industry in Juárez." The Barrio family is headed by Francisco Barrio Terrazas, who in 1983 was elected municipal president. Bermúdez Cuarón supported him, and the Bermúdez family is one of the owners of Lote Bravo, the parcel of land where the first murdered women were found. It was Francisco Barrio who, as governor of Chihuahua, invited Ressler to consult on the investigation of the murders. A few days later, the solicitor González Rascón, violating the confidentiality the investigation warranted, "announced . . . a macabre detail of the serial homicides: on five of the bodies it was observed that a tuft of hair had been cut from the back of the head. Likewise, the victims died of asphyxiation by strangulation" (González Rodríguez 2006, 234). Other bodies from the cotton fields "preserved similarities with respect to the lesions inflicted . . . , for example, the mutilation of the breasts" (236). González Rodríguez notes that "in front of the [cotton] fields is the Maquiladora Association," and he suggests that "the bodies planted there were a morbid message to all those who knew how to read it" (233). Murder, it seems, is always a message, an open letter that remains to be deciphered. Writing of the murder on 11 September 2004 of Rodolfo Carrillo Fuentes, the brother of Amado and Vicente Carrillo Fuentes, Washington Valdez remarks, "The date gunmen picked to eliminate Rodolfo Carrillo Fuentes . . . was an obvious message. But for whom?" (2006, 110).

In Ciudad Juárez murders are messages sent from whom we do not know to unidentifiable addressees. Every murder is a dead letter, both legible and illegible, open and closed, signed and anonymous. The marks repeat themselves, thereby becoming legible as the same, as a signature, as a trace that nonetheless remains illegible, without sense, without meaning. The bodies, the corpses, are caught between existence and being, neither meaningless objects nor meaningful beings. The noncoincidence or noncorrespondence with itself of the body, the temporal disjunction that divides the body from itself, dividing existence from being, meaninglessness from meaningfulness, body from name, instances the logic of the secret, which names the separation from self that makes possible self-identity, guards and protects it, even as it surrenders it. Noncoincidence or noncorrespondence—which means that we only ever correspond to or with ourselves, that we are not immediately given either to ourselves or to others—also means that at the heart of all identity or identification is delay and deferral, a certain structural and unrelievable suspension. Because delay and deferral are structural, there will always be the need for the name and the impossibility of its coinciding with that which it names. The noncoincidence of the name and the singular being it nominates results in the necessity and impossibility of mourning.

In his account of the 1995 discovery of "the semi-nude body of a murdered young woman . . . found on the outskirts of Ciudad Juárez," González Rodríguez unwittingly announces the problem of the name and the impossibility of doing justice to the memory of the dead. He writes:

> *Symbolic of other murders*, it had been discarded in an abandoned area amid shrubs and trash. Judicial records indicate that the body was found "lying face down, her head oriented toward the north, the right arm bent beneath the abdomen and the left bent somewhat lengthwise; her legs spread." Death by strangulation was confirmed, and according to the forensics exam, it occurred at the same instant as the rapist's orgasm. Despite the decomposition of the remains, a "triangular cut wound" was observed "in the coccyx region, extending to the inner part of both gluteal regions, and the dilated anus." The criminal's signature. (2012, 90; emphasis added)[18]

The forensics report reveals a perverse—and fantastic—precision that illuminates both the empirical and transcendental problem of time or delay. The detail that the victim's death—the time of her death—coincided with the instant of the rapist's orgasm is both sensational and unverifiable. Because empirical methods for determining the time of death (body temperature and rigor and livor mortis) are always approximate, providing merely a narrower or broader time range within which death occurred, it is impossible to specify that the rapist's orgasm coincided with the victim's death.[19] The interval of time that the forensic report occludes (which González Rodríguez reports without questioning) is important for the feminicide and the maquiladora culture of Ciudad Juárez, in which intervals of time or delay—arriving, both coming and being, late—literally result in being "late," dead. In the testimonies collected in Monárrez's *Trama de una injusticia*, the problem of time, its calculus, provides the key to the murders—that is, to the culture of waste or expendability in which women can be used up and disposed of like so much industrial refuse.

The logic of temporal delay informs the culture of feminicide. On the one hand, there is the unrelievable, unmitigable demand to be *on time*, to arrive at the appointed hour; on the other hand, one always arrives too late and too soon. The maquiladora environment is organized temporally, in terms of both the laborers' shifts and the production process itself, which demands that workers meet certain production quotas, which in turn requires them to maintain a certain pace of production. The machine—the apparatus, its supervisors, and the capitalist machine itself—ultimately sets the pace in which the female worker "is, after all, an insignificant cog in the wheel of production" (Arriola 2010, 39). The female body is (part of) the machine. The maquiladora calculates with and against time. The clock never stops ticking and those who fall behind lose their jobs, sometimes their lives. "It's a system," writes Monárrez, "that is sustained with the reproduction of disposable women: when their labor performance slows down, their fingers become stiff, they suffer from stress or headaches among other symptoms, it's the moment to fire them without having to indemnify them" (2009, 76). It is always a question of taking too much time and thus of losing time. The case of Claudia Ivette González Banda makes explicit the disposability of women who do not arrive on time.[20]

On 10 October 2001 Claudia Ivette "arrived . . . two minutes late at her job at the Lear Corporation maquiladora; they didn't let her enter for her shift and no one knew anything about her" (Monárrez 2009, 142). The maquiladora denied her entry for arriving (*being*) two minutes late despite her having won an award for attendance. The award marks or indicates, but also measures, her attendance, her presence over time, her being-on-time or being-there, without, however, giving her any credit for being timely. Consequently, the award does not amount to time saved in the name of or in the account of Claudia Ivette; the time saved is not credited to her. It does not add up to a time that could have been spent later to make up (or account) for time lost. The time that the award counts—for which it accounts—is not enough to save her life. Put another way, the maquiladoras make extra time (*tiempo extra*, overtime) available for the workers, thus making themselves larger profits and, ultimately, saving (themselves) time, but they never allow that savings to be spent by the workers. The women have no credit. Women save time for the maquiladora, but they only ever lose time for themselves. The extra time a woman works is time lost. To gain time is to lose time: the women of Juárez are always already late, posthumous.

Such systemic, structural belatedness is legible in the case of Lilia Alejandra García Andrade, who "was sequestered on 14 February 2001" (Monárrez 2009, 140).[21] Valentine's Day. For three months, after separating from her partner, Lilia Alejandra had been living with her mother and father. On the morning of the day of her disappearance, she asked her mother for money for the bus. Her mother, Norma Andrade de Garcia, was upset with her and "was punishing her" (141). Because it was Valentine's Day and she believed her daughter would go out with her new boyfriend after work, and because she was upset with her about the new boyfriend, she decided not to pick her up at work, thinking she would end up wasting her time waiting for her daughter. "I'm not going to go for her. . . . I know in the end Leonardo is going to bring her, and she is going to think that I'm playing the fool. . . .

I said it's a way not to lift the punishment" (141). Indeed, Norma admits that even as time passed (*"vio correr el tiempo"*) and her daughter did not return home, she was most concerned with the punishment, which she figured as payment or debt: "Ah, but, damned Alejandra, when you get home you're going to pay for this. I was really upset, because I believed that she was running around with that boy" (141). What she did not know, however, was that Alejandra and Leonardo did not work the same shift, and "Alex, when she left the maquila . . . she stayed there talking with him for about an hour, and at eight she left, she left alone, and she didn't call me. Because she thought, well, I don't know, I think she must have thought that, because I was angry, for that reason I hadn't gone, right?" Subsequently, Norma would learn that Alejandra "didn't stay to work overtime [*tiempo extra*]" (141). Lilia Alejandra García Andrade was out of time. Monárrez writes, "The mother realized that the notion of time regulated by others and the meaning of time regulated by Lilia Alejandra herself have been disturbed. Alex is no longer part of those times; therefore, she is left with the anguish about where her daughter might be" (2009, 142). This is the upshot of a woman's life on the Mexico-US border: time is regulated by multinational, transnational capital. Writing of the murder of Claudia Ivette, Monárrez concludes, "We could venture to say that the fragmented body of Claudia Ivette loses the possibility of continuing its existence in historical time by not complying with the regulation of time marked by the aims of capital" (2009, 144). Or, as Jean Franco remarks, "What some people have termed 'savage capitalism' keeps its eye on profit, not on people" (2013, 225). Out of time or out of step with time counted or marked by capital, by its interests and aims, its intentions, no one knows *where* or *if* you are.[22] This is what it means to be late: there is no *extra* time. Women live on *borrowed* time. They are, then, always in debt to a system that abuses them. Women pay (for) the interest of capital with their bodies, with their lives.

Whereas to arrive late means to be out of time, to arrive early, which ought to result in more time, a certain surplus or savings, in fact results in less time. The victim-survivors who seek justice for their lost (murdered, disappeared) beloved daughters are too often told to *wait*, that *not enough time has passed* to determine whether something—an event, a sequestration, a murder—has happened.[23] And once enough time has passed, it is too late. This is not simply the case for the women who have been murdered and their families, the survivors, who are also victims. It is also the case for justice, which demands that one act—respond—immediately, as soon as possible. At the same time, however, it requires that one calculate, investigate, learn as much as possible—in short, that one delay, that one take all the time necessary for justice. Justice is always caught between the mutually exclusive demands for precipitation or urgency and patience or delay. But in Mexico the delay results not from the state's internal demand for investigation, its desire to come to the right decision and judgment. Rather, it comes from incompetence and impunity, from a "fatal indifference" that is not disinterested but masks an interest in maintaining the culture of feminicide in which women are disposable objects.[24] In other words, the delay results from a desire to maintain the status quo or the performative-constativity of *what is*, of a certain understanding of power (*pouvoir*, *puissance*, *poder*) as presence, of being-present, thus of always already being-on-time. Capital imagines itself as present, ubiquitous, omniscient. It figures itself as the living present, an actuality or reality that "poor, brown females," as Alicia Gaspar de Alba calls them, too often do not survive.[25]

Although the examples of temporal disjunction—whether the impossibility of determining with any precision the simultaneity of the violator-murderer's orgasm and the victim's death or of delimiting the temporal regulation of feminicide culture—are all empirical, they accord with a transcendental principle that is not unrelated to the double law and the double bind of the name. It is a fact of mortal being that we always arrive at death too soon—in anticipation of it—and too late (which means death comes too soon to us) for us to experience it "as such." In *Dying for Time*, Martin Hägglund observes, "The same structure of deferral and delay characterizes temporal experience in general." This is so, he remarks, because "a temporal event can never be present as such, since it comes into being only by becoming past and becoming related to the future." As a consequence of this logic, "the experience of the event is always given *too late* (in relation to what is no longer) and *too soon* (in relation to what is not yet)" (61). This holds for all experience, including orgasm, for sure, but also for the experience of pain, which is why all pain is, from the beginning, painfulness, hence, symbolic. The temporal logic of delay or belatedness instances the anachronism of the event, not because the event lies outside time but because temporal succession depends on deferral and delay, *spacing*, such that every event, as Hägglund argues in *Radical Atheism*, is destroyed in its coming-to-be.[26] The possibility of any event thus demands that it happen or arrive both too soon and too late, which means the event never coincides with itself in any given simplicity or self-presence. The non-self-coincidence of the event demands the name. The event is comprehended, both lost and found, always in anticipation and belatedly, in the name and in the signature that leaves a trace in and as the world.

Temporal delay informs the logic of the name that troubles González

Rodríguez's determination that this particular murdered woman is "*symbolic* of the other murders." González Rodríguez is not the only commentator or analyst, whether journalistic or academic, to refer to the idea of symbolization to help explain the murders and the culture of feminicide. For example, Diana Washington Valdez writes that the murder and mutilation of Javier Felipe "El Negro" Lardizabal "is a powerful symbol in the history of the Juárez women's murders" (2006, 114). Found in November 1993 in Lote Bravo, which would later become a "cemetery" for murdered, mutilated, and raped women and girls, Lardizabal had disappeared in May 1993 "while conducting an undercover investigation into corruption within the Chihuahua state police" (113). According to Washington Valdez, "After Lardizabal's murder, there would not be another local investigation of Juárez police corruption until 2004. His death was symbolic because it set the stage for what was to come for the next dozen years" (114). In other words, Lardizabal's murder symbolizes not the beginning of the feminicides, although it more or less coincided with their beginning, but rather the impunity of the perpetrators. His murder "heralded the emergence of the Juárez police cartel" (114), which is implicated in the feminicides and, more generally, in the lawlessness that reigns in Juárez and northern Mexico, whether through negligence, incompetence, corruption, and/or active participation in the sequestrations, torture, and murder of women and girls. Washington Valdez writes: "I once asked Susie Azar, a former El Paso mayor who had operated a maquiladora in Juárez, for her thoughts on the disappearances in broad daylight with no one seeing or hearing anything. Without hesitation, she replied, 'The police are doing it. If no one sees or hears anything, then the police have got to be doing it'" (127).

The murder of Lardizabal symbolizes, according to Washington Valdez, the rise of the police cartel, which itself figures or announces systemic violence, the new order of everydayness in which "justice," nominally the responsibility of the state and its judicial apparatus, can no longer be expected from it. That is, in Ciudad Juárez "justice" does not come from the state, nor does it happen by chance or accident; it results instead from criminal activity, which means, simply, "justice" is more of the same. In 1993 Rosa Lardizabal, the sister of Javier Felipe Lardizabal, "accused Jésus Buil Issa, a Chihuahua state judicial police commander, of being involved in the disappearance of her brother" (Washington Valdez 114). In 2005 "Jésus Buil Issa was abducted in Juárez by one of the mysterious armed commandos that roam the region. . . . Rosa Lardizabal said she did not wish on anyone what happened to Buil Issa. But she nonetheless viewed his death as a form of justice for her brother's kidnapping, torture, and murder at the hands of police" (114–115). To declare that the violation of another *is* just, or is a *form* of justice, presupposes the constative-performative presence of an undivided sovereignty that realizes or actualizes itself—absolutely, *without remainder and without delay*, immediately—in *act*; it is an intention that would be absolutely transparent, without reservation, without secret. It would, in effect, be a justice without decision, since a decision always takes time, which negates the possibility of immediacy. Such justice would be terror—and thus unjust—in that it would be automatic, mechanical, without delay, without reserve, without secret, without any possible deliberation or appeal.

Such a conception of justice would ultimately make it impossible to distinguish the state from criminal organizations, justice from injustice. There would be no difference between them, but, importantly, there would also be neither hope for nor expectation of a difference. Put simply, were sovereignty absolute and undivided in itself (not unlike Segato's understanding of the signature, for instance), the expectation that the state should protect its citizens would make no sense, because an absolute sovereign could only ever *be* (constative) what it *does* (performative). If—but only if—sovereignty were absolute, the "paradox" Ileana Rodríguez identifies would make sense. Jean Franco explains that Rodríguez "astutely points out that 'cultural analysts interrogate the nature of the state by denouncing its indifference to *feminicidio*, yet they simultaneously demand that justice be served to the bereaved families of these women and that protection be given to all the nation's citizens. Thus, while they rebuff the state, they hold it accountable to the well-being of the community'" (Franco 2013, 223, quoting Rodríguez 2009, 158).[27] These positions are incompatible only if the state is absolutely identifiable with its acts. But no sovereign entity—whether the state or any other—has ever been simply or absolutely identifiable with its acts, as if intention were transparent and undivided. Because the state is not simply or unequivocally what it does—because sovereignty is necessarily divided in order that it act in the first place—no state, no sovereign, can guarantee protection and justice for its citizens; it can only ever promise protection and justice. But because protection and justice are promised, no matter how corrupt the state is, it must always be held accountable by its citizens, who, in turn, must demand that which has been promised. However, it is impossible that such a promise be fulfilled once and for all, insofar as the guarantee of fulfillment would mean the state was absolute. Put simply, the state will always disappoint its citizens because justice and protection cannot be present, guaranteed; yet such disappointment is also the only possibility for justice. Further, the impossibility of protection and justice does not and cannot mitigate the demand for protection and justice *here and now*.

In *La culture de la peur*, Marc Crépon refers to the impossibility of the state's promise to its citizens as abandonment, and he writes that "liberalism is, among other things, the name we give to the ideology of that *abandon*" (1:2008, 79). From the moment the state "claims to protect some from one or another of [its citizens], it exposes and abandons them to those whom it does not take in hand—those whom it judges ineluctable, in the name of the laws of history or of economy, or those it esteems are not within its competence" (79). According to Crépon, therefore, the liberal state can only ever promise its citizens their well-being or security: what, for example, the United States calls the *right* to life, liberty, and the pursuit of happiness, or what France calls "*liberté, égalité, fraternité.*" Yet, as Crépon points out, "According to its essence, every promise of protection, circumscribed to a determined domain, contains in itself a threat of this very *abandon*. This is why human security's retreat [*le repli*] to the state's protection is not separable from its negative effects" (79–80). Although Crépon identifies this abandonment with the liberal state, insofar as the promise of the state has been the same at least since Hobbes's theorization of it in *Leviathan*, it is hard to imagine a state structure that does not abandon its citizen-subjects as the cost—the collateral damage—of both their protection and its institution. In other words, the state protects itself (and many of its citizens) by abandoning many of its citizens, thereby jeopardizing itself, threatening itself. Such abandonment instances the autoimmunity of state sovereignty. The more the state attempts to preserve and protect its citizens, thereby preserving and protecting itself, the more it necessarily turns away from (some, many) citizens thereby threatening itself. The state destroys itself protecting itself.[28]

Jean Franco, too, takes up the self-destructive state and does so by turning to symbolization in her analysis of the cruelty of modernity, suggesting that "the symbolic significance" of the increasingly common practice of beheading or decapitation "goes right to the issue of sovereignty, making it a dramatic statement of the mutilation of the sovereign state" (2013, 227). In 1789 Joseph-Ignace Guillotin proposed decapitation by guillotine as the universal punishment in France for capital crimes. The proposal and the practice were formally adopted in 1791, making it the French state's official and universal method of capital punishment; it was first used on 25 April 1792, which means the practice has its place—alongside the Declaration of the Universal Rights of Man (1789)—in the history of the Enlightenment (with the democratic movements and the institution of literature it inspired).

Indeed, Guillotin proposed to modernize "a simple machine" already widely in use in other countries (Arrasse 1987, 23) in the name of "the 'philosophical' humanization of justice" (26). He claimed that the guillotine was more humane than other forms of execution in three ways. First, although it inspires fear in the condemned, it kills softly and quickly, in the blink of an eye ("*clin d'oeil*") and with "the least pain." According to *Le Moniteur*, which reported on the assembly session at which Guillotin described the machine's efficaciousness, Guillotin remarked, "The form of execution I have invented is so gentle that one would not know what to say if one were not expecting to die and that one would believe to have felt only a slight chill on the neck" (Arrasse 1987, 35). Second, the guillotine would spare the public the horrible spectacle that accompanied, for instance, the execution of Robert-François Damiens (28; for a description, see Foucault 1975, 9–12). Third, it would spare the executioner the traumatic intimacy of execution. In addition, Guillotin's proposed Article 6 (the one that required the most time for ratification) stipulated that "in every case where the law pronounces the death penalty against the accused, the form of execution will be the same, whatever the nature of the crime for which he will be rendered culpable. The criminal will be decapitated; it will take place by the effect of a simple machine [il le sera par l'effet d'une simple mécanique]" (Arasse 1987, 26). The universality of decapitation effectively annulled the privilege accorded to the aristocracy, for whom it had been previously reserved, making the guillotine an instrument of democracy. The most humane and the most democratic killing machine, the guillotine was also the most efficient. As such, it could be argued, it represented the sovereign promise for a better, more just, and more humane state.

Immediate and impersonal, it is also—as is any form of death penalty—without appeal. The guillotine is unaffected, unmoved. It is fatally indifferent. This indifference—the mechanicalness and automaticity of its execution, its strict impersonality—makes it the symbol of both justice and terror, of a justice that cannot be distinguished from terror.[29] In other words, the chance for a more democratic and humane, a more just state is the threat of a more autocratic and inhumane, a less just state.

Franco would agree, remarking, in the wake of sovereign mutilation, "The headless societies are dominated by fear" (1987, 227). But fear—which is to say, the care for a life constitutively threatened—is existential and without relief. Hobbes understood this. We are as afraid *within* the sovereign state as we are *without* it.[30] This is the double bind of sovereignty, which Franco apparently believes was once held in check: "Once we strip humanity of transcendental destiny, once the utopian has been discredited, once we take away the ethical imperatives of either religious belief or humanism, there is nothing to rein in our infamous desires" (235). Thus, the cruelty of modernity depends on our having lost our faith. In a faithless world—without transcendental destiny, utopias, and ethical imperatives—we are threatened by our "infamous desires," hence by a sovereignty ("I can," "I will," "I want") without limits. "What freedom has brought about," Franco laments, "is self-destruction through the quest for pleasure that leads to boredom or worse" (235). A "transcendental destiny" refers either to religious faith (that is, faith in some destiny beyond the strictures of time and space) or to a Kantian moral law that regulates our lives from beyond the limits of our pathological investments. It is, then, the idea of an eternal destiny, whether religious or humanist, expressed in the idea of eternal progress toward perpetual peace. But the absoluteness of such a transcendental destiny demands an indifference to life in the name of an absolute good (eternal salvation or the moral imperative). There can be no doubt that the ethical imperatives of both religious belief and humanism are more pernicious than benevolent, justifying, as they have always done, religious and secular wars, racial and ethnic hatred, religious intolerance, domestic violence, feminicides, the death penalty. The list could go on, but the question would remain the same: How does the indifference to human life inspired by the ethical imperatives of religious faith and humanism differ from what Franco condemns as the lack of empathy for and carelessness of human life that results from "freedom"? Isn't rather the promise of religious belief and secular humanism—in short, the promise of a transcendental destiny—the threat of evil? And the evil is not only that religion has gone over, as Franco puts it, "to the dark side," and in doing so that it "sanctifies . . . this absolute indifference to the life of another" (228, 229). One wonders when religion and its insistence on a transcendental destiny will not have promoted such indifference to life? In other words, Franco conflates "freedom" with the dark side toward which religion will have turned, failing to understand that freedom is the condition of both sides. It is the condition of possibility both of caring for the other and of being indifferent to the other. But only the notion of freedom—contrary to the idea of a transcendental destiny—opens onto the ideas of justice and responsibility.

Unlike González Rodríguez and Washington Valdez, who are both journalists, Jean Franco is a Latin American cultural and literary critic, but like them she quickly recurs to the idea of symbolization to help explain or comprehend the murders and the events taking place in Ciudad Juárez.[31] Whether it is a beheading or the murder of an undercover officer investigating police corruption or the murder of a young woman, these acts become symbols of other murders, of other acts or practices, of cultural/social processes, of the state of sovereignty, of the state of violence. Despite consistent and near universal recourse to symbolization, no one asks how a symbol is constituted or what it means to be a symbol, what is gained and what is lost in such a determination. Julia Monárrez perhaps comes closest when she turns to Bourdieu to explain the effects of symbolic violence:

> Pierre Bourdieu argues that even when domination is founded on the conduct of force, it always possesses a symbolic component. In symbolic violence, the acts of submission and obedience are present and they are exerted by the support that the dominated cannot cease to grant to the dominant and the domination in general. . . . This structure of power relations becomes an instrument for advancing hegemonic schemas that come to seem natural. . . . Such categories order and maintain social structures and perceptions, and they ultimately come to be defined by structures of inequitable capital. (2010a, 184–185)

On the basis of an analysis of "comments made by privileged groups in 2004," Monárrez claims to have been "able to confirm how symbolic power constructs reality and how it establishes a set of beliefs and legitimate knowledge" (185). In her use of "symbolic violence" and "symbolic power," the "symbolic" refers to a capacity for and control of representation. The symbolic is meaningful. Symbolic violence refers to meaningful violence, on the one hand, and, on the other hand, to a violence that is ostensibly "less" violent than "real" or nonsymbolic, nonrepresentational violence. Yet, the representation of women as lazy, as unreliable, as late, as sexually promiscuous is symbolic violence that does real violence to women. In short, symbolic violence is real violence and real violence does symbolic work. Despite the impossibility of rigorously distinguishing symbolic from nonsymbolic violence, Monárrez's analysis is necessary, not least because, as she remarks, the effect of the hegemonic determination of symbolic violence and symbolic power has "consequences for the attainment of justice" (2010a, 185).

Yet if power is irreducible, if it inheres in every relation, and if every relation of power ineluctably "possesses a symbolic component," then the attainment of justice is constitutively violent and itself necessarily symbolic. It is therefore essential to understand the constitution of the symbol and, more so, its relation to the singular body and being—the singular life—of the murdered, who, through no interest or intention of her own, becomes a symbol in various discursive contexts. Symbolization—a certain symbolic violence and symbolic power—is not simply the work of hegemonic discourses. On the contrary, those who seek justice, those who strive to understand and explain the cultural phenomenon of the feminicides—those who, Monárrez suggests, seek to calculate "the responsibility that corresponds to" everyone implicated (more or less) in the economy of femicide—also have recourse to symbolization and, thus, to a symbolic violence and symbolic power. Everyone turns victims, dead bodies, into symbols. What is at stake in this irreducible, unavoidable gesture? For instance, in the case of González Rodríguez's account, what does it mean to say that *this* murder—*this* found body—is "symbolic of other murders"? How does one see in *this* body, in the *singular* death of *this* young woman, the *symbol* of other murders and other *singular* deaths? How is it that a young murdered woman substitutes for or "represents" others?[32] How is it that through the gesture of symbolization, many singular murdered women add up to one?

If this body symbolizes others, how is the relation between the bodies to be thought? It is well known, for instance, that Mexican authorities substituted one body for another, as if any body would do, as if each was, finally, always the same body; but we also know that the police sought to diminish any relation between the bodies (that is, between the murders), routinely denying the possibility of their seriality or of any connection between them. For example, as Washington Valdez points out, "The state police file for Elizabeth Castro says she had a triangle carved on her back, a mark the killer or killers also left on several of the previous Juárez victims. But Chihuahua state authorities held firm. They said the deaths were not related" (2006, 49). Later, she attests, "Multiple bodies were found at Lote Bravo in 1995 and in Lomas de Poleo in 1996. In between, other brutally murdered victims were found in the outskirts of the city, on city streets, and in motels. And each time, the authorities were adamant that there was no connection" (69). For the Mexican state, each murder was absolutely singular, without reference to any other murder. Each murder was so singular as to be beyond any possible count or account. The bodies, the murders, do not add up.

To name one body the *symbol* of others, as González Rodríguez does, diminishes the singularity, the irreplaceability, of each, but it is impossible to bear witness to the murdered women without making each murder symbolic of others, precisely in order that they pass between us, that we take account of them. This is the unavoidable effect of the signature, of the iterability constitutive of both its singularity and its universality, its authenticity and authority. In other words, each murder is symbolic not only of other murders in Ciudad Juárez, but of all the murders in the world. Every murder refers or remits itself to all murders, as if each murder were not only the *last* in the incalculable series of murders but also the *first*. Every *singular* murder, *qua* symbol, recalls every murder that ever was and anticipates every murder to come.[33]

To call the corpse of a murdered woman (of this singular murdered woman) a symbol of other murdered women, however necessary and well-intended the gesture, is never innocent or without violence. And if it is true that the violence of symbolization or of naming is not the same as the violence of murder, it is also true that any analysis of the Juárez feminicide—any analysis of any feminicide or genocide, or for that matter of any murder—requires the negotiation of the paradox of the name, of the symbol. It is necessary to name the violated in order to do justice to the victims and to mourn them. But in naming them, we cannot *avoid* doing violence to them, to their memory and to their survival, as the very condition of their memory and survival. And this means in doing justice to the murdered, we nevertheless do them an injustice. Thus, in *accounting for* the feminicide, which means in *counting* the bodies and *recounting* the names, how do we take an *interest* in the victims, how do we *pay attention* to them, without violating them once more by diminishing the absolute singularity and irreplaceability of their lives?

But if justice and mourning depend on the *interest* we take in the victims, then the issue becomes the *use* of the other; it becomes a problem of usury. This is what is at stake in Roberto Bolaño's *2666* when one character recalls that another had observed, "No one pays attention to these murders, but in them is hidden the secret of the world [Nadie presta atención a estos asesinatos, pero en ellos se esconde el secreto del mundo]" (2004, 439).[34] The idiom "*prestar atención*" is correctly translated as "pays attention," but it literally refers to lending: "No one lends attention to these murders." A *préstamo*, for example, is a loan. It is a matter not simply of *paying* but of *lending* attention. It is a matter of *interest*.[35] The symbol is usurious; it is the mechanism of verbal usury, which refers to an increase in meaning that results in the loss of meaning.[36] The symbol means both more and less at the same time. It will be impossible *not* to participate in this economy of the name (the signature, the symbol) and of the world, for the name gives meaning to the world even as, always inflationary, it shows the world to be counterfeit coin, that which cannot be legally tendered to another in exchange, that which, when rendered to another, renders all community and communication suspect.

Later in *2666* the character named Sergio, who writes for the "culture and gossip" section of a newspaper and who is based on Sergio González Rodríguez, claims that those who listened to him recount his interest in the feminicide, did so "like children who hear for the umpteenth time the same story that terrorizes and immobilizes them, assenting gravely with their heads, accomplices in the same secret" (706). Accomplices in the same secret, they are murderers, like us. This is what it means to be welcomed into and to form part of a community. At the end of Bolaño's *Los detectives salvajes*, Juan García Madero reports a conversation he had with Lupe, the Mexico City prostitute that Ulises Lima, Arturo Belano, and García Madero help escape from her *padrote*, Alberto, in the Sonoran Desert where so much of *2666* takes place. "Before we left Lupe said that we could return to Villaviciosa whenever we wanted. Why?, I ask. Because the people accept us. They are murderers, the same as we are. We aren't murderers. I say. The Villaviciosans aren't either, it's just a way of speaking, Lupe says" (1998, 608). We are welcome because we are all murderers. We are all complicit, accomplices, in the story (*cuento*) and the account (*cuenta*) of the murders. It is a story and an account that we always tell/pay too soon and too late, with too little and too much interest. This universal culpability haunts the protagonist of Alicia Gaspar de Álba's novel *Desert Blood: The Juárez Murders* (2005), who concludes, "This thing implicated everyone. No wonder the crimes had not been solved, nor would they ever be solved until someone with much more power than she, with nothing to lose or to gain, brought this conspiracy out into the open" (335).[37] What does it mean to await someone with nothing to lose and nothing to gain? One wonders if such a person—someone completely uninvested, uninterested, disinterested—could ever be compelled to care.[38]

Since 1492 this interest—the chance of gain, the threat of loss, the promise of the world—is Columbus's legacy. In his last will and testament—notarized in Valladolid 19 May 1506 by Pedro de Ennoxedo—Columbus leaves to his heirs two things: all the rent (*renta*) owed him on his share of the New World and his debts: "I tell and order Diego, my son, or *to whomever inherits*, to pay all the debts that I leave here in a memorial, in the form indicated there, and also the others that will justly appear that I left" (Colón 1992, 536, emphasis added). We sign in his name and for his debts. The interest of this inheritance—the gain and the loss—remains incalculable.

CHAPTER 3

AS IF . . . LITERATURE BEFORE THE WORLD

Lo que nos importa es la intención, el rumbo del flujo.
ALFONSO REYES, *LA EXPERIENCIA LITERARIA* (1941)

La idea de la ficción . . . yace completamente en ese pedestre y desconcertante como si. *El* como si *que nuestro cerebro aplica a diario para que nuestro cuerpo se mueva razonablemente por el mundo, para que descubra nuevas fuentes de energía y consiga salvaguardarse de depredadores y enemigos. El* como si *que nos impide tropezar a cada instante, que nos mantiene en equilibrio y nos impide estrellarse contra una ventana o caer de una escalera. El* como si *que nos permite relacionarse con los espectros ambulantes de los otros.*
JORGE VOLPI, *LEER LA MENTE* (2011)

La possibilité de la fiction ne se dérive pas.
JACQUES DERRIDA, *LIMITED INC* (1990)

THE INTENTION OF LITERATURE

If Roberto Bolaño is correct that we do not lend or pay attention to the murders of women in Ciudad Juárez, yet within them hides the secret of the world, then the problem of the symbol—its constitutive seeming or fiction, its ineluctable violence, its remainder—begs the question of the relation of literature to the world, of literature's interest in the world and of the world's interest or investment in literature.[1] How is the secret of the world "kept"—"revealed," "shared"—by murders to which we pay no attention or interest? Is it possible to pay or to lend attention to—to take interest in—*this* murder, *this* death, *this* life? What of the world that opens and closes with every birth, every murder, every death, every life? How to account for the world that opens only through the movement of symbolization (simulacrum, counterfeit, spectrality, fiction), which secretes us from and in the world? How is the world revealed to us even as it is kept from us?

In the wake of Mexican philosopher Antonio Caso's challenge to state-sanctioned positivism, the reinvestiture of philosophy as an academic discipline in Mexico, and the discipline's subsequent engagement with Husserlian phenomenology, Mexican polymath Alfonso Reyes explicitly posed the question of literature's relation both to other discursive constructs and to "reality."[2] In *La experiencia literaria*, Reyes distinguishes "the principal activities of spirit" in the following way: "Philosophy concerns being; history and science, real events . . . ; literature, an imaginary event, although comprising elements of reality, the only material available to us for our creations" (1962, 82).[3] Later, in *El deslinde* (first published in 1944), his phenomenographical "prolegomena to a literary theory," he reasserts literature's dependence on and appropriation of a "minimum of reality [*mínimo de realidad*]" (1963a, 197): "The servility of fiction is simply said in Goethe's confession: 'I, original? I do nothing more than recompose in my way what the world lends me'" (205).[4] On Reyes's account, literature depends on what the world *lends* an author, and even if said author does not borrow much—only the necessary "minimum of reality"—the debt always comes due. Literature pays (with) interest.

According to Reyes, literature—like every other modality of expression—has a semantic value (its meaning or "*significado*") and a formal value (its "linguistic expressions") (1962, 82). These two values are themselves functions of intention: "The common denominator of both values is in the intention. The semantic intention refers to the fictitious event; the formal intention refers to the aesthetic expression. There is only literature when both intentions come together. We will call them, for short, fiction and form" (82). Literature instances the synthesis of meaning (fiction) and linguistic embodiment or expression (form). Importantly, on Reyes's account, unlike history or philosophy or scientific discourses, only literature depends on the absolute synthesis of meaning (the semantic intention) and expression (the formal intention). The insistence on the synthesis of fiction (meaning) and form (expression) has two consequences. *First*, the lack of a gap or interval, of difference or delay, between spirit and letter means that, strictly speaking, literature is untranslatable.[5] In other words, literature manifests the absolute singularity of meaningful expression: that which cannot be said otherwise and still say the same thing. *Second*, the acknowledgment that literature results from the synthesis of fiction and form means that they do not coincide: a synthesis necessarily takes time and marks a spatial-temporal relating of fiction and form. As a result, literature is the fiction of the absolute coincidence of meaning and expression. It is as if "literature" named an absolute singularity that was nevertheless legible, that which could not be translated and yet could be read. It would be a symbolic structure whose material support (its expression) nevertheless failed to suggest anything other than its symbolic meaning. Literature would be the sign that signed only itself, that never pointed toward anything other than itself. Literature would be absolutely self-referential. Yet it is clear (given Reyes's insistence on the minimal borrowing from reality) that this cannot be the case: literature must refer beyond itself, at least to the extent it borrows from reality.

Reyes calls literature a fictive rather than a mimetic art, because, he contends, "mimesis" is too easily misconstrued as the imitation—the mere copying or the dead repetition—of reality. For Reyes, "fiction" names three related operations that combine to produce and to reproduce the world. First, fiction "indicates that we add a new structure—probable or improbable—to those that already exist." Second, "It indicates that our intention is to feign ignorance of the real event." Third, "It indicates that we translate a subjective reality," which Reyes calls "a psychological truth" (1962, 82–83). Literature *translates* a *subjective reality* that *subtracts itself from* and *adds itself to* an already existing reality characterized as the "set of acts exterior to our spirit" (83). As an intentional structure, fiction *distances* us from reality—by feigning ignorance (*desentenderse*) of it, without, however, negating entirely one's relation to it, since, as Reyes notes, literature or fiction must include a "minimum of reality." On the basis of this understanding of fiction—its specific intentionality, its intentional ignorance of and thus subtraction from and addition to reality—Reyes calls literature both a "*mentira práctica* [practical lie]" and "*la verdad sospechosa* [the suspect truth]" (83).[6]

Reyes thus makes two important claims about literature. The first is ontological: "Like language itself, [literature] is in essence oral. To write—Goethe said—is an abuse of the word. Speech is essence; the letter, contingency" (83). Language is essentially speech, and literature, despite being characterized by the letter, is essentially oral. In *El deslinde*, Reyes writes:

> We preserve, then, the current term "literature," certain that no one will be perturbed by the etymological origin of the word, the limitation of the "letter" or written character, and that everyone knows that literature is as oral as written. Strictly speaking, [it is] oral in essence (and not only by generic origin), as the graphic character refers to the spoken word and

> from which it takes its meaning, and the word is only written by accident [*por accidente*], as an aide to memory. (1963a, 37)

The first two sentences of *La experiencia literaria* make clear writing's accidental relation to language: "To write . . . is no more than a diversion. Writing, accident of language, may or may not have been: language exists without it" (1962, 21). Reyes's insistence on the essential orality of literature, as if literature's materiality were simply accidental, allows him to posit literature as the perfect synthesis of meaning and expression, such that each is exhausted in the other without remainder. This determination of literature in turn permits him to link literature to what he calls a "primitive" moment of communication without the phenomenon of language, therefore without the necessity of language passing between us and becoming worldly. Such unmediated communication, without the passage through the world, marks the fantasy of a world without difference, without violence, without equivocation. Everyone would "share" the same thoughts, except this would not be sharing since insofar as there would be no difference between us, there would be no exchange. In *La experiencia literaria* Reyes calls this "telepathy" (1962, 23). For Reyes, then, literature—the experience of literature—would name the possibility, after the fall into language, of the return to a "time" before the difference language makes. On Reyes's account, "literary experience" signals the chance of direct perception, of an unmediated intuition. The experience of literature would return us to the thing itself.

Yet Reyes makes clear that even if language is capable of existing without writing, civilization is not: "Writing, by fixing the fluidity of language, establishes one of the indispensible bases for a true civilization" (1962, 21). Not only civilization but existence itself requires the possibility of tradition, of inheritance, thus, of conservation: "A certain dose [*una cierta dosis*] of conservation in the things seems to us a *sine qua non* clause in order to accept the contract of existence" (21).

Existence depends on "a certain dose of conservation" in order for the "contract of existence" to be accepted, which means existence always takes the form of a countersignature. Existence is belated, delayed. Whatever exists must leave a remainder; it must have at least a certain dose of conservation. Consequently, existence—the contract of existence—comes after itself. It follows, then, that existence instances the countersignature of what remains. We are always already "in"—a party to—the contract; we sign belatedly, countersign, and thus "accept" a contract that already binds us to the time of existence. Therefore, the existence of language—its specific "there is," the essentially oral word—must remain, and thus depends upon a "certain conservation," to survive as language in the first place. Reyes contends that because it is the purest expression of spirit, the spoken word goes up in smoke at the moment it leaves the mouth: "The *word*—smoke from the mouth in the Chinese hieroglyph—wants to disperse itself in the air" (1962, 21). The voice ("*la voz*") requires, therefore, a material support (inscription) so that it may remain as language, thereby making possible the "contract of existence" between human beings, which Reyes figures as the possibility of rights against the sovereign's capriciousness: "In order for the word to persist, in order that it bind and commit the conduct of the one who proffers it, the bureaucratic right was born that, while constitutional right was still arriving, at least obliged the sovereign not to recant constantly. In order that the creations of the word were not lost . . . the fixing of language was invented" (21). The bond of community, the binding of sovereign to subject (the law), takes place in and through the fixing and binding of writing, which, according to Reyes, conserves what spoken language creates but cannot sustain.

One of the creations of language, which the written word fixes and conserves, is the human being itself and the society in which it survives, "as if man, each man and human society, were something other than constellations of words" (1963b, 214). Just a page later, Reyes reaffirms that "man is a speaking being" (215). In "Hermes o la comunicación humana," the first chapter of *La experiencia literaria*, Reyes wonders whether "mute man, anterior to language . . . communicated with his peers through a certain radiation that goes from one mind to another, emitted and received through the nerve antennas" (1962, 22). Despite acknowledging that such communication has not been established by science, he nonetheless wants to retain it as a "metaphor" (22) of a primitive or animal nonverbal form of communication that we—humans—have lost, the sign of a divine power lost through human sin (23). We were closer to the gods before we spoke. The exchange of words *promises* existence, inheritance, and living tradition. As Reyes has already suggested, however, writing not only makes survival possible by preserving the word but also abuses the word, which means the *exchange* of words, which Reyes calls "coin [*la moneda*]" (1963b, 268), results in both gain and loss. Gained is the archive (hence conservation or survival), freedom of expression (which Reyes also calls "improvisation" [269]), and law, all of which (archive, freedom of expression, and law) writing makes possible. Lost, however, is the immediacy or presence of life experienced in the recitation of the poem that has not been corrupted—mediated or delayed, hence conserved—by "graphic signs" (269).

It is important not to lose sight of Reyes's fundamentally ontological claim: because existence is economical and contractual, delay or deferral—time or temporalization—must be inscribed at the heart of existence or being. Whatever is, whatever exists, arrives late; existence is belated, delayed, posthumous. This is his essential claim, but it is no less important to stress Reyes's specific exemplification of the economy of existence through the example—which is not one example among others—of language and the particularity of the *spoken* word, on the one hand; and, on the other hand, the necessity of the *written* word for the possibility of freedom of expression and law. In sum, for Reyes the example of existence is human being, and that which most exemplifies human being is language. Language, however, is possible only insofar as it is economical or contractual, hence insofar as it has the structure of the promise. Consequently, even if, as Reyes argues, language is essentially oral, it must nonetheless come after itself as writing in order to remain and thus *be* in the first place. This delay is without mitigation. It is the price of human being, of life, of civilization.

Reyes's second claim about literature is methodological: "It is undeniable that between the expression of the literary creator and the communication that he transmits to us there is no mathematical equation, a fixed relation. The representation of the world, the psychological implications, the verbal suggestions, are different for everyone and determine the personal being of each man. For this reason," Reyes writes in *La experiencia literaria*, "the study of the literary phenomenon is a phenomenography of the fluid entity" (1962, 84–85). Although Reyes insists that literature names the discourse in which there is no gap between meaning (fiction) and expression (form), which means literature always says exactly what it means and means exactly what it says, an irreducible distance nevertheless separates author (sender) and reader (receiver). This interval complicates the arrival of literature. Importantly, for Reyes the gap lies only between author and reader, that is, *between* us and not *within* us. Reyes suggests that even if, by the time literature arrives at its destination, the reader may not understand it before it is sent off, it still says what it means and means what it says. Misunderstanding, then, is an effect of the spatial-temporal disjunction between two (or more) human beings, but it is not constitutive of literature *as such*. Indeed, in *El deslinde* Reyes argues that although literature can eschew neither the poetic (the formal) nor the semantic (the meaning or content) elements, neither is strictly essential to it. The essence of literature (and what therefore ought to be the object of literary theory) is intention, pure and simple. It is precisely literature's specific intentionality that makes its meaning and expression indivisible. For this reason, Reyes affirms, "intention will never be insisted upon enough" (1963a, 83).

For Reyes there is a literary intention that becomes phenomenal in but cannot be reduced to either meaning or expression. This explains why literature can, in fact, appear in *any* form and with *any* content. Reyes writes: "The mental process of the historian who evokes the figure of a hero and that of the novelist who constructs a character can turn out to be the same; but the intention is different in one and the other case" (83). Literature thus names a specific intention capable of animating whatever form or content. Therefore, although it is essential that literary intention appear in some form, the form in which it appears always comes after the intention. More than once Reyes remarks that the literary intention or the noetic act of literature takes place in the mind, in consciousness, before it appears or manifests itself in the world. Indeed, this is the gap to which Reyes refers when he notes that there is no "mathematical equation" for calculating the gap between "expression" and what is "communicated" to us. There is no formal principle for gaging the relation—the economy of what is gained and lost—of an author's literary intention in its delivery or transmission to the reading public. The intention of the "literary creator" remains cut off, isolated or secreted from us, even though it takes place as the indivisibility of meaning and expression and as the literary object, that is, as the possibility of a certain secretion between us.

The upshot of Reyes's argument is paradoxical in that if the essence of literature is purely and simply intention, the *appearance* of literature is accidental, which means literature *as such* need not appear in the world in order to be. And yet, on Reyes's own account, without its necessary "transcription" or "transliteration"—without its becoming-lettered—neither literature nor language (both of which are essentially oral, according to Reyes) *remains*. The logic of Reyes's account thus suggests that there is a distance and tension between a nonphenomenal literary intention that never appears in the world and a phenomenal literary object (the institution of literature) that appears in the world so that intention might survive.

But if literature is essentially intention, and if the task of any literary theory would be the calculation of intentionality, why does Reyes distance himself from Husserlian phenomenology? After all, Husserl remarks, "intentionality is the name of the problem encompassed by the whole of phenomenology. The name precisely expresses the fundamental property of consciousness. . . . Phenomenology begins with problems of intentionality" (1983, §146:303). In the second edition of *La experiencia literaria*, published in Buenos Aires in 1952, Reyes added a footnote explaining his use of the term "*fenomenografía*" rather than "*fenomenología*": "In order to avoid confusions with the modern [term] 'phenomenology' (Husserl),

I prefer to use this term, which has Mexican antecedents in Porfirio Parra's *Logic*" (1962, 85n).[7] And in the brief text "El espejo de Husserl" (1942)—first published in *Cuadernos americanos*, in the interval between the publication of *La experiencia literaria* and *El deslinde*—Reyes suggests that his reluctance to have his methodology confused with Husserl's phenomenological method stems from his complaint that "the phenomenologists are seasoned at removing the bulk from the horns of reality" (2009, 331). Reyes is concerned that phenomenology threatens to become an absolute idealism (330). He accuses Husserlian phenomenology of being too refined, polished, and delicate. It is, he says, "a squeamish philosophy" (331).

Reyes's ontological determination of being in terms of a contract of existence—which inscribes delay as the possibility of existence and which therefore demands, not as a derivative of existence but as its possibility, a remainder that must take the form of a passage through inscription or materialization—is incompatible with his methodological determination of a purely spiritual literature without necessary materialization and, therefore, without necessary delay or remainder. On the one hand, there is the demand for literality, for the becoming-letter of language, in order for language to *be* at all. This is Reyes's example of the contract of existence. It is also his example of the possibility of free expression and law, hence, of community, sovereignty, and the chance of democracy. Consequently, despite Reyes's characterization of it as secondary, writing cannot be derivative of or ancillary to speech. On the other hand, the being of *literature* depends not on material inscription but on an intention that, in principle, has no necessary relation to either its formal or semantic determinations. At stake is the same tension identified above in Reyes's three-part description of literature: namely, the translation of an already subjective reality into a practical lie that nonetheless corresponds to or refers to a minimum of reality—that is, to a "reality" external to consciousness of which the literary intention pretends to be ignorant. In the necessary relation between external reality and the "*verdad sospechosa*," nothing less is at issue than the bulk—the weight—of the world.

Although Reyes jettisons Husserl's phenomenology in favor of a Mexican *fenomenografía*, he does not, in fact, assess the status either of the reality outside of consciousness or of fiction's (the practical lie's) relation to it except insofar as he claims that fiction or literature depends on this reality and is therefore derivative of it, even as it feigns ignorance of it. In short, for Reyes literature needs a reality that has little use for literature. And only a *fenomenografía* can spell out their difference and assign to literature its proper value and place. Reyes never asks, however, about the limits of his critical method, which depends entirely on the assumption that literature is *essentially* intentional and that *fenomenografía* is the proper method for discovering this intention. But if, as Bolaño suggests in *2666*, it is always a question of not having *lent* sufficient attention to, thus of not having taken sufficient interest in, the world, then the task of understanding the relation of literature to the world as a problem of intention remains pressing. If literature is essentially intention (and this is not given), then what literature intends is the world *of* literature, the world *as* the world *of* literature.

ADVENTURES OF THE NOEMA

Reyes's criticism of Husserl's phenomenology as too delicate and dismissive of the world, hence as an idealism, follows from a difficulty that Husserl himself recognized: namely, how phenomenology understands consciousness's relation to material or transcendent (hyletic) reality. Husserl himself wondered, "To what extent . . . is the *material world* something of an essentially different kind excluded from the *essentiality proper of mental processes*? And if that is true of the material world, if the material world stands in contrast to all consciousness, and to the own-essentiality of consciousness, as '*something alien*,' the '*otherness*,' then how can consciousness become involved with it—with the *material* world and consequently with the *whole* world other than consciousness" (1983, §39:70)? In reply he invokes the noema, the status of which remains a matter of some debate.[8] As early as his 1954 thesis *Le problème de la genèse dans la philosophie de Husserl* (1990), Derrida recognized the difficulty the noema posed for phenomenology. And in an important note to his introduction to Husserl's "The Origin of Geometry," Derrida calls "the non-reality of the noema"—which characterizes "the type of intentional inclusion of every noema in conscious lived experience, whatever the intended type of existent may be and however it may be intended, even if we are dealing with the perception of a real thing"—"a very difficult and decisive notion" in Husserl's phenomenology (1962, 57n1/1978a, 66–67n61). Furthermore, in "'Genesis and Structure' and Phenomenology," Derrida asserts that the two intentional moments of consciousness—the noesis and the noema—can be distinguished from each other insofar as the noema "does not *really* belong to consciousness" (1967b, 242/1978b, 162–163). He writes that the noema "is neither the determined thing itself, in its savage existence, of which the noema is merely the appearance, nor a properly subjective moment" (242/163). On Derrida's account, "There is *within* consciousness in general an agency that *does not really* belong to it" (242/163).

More recently the noema has troubled Jean-François Courtine, who in *La cause de la phénoménologie* recurs to early Husserl in order to explain the importance of the distinction between the object *such that* (or *as*) it is intended (*"l'objet tel qu'il est visé"*) and the object *that* is intended (*"l'objet qui est visé"*) (2007, 92). Maintaining this distinction, which ultimately depends on a "supplement" (82) of signification or sense, is crucial for understanding Husserl's concept of intentionality.[9] In a move reminiscent of Reyes's, Courtine notes that this supplement (or *plus*), which is added to the object, in fact does not add up. On the contrary, it subtracts material reality. This "intentional content"—which Husserl begins to call the noema or noematic sense in 1908 (2007, 92)—does not mediate the given materiality (color, sound or, any *"donnée simplement hylétique"*) and consciousness; rather, "it is reduced to a real component of immanent lived experience" (82). Courtine rightly targets the "as" (*comme, als*) as the key term in what might be called Husserl's nonmediating directional intentionality. The "as" marks or instances the intended or interpretative appearing of the object, but, importantly, Courtine argues that such interpretative intention "does not constitute just a middle term, an intermediary or a mediation. It is a 'function'" (88).[10] As a function of consciousness, such sense would not mediate consciousness and material reality; it would be entirely immanent to consciousness.

Despite his apparent certainty that the intentional content (and with it, consciousness) remains cut off from hyletic reality, Courtine wonders whether perhaps what Husserl calls "sense" (*sens*, *Bedeutung*) or "noematic sense" (*sens noématique*) does not in fact reintroduce "the mediation of the intentional content" (2007, 95); nevertheless, he leaves this "difficult question" aside.

Husserl's own remarks, in *Ideas I*, §49, appear to support both Reyes's criticism of phenomenological idealism and Courtine's analysis of a nonmediating sense that remains immanent to consciousness, hence cut off from the material world. In a gesture reminiscent of Descartes sitting by the fire, Husserl writes, "Let us recall the possibility of non-being of everything physically transcendent: it then becomes evident that *while the being of consciousness*, of any stream of mental processes whatever, *would indeed be necessarily modified by an annihilation of the world of physical things its own existence would not be touched. . . . Consequently no real being*, no being which is presented and legitimated in consciousness by appearances, *is necessary to the being of consciousness itself*" (1983, §49:91–92). Untouched by the transcendent world, consciousness is purely immanent to itself and, as such, its presence to itself is, as Husserl says, "guaranteed" (§46:85): "A veritable abyss yawns between consciousness and reality. Here, an adumbrated being, not capable of ever becoming given absolutely, merely accidental and relative, there, a necessary and absolute being, essentially incapable of becoming given by virtue of adumbration and appearance" (§49:93). Consciousness is literally cut off from the accidental or contingent world of appearances that it nevertheless intends or means. Indeed, it is separated or excluded from the empirical possibility of its own self-presentation. Husserl calls this an "eidetic law": "*Over against the positing of the world, which is a 'contingent' positing, there stands then the positing of my pure Ego and Ego-life which is a 'necessary,'* absolutely indubitable *positing. Anything physical which is given 'in person' can be non-existent; no mental process which is given 'in person' can be non-existent.* This is the eidetic law defining this necessity and that contingency" (§46:86).[11] The quotation marks bracketing the "in person" have already done away with any empirical contingency of experience. The "in person" is nowhere other than *in* consciousness. Consciousness is thus invulnerable to anything other than itself:

> In spite of all our assuredly well-founded statements about the real being of the *human* Ego and its mental processes, in the world and about everything in the way of "psychophysical" interconnections pertaining to them—that, in spite of all that, consciousness considered in its "*purity*" must be held to be a *self-contained complex of being*, a complex of *absolute being* into which nothing can penetrate and out of which nothing can slip, to which nothing is spatiotemporally external and which . . . cannot be affected by any physical thing and cannot exercise causation upon any physical thing. (1983, §49:93)

Because consciousness is both unaffected by and impotent to affect the world, phenomenology directs its "seizing and theoretically inquiring regard to *pure consciousness in its own absolute being*" (§50:94). After reducing "the whole world with all physical things, living beings, and humans, ourselves included," that is, everything in the world and the world itself, too, what remains is the "phenomenological residuum": "Strictly speaking, we have not lost anything but rather have gained the whole of absolute being which, rightly understood, contains within itself, 'constitutes' within itself, all worldly transcendencies" (§50:94). Cut off from the world, consciousness constitutes within itself the world *as* transcendent. In arising out of its own activity alone, from its autogenesis, consciousness also raises the world. Consciousness secretes the world.

On the basis of such remarks, Derrida claims that "a *purely and exclusively active* intentionality" is "mutilated" (1990a, 151/2003d, 85), hence, decapitated.[12] But Derrida also points out that were intentionality so mutilated—were consciousness purely active—it would *not* be intentional: "Ultimately, we can even say that pure intentional activity is the contrary of intentionality. Because we would no longer comprehend why noetic activity would still require a noematic correlate nor why that correlate would be grounded on an object given 'in person' in perception. A purely active perception should not have any meaning [*sens*] for Husserl" (151/85). If intentionality is not purely active, then, by definition, consciousness must be marked from the beginning by "a primitive passivity" (151/85). It is here that the question of the noema opens onto "the mysterious relations between sensuous 'hylē,' a real [*réell*] and nonintentional component of lived experience; intentional and noetic 'morphē,' which comes to animate it; and the intentional non 'real' noema, which is constituted from them" (152/85). The noema is "the veil" (152/85) that Husserl uses to hide the difficult relation of *hylē* to *morphē*. Thus, the noema both signals the relation between matter and form, insofar as it is constituted *from* them (*à partir d'eux*), and hides that relation.

The stakes are high for Husserl. The decision concerning the relation of priority between sensuous *hylē*, "*which has in itself nothing pertaining to intentionality*" (1983, §85:172), and sense-bestowing, intentive *morphē*, which animates the nonintentional stuff, is important for determining the genesis of consciousness, but also for sustaining Husserl's argument that phenomenology is not simply another psychologism.[13] Husserl suggests that *hylē*, while not itself intentional or "consciousness of something," nevertheless "bears" intentionality: "As the content that is 'presentive' with respect to the appearing *white* of the paper, it [the datum of sensation] is the bearer of an intentionality; however, it is not itself a consciousness of something" (§36:65). Husserl's assertion, which Derrida characterizes as "very obscure" (1990a, 154/2003d, 86), opens onto serious problems for phenomenological consciousness. Derrida explains:

> One does not know if this "bearer" [*porteur*] of intentionality precedes intentionality or is constituted as the bearer by the intentional act. If it precedes it, what is the original autonomy of intentionality? . . . If, on the contrary, it is intentionality alone that constitutes hylē as hylē, as *a priori* substrate of intentional meaning, one loses from view all the original reality of hylē. One no longer knows what distinguishes it from the noema, which is included in lived experience as non-real (*reell*). If hylē is, as non-intentional, a real (*reell*) component animated with a meaning by a noetic intentionality, isn't it necessarily identical to a "noema"? All the

> reality (*reell*) of lived experience would then be reduced to its constituted meaning. (154/86–87)

In other words, Husserl's claim that *hylē* "bears" intentionality results in two untenable and mutually exclusive possibilities. *Either* sensuous data (*hylē*), which is not intentional, makes possible—by bearing it—intentionality, which means consciousness arrives to itself from another that is always before it; thus consciousness is not constitutive but rather dependent upon an already constituted passivity. *Or* consciousness is constitutive but at the cost of the world inasmuch as *hylē* becomes indistinguishable from noema, which means phenomenology becomes indistinguishable from intentional psychologism. Ultimately, Husserl sets the question aside while nevertheless affirming that "this remarkable duality and unity of *sensuous* υλη [*hylē*] and *intentive* μορφη [*morphē*] plays a dominant role in the whole phenomenological sphere" (1983, §85:172).[14] These "concepts," he claims, "force themselves upon us if we presentiate to ourselves any clear intuitions or clearly effected valuations, acts of liking, willing, or the like." They do so, moreover, "as unities by virtue of sense-bestowing." Hence, Husserl observes, "sensuous Data present themselves as stuffs for intentive formings, or sense-bestowings" (§85:172). He thus concludes, "As for the possibilities left open above [namely, in his inability to decide the priority of matter and form], they should be entitled accordingly *formless stuffs* and *stuffless forms*" (§85:173).[15]

It is an important problem, one that signals the difficulty that the noema poses within Husserl's system, because even if the noema names a nonreal intentional content, which would seem to put it entirely on the side of noetic activity or of consciousness, the content nevertheless must come from someplace else, from hyletic reality; otherwise, Husserl's critique of psychologism is empty. But if the content—sensuous *hylē*—presents itself *as such*, that is, as sensuous *hylē* or as formless stuff, then it must do so as already bearing in itself a certain—however minimal—form. If sensuous *hylē* presents itself *as such* to the sense-bestowing form of noetic activity, then it follows that consciousness receives this minimal form as the becoming-possible of its own formalization. Put another way, the passive reception of matter (*hylē*) marks the formation of form *as such*, *as* sense-bestowing. Form (*morphē*) thus becomes itself belatedly, as the effect of a passivity that presents the possibility of form. The becoming-form of form—or the possibility of "form *as* form," the noematic sense of form—would be a correlate not of noetic activity or of intentionality but of matter or passivity. Yet the priority of *hylē* is complicated by the necessity that in order to present itself *as such*, such that it might be passively received by consciousness, *hylē* must already be *as if* it were formed; it must always already appear *as hylē*. As a consequence, the passivity of *hylē* is contaminated from the start by activity or by form, and this means that *hylē* becomes itself *as such*, such that it can present itself to consciousness, belatedly. In a certain way, then, it is always too soon and too late for both *hylē* and *morphē*, for both passivity and activity, each always coming before and after the other.[16]

Husserl rejects the idea that noetic activity—through the intentional Object of consciousness—simply portrays or copies external reality.[17] Were consciousness simply to copy a reality external to and absolutely independent of it, consciousness would be entirely dependent upon (and thus completely derivative of) an already constituted reality. There would be no possibility, for example, of reflection, of taking a stand with respect to the world, in short, of thought or freedom. On the contrary, consciousness would belong to the world; it would be completely subordinate to it and as such absolutely immersed in it. The result would be an infinite regress, a repetition without ideality.[18]

To argue that the intentional act of consciousness (noesis) neither portrays nor copies external reality, however, does not explain how consciousness relates to the world outside it without falling into either skeptical empiricism or speculative idealism. Husserl's answer is the noema, which marks the limit of sensuous *hylē* and intentive *morphē*: "Corresponding in every case to the multiplicity of Data pertaining to the really inherent noetic content, there is a multiplicity of Data, demonstrable in actual pure intuition, in a correlative '*noematic content*' or, in short, in the '*noema*'" (1983, §88:181–182). That is, in every intentive or intentional act of consciousness, the noema appears as a correlate. Or, as Husserl puts it, "The eidetic law, confirmed in every case, states that there can be *no noetic moment without a noematic moment specifically belonging to it*" (§93:193). This is the case for noetic acts at every level, from the lowest to the highest. Moreover, even if the content differs from one level (say, the level of sense perception) to the next (say, that of judging or willing [§§94–95:194–199]), or from one domain (that of objects simply in the world) to another (the experience of another subject or alter ego), the structure of the noema remains the same.[19] Husserl writes,

> Even in the case of noeses of a higher level—taken in concrete completeness—there at first emerges in the noematic composition a central core thrusting itself to the fore in a predominate way, the "meant Objectivity *as* Objectivity," the Objectivity in inverted commas as required by the

> phenomenological reduction. There this central noema must also be taken precisely in the modified Objective composition in which it is just that noema, something intended to *as* intended to. (1983, §93:193, emphases added)

Husserl calls the noematic as-structure, "sense," but "in a very extended signification," and he claims that "sense . . . is to be taken precisely as it inheres 'immanently' in the mental process of perceiving, of judging, of liking; and so forth; that is, just as it is offered to us when we *inquire purely into this mental process itself*" (§88:182).[20]

Everything depends on the "very extended signification" of "sense" and the notion of "immanence" at work here, because although Husserl repeatedly affirms that the noema is sense or meaning, such a claim ultimately proves problematic. Undoubtedly, there is no sense or meaning without the noema, but the noema is not sense. If, as Husserl argues, the noematic *as*-structure presents the objects that consciousness intends *as they are*, that is, *as* objects *for* consciousness, it does so, as Derrida points out, as that which "permits the repetition of sense as the 'same' and renders possible the idealization of identity in general" (1962, 57n1/1978a, 66–67n61). In short, the noema instances originary repetition, but it does not simply reproduce a self-identical sameness (or "sense") that is there before it. Rather, by force of repetition the "same"—or identity, essence, ideality, the "as such" of sense—becomes possible. Through originary repetition or repeatability differences appear *as* the same. Whatever appears does so *as* it is. The noematic *as*-structure, Husserl argues, does not portray or copy actual objects existing outside consciousness; rather, it presents these objects as they are, *as* objects, *for* consciousness. In the noema, consciousness touches the world, but not in the sense that the noema—as if it were something in itself—mediates consciousness and the world. The noema takes place *as* the taking place of intentionality, which means the noema happens as the possibility of consciousness's "intending" the world. The noematic core or the noematic structure, the *as*, thus informs all objectivation and, therefore, all ideation. There is no object of consciousness, no intentionality without the noema. In formulations like "perception as perception" or the "judged as judged," or more generally, "the meant Objectivity as Objectivity," the *as* constitutes the *sense* of the "thing" (perception, judgment, objectivity) intended, hence its being *for* consciousness. Accordingly, the noema is neither the noetic act itself nor a copy of the thing intended. Nor is the noema constituted in a noetic act of reflection.[21] It follows, then, that the relation between noesis and noema is not causal; they are correlates of one another. The noema—*qua* the promise of sense—makes possible the presentation of the "thing"—whether as perception, judgment, liking, negation, doubt, etc.—to consciousness or, more exactly, *for* consciousness: "Just as every intentive mental process has a noema and therein a sense by which it is related to an object, so, conversely, everything which we call an *object*, of which we speak, which we confront as actuality, which we hold as possible or probable, no matter how indeterminately we think it, is precisely therefore already an object of consciousness" (1983, §135:278).

If the noema "belongs"—as Husserl says it does (§93:193)—to consciousness, such belonging nonetheless remains equivocal. Indeed, Husserl makes it "perfectly clear" that although "there belongs to the essence of the mental process of perception in itself the 'perceived tree as perceived,' or the full noema," the noema remains foreign to the mental process: "However, this *noema*, with its 'tree' in inverted commas, *is no more contained inherently than is the tree which belongs to actuality*" (§97:202). Mental processes refer to "*not really inherent*" moments of consciousness "by means of the heading of sense" (§88:181). In other words, the noetic act does not bestow or give "sense" to what it perceives (or judges or likes, etc.) through a noema that is simply or unequivocally the property of the mental processes. Rather, what is "not really inherent" to consciousness manifests itself *for* consciousness *as* what it is, that is, *as* itself or *as* sense. This is why Husserl can claim that although the "posited actuality is indeed not there for us in consequence of judging" (i.e., in the act of judging the judged *as* judged), nevertheless, "everything remains as of old. Even the phenomenologically reduced perceptual mental process is a perceiving *of* 'this blossoming apple tree, in this garden,' etc., and likewise, the reduced liking is a liking of this same thing. The tree has not lost the least nuance of all these moments, qualities, characteristics *with which it was appearing in this perception*" (1983, §88:183).

That the noema does not belong to consciousness does not mean, however, that it originates in the actually existing world beyond consciousness as, say, merely the effect of an actually existing object. Were the noema an effect of an actually existing object, it would be affected by that object's disappearance. But it is not. Husserl writes: "The *tree simpliciter*, the physical thing belonging to Nature, is nothing less than this *perceived tree as perceived* which, as perceptual sense, inseparably belongs to the perception. The tree simpliciter can burn up, be resolved into its chemical elements, etc. But the sense—the sense of *this* perception, something belonging necessarily to its essence—cannot burn up; it has no chemical elements, no forces, no real properties" (§89:184). Simply put, the noema "is not touched by excluding the actuality of the tree and that of the whole world" (§97:202). It follows, therefore, that the noema—or the intentional object, which cannot be conceived without it—belongs "neither to the world nor to lived experience" (Derrida 1967a, 90/1974, 64).

The noema is cut off, separated and segregated, secreted, from both subject and object. Neither in the world nor in consciousness, it names "the root and the very possibility of objectivity and of meaning [*sens*]" (Derrida 1967b, 243/1978b, 163). It therefore instances "the common root of activity and of passivity" (235/158). The "as," or the *as*-structure, can be reduced neither to an effect of consciousness (or intentional activity) nor to inchoate reality outside consciousness. On the contrary, both nonintentional reality and consciousness are effects of the "as." This means that the "as," which has no sense of its own and which instances the virtuality of the virtual, nonetheless has a certain force.

OF THE INTEREST IN AND OF LITERATURE

Nearly forty years after he wrote *Le problème de la genèse dans la philosophie de Husserl* and thirty years after the publication of his introduction to Husserl's essay "The Origin of Geometry," Derrida returned to the noema, this time in order to complicate the idea of literature.

What about literature interests Derrida? The answer is complicated, but it begins with Derrida's recognition that "there is no text that is literary in itself" (1992, 44). For Derrida, "Literarity is not a natural essence, an intrinsic property of the text" (44). Because literature has no essence, the literary space can accommodate any statement: "One can always reinscribe in the literary space any statement—whether a newspaper article, a scientific theorem, a snatch of a conversation" (45)—without compromising the institution of literature.[22] Although literature may include scientific, philosophical, or conversational discourses, "it will never be scientific, philosophical, or conversational" (47). On the one hand, there is no self-identity or essence of the literary text; there is no "intrinsic property" that identifies it as such, which means literature depends on what Derrida calls "nonliterary powers" (1999, 208/2008b, 157), thus on context and conventions, on norms and safeguards without which literature—the modern institution of literature—would not have been possible. On the other hand, the incorporation of statements that originate in other discursive formations does not compromise the literary text. Literature names an institution, the laws of which permit it to say everything in any way, on the condition that whatever it says be "literature," that is, that it can be dismissed as a fiction.[23]

Literature, then, is powerful in that it can say everything and impotent in that it makes no claim to truth. Consequently, one can always act as if literature makes no difference. Nevertheless, without relinquishing its specific fictionality, and thus without being anything other than the institution of literature, literature also exceeds its institutional frame. "To say everything," Derrida remarks, "is also to break out of [*franchir*] prohibitions. To *affranchise oneself* [*s'affranchir*]—in every field where law can lay down the law. The law of literature tends, in principle, to defy or lift the law. . . . It is an institution which tends to overflow the institution" (1992, 36). Because literature has no essence, because it never shows up *in itself* or *as such*, every attempt to target literature *as such* necessarily misses the mark. "The space of literature is not only that of an instituted *fiction*," as Derrida remarks, "but also a *fictive institution*" (36). It will only ever be *as if* there is literature. At the same time, literature "allows one to think the essence of the law in the experience of" literature's "power to say everything" (36, 37). It is this *power* to say everything—which is indissociable from but also irreducible to the *right* to say everything—that results in literature's exceeding its own institutional limits. It is what allows literature to haunt every other discourse. The institution of literature, then, does not coincide with itself; it comes both before and after itself. It comes before itself insofar as it instances a power that makes its institutionalization possible; it comes after itself insofar as it exceeds the institution—that is, the convention and context—that would limit it.

It follows, therefore, that the power of literature is not constative. Literature makes no claim to describe anything as either true or false, even in such cases where all of its resources—statements—are historically verifiable as either true or false. Consequently, if literature names a certain power, it is *perhaps* performative. It is "perhaps" performative, because literature's specific performativity complicates the thetic unity of intention that, classically, governs the concept of performance.[24] Indeed, a certain performativity is already legible in Derrida's claim that the reinscription of any statement within literary space depends upon an *attitude* to the text, one that instances "a literary *functioning* and a literary *intentionality*" (45). Derrida argues, moreover, that the specific intentionality of the literary text enables the suspension of what he calls the "'thetic' and naïve belief in meaning and referent" (45). In other words, the experience of literature, which can always *not* take place, allows for "a nonthetic experience of the thesis, of belief, of position, of naivety, of what Husserl called the 'natural attitude'" (46). In other words, because literature suspends the claim to truth, because it posits itself as fiction, it facilitates the "transcendental reduction" of the assumption of meaning and referent as given or natural.

Although literarity "is the correlative of an intentional relation to the text," Derrida insists that it does not depend on the "empirical subjectivity or caprice of each reader" (1992, 44). Despite depending on a specific *attitude* to the text and being marked by intentionality, literature is not simply subjective. Derrida observes:

> The literary character of the text is inscribed on the side of the intentional object, in its noematic structure, one could say, and not only on the subjective side of the noetic act. There are "in" the text features which call for the literary reading and recall the convention, institution, or history of literature. This noematic structure is included (as "nonreal," in Husserl's terms) in subjectivity, but a subjectivity which is non-empirical and linked to an intersubjective and transcendental community. (44)

That the "noematic structure" of literature is included in a nonempirical subjectivity and is "linked to an intersubjective and transcendental community" establishes the condition of possibility of its being determined institutionally (hence, normatively) and of its having a history. However, without the noematic structure known as "literature," such an intersubjective and transcendental community could not happen at all. As a noematic structure, literature makes possible the subjectivity or intentionality that determines and limits it. For this reason Derrida suggests that "literature perhaps stands on the edge of everything, almost beyond everything, including itself. It's the most interesting thing in the world, maybe more interesting than the world" (1992, 47). To take stock of this assertion, and thus to comprehend the peculiar "power" of literature, it will be necessary to understand the stakes of Derrida's claim that literature is a noematic structure. That literature is a noematic structure means that literature has a complicated relation to consciousness and intentionality. If, as Husserl claims, intentionality "expresses the fundamental property of consciousness" (1983, §146:303), then literature, as a noematic structure, does not unequivocally belong to consciousness. It is an effect of consciousness that exceeds consciousness, which means literature names *both* an object *in* the world (an object targeted or intended by consciousness) *and* that which is not simply in the world. Rather, literature is "perhaps" (Derrida says) that which *opens* the world and is thus more interesting than it.[25] Yet if literature opens the world, it does not do so from beyond the world.[26] Literature, then, would be before the world without being beyond it.

IN THE NAME OF LITERATURE

The noematic structure of literature can already be read in Husserl, who ascribes to literature the possibility of repetition and ideality and, therefore, the chance for community and tradition. In "The Origin of Geometry" (1936), Husserl announces that "literature, in its broadest concept," includes "the entire class of spiritual products of the cultural world," because "it belongs to their objective being"—hence, to their ideality—"to be expressed and repeatedly expressible in a language" (1978, 160, 160n). What makes possible the objective being of the spiritual products of the cultural world? Husserl answers: "Everyone can talk about what is within the surrounding world of his civilization as objectively existing," because "everything has its name, or rather everything is nameable in a very large sense, that is to say, expressible in a language" (162). Husserl is not far from Hegel, who, in *The Philosophy of Mind*, asserted that the name is the fundamental desideratum of language and that we think in names.[27] Ideality *happens* in the name; that is, the name (or the word) is an ideal entity: "Thus, the word has an ideal Objectivity and identity, since it is not identical with any of its empirical, phonetic, or graphic materializations" (Derrida 1962, 58/1978a, 67). Ideality, therefore, is "the element of language in general" (56/66). The word or the name "supposes a spontaneous neutralization of the factual existence of the speaking subject, of words, and of the thing designated. Speech, then, is only the practice of an immediate eidetic" (58/67).[28] Without the eidetic reduction effected in the name, there would be no possible ideality, consequently neither subjectivity nor objectivity. Moreover, because the eidetic reduction—which names the movement of becoming-ideal—is "immediate," it is necessarily spontaneous; it is mechanical and automatic.

At stake is the relation between the name (or the word), the noema, and writing. Although the name and the noema are irreducibly heterogeneous, they are nonetheless indissociable. For instance, even if Husserl never says as much, it is obvious that the spontaneous eidetic reduction effected in the name, which makes possible the repeated expression of empirical (and therefore *different*) instances of the word *as* the same, necessarily "repeats" the power of the noema, which Derrida identified as the power of repetition of the non-self-same *as* the same. Consequently, as the possibility of repetition and ideality—as Husserl's example of the burned up tree and the end of the world spell out—the noema "informs" the ideal object, which can only ever be expressed in the name.[29] Yet part and parcel of the noema, and precisely what separates it from noetic activity pure and simple, is *hylē*, which, insofar as it is not immanent to consciousness, is not active but passive. It *remains*. And in remaining, it links name and noema to writing.

Husserl both recognizes the need for a remainder and dismisses it. The dismissal takes place in the complex determination of ideality through the tripartite reduction of language, which results in a transcendental or pure language. The first reduction is the spontaneous, eidetic reduction: "For example, the word *Löwe* occurs only once in the German language; it is identical throughout its innumerable utterances by any given person who intends it" (1978, 161). No matter how many times the word "lion" is said, it is always the same word. Nevertheless, the ideality of the word *Löwe* remains tied to a specific language, German, and to a specific historical community.[30] It remains, therefore, subjectively determined and, as a consequence, subject to equivocation. The second reduction brackets the materiality of the word in favor of its ideal or intentional content. It is no longer a question of the ideality of the word in its articulation but of the ideal content, that is, what is meant. Although this second reduction allows for translation between languages (*Löwe* can be translated as *lion* or *león*, for instance, because they all "mean" "lion"), it does not reduce equivocation, because intentional contents remain subjectively determined: not all lions (even within the same language) are equal. One person's lion (African lion, mountain lion) can always be another person's house cat. In other words, both the eidetic and material reductions result in idealities that are enchained; such ideality remains normative in that it is contextually and conventionally determined. The third—transcendental—reduction results in the "free" ideality of the object as such. This form of ideality is, Derrida notes, "absolute and without limit of any sort. . . . All adherence to any real contingency is suppressed" (1962, 64/1978a, 72). It follows, then, that the translation and transmission of the ideal object itself is also absolute and infinite. Husserl claims, "The Pythagorean theorem, indeed all of geometry, exists only once, no matter how often or even in what language it may be expressed. It is identically the same in the 'original language' of Euclid and in all 'translations'; and within each language it is again the same, no matter how many times it has been sensibly uttered, from the original expression and writing-down to the innumerable oral utterances or written and other documentations" (1978, 160). Whereas Husserl explicitly claims that only the ideality of the geometrical object is so constituted, Derrida argues that, in fact, for Husserl this is the form of the ideality of the object itself (1962, 65/1978a, 73).[31] In effect, in the transcendental reduction constitutive of the ideality of the object as such, Husserl reduces language altogether, which results in the reduction of all factual communities and cultures.

The reduction of language is a necessary step that enables the (re)turn to language essential for the constitution and transmission of absolute ideality. In other words, if the fundamental question of "The Origin of Geometry" is "How does geometrical ideality . . . proceed from its primary intrapersonal origin, where it is a structure within the conscious space of the first inventor's soul, to its ideal objectivity?" then the answer can only be "through the mediation of language" (1978, 161). Yet this return to language cannot be that of an "extrinsic and accidental" (Derrida 1962, 70/1978a, 77) fall into an empirical language. Speech can no longer be "the expression . . . of what, without it, would *already* be an object: caught again in its original purity, it *constitutes* the object, it is a concrete juridical condition of truth" (70–71/77). Derrida signals the "paradox" of Husserl's solution to the problem of the constitution of the ideal object and its possible transmission: "Without what appears as a fall back into language—and thereby into history—a fall which would alienate the ideal purity of sense, sense would remain an empirical formation imprisoned as a fact in a psychological subjectivity, *in the inventor's head*. Instead of enchaining it, historical incarnation frees the transcendental" (71/77).

This paradox must be thought in two ways. On the one hand, historical and empirical incarnation is necessary for the possibility of transmission beyond empirical psychological subjectivity or historical context. On the other hand, freedom from historical context is necessary for the constitution of such empirical determination. On the one hand, there must be the possibility of the infinite repetition of the same, hence, absolute ideality; on the other hand, there must be the chance of a remainder, hence, of historical determination. Without these two conditions, which appear to be incommensurable and mutually exclusive, there is no possibility of the constitution of an ideal object and its transmission, no possibility that it will get either into or out of the inventor's head.

If the absolute ideality of the object depends on "transcendental language," this is so because only a transcendental language—absolutely cut off and unchained from empirical language and historical circumstances—affords the possibility of infinite repetition and translation without the resistance or friction of cultural specificity or empirical subjectivity. On Husserl's account, there is no drag or delay in the "transmission" of such a transcendental language. Yet Husserl acknowledges that "the original being-itself-there" of any object "in the immediacy [*Aktualität*] of its first production" does not result in "persisting acquisition . . . that could have objective existence" (1978, 163). This is so because a purely transcendental language—which is modeled on the presence-to-self of spoken language—immediately passes over into what is no longer, that is, "what-has-just-now-been" (163). It is clear, then, that without the possibility of its persistence over time, a purely transcendental language could not produce an ideal object that could be either invented or shared. This is as true for *intra*subjective reality as for *inter*subjective reality. In short, "the original being-itself-there" of any object must become a "retention" that can be reactivated.[32] Such reactivation results in "the self-evidence of identity": "What has now been realized in original fashion is the same as what was previously self-evident" (163). For Husserl, the capacity for reactivation also establishes "the capacity to repeat the structure at will in the self-evidence of identity (coincidence of identity) throughout the chain of repetitions" (163). The possibility of repetition—which depends on a trace of what is no longer remaining for a future that is not yet, thus remaining for an other that survives "me"—establishes the minimum ideality (and, with it, identity) necessary to "have" a thought in the first place, hence for the intra-subjective "invention" of an ideal object. At the same time, however, because the possibility of repetition depends on a remainder that must be open to a future, repetition effectively constitutes the intrasubjective through the intersubjective. That is, the remainder of repetition composes the inside from the outside. The intrasubjective is always already the intersubjective. Consequently, ideality and identity are not effects of absolute self-presence but of constitutive non-self-coincidence or delay, what, in *De la grammatologie*, Derrida calls "*the dead time* in the presence of the living present" (1967a, 99/1974, 68).

Although in "The Origin of Geometry" Husserl describes only the primary stage of ideality and thus the moment of eidetic reduction, what is important is the structure of language and its irreducible dependence on repetition (thus temporalization, delay) for the constitution of ideality and, therefore, of identity and communicability. This structure and dependence never changes. It remains the same whether Husserl describes the intrasubjective invention of an ideal object or its intersubjective transmission: "The production can reproduce their likenesses from person to person, and in the chain of the understanding of these repetitions what is self-evident turns up as the same in the consciousness of the other. In the unity of the community of communication among several persons the repeatedly produced structure becomes an object of consciousness, not as a likeness, but as the one structure common to all" (1978, 163–164). For an ideal object to be constituted or transmitted, there must be a remainder. Husserl calls the possibility of such persistence "writing": "What is lacking is the *persisting existence* of the 'ideal objects' even during periods in which the inventor and his fellows are no longer wakefully so related or even are no longer alive" (164).[33] Thus, for tradition and inheritance to be possible, the ideal object must survive the death of the inventor and, indeed, of everyone else. It must be retained (archived) and remain capable of reactivation even if the inventor and his fellows are dead. "The decisive function of written, documenting linguistic expression is that it makes communications possible without immediate or mediate personal address; it is . . . communication become virtual" (164). Writing is virtualization. It makes possible "a continuity from one person to another, from one time to another"; it makes an ideal object "ever capable of being handed down" (169). In short, the "dead time"—anachronism, delay—that makes repetition both possible and necessary marks both intrasubjective psychic reality and the intersubjective world. The *inter*subjective is possible because the *intra*subjective was always already marked by exteriority, that is, by the repetition of the non-self-same that institutes the "same."

The importance of such virtualization cannot be overemphasized. If writing—understood in its most traditional sense—instances the virtualization of intersubjective communication, it does so because intrasubjective communication (what one thinks or feels, conceives or perceives, in oneself) is already marked by virtuality. Husserl himself notes the constitutive movement of becoming-ideal or becoming-truth—thus the movement of virtualization—in the irreducible movement (alteration) of the self-same, that is, in his insistence on the noema. The noematic "as" (*als*)—something *as* something—accompanies Husserl along every step of his phenomenological journey. There is neither perception nor the reduction or bracketing of perception without this mechanical, automatic repetition that "adds" nothing to the object but, in repeating it—this (*as*) this—(re)produces its self-identity and its sense *as such*. Nothing happens, nothing takes place, without or before the "as." No consciousness, no world, no object or objectivity that is not already doubled, repeated, in order to be *as* it is: consciousness *as* consciousness, world *as* world, the living *as* living, the other *as* other.

The "as" underwrites the virtualization of perception and conception, of sensibility and intelligibility, hence, of all possible experience. Nevertheless, Husserl attempts to secure the presence-to-self of experience by positing an "expression" (*logos*) coincident with the noema. Were such coincidence possible, however, it would obviate the constitutive anachronism—the delay—of the "as." Husserl explains: "'Expression' is a distinctive form which allows for adapting to every 'sense' (to the noematic 'core') and raises it to the realm of 'Logos,' of the *conceptual* and, on that account, the '*universal*'" (1983, §124:257). Although Husserl distinguishes expression from the noema by claiming that expression is "adaptable" to every "sense," insofar as expression happens through significations, it necessarily entails the noema as its starting point: "Anything 'meant as meant,' anything in the noematic sense (and, more particularly, as the noematic core) pertaining to any act, no matter which, is *expressible by means* of '*significations*'" (§124:257). Significations (meaningful signs, signs *as* signs) necessarily take their point of departure from the noema, that is, from the "as." Importantly, the expression of what is "meant as meant"—hence, the noema—is absolute, both exhausted in the expression and perfect, which means the noema and its expression are irreducibly bound one to the other: "Apart from the fact that it confers expression precisely on all other intentionalities, the stratum of expression . . . is not productive. Or, if one wishes: *its productivity, its noematic production, is exhausted in the expression*" (§124:258). Under such a regime of signification, nothing would remain of expression; there would be no excess. "As a consequence," Husserl asserts, "the expressive stratum . . . is perfectly identical in essence with the stratum undergoing the expression" (§124:258). This would be the absolute coincidence of expression and meaning. In the instance of expression, the object (the object *as* object) presents itself *as such* and, because expression exhausts itself in the expressing, nothing ought to be left behind. Expression and what is expressed ought to be seamless. We are close, here, to Reyes's dream of literary expression—and the experience of literature—in which the meaning or sense coincides absolutely with the expression such that there is nothing left over, no seam or fissure that would make translation both possible and necessary. Under the condition of such absolute coincidence wherein the expression is exhausted in the expressing of meaning, there is no chance of the meaning being said "in other words," no possibility of saying the "same" otherwise. No repetition. There is no remainder of expression, thus no equivocality, no confusion. In short, in attempting to bracket the "as," both Husserl and Reyes seek to secure certain forms of expression from the deleterious effects of delay, from repetition: Husserl in the name of science and phenomenologically exact expression, Reyes in the name of literature. The upshot would be the absolution of singularity in pure universality. In principle, nothing singular would impinge upon or impair, limit, communicability.

According to their respective advocates, both science and literature ought to instance full or complete expression. Husserl admits, however, that this is not the case. Incompleteness, he remarks, "belongs to the essence of expression as expression, that is to say, to its *universality*" (§126:261). The essence of expression *as* expression, hence the noematic core or the *as such* of expression, is not simply to exhaust itself in the expressive act or in the noetic act. Essence in principle ought to absolve the difference—the gap or delay—between noesis and noema, thereby allowing consciousness to catch up with itself. On the contrary, the essence of "expression as expression"—which Husserl calls "universality"—requires the noncoincidence of expression and noematic sense. "It is inherent in the sense of the universality belonging to the essence of expressing that all the particulars of the expressed can never be reflected in the expression. The stratum signifying is not, and of essential necessity cannot be, a kind of reduplication of the substratum" (§126:261–262). If incompleteness belongs to the essence of expression ("expression as expression"), thus to its universality, then it follows that expression can never coincide completely with the sense of perception, that is, with the meant *as* meant; to do so would be to remain at the level of particularity. Paradoxically, the chance for direct intuition is the expression that makes it impossible. Expression operates the spontaneous, mechanical, eidetic reduction of the singular object in the word or name. What remains, however, is the "as," which determines both strata: that of expression (expression *as* expression) and that of sense (the meant *as* meant). Expression, then, is both more and less than sense; the act of expression both adds to and subtracts from sense. It is *more* in that only through expression can communication take place, with oneself or with others. It is *less* insofar as expression universalizes sense in order to express it *as* sense. Both more and less, because expression makes it possible to share sense, to communicate *my* self with another and with myself, but at the cost of reducing my sense to *no one's* sense. Put another way, because we can only ever *express* what we sense or mean, we can never express what we *sense* or *mean*.[34] As Derrida puts it in *Passions*: "As soon as there are words—and this can be said of the trace in general, of the chance that it is—direct intuition no longer has any chance" (1993c, 68/1995b, 30).

Again, the importance of this ought not to be underestimated. The structural delay marked by the "as" opens the possibility of sense and ruins it in the same stroke. Because the "as" is an effect of delay or anachronicity, it instances the originary repetition that can only *promise* ideality, identity, self-sameness, and, therefore, sense. The "as" thus instances the force of virtualization. It thus instances originary, constitutive fiction: literature. The "as" thus opens the world, but because it does so virtually, by disappearing whatever is in order that it be in the first place, it does so as fiction, as literature, as if there were world.

A WORLD OF HOMONYMY

The incompleteness necessary for universality is structural and goes all the way down to the noematic core. Through its power of repetition, the noematic "as such" (expression *as* expression), constitutive of the self-same, of whatever is *as* what it is, inscribes incompleteness at the heart of the possibility of sense. Hence, the possibility of sense is its impossibility. Derrida spells this out near the end of "Et cetera," an essay devoted to the syncategorema "and" (*et*) and, ultimately, to its homophonic relation, in French, to being (*est*), a relation that provokes a certain undecidability (*eh . . . eh*).[35] He turns to the "as" (*comme*) to figure the stakes of deconstruction: "Each time that I say 'deconstruction and X . . . ,' it is the prelude to a very singular division that makes of that X, or rather makes appear in that X an impossibility that becomes its proper and only possibility, so that between the X as [*comme*] possible and the 'same' X as [*comme*] impossible there is no more than a relation of homonymy of which it is still necessary to take account" (2004, 32). The "as" inscribes homonymy—thus virtuality—at and as the origin of experience and sense. In the noema "tree as tree," for instance, the "tree" before the "as" is not the same as, and thus has no relation to, the tree that comes after the "as." In the repetition or doubling (tree as tree), phenomenological self-sameness is produced as virtual, as fiction, as if what comes before and after the "as" were the same, as if anything came before the "as." In "the meant *as* meant," which instances intentionality, sense begins in homonymy, in a doubling or repeating that promises sense where it is impossible: "Between X *and* X . . . between the X as possible *and* the X as impossible, there is only a relation of homonymy, hence of a relation that is neither semantic nor of synonymy, a relation without relation" (32). It is not until the end of "Et cetera," however, that Derrida draws attention to the "as" (*comme*): "I will add one more word, before forgetting: deconstruction is not only plural, at once possible *and* impossible, because possible *as* impossible" (32). Whatever happens ("*ce qui arrive*") does so *as* impossible (32). It is only ever as if the "as such" were possible. The "as if" instances the impossibility of the event as such.

According to Husserl, syncategorematic elements are "words" that are not self-sufficient: "The isolated 'and,' 'if,' the isolated genitive 'of the heavens,' are comprehensible and yet non-selfsufficient and in need of completion" (1983, §126:262). In the *Logical Investigations*, he "ranks the syncategorematic parts of expressions on a level with quite different parts of expressions, with the letters, sounds, and syllables which are in general meaningless." He adds: "In the vast majority of cases, they are not parts of an expression *qua* expression, i.e., not its significant parts; they are only parts of the expression as a sensuous phenomenon. Syncategorematic expressions are therefore understood, even when they occur in isolation; they are felt to carry definite 'moments' of meaning content, 'moments' that look forward to a certain completion" (2001, 186). As both meaningless and sensuous, syncategoremata instance a kind of syntactical resistance that makes meaning possible even as it jeopardizes its univocity. This is so because syncategoremata inscribe incompleteness—temporality—within the possibility of sense.

For instance, in the noematic *as*-structure X *as* X, in which the second X appears as the "as such" of the first X (which means, in a certain way, the second X comes before the first), the "as" instances the spatial-temporal—syntactical—pivot upon which sense (and all experience) turns. In the syntagm "world as world," the first "world" becomes what it is (*as such*) only in the wake of the passage through the "as." The world becomes what it *is, as such*, only by means of the repetition effected through the "as," which is itself meaningless but which promises a sense to come. But because sense is always to come, it can never be guaranteed. Put simply, if the world *as such* names the world *as it is*, then the sense of the world would be univocal. There could be only one meaning of the world. And this one meaning of the world—the world *as such*—would guarantee sense in general. The complete annihilation of the facto-historical world, without touching consciousness, leaves the world *as such* in place as the guarantee of sense.[36] Quoting Husserl, Derrida observes: "As the infinite horizon of every possible experience, the world is consequently 'the universe of Objects which is linguistically expressible in its being and its being-such'" (1962, 78/1978a, 82). Consequently, the world that remains after the end of the world—the total annihilation of the physical, factical world—supports the consciousness that bears it. As the ground of the ground, nothing appears more stable, more certain than the phenomenological world, the world reduced such that it is *as* it is, without, however, it being subject to contingency, to the possibility of castrophe. Yet the fact that sense is always to come, thus not guaranteed, jeopardizes the univocity of the sense of the world. It jeopardizes the world as the guarantor of sense, as "the ground of grounds, the horizon of horizons" (Derrida 1962, 80n/84n87).

That ambiguity threatens the ground of the world as the ground of sense disturbs Husserl, and he attempts to reduce it by limiting its effects to "the facto-cultural phenomenon preceding the reduction" (Derrida 1962, 102/1978a, 101). In short, Husserl wants to limit equivocation to the everyday use of language, as if the phenomenological reduction could rid language of ambiguity. In the *Logical Investigations* he takes as his example the German word *Hund*, which means both dog and a truck used in mines. Husserl explains,

> The class of ambiguous expressions illustrated by this . . . example [is] what one usually has in mind when one speaks of "equivocation." Ambiguity in such cases does not tend to shake our faith in the ideality and objectivity of meanings. We are free, in fact, to limit our expression to a *single* meaning. The ideal unity of each of the differing meanings will not be affected by their attachment to a common designation. (2001, 122)

In "The Origin of Geometry," Husserl goes further:

> Now one will say that in the sphere that interests us here—that of science, of thinking directed toward the attainment of truths and the avoidance of falsehood—one is obviously greatly concerned from the start to put a stop to the free play of associative constructions. In view of the unavoidable sedimentation of mental products in the form of persisting linguistic acquisitions, which can be taken up again at first merely passively and be taken over by anyone else, such constructions remain a constant danger. This danger is avoided if one not merely convinces oneself ex post facto that the particular construction can be reactivated but assures oneself from the start, after the self-evident primal establishment, of its capacity to be reactivated and enduringly maintained. This occurs when one has a view to the univocity of linguistic expression and to securing, by means of the most painstaking formation of the relevant words, propositions, and complexes of propositions, the results which are to be univocally expressed. (1978, 165)

Already in 1962 Derrida recognized that what Husserl calls "ambiguous expressions" trouble the world as the stable ground of sense: "If, in fact, equivocity is always irreducible, that is because words and language in general are not and can never be absolute objects. They do not possess any resistant and permanent identity that is absolutely their own. They have their linguistic being from an intention which traverses them as mediations. The 'same' word is always 'other' according to the always different intentional acts which thereby make a word significant" (1962, 106/1978a, 104). At stake in such ambiguity is irreducible homonymy, which, according to Aristotle, is both the condition of the possibility of language and destructive of the possibility of making sense.[37] The noematic "as"—the power of repetition—inscribes homonymy and thus equivocation, ambiguity, but also fiction, virtuality, spectrality, at the heart of whatever is as such.

Because it looks forward to completion but is not complete, the "as" of the "as such" as much as the "as" of the "as if" is already conditional, uncertain, insecure. The "as" already bears within itself, as the condition of its possibility, the "if." The "if" marks the precariousness of temporal synthesis always already inherent to the "as." The "as," then, is the non-self-sufficient, incomplete mark of constitutive virtualization, of fiction, of narrative, of temporalization. No doubt this is why more than forty years after first signaling the importance and difficulty of the noema, Derrida claimed, "This small word, the 'as' of the 'as if' as much as the 'as' of the 'as such'—whose authority founds and justifies all ontology as much as all phenomenology, all philosophy as science or as knowledge—this small word 'as,' could well be the name of the true problem, not to say the target of deconstruction" (2001, 74/2002b, 234).[38]

AS IF (THE SECRET OF) THE WORLD

The force of the "as"—the force of originary virtualization or fiction, the force of "literature," then—while not opposed to the institution of literature and its *right* (*droit*) to say everything, should not be confused either with that institution or with that right. Derrida points out that literature is "a modern invention" (1993c, 64/1995b, 28) and that it is linked "to a certain non-censure, to the space of democratic freedom" (65/28); consequently, there is "no democracy without literature" and "no literature without democracy" (65/28). However, this does not mean that the trace of either literature or democracy awaits the modern invention of the institutions of either literature or democracy. On the contrary, Derrida claims in *L'Université sans condition* that "as soon as there is a trace, some virtualization is under way" (2001, 25/2002b, 210)—a claim that parallels the suggestion in *Voyous* that "there is always some trace of democracy, every trace is a trace of democracy" (2003c, 64/2005a, 39). He means that "literature" and "democracy"—virtualization, fiction, spectrality, thus absence and death—mark the opening of whatever or whoever comes. This force of virtualization necessary to literature and democracy makes possible the institutions of literature and democracy and the right (*droit*) to say everything. The force necessary to say anything, to say "there is," the force necessary for anything to appear *as it is*, comes before the right to say everything: the impossible force—the force of death, of finitude, of "tropic movement" or syntactic resistance—precedes the possibility of saying; that is, the impossible force comes before the possible.[39]

While the impossible force of the "as" is unconditional, the right to say everything—the right of the institution of literature—is necessarily conditional, being afforded to the institution of literature and to its "authors" only under cover (under the protection) of fiction, as if whatever is said in a literary text made no reference to the world beyond its covers.[40] As if this were possible. In sum, the force of virtualization, which makes it impossible for anything to be in itself or as such, makes possible the institution of literature and its right to say everything insofar as it does so as a fiction, that is, as *intentionally* simulacral, symbolic. The force of fiction opens onto the fiction of force and literature's plausible deniability: namely, that it does not refer to anything outside it, that it makes no difference. It is always possible to act as if literature made no difference.

If the force of the "as" is coeval with the trace, then virtualization (fiction, literature, death) instances the beginning of life, the beginning of the world. In *De la grammatologie* Derrida suggests that life is virtual, always already spectral, when he writes that in the not unrelated experiences of writing and onanism, "the possibility of auto-affection manifests itself as such: it leaves a trace in the world. The worldly residence of a signifier becomes impregnable. That which is written remains, and the experience of touching-touched admits the world as a third party. The exteriority of space is irreducible there" (1967a, 227/1974, 165). There is no auto-affection without the passage outside, without the relation to exteriority. This passage does not simply leave a trace of itself *in* an already given world. Rather, the passage outside opens the world. There is no world without auto-affection, thus without the singularity of life, of this life here and now, which is divided in itself from itself. The chance, the accident of auto-affection leaves a trace in and as the world: "Within the general structure of auto-affection . . . the operation of touching-touched receives the other within the narrow gulf [*la mince différence*] that separates doing from suffering" (227/165). "The narrow gulf," delay (spacing, temporization, death) marks the impossible possibility of auto-affection and, with it, of the world. Noncoincidence with self—the spacing of the passage through the other—instances auto-affection *as* impossible. The spacing of touching-touched both opens the chance of and threatens auto-affection in that auto-affection is possible only through the suspension of its immediacy, only through the mediation of touching-touched, thus through its interruption. This suspension leaves a trace of the other, of the world, that the living being bears within itself as the promise of auto-affection.

"And the outside," Derrida writes, "the exposed surface of the body, signifies and marks forever the division that shapes auto-affection" (1967a, 227/1974, 165). The body, as the scene of touching-touched, poses the limit or horizon of virtuality, as if there were a limit that had not already been crossed and double crossed, crossed out in the instance of its inscription. Where to draw the line between touching-touched, between act and passivity? Auto-affection names the virtualization of life, the becoming-virtual that instances living being. "Auto-affection is a universal structure of experience. All living things are capable of auto-affection. And only a being capable of symbolizing, that is to say of auto-affecting, may let itself be affected by the other in general. Auto-affection is the condition of an experience in general" (228/165). Life is symbolization. It is the force of virtualization, of the *as* and of the *as if* of fiction and of the impossible. Only a being capable—hence with the *power* or faculty—of symbolization can auto-affect. Virtualization, death, the "as" and the "as if," are already at work *as* the promise of life and the impossible possibility of the world:

> Death declares each time *the end of the world in totality*, the end of every possible world, and *each time the end of the world as unique totality, thus irreplaceable and thus infinite*. . . . As if the *repetition* of an infinite whole were still possible: the end of the world *itself*, of the only world that is, each time. Singularly. Irreversibly. That's what the "world" would mean. (Derrida, 2003b, 9).[41]

Death makes the world—and what it carries, what it bears or supports—unique, singular, irreplaceable.

If the singularity of death makes each life and each world absolutely singular, unique, irreplaceable, then no life is livable and no world is inhabitable *as such*. If life is symbolization, thus constitutive division and sending-off without return, then life is virtual. The singularity and irreplaceability of life is such that *as such* it is not. Life is what cannot be lived *as such*. This holds as well for the world. There is no world *without death*, and yet, at the same time, there is no world *with death*. Death instances the end of the world, the impossibility of the world, as the only possibility of the world. And insofar as death does not simply await us at the far end of life as such, of a life without death, death names the suspension of life *as* life. Hence Derrida's claim, in *De la grammatologie*, that archi-writing or the trace "marks *the dead time* in the presence of the living present" (1967a, 95/1974, 68).[42] To say that there is no world—there is no singular, unique world—*without death* means the irreplaceability of life, the singularity and uniqueness of life, depends on finitude, on death. And if in its most minimal sense the world means *that in which* (*ce dans que, ce en que*) living beings are carried, then the world, insofar as it carries each living being in its uniqueness, must necessarily be unique, coterminous or coeval with the unique being it carries. The world is finite, neither before nor after death, no world with or without death, no world without end.[43]

Death is at work *as* the possibility of life, *as* the unrelievable singularity of life and the world. The singularity of death makes each death the end of the world. The absolute singularity of life/death means, however, that the world is not shareable. There is no *common* world, no common *sense* (neither perception nor meaning), thus no shared experience, of the world. Some forty years after his introduction to Husserl's "The Origin of Geometry," thus forty years after suggesting that irreducible equivocation ruined from the start the idea of the world as the ground of the ground of sense, Derrida writes:

> *There is not the world*, that nothing is less certain than the world itself, that there is perhaps no longer a world and no doubt there never was one as totality of anything at all, habitable and co-habitable world, and that radical dissemination, i.e., the absence of a common world, the irremediable solitude without salvation of the living being, depends first on the absence without recourse of any world, i.e., of any common meaning [*sens commun*] of the word "world," in sum of any common meaning at all. (2010, 366/2011, 266)

Or, as Derrida put it earlier in the same seminar: "There is no world; there are only islands" (31/9). The uniqueness, the singularity of my death—which is never simply my own, of which I never have an experience except in and through the death of the other—opens (to me, as mine) the singular and unshareable world, what I call "my world." Yet, because my world is never my own insofar as my death (hence my life) is never mine, I am always cut off from my death and, therefore, from "my (own or proper) world." The world names the place I am not *at home*: "We would have to conclude that this world, what we also call the entirety, the whole and the everywhere, the everywhere of the world, is where we are not at home" (159/104).

The living being cannot *not* be in the world and yet is never *at home* in the world. I have only one world, but it is not my own: this is the paradox or aporia of singularity. The same paradox is legible as the logic of the secret, of the name, of the signature. And of language: "*I have only one language, yet it is not mine*" (Derrida 1996b, 15/1998b, 2). This fact—that I only ever speak one language, but that language is not my own—results from the differantial relation of *langue* (language *qua* structure) to *parole* (speech, the historical incidence, the event, of language).[44] This impossible relation opens the possibility of the idiom, that is, the singularity of one's insertion into and relation to language. But this singularity is ruined from the start by language's ideality, hence its necessary repeatability or iterability. Indeed, this is language's *promise*: it provides the opportunity for our becoming-singular, thus for our freedom; and, at the same time, it subjects us to the law.[45] As Derrida explains: "The monolingualism of the other would be that sovereignty, that law originating from elsewhere, certainly, but also primarily the very language of the Law. And the Law as Language" (1996b, 69/1998b, 39). Because the law appears *as* language, it is always *as if* I give myself the law, as if it originates in me, in my sovereign—singular—speech. Yet, because the language I speak is not my own, the law always comes from elsewhere, from another, from a language that precedes me and that thus imposes the law on me. Consequently, language is that which both *saves* and *threatens* us: "This is the most difficult paradox to assume: it is owed to the abyssal imbalance between *the language that destroys*, with its infinite power of seduction, and *the language that saves*, between the disastrous power of ideology, as well as all the forms of violence inscribed in our relation to language, and the weakness if not the impotence of a word that still wishes to oppose it" (Crépon 2014, 20–21).

On Crépon's account, "Literature and philosophy find their place in the gray zone that separates the language that destroys from the language that saves" (24). In other words, literature and philosophy take place in and as the irreducible invention—event—of singularity (the language that saves) even as they are determined by the law of language and language *as* the law (the language that destroys). Literature and philosophy invent that which destroys them and betray that to which they respond. They necessarily submit to the law from which, in their singularity, they are subtracted *in* and *as* its institutionalization. Language happens, therefore, only in the singular invention it both destroys and makes possible. Crépon writes, "Here is already that by which literature and philosophy are confronted: the undeniable and irreducible fact that we are, in more than one way, *possessed* by languages that are not truly ours and *threatened* by that which this possession is susceptible of ordering" (25). If literature and philosophy resist this possession and threat, they do so only by assuming them: philosophy by means of "critique"; literature—"every literary work worthy of the name"—by affirming that "the 'idiomatic' invention of singularity . . . is possible, with and in language" (27).

If "our experience of language" is marked by "constitutive violence," as Crépon claims it is, then there can be no "gray zone" in which literature and philosophy might reasonably harbor "the secret hope of escaping violence for as long as possible" (27). To put it simply, if our experience of language is constitutively violent, and if the relation to language determines both our singularity and our relation to the law, then there is no possibility, no chance and no hope of escaping violence. What would be the condition for a nonviolent delay, for the "as long as possible," given that delay instances violence? Because the violence of language (language as law and law as language) conditions all relations—both to every other and to ourselves—there can be no instance of nonviolence. The invention of singularity, in other words, is not the effect of a consciousness itself always already marked by the relation to language; rather, singularity is an effect of the relation to language constitutive of the impossible possibility of consciousness. If there is singularity, it does not arise from a "secret hope" that could itself be only the effect of the language that will always already have destroyed it. In every instance, then, language ineluctably invents—inscribes—the singular relation to that which, *qua* other *as* other, cannot be known or determined in advance. This singular relation to the other *as* other *to come* instances the event of language as the demand of/for the name and the call of/for justice. The mistake is to think that either the name or justice is nonviolent.

CHAPTER 4

KILLING TIME

Jet Lag, or the Anachronism of Life

El asesino en serie deja su firma, ¿entienden?,
no tiene un móvil, pero tiene una firma.
ROBERTO BOLAÑO, *2666* (2004)

Je suis tout à fait ailleurs.
JACQUES DERRIDA, *LA CARTE POSTALE* (1980)

There is *one* world, but it is neither *mine* nor *ours*. I am not at home in the world I cannot live without; I am, as Derrida observes, completely elsewhere. If the life of the living being depends on auto-affection and if only those beings are capable of symbolization, then life is necessarily speculative in that symbolization is marked by the structure of referral, of sending-off, of deferral. Indeed, in *De la grammatologie* Derrida observes that "auto-affection," which is another name for life, "is pure speculation" (1967a, 221/1974, 154), which means life is spectral or specular (phantasmatic) and economic (a question of interest, of gain and loss, of credit, of paying and lending). Speculation is an effect of delay. The symbol is speculative. Yet *qua* the impossible possibility of auto-affection, Derrida makes clear that "the symbolic is the immediate" (222/154). Immediacy, then, has the structure of the symbol, which means, simply, the immediate is not pure: it is not unmarked by the delay that opens the promise of symbolization. As a consequence, symbolization does not befall an already living being immediately in touch with itself.[1] Rather, symbolization is immediate in that it names the structural incompleteness of the living being. The immediacy of mediation exposes the living being to the outside, to exteriority in general, as the impossible condition of the possibility of interiority: life necessarily exceeds the living being. Life comes from the other. Hence, if symbolization is immediate to the living being, the living being is cut off, separated, divided from itself. Life is *posted*, sent off.

TELEPATHY AND HISTORY: ALFONSO REYES

In *El deslinde* Alfonso Reyes sought in literature the absolute coincidence of meaning and expression. Yet because this coincidence is synthetic, it is necessarily differential, thus requiring a spatial-temporal referral that ineluctably instances delay, deferral, thus noncoincidence, disjointure. In a word, anachronism. The fact that literature derives from a synthesis of meaning and expression makes translation both necessary and impossible. On the one hand, without the chance of translation, that is, without the possibility of repetition *in other words*, "literature" would be unrecognizable. In short, if literature were to put off universalization (as Crépon says it secretly hopes to do), "for as long as possible," were it, then, absolutely singular such that it could not be translated—whether inter- or intralinguistically—it would not be literature; it would not be anything. On the other hand, because there is delay, translation is impossible. The difference from itself of every articulation, of every expression, means translation never catches up to that which it targets. Necessary and impossible, the movement of translation (*tra-ducción*) is both originary and belated. The desire for a literature that coincides with itself without delay is the desire for pure presence. It is the desire for a literature that is not sent off, delivered, posted.

In the first chapter of *La experiencia literaria*, "Hermes o de la comunicación humana," Reyes offers what he calls "an explanatory fiction" of the process through which writing and intersubjective communication develop. The story begins in silence: "The mute man anterior to language, perhaps he communicated with his neighbors through a certain radiation that went from one mind to another, emitted and received through the nervous antennas?" (1962, 22). Reyes understands such communication to take place "anterior to the word," and although it is "emitted and received" and thus passes between us, it leaves no trace of its passage in the world. Communication "before the word" never exteriorizes itself, consequently it suffers no corruption in the transference from one to another. This would be the "Adamic ray" (22) or what Reyes identifies as "telepathy" (23). Reyes remarks that "language and all the actual means of communication work directly against this animal or primitive faculty; they are atrophying it through disuse and, save exceptional surviving instances, they end up extinguishing it" (23). Despite claiming that what he recounts is an "explanatory fiction" rather than a history, Reyes nonetheless refers to contemporary research and the question whether "inheritance and instinct, today automatic repetitions incrusted in the memory of the species, are not phenomena of telepathic origin, solicitous transmissions of teachings, whose secret the paternal generation deposits in the functional centers of the filial generation" (24). Telepathy instances a modality of inheritance without critical or aleatory intervention, a secret deposited without resistance in the next generation.

The unacknowledged relation to Husserl is apparent. After all, Reyes's "explanatory fiction" pursues the same problem as Husserl's account of the origin and inheritance of geometry: how to pass on, communicate, the truth without interference or friction, without corruption or delay. Both Reyes's *fenomenografía* (although here not called by this name) and Husserl's phenomenology explain the possibility of inheritance through a reduction of language (historical, empirical languages) that cannot fail to reimport language at the decisive moment as the key element for the transmission of truth. (Recall that in Husserl the reintroduction of language, now purified of all empirical, subjective determination, takes place as writing.) For his part, Reyes imagines a moment of communication *anterior to the word* that makes possible pure communication, the absolute transmission—without loss or remainder—from one to another without the risk of any historical, empirical accident jeopardizing it.

In principle, in neither Husserl nor Reyes is this purified language (whether transcendentally reduced *à la* Husserl or anterior to words *à la* Reyes) exposed to the world. In neither case would such language leave a trace—a track or trail—in and as the world. Both reduce, bracket the world. For Reyes, this is telepathy. It instances the possibility of a communication *between us* (thus constitutive of community) that does not *pass through* the world. In sum, at stake for Reyes is the possibility of a pure communication, one that remains uncontaminated by words and by the passage through the world and yet that does not jeopardize the world *as such*. On the contrary, such pure—telepathic—communication instances the possibility of the *one* world that is *ours*, shared between us that nevertheless does not come between us. Only telepathy would allow for a communication without friction or resistance, without loss or gain.

The story (*cuento*) Reyes tells in "Hermes o de la comunicación humana" follows the typical plot. It moves from this telepathic communication through progressive stages of exteriority: the development first of hand gestures and then of spoken language in the word, followed by the problems associated with the rise of multiple languages (translation) and the development of writing, which, again, follows the classical genealogy from the ideogram to the hieroglyph to the phonetic character or the letter. The story concludes with the suggestion of the development of a communicative technology that would be the opposite of the telepathy with which human communication began, but which would nonetheless have the same effect. After referring to recent developments that reduce only the time it takes to produce written texts (typing and stenography, for example), Reyes turns to those developments that reduce the time of transmission, "'pneumatic' mail and the telegraph" (1962, 50). These are technical developments that, on Reyes's account, ultimately signal only their own limitations. He argues that the "modifying mechanisms of the spoken word" (51), such as the telephone, the radio, and the megaphone, which overcome the "natural" limitation of the transmissibility of the spoken word, in fact "never become more than a sad confession of impotence" (51). In other words, such developments remain within the limited confines of writing in that they are technical developments meant to project the spoken word across greater distances more efficiently (more rapidly, but never without delay). But more than anything else, for Reyes, they signal the limitation of the spoken word and of language itself. For language is always marked by absence. Language never presents, even in the co-presence of interlocutors, either the things themselves or the ideas themselves, in their purity, without the mediation of a technical support, namely, the word, whether spoken or written, whether delivered via telegram or telephone.

Reyes begins his story of communication with the myth of a wordless, perfect communication, but he ends it with the dream of pure presentation, a presentation that obviates the need for the "as" and the "as if." Pursuing to its logical conclusion Paul Valéry's suggestion that in "a not distant future," there will be "home radioplasty, a service that will be able to send, from the museum to the home of the member, through a system of waves, the material reproduction of a painting or statue" (51), Reyes arrives at Adolfo Bioy Casares, who anticipates, "in *The Invention of Morel*, the integral uptake of human bulk with all its attributes of presence, form, consistency, color, movement and voice: a perfect double of each one of us." As a result, "the absent or already disappeared man will be able then to reproduce himself indefinitely in his recorded scenes. One would arrive at the integral repetition of history" (51). The beginning and the end are the same. A pure interiority (a communication that "passes" between us without ever getting out of our heads) becomes a pure exteriority (the infinitely repeatable material reproduction of ourselves in all our historical moments). We move from having no need for a technology of representation because all our thoughts would be the same (your ideas would be my ideas) to having no need for thoughts because, insofar as we are infinitely repeatable in our historical determinations, we are always present without delay both to ourselves and to others. In both cases, it is a question of the absolute reduction of time and space and, with it, of history.

On Reyes's account, like animals and primitive beings we would bear a striking resemblance to divine or angelic beings (23). In Valéry and Bioy Casares, words will have disappeared as well, but thoughts are no longer in the head; they are the things themselves. I don't send my words to you as the representation of my thoughts or of the things before me; rather, the thing itself appears before you. In short, the promise of the most advanced technology signals a return to the most primitive, which means a return to our divine or angelic nature. And the way back and forward (they are the same, finally, in Reyes's "fiction") is to remove time and space from communication. Yet communication without mediation (without delay or transmission) would also spell the end of alterity, for the other would be reduced to the same.

At issue in Reyes's "fiction" of the twin poles of communication—the mythological origin of a communication anterior to the word and the "end" (*telos*) of communication in which the things themselves are always present—is the absolution of the postal principle, which would also signal the "end" of literature. Recall that on Reyes's account, literature—unlike, say, history or philosophy or any other form of discourse—instances the absolute synthesis of meaning and expression. Literature, then, is that which cannot be said in other words, which means it refers only to itself or, rather, in principle, it does not refer at all, insofar as referral amounts to corresponding—to a sending-off—to that which is not present, to that which is no longer and not yet. Reyes's understanding of literature admits no delay, no difference. The end (*telos*), however, is also the end. Literature's absolution is disastrous. As Derrida remarks in *La carte postale*, "The end of a postal epoch is doubtless also the end of literature" (1980, 111/1987a, 104). And the end of literature is the end of the world in that literature begins *in* and *as* the trace of symbolization, the minimal mark of exteriority necessary for auto-affection. Literature names the asymmetrical inscription of the world. The world is before us.

Reyes's account of literature, however, as that which is perfectly self-identical, strictly speaking—and despite his claim that it cannot do without a "minimum of reality"—has no need for the world. As absolutely coincident with itself, literature, for Reyes, instances an intentional consciousness invulnerable to and untouched by the absolute destruction of the world.[2] As if consciousness—literature—had no need of the world, as if there could be literature without world, without the openness to an exterior in general that leaves a trace in and as the world. Without the exposure to the outside, literature—if there were any—would be telepathic. Without a necessary passage through the world—which means the world would disappear but literature (intentional consciousness) would remain—literature would instance the pure presentation of the absolutely self-same. It would have no need for the "as" or the "as if." Such would be the condition of what might be called an absolutely sovereign literature that could only be indifferent to the world. There would be no event of the world. It is hard to reconcile this understanding of literature, which is a necessary consequence of Reyes's dream of telepathy, with his understanding that literature must always bear a "minimum of reality."

This understanding of telepathy—thus of the absolute coincidence of consciousness with itself (the coincidence, then, of meaning and expression or form and matter)—leaves its mark in Reyes's attempts at historical understanding. As Gareth Williams points out, in Reyes's "Pasado inmediato," which he wrote in September 1939 and included in the eponymously titled volume in 1941, Reyes was "writing at an extraordinary moment: a moment of maximal nomic danger both for the national context as well as for the stage of world affairs" (2011, 97). According to Williams, "Pasado inmediato" responds "to the perceived fracturing of, or decline in . . . the decisive ethical (and therefore cultural) state form" (96). In other words, "Thirty years after the outbreak of what would become a decade of revolutionary upheaval, 'Pasado inmediato' restores the jurisdiction of genealogical friendship to the revolution" (96). And, in a note, Williams remarks that the essay constitutes "a response to the decline in the function of the master, an attempt to turn the clock back on Hegel and his philosophical, historical, and political legacies" (199–200n11). To "turn the clock back," however, is to kill time, to absolve the difference time makes. The movement of the argument is not without its irony, however, in that in order to kill time, Reyes must first acknowledge the anachronism or contretemps of the Díaz regime (which will be suspended by the revolution), which appears to inaugurate a "historical" moment that is completely coincident with itself.

Reyes begins by acknowledging the problem: "The history that has just passed is always the least appreciated. The new generations fight against it and tend, by mental economy, to summarize it with a single emblem in order once and for all to liquidate it" (1960b, 182). Reyes calls the "immediate past" "the verb's most modest tense [*tiempo*]" and although those prone to hyperbole or exaggeration ("*los exagerados*") sometimes call it "the absolute past," Reyes himself does not think it warrants exaltation as "a present perfect [un *pretérito perfecto*]." Rather, he suggests it should be considered "a defined past [*un pasado definido*]" (182). The immediate past is the verb tense that refers to events that have been completed (and are therefore past) in a moment virtually contiguous to the present instant. In Spanish, although the present indicative is often used to describe or narrate such moments, the tense is formally indicated by the structure "*acabar* de + infinitive," meaning "just to have" done something: "Acabamos de terminar la cena" (We *just* finished dinner). The question is the relation of past to present. The immediate past attempts to articulate a relation in which the past, though past, remains present in (or immediately close to, near) the present-present and is both (absolutely) past and (still) present.

The "immediate past" to which Reyes refers is 1910, some twenty-nine years prior to the present in which he was writing the essay. In this moment, here and now, "the symbols of chronology want to come to objective life [*cobrar vida objetiva*]" (182). By 1910 "the old regime . . . was showing signs of expiring and had endured what nature appeared to consent. The dictator frankly had entered on that path of solitude that is old age. Between him and his people had deepened a chronological abyss" (183). The assumption of a natural term for political regimes forgets that death—*caducidad* and anachronism or chronological abyss, the dead time at the heart of the living present—is at work in life as its promise, which means, on the one hand, that every living being (whether natural or political) strives to defer the death that makes it possible, and, on the other hand, that the condition of sovereignty is the "chronological abyss," that is, a gap between sovereign and subject. In short, nothing is more natural than this unnatural fact of life, whether that of living beings or that of political regimes. Insofar as *caducidad* is mortality and therefore life, there will never have been a life that did not suffer—and sustain itself through—a chronological abyss. Death is the *suspension* of life. There is no life, but also no politics that is not suspended. But because life is suspended, at every moment "life"—here understood as political life during Porfirio Díaz's thirty-five-year regime (1876–1911)—is threatened. Its own "succession"—its endurance—suspended: "The problem of an inescapable succession was already distressing" (183).

Strictly speaking, this is the condition of any political regime even in times of peace: "The leader of the peace, of the long peace, had proposed solutions offering candidates to the people. But one is not dictator in vain. The dictatorship, like poison, is the desperate recourse that, to perpetuate itself, poisons the one who distributes it as much as those who take it. The dictator was jealous of his own children and devoured them like Saturn"

(1960b, 183). It is easy enough to see what is at stake in this passage. Reyes effectively describes the autoimmunity of the state form in general and of the Díaz regime in particular. Because succession is necessary for the survival of any (living) political regime, Díaz must necessarily name an heir. Yet because any possible heir threatens the survival of his regime in his name, he devours or destroys his own successors. In order to save itself, the regime destroys itself. Ultimately, and against the regime's desire for survival, "the people, in waking from a long dream, now wanted to choose for itself, it wanted to use its own hands and know itself to be the owner of its own muscles" (183). The Mexican Revolution occurs because the Porfiriato attempts to immunize itself against its own decline and death by naming its own successor, only to see this immunological response turn against itself by perceiving in its self-determined succession a threat to itself and consequently moving to undermine it. This opens the space for "*el pueblo*" to assert itself—its sovereignty—against the regime. Importantly, Reyes understands this possibility as an effect of the peace and stability of regimes that long endure: "*Pax.* These long-lived governments so characteristic of the century—Victoria, Franz Josef, Nicholas—I don't know what dormant virtue they carried with them. Under the sign of Porfirio Díaz, in those last years, history stops, the future makes a stop. Already in the country nothing happened or nothing seemed to happen, on the unfolding plane of that solemn routine" (183–184). Not unlike the British, Austrian-Hungarian, and Russian empires, Mexico rests in peace. Or appears to do so. And this makes sense. A certain peace hides the fissures that destroy from within the state form. The state is a ruin, always already fossilized: "History, that is to say, the succession of transcendent events in the life of peoples, seems a remote thing, something already finished forever; history seems a part of prehistory. Mexico was a mature country, not liable to change, in final equilibrium, in the state of civilization. Mexico was peace, understood as a kind of immobility" (184). Further, this peace resulted in the decline of Mexican culture, which manifested itself in the perceived division between theory and practice. Peace was

> a symptom, small only in appearance, of that decomposition of culture: it became popular . . . to consider that there was a schism [*cisma*] between theory and practice. Theory was the lie, falseness, and it belonged to the age of metaphysics, if not that of theology. Practice was reality, the true truth. Expression, all of it, of a reaction against culture, of a love of the lowest ignorance, that which ignores itself and in itself it strokes and pleases itself. When society loses its confidence in culture, it regresses toward barbarity at the speed of light. (1960b, 193)

Despite the chronological abyss between the dictator and the people, despite the schism between theory and practice—both of which mark the anachronism (the non-self-coincidence) necessary for something, anything, to happen—Reyes recurs to a different model to describe the event of the revolution: "To present only some of its partial aspects is to mutilate reality. The dignity of history consists in arriving at the parallelism of ideas with events, ruling people here with the same golden rule that the *Epístola moral* proposes: 'Make thought equal to life'" (186). This is the gesture of interest: a nonmutilated reality, the unity or parallelism of thought and life, of theory and practice, of idea (form) and action (expression or matter), as if history were not cut off from itself, as if history were not constitutively anachronistic. Here, in "Pasado inmediato," history catches up to itself. The revolution is no accident, even if, as Reyes points out, "it was born almost blind like children and, like children, afterwards it was opening its eyelids" (186). Even if, as Williams hypothesizes, Reyes seeks "to turn the clock back on Hegel" and restore the master to its proper place, he does so via a certain Hegelian gesture, for what is the Mexican Revolution but the moment in which the idea becomes actualized, concrete, the moment in which the idea coincides with itself, thus overtaking and reconstituting accidents into history. Mexico opens its eyes and becomes conscious of itself. "It is true," Reyes writes, "that the Mexican Revolution erupted from an impulse much more than from an idea. It wasn't planned" (185). Yet even as it advanced blindly, accidentally, by impulse, "intelligence accompanied it . . . ; sometimes it merely suffered it, until the day arrives in which it illuminates it" (186). This is the cunning of reason, in which everything that happens does so for a reason and on account of reason. Understood this way, history instances the self-unfolding, the self-determination, of reason and thus of the *appearance* of freedom in the world. But it is possible, on Reyes's account, only insofar as the necessity of the idea coincides with the accidentality of its historical expression.

The appearance in the world of an idea that will have governed the accidents of history, what Hegel calls the cunning of reason, is always only the effect of historical "upstreaming," of understanding what happened farther "upstream" from our perspective already farther "downstream." The concept of "history" entails this movement upstream from downstream. Historical narrative seeks to make sense of what (will have) happened from a perspective subsequent to that happening, which means it is always written from a point downstream that looks back toward a point upstream that *must* arrive "here"—downstream. So, for instance, only from the perspective of 1939 can Reyes claim that the 1908 demonstration in memory of Barreda was "the first patent sign of a public consciousness freed from the regime" and that "in the theoretical order, it is not inexact to say that the revolution was born there" (1960b, 209). Only in 1939 could he assert that the dialogue between Mexican philosophers Antonio Caso and José Vasconcelos had "already erased the difference that never should have existed and that caused so much damage to the generation that follows us"; their dialogue will be, he writes, "with time, one of the most beautiful chapters of Mexican culture" (213). The desire—against that which seems to predominate—*not* to forget 1910 and what it *will have* wrought, what it *will have* inaugurated, what it *will have* symbolized, is possible only through a certain forgetting.[3] Reyes will have had to forget the differences that history both makes and is. Only by forgetting the differences—that should not have existed—between Caso and Vasconcelos will their correspondence be one of the most beautiful chapters of Mexican culture. Only *with time* (*con el tiempo*) will differences have been resolved. In other words, it is only through a certain *tele*graphy or a long-distance *tele*phone call from a past that is no longer to a future that is not yet that differences *may be—but will not have been*—resolved into a beautiful chapter of Mexican culture. But it is precisely this telecommunication, this *sending*, that Reyes seeks to displace in favor of a telepathy that absolves time (the chronological abyss) and the difference it makes in an undifferentiated present. This is the absolution of time. The immediate (or absolute) past is the absolute present.

Writing in 1939 of the year 1910 (which he claims already seems far off from the present) and the decade that followed, Reyes remarks: "Literature *continues* as it *can* in the middle of civil struggles. In the worst years, from 1914 to 1916, the editorial labor of Mexico *is* overwhelming and superior to what we *had known* until then. Later *will come* Vasconcelos's formidable educational work, Genaro Estrada's excellent organizational work. New names *will appear*: Ramón López Velarde, shooting star in our poetic sky. Diego Rivera, who is an entire epoch by himself, *returns* from Europe. The country *becomes* aware of its own character" (1960b, 215–216, emphases added). With the exception of one instance of the past perfect, "had known [*habíamos conocido*]," necessary for indicating what will have been the case up to a past present moment, and two instances of the absolute future announcing what will happen (and from the vantage point of 1939 that can be known to have happened—the appearance on the scene of Vasconcelos's educational work, the organizational efforts of Genaro Estrada, and López Velarde's poetry), the other verbs are conjugated in the present tense and yet describe a past (the year 1910) that Reyes has already indicated seemed far off, thus not immediate. Thus the "present" of 1910 orients the past perfect (it is past in relation to 1910) and the future (what happens subsequent to 1910 but is the future only with respect to 1910). The last sentence troubles this historical frame, however: "The country becomes aware of its own character [El país cobra conciencia de su carácter propio]."

Unlike the events narrated as occurring in the present tense or time (*tiempo*) and those narrated as being either past or future in relation to 1910, the last sentence remarks *as present in 1910* what it will have been impossible to know until later, perhaps as late as 1939. The claim that "the country becomes aware of its own character" does not unambiguously refer to the events of 1910 or even to the years immediately succeeding it, not least because it would be impossible in 1910 to know that the country was becoming, at that moment, self-conscious. Rather, the sentence performs the telepathic absolution of time in which the absolute past (1910) *is* the absolute present (1939). The year 1910, which is already far off, becomes the immediate past of 1939, as if they were so contiguous as to be comprehended within the same time or tense. The revolution is (always) present, is (always) in the present tense or time, then and there, here and now. There is no difference between 1910 and 1939. Or, rather, the difference between them makes no difference. There is no *contretemps*, no *cisma* or delay, between them. The one (passes) seamlessly, immediately, (into) the other. The one (is) the other.

For Reyes, then, telepathic history manifests itself in the figure of a national self-consciousness that is (always) present to itself. One present (1910) is another (1939); between them nothing passes, happens: *no pasa nada*. Consequently, the national patrimony is absolute. It cannot be passed on because it cannot pass away. Mexican inheritance is uncritical, not just between 1910 and 1939 but from the beginning. In *Visión de Anáhuac (1519)*, first published in 1915, Reyes suggests that what unifies Mexico and Mexicans across history and thus what connects postindependence and post-Porfiriato Mexicans with "the race of yesterday" is not "the indigenous tradition," nor is it a question of blood ("without speaking of bloods"). Rather, it is a question of "the everyday emotion before the same natural object. The shock of sensibility with the same world styles begets a common soul" (1960a, 34). Mexican community, on Reyes's account, is grounded not in "blood" or shared language but rather in the idea—effectively Aristotle's—of an essential sameness.[4] Only by grounding historical community on a sameness that is uncorrupted by the accidents of history (historical languages, races, classes, etc.) and that is thus "shared" telepathically, via the experience of the things of nature rather than through language, is Reyes able to think the identity of 1519 and 1915. This is telepathic community, telepathic tradition, based on the "minimum of reality": the encounter with the objects of nature. It is a tradition that bears no mark of time. It is all the same to Mexican self-consciousness. In its silent relation to nature, what we call "Mexico"—the national identity—is present to itself in the same way and as the same in 1519 and 1915.

Only via such telepathy is the nation-state able to become aware or to acquire (*cobrar*) consciousness of itself in such a way that every present instant is the same (to it). But what does this mean? Although in the phrase *cobrar conciencia* (to become aware) *cobrar* means to become or to acquire, its primary signification is "to charge," in the sense of how much something is going to cost. It can also be used in the calculation of punishment in the adjudication of a crime: what the crime will have *cost*. In short, *cobrar* instances economization (give and take, gain and loss). It designates structures of interest, credit, and exchange. If Mexico becomes aware, acquires consciousness of itself, it does so in and through economization, which means delay, deferral. The telepathic present—the presence to self of national consciousness—takes time; it *costs* time. It results from an economy in which the "present" appears on credit, as the possibility of interest gained and capital lost. The *darse cuenta* (the "giving (oneself) account/bill" and thus the structure of self-consciousness) *renders* interest. It renders account (*rinde cuenta*): the ghost or simulacrum of presence and of the present. When will the present not have been taken on faith, on credit, with everything gained and lost in the interval, the suspension, of consciousness?

Credit and interest, gain and loss: these are effects of the *tele-* (telepathy, telephone, telegraphy, telecommunications, Teletype, telex, television) that instances unrelievable and irreducible *sending*, separation, division, a certain suspension and speculation. *Tele-* always signals distance, remoteness, delay, difference, no matter how reduced and immediate it appears to be. Indeed, the apparent immediacy of the *tele-* (telecommunications in general) is an effect of this delay, for without it, there would be no correspondence, no communication, no exchange. There would be no possibility of response, thus of responsibility and justice. Yet to what, to whom, does this response respond? Literature names the asymmetrical response to an absolutely singular call, a demand that is always before it, always (in) secret, in anticipation of or before the "one" that responds. This is the responsibility of literature.[5] This is telepathy: the singular sending that catches the receiver off guard, at a loss, indebted to respond to what no one—neither oneself nor any other—will ever know or hear or experience, with everything to gain *and* to lose. Literature instances the speculative moment.

This is not Reyes's conception of telepathy, however, inasmuch as for him literature—as aesthetic form—names the absolution of the difference between meaning and expression, hence the telepathic or immediate relation of form and matter that *El deslinde* attempts to formalize and "Hermes o de la comunicación humana" pushes to its logical extreme, thereby announcing a nonresponsive literature, one of absolute transparency in which there is no secret. In both its literary and historical manifestations, Reyes's telepathy works to preserve the purity and transparency of sense. His telepathy puts the nation-state immediately in touch with itself in both its historical and aesthetic determinations. Yet because the *tele*pathic instances structural delay—which is another way to say symbolization—in order to constitute the possibility of sense (*pathos*, *aisthesis*) and with it of its presence in the present, it necessarily touches itself through the other-than-itself. Telepathy is mediation. All sense is *tele*pathic, cut off from itself in order to touch itself for the first time. Sense—in all its senses—arrives, if it ever does, from long distance.[6]

For Reyes telepathy is nonspeculative, noneconomic, without interest. It instances the perfection of communication and of aesthetic experience—of the arts, then—in the absolute reduction of the time of correspondence and thus the possibility of equivocation; it is the end of secrecy and of speculation, hence, of interest. In itself, by itself (*qua* telepathic in Reyes's sense), literature pays no interest. Why? Because it would be unable to bear the "minimum of reality." That is, literature must always bear that which is not literature in order to be literature. And this means that in its necessary referral to the world, to what is outside literature, the "literary" cannot ever simply be transported or transferred without material support. It must carry—and thus be carried away by—the minimum of reality. The interest of literature depends on the *tele*pathic *qua* temporal delay, deferral, referral; thus, it relies on the *tele*pathic as that which traverses an irreducible distance and which is therefore exposed to the other, to alterity in general.

THE TIME OF THE *TELE-*, OR THE ANACHRONISM OF LIFE

Reyes is one of the few Mexican writers who survives Bolaño unscathed. In *Los detectives salvajes* (1998), on 10 December Juan García Madero catalogues the books he has stolen from Mexico City bookstores. The list ends with those stolen from *Librería El Mundo*: "Selected poems by Byron, Shelley, and Keats; Stendahl's *The Red and the Black* (which I've already read); and Lichtenberg's *Aphorisms*, translated by Alfonso Reyes. This afternoon, as I arranged my books in the room, I thought about Reyes. Reyes could be my little refuge. A person could be immensely happy reading only him or the writers he loved. But that would be too easy" (1998, 103–104/2007, 102–103). In the posthumously published *Los sinsabores del verdadero policía* (2011), at the airport, as he departs from Barcelona, the poet Pere Girau remarks, "Mexico is a truly exotic country, the promised land of Artaud and the Mayas, home of Alfonso Reyes and Atahualpa" (2011, 57/2012, 32). Rosa corrects him: "Atahualpa was an Inca, a Peruvian Inca" (57/32). Elsewhere, however, Bolaño's affirmation of Reyes is more interesting. Again in *Los detectives salvajes*, during Juan García Madero's first visit alone to see María Font on 17 November, he encounters her father, Joaquín (Quim) Font, who cautions García Madero:

> "She has some friends that—but there's no point getting into it, you'll meet them," he said. "In some ways, it doesn't bother me. A person has to get to know people from all walks of life. At a certain point you need to steep yourself in reality, no? I think it was Alfonso Reyes who said that. Maybe not. It doesn't matter. But sometimes María goes overboard, wouldn't you say? And I'm not criticizing her for that, for steeping herself in reality, but she should *steep* herself, not *expose* herself, don't you think? Because if one steeps oneself too thoroughly, one is at risk of becoming a *victim.* I don't know whether you follow me. . . . A victim of reality, especially if one has friends who are, how to put it, magnetic, wouldn't you say?" (1998, 53/2007, 47)

How much reality must one have, must one bear, to be *soaked* or *steeped* in it without, however, being *exposed* to it? Where to draw the line between too little reality and too much? How much reality is necessary? What is the "minimum of reality" that allows one to be immersed in it without becoming a victim of it? Whereas Reyes limits his interest in the "minimum of reality" to what literature—and not life—must bear, in his gesture to rethink the relation of literature to life, thus to rethink the limits of sense, Bolaño extends Reyes's question from literature to life. Effectively, *Los detectives salvajes* asks how much reality (a) life can bear.

Although he nowhere associates Reyes with it, Bolaño refers throughout his work to telepathy. The most extensive instance occurs in *2666*, in "The Part about Amalfitano," when Amalfitano—already hearing the voice of his grandfather/father—"thought about telepathy. He thought about the telepathic Mapuches or Araucanians" (2004, 276/2008, 216). According to Lonko Kilapán's *O'Higgins es araucano: 17 pruebas, tomadas de la Historia Secreta de la Araucanía*, which Amalfitano read (Bolaño 2004, 276/2008, 216), the Araucanos had at least three writing systems: *adkintuwe* (based on the movement of tree branches and which allowed Araucanians to know what was happening in Concepción and Santiago), *Prom* (a system of knots), and *Adentunemul* (a secret writing composed of triangles) (283–284/221–222). They also relied on telepathy, which, according to Kilapán, the Spaniards never suspected (283/221). The story is familiar. Bolaño relays the same tale Reyes tells: "'Primitive man was ignorant of language; he communicated by brainwaves, as animals and plants do. When he resorted to sounds and gestures and hand signals to communicate, he began to lose the gift of telepathy, and this loss was accelerated when he went to live in cities, distancing himself from nature'" (283/221–222). Yet despite their increasing urbanization and the development not only of spoken language but also of writing as a means to preserve thought and communicate across temporal and spatial distances, the Araucanians—and in particular the Kügas—continued to cultivate telepathy.

The Kügas were distributed throughout the Americas, the Pacific islands, and the far south in order to form a telepathic network that would make it impossible for an enemy to take them by surprise. Moreover, "'By means of telepathy they kept in permanent contact with the Chilean migrants who first settled in the north of India, where they were called Aryans, then headed to the fields of ancient Germania and later descended to the Peloponnese, traveling from there to Chile along the traditional route to India and across the Pacific Ocean'" (283/222). Kilapán describes a telepathic early warning system, a global telecommunication network that, contrary to the post or to a postal network, allows the Kügas to remain in "permanent contact" with others. The claim of permanent contact, which is the dream of absolute presence, is the naïve idea of telepathy, as if telepathy were able absolutely to reduce the delay between us, as if, via telepathy, one no longer touched the other/oneself from a distance. As if all contact were not always already *tele*pathic, sent off, long distance, delayed.

The relative strength of our telepathic faculty indicates the state of our alienation not only from nature but also from ourselves in that the diminution of our telepathic capacity means our thoughts have become mediated by a language that separates us from ourselves. Amalfitano draws certain conclusions from his reading of Kilapán, the most interesting of which are perhaps the seventh and the ninth: "7: . . . telepathic communication was never discovered and if at some point it stopped working this was because the Spaniards killed the telepaths. . . . 9: should one deduce from this that Bernardo O'Higgins was also a telepath? Should one deduce that the author himself, Lonko Kilapán, was a telepath? Yes, in fact, one should" (285/223). Telepathy remains secret, absolutely secret, because, strictly speaking, not even telepaths could discover or know of their telepathic powers. Insofar as telepathy takes place without the mediation of language, without any material support, without any temporal deferral, even were it possible to "transmit" thoughts directly, neither the sender nor the receiver would know either what the "ideas" were or whence they came. Without the name—the word *par excellence*—to identify the idea or concept or thing (and also to identify the sender and the receiver and thus to determine the posts between which thoughts are posted, sent), thoughts (were they possible in the first place) would simply "appear" *ex nihilo*. But they would appear without appearing, because the possibility of appearing is spectral, hence delayed and deferred.

The lack of a "signature"—the chance therefore that thought could take place without any material support, that it might arrive *ex nihilo*—means that thought would be spurious, without relation to any context. Yet without the necessary limitation of context, thought would be incapable of any meaning or sense whatsoever, because it would not refer to anything, not even, finally, to itself in that without soaking itself in (*empaparse de*)—to say nothing of exposing itself to (*exponerse a*)—a minimum of reality, thought would be nothing at all. Indeed, it could never be said to happen; it would leave no trace of itself anywhere. In short, Amalfitano's deductions would be impossible if one were telepathic, because they would have no context, no relation to the world. For instance, "1978," the year of publication of Kilapán's book, would not refer to the historical context of the Chilean dictatorship. Such referral is possible only insofar as thought is constitutively exposed to exteriority, soaked in reality. Without such exposure, thought could think only itself, but in thinking only itself, thought neither leaves nor takes any impression of itself.[7]

Bolaño has reservations about telepathy. He invokes it as a possibility no fewer than three times in *Los detectives salvajes* and each time the narrative undermines it.[8] In each instance—and this is also the case in *2666*'s Araucano examples—material forms of correspondence supplement telepathy. No doubt this is necessary, because, like all forms of correspondence (all of which have the structure of *tele*communication), *tele*pathy structurally never arrives at its destination. It may always not arrive at its destination. Indeed, in Bolaño's examples telepathy's apparent purity and immediacy, its ostensible incorruptibility, depend—again, like all telecommunication—on delay and, therefore, on noncorrespondence. Bolaño marks the impossibility of telecommunication through the supplement of *more* telecommunication (the Araucanians use of three writing systems despite their telepathic abilities, for instance) that nevertheless results in *less* correspondence. In short, telepathy—understood according to Reyes's logic of immediate, pure correspondence—necessarily fails because it is always already inscribed within an economy of loss and gain, of an exchange that takes place via temporal delay and spatial difference. It is speculative. And this means telepathy is another name for differ*a*ntial correspondence: it instances a sending-off that neither arrives at the addressee nor returns to the sender.

Bolaño thematizes the relation of noncorrespondence and delay to telecommunication, to writing. The first story in *Llamadas telefónicas*, "Sensini," recounts an unnamed narrator's curious correspondence with the Argentine writer Luis Antonio Sensini. Each letter the narrator sends elicits a response from Sensini that is returned to the narrator always with a delay of one week, or, as the narrator says, "As always, the reply arrived by return mail" (1997, 18/2006, 6). Sensini, like Bolaño and like the anonymous narrator, lives off prize money from literary competitions. His oldest son, Gregorio, had been disappeared in Argentina during the military dictatorship. When Sensini writes saying that Gregorio's cadaver had probably been found in a clandestine cemetery, the narrator confesses his reluctance to respond, doing so with only a brief note in which he expresses his condolences and the suggestion that perhaps "Gregorio's cadaver was not Gregorio's" (24/13). It is easy to understand both the reluctance to write (What can one say, after all?) and the desire that the cadaver not be that of Sensini's son.[9] Then, at the end of August, after a summer during which the narrator worked at a resort hotel and had no correspondence with Sensini, he sends Sensini a card indicating that he may visit him in Madrid when the season is over. Upon returning to his home in Girona in the middle of September, the narrator finds a letter from Sensini dated 7 August, indicating that he was returning to Argentina. Letters arrive without corresponding, each arriving before and after the other. A letter dated 7 August that arrives both before and after a letter written in late August that arrives both before and after the one written on 7 August. The law of the post is delay, noncorrespondence: upon receiving the 7 August letter, the narrator claims,

> I wrote to him immediately, at the only address I had, but received no reply. Gradually I came to accept that Sensini had gone back to Argentina for good and that, unless he wrote to me again, our correspondence had come to an end. I waited a long time for a letter from him, or so it seems to me now, looking back. The letter, of course, never came. I tried to tell myself that life in Buenos Aires must be hectic, an explosion of activity, hardly time to breathe or blink. I wrote to him again at the Madrid address, hoping that the letter would be sent on to Miranda, but a month later it was returned to me stamped "Addressee Unknown." (24–25/13)

A dead letter—dead on arrival, returned to sender—arrives without arriving, addressee becoming sender, sender becoming addressee, but each as absent as the other. *Je suis tout à fait ailleurs.* One is never at home to receive the letter one will have sent.

The separation between one and another results in asymmetry. "B is in love with X. Unhappily, of course. There was a time in his life when B would have done anything for X, as people generally say and think when they are in love. X breaks up with him. She breaks up with him over the phone [*por teléfono*]" (63/54). In principle, the telephone—like the telegraph and the post, like email and text messages and Skype and every other mechanism of communication—reduces temporal distance, making it possible for B and X to communicate from one end of Spain to the other. But the telephone also separates them: "The next day he phones X again. And the day after. X's attitude is increasingly cold, as if B were receding further into the past with each phone call. I'm disappearing, thinks B. She's erasing me" (64/55). The telephone both reduces and increases distance. It makes possible long distance intimacy previously unimaginable even as it disappears us one from the other, stretching out the distance between us. "Time—the time that separates B from X and that B does not like to think about—passes through the telephone line; it is compressed, stretched, revealing a part of its nature" (65/56). Moreover, the time that passes through the telephone imposes an anonymity that kills. Time not only distances us from each other, it disappears us from each other. In "Llamadas Telefónicas," X is murdered by an anonymous caller. In *2666* Bolaño explains: "All names disappear. Children should be taught that in elementary school. But we're afraid to teach them" (2004, 755/2008, 605). Yet the name that disappears also survives the living being who bears it: "The name is made to do without the life of the bearer, and is therefore always somewhat the name of someone dead. . . . When I called you . . . you were dead. *As soon as* I named you, as soon as I recalled your first name" (Derrida 1980, 45/1987a, 39). The interval or gap—in French, *écart*, which, Derrida points out, anagrammatically spells *carte* (card, as in postcard)—instances the "dead time" of life, of correspondence, of identity. This gap or interval is jet lag, what Derrida calls "*décalage horaire*": "jetlag [*Le décalage horaire*] is in me, it is me. It blocks, inhibits, dissociates, arrests—but it also releases, makes me fly" (115/108). Or, more succinctly, "This delay kills me, and it also makes me live, it is pleasure itself" (118/111).

JET LAG

Llamadas telefónicas begins with Arturo Belano's confession that jet lag defines his experience of the world: "I had practically no friends and all I did was write and go for long walks, starting at seven in the evening, just after getting up, with a feeling like jetlag—an odd sensation of fragility, of being there and not there, somehow distant from my surroundings" (1997, 13/2006, 1). Jet lag refers to the disjunction produced by a too-quick displacement across time zones that results in the traveler being both ahead of and behind herself. This spatial dislocation that results in temporal disjunction produces the effect in the traveler of occupying two "presents" at the same time. On the one hand, her body remains subject—until it becomes sufficiently adjusted—to the temporal routines of the place to which it was attuned but in which it is no longer. On the other hand, she must accede to the demands of the time in which she currently is. This double occupancy forces her to oppose herself in order, *over time*, to meet or catch up to herself, hence to coincide with herself.[10] Consequently, only more time makes possible the "*ajuste de cuentas*" (Bolaño 2004, 748/2008, 599) or the adjustment of the two times between which the traveler "lives," allowing her to forget the jet lag of everyday life. Consequently, the solution to the problem is the problem, for time is constitutive displacement, delay, deferral, disjunction.

In *2666* Bolaño thematizes jet lag in "The Part about Amalfitano" in the context of the mysterious appearance of Rafael Diesti's *Testamento geométrico* in a box of books Amalfitano will have sent to himself from Barcelona. Amalfitano remembers having neither bought nor read Diesti's treatise. He does not remember packing it in a box upon his and his daughter Rosa's departure for Santa Teresa. "Had the book disappeared from his memory while he and his daughter were flying east to west? Or had it disappeared from his memory as he was waiting for his boxes of books to arrive, once he was in Santa Teresa? Had Diesti's book vanished as a side effect of jetlag?" (2004, 243/2008, 188).

Amalfitano's ideas about jet lag are "rather peculiar" (243/188). Rather than disrupting the solitary traveler in his or her singular relation to the world, jet lag affects all those who will have been surprised by the traveler's arrival. According to Amalfitano, who "believed (or liked to think he believed) . . . that when a person was in Barcelona, the people living and present in Buenos Aires and Mexico City didn't exist. The time difference only masked their nonexistence. And so if you suddenly traveled to cities that, according to this theory, didn't exist or hadn't yet had *time* to put themselves together, the result was the phenomenon known as jetlag" (243/189).

By arriving precipitously, unexpectedly, without anticipation or prior notice, the traveler cuts short and thus deprives those who do not anticipate her arrival of the time necessary to compose themselves, to stand up and "put themselves together" correctly.

If, as Borges put it in *Historia de la eternidad*, time is delay (*demora*) (1996, 1:361/2000, 132), then jet lag names the law of life. It designates our existential condition. Insofar as we never coincide with ourselves, we are ghosts haunting ourselves and others. We always arrive both too soon and too late. At the same time, however, jet lag also opens the possibility for the relation to the other.

> These ideas or feelings or ramblings had their satisfactions. They turned the pain of *others* into *one's own* memory. They turned pain, which is natural, enduring, and eternally triumphant, into personal memory, which is human, brief, and eternally elusive. They turned a brutal story of injustice and abuse, an incoherent howl with no beginning or end, into a neatly structured story in which suicide was always held out as a possibility. They turned flight into freedom, even if freedom meant no more than the perpetuation of flight. They turned chaos into order, even if it was at the cost of what is commonly known as sanity. (Bolaño 2004, 244/2008, 189)

In other words, jet lag, delay, makes possible the becoming-meaningful, the becoming-sense, of life. It makes possible the empathetic relation to the other such that another's suffering can become my memory, but at the same time it also mitigates one's own suffering, a suffering or passion that lasts a lifetime and that, in every case, defeats us. Jet lag opens the time and space of narrative, which turns an incoherent howl into "a neatly structured story," which turns flight into freedom. What is important, however, is the structure of experience. Constitutive jet lag means that whatever happens to us always happens both too soon and too late. Pain becomes memory. A howl becomes meaningful, coherent. Flight becomes freedom even if one continues to flee. Jet lag inscribes the structural belatedness that makes repetition both possible and necessary. Only through repetition or reiteration, only through narrative, can pain, incoherence, and flight become memory, meaning, and freedom. Only through narrative—however minimal—do we become what we will have been. We are born posthumously.

Identity, then, is predicated upon the possibility of repetition and therefore of alteration, in that all repetition takes time and thus differs from and defers itself. It follows that rather than offering the security or guarantee of a given and indivisible self-identity, identity is speculative, a question of interest and credit. The structural delay of jet lag informs the symbolism or virtuality of names and bodies, of words and things, of experience "itself." In putting us in touch with ourselves only through the relation to an outside, hence in constituting auto-affection through hetero-affection, jet lag determines all relations as asymmetrical. We are cut off from ourselves and others. We are cut off from the time of our life.

We always have either too much time or too little, which means we are always making adjustments to and settling our accounts (*cuentas*). *2666* registers the adjustment—the economization—of time, remarking the need either for more or less time, more to make up for a shortage of time, less to do away with an excess of time. In "The Part about the Critics," the day after Pelletier and Espinoza's attack on the Pakistani taxi driver in the name of Liz Norton's honor—and as a way finally to experience the *ménage à trois* they had imagined ("It was as if they'd finally had the ménage à trois they'd so often dreamed of" [103/74])—"To kill time," the two critics "went out for a walk around the neighborhood" (105/75). In the aftermath of the attack, they have too much time on their hands; any time is too much time. Killing time saves them from themselves: "Time, which heals all wounds, finally erased the sense of guilt that had been instilled in them by the violent episode in London. One day they returned to their respective labors as fresh as daisies" (117/85). But the critics are not the only ones who kill time: in "The Part about Amalfitano," Lola "killed time writing long letters to Amalfitano in which she described her daily life in San Sebastian" (226/175). In "The Part about Fate," when Chuck Campbell describes his relationship to Jimmy Lowell, he notes, "Compared to the others, he's pretty decent, has an open mind. It's just that every so often, to kill the time, we act like assholes [*jugamos a ser canallas*]. But we don't mean anything by it" (367/290). How to tell the difference between *being* a *canalla* (rogue) and *playing* one? That's one thing, but the other is, simply, that one "plays" at being a rogue *to kill time*, to do away with a time that is itself already dead, useless; a time to get through or across, not unlike the old plaza in Santa Teresa, which people cross and cross again "for work or to kill time" (773/619). The time it takes to cross and recross the plaza can be both a waste of time, thus an act of killing time, and productive time, time spent working. Both acts—the labor and the murder—take time, take the time they either need (one needs time to work: labor is time) or want to kill. Which is why we need more time, why we never have enough time. Chucho Flores tells Fate that Santa Teresa

> is a big city, a real city. . . . We have everything. Factories, maquiladoras, one of the lowest unemployment rates in Mexico, a cocaine cartel, a constant

> flow of workers from other cities, Central American immigrants, an urban infrastructure that can't support the level of demographic growth. We have plenty of money and poverty, we have imagination and bureaucracy, we have violence and the desire to work in peace. There's just one thing we haven't got. (362/286)

Fate thinks that what they are lacking must be gasoline, since they are driving in the desert. But he nonetheless asks, "What don't you have?" And Flores responds, "Time. . . . We haven't got any fucking time." Fate wonders, "Time for what? . . . Time for this shithole, equal parts lost cemetery and garbage dump, to turn into a kind of Detroit?" (362/286). In other words, Santa Teresa needs more time to become a ruin, to die. The desire for more time, the desire that Santa Teresa might have more time, suggests, on the one hand, that Santa Teresa is out of time; and, on the other hand, given Fate's response, that more time is nevertheless less time, that time is destructive.

Time destroys. Killing time is the time of survival; but the time it takes to survive, surviving time, destroys what it saves. To desire less time, the desire to kill time, is the desire for more time, the time it takes to kill time. To desire more time, the desire to survive, is the desire for less time, the time it takes to ruin or destroy that which one hopes will be saved. We live in the interval between too much and too little time, between the desire to kill and to save time. Life and death are the names for the endless *ajuste de cuentas* (settling of accounts) that time—delay, deferral, jet lag—demands. "The dead woman's name was Angélica Ochoa and, as he was told by the policemen who were cordoning off the street, it looked more like a settling of accounts than a sex crime. Shortly before the crime was committed, two cops saw a couple arguing heatedly on the sidewalk, next to the club El Vaquero, but they didn't want to intervene, thinking it was a normal lovers' spat" (748/599). Delay marks the scene: the police hear the shots and return too late to the scene, finding only the murdered woman. The presumed murderer, La Venada, Angélica Ochoa's husband, heard she was going to leave him and killed her. She will have left too late. She will have died before she left.

Delay instances the general condition not only of life but also of whatever is or appears to be. Late in *2666*, Ingeborg tells Archimboldi, we are "on the mountain . . . but we're also in a place surrounded by the past. All these stars . . . Can you possibly not understand, clever as you are?" (1040/831). And when Archimboldi asks what there is to understand, Ingeborg tells him to look at the stars:

> All this light is dead. . . . All this light was emitted thousands and millions of years ago. It's the past, do you see? When these stars cast their light, we didn't exist. This light was cast a long time ago. It's the past, we're surrounded by the past, everything that no longer exists or exists only in memory or guesswork is there now, above us, shining on the mountains and the snow and we can't do anything to stop it. (1041/831)

To be surrounded by the past is to be "surrounded by ghosts" (295/231). The light of the world arrives late; the present is illuminated by the past, by phantoms. Indeed, according to Barry Seaman, the light that illuminates the night sky emanates from stars that may or may not be dead: "It might be a live star or it might be a dead star" (2004, 321/2008, 252). But we speak of these stars only metaphorically, Seaman remarks: "Really, when you talk about stars you're speaking figuratively. That's metaphor" (322/253). On Seaman's account, "Metaphors are our way of losing ourselves in semblances or treading water in a sea of seeming. In that sense a metaphor is like a life jacket" (322–323/254). The problem, he claims, is that "one must not forget that there are life jackets that float and others that sink to the bottom like lead" (323/254). The idea that metaphor allows us to remain immobile in the sea of appearances recalls Aristotle's classic example of metaphor, "Here stands my ship" (*Poetics* 1457b10, which he cites from Homer's *Odyssey* 1.185 and 24.308). One of the most famous examples of metaphor, then, is the metaphor of arresting the movement of metaphor. Put simply, it is clear that metaphor instances the capacity to see similarities where there are only differences; thus, it is the operator of identification. As such, for Seaman, metaphor is the lifesaver par excellence, making it possible for us to remain afloat in the sea of appearances. And yet metaphor also drowns us, carrying us to the bottom. It is not necessarily possible to distinguish the life-saving metaphor from the drowning metaphor, just as it is impossible to distinguish the light from living stars and dead stars, all the light being always already dead on arrival. What metaphor, then, is not, by definition, a dead metaphor?

Seaman claims there is but one. Or, rather, there is only one star that is not a metaphor: the sun. "But really there's just one star and that star isn't semblance, it isn't metaphor, it doesn't come from any dream or any nightmare. We have it right outside. It's the sun. The sun, I am sorry to say, is our only star" (323/254). But if the sun were the only star, and thus not a metaphor, the sun would be identical to itself without delay. And its light would not be dead, arriving to us not as an appearance but as what it is, without mitigation or mediation. The sun would be telepathic in Reyes's sense. But we know what happens if we get too close to the sun. Seaman recounts the plot of a science-fiction movie he saw in his childhood:

> A rocket ship drifts off course and heads toward the sun. First, the astronauts start to get headaches. Then they're all dripping sweat and they take off their spacesuits and even so they can't stop sweating and before long they're dehydrated. The sun's gravity keeps pulling them ceaselessly in. The sun begins to melt the hull of the ship. Sitting in his seat, the viewer can't help feeling hot, too hot to bear. Now I've forgotten how it ends. I think they are saved at the last minute and they correct the course of that rocket ship and turn it around toward the earth, and the huge sun is left behind, a frenzied star in the reaches of space. (323/254)

In short, where there is no metaphor, there is no possible survival. The absolute presence of the sun, the absolute reduction of differing and deferring, of spacing, instances the absolute destruction of life. The only way to save oneself from the literality of the sun, the only star, is to turn away from it, to return to earth, leaving an immense space—the space of metaphor, of appearance and thus of ghosts, of phantasms and of dead light—between us and absolute self-presence. To survive the sun, the sun must be reduced to metaphor, to simulacrum, to what appears on the horizon or in the noon sky. The sun must always arrive belatedly, from the past of its own posthumousness. And its posthumousness is inscribed in its name, for the "sun" is merely another name for the star that can be identified only as singular, as unique, through an act of naming that cannot not displace the star into what it is not, the sun. The moment the only star is called the sun, its light has already gone out; it is already dead. The light of the sun, deferred, archives a past that never was present.

In response to Ingeborg, Archimboldi points out that it is not only the light of the stars that is dead on arrival. "An old book is the past, too. . . . A book written and published in 1789 is the past, its author no longer exists, neither does its printer or the ones who read it first or the time when it was written, but the book, the first edition of the book, is still here. Like the pyramids of the Aztecs" (1041/831). The book archives time. It "saves" time, the past, from the death that comes for its author, printer, and first readers. It saves the time of those who are no longer for those who are not yet. Even if, as Seaman remarks to Oscar Fate, "reading is never a waste of time" (325/255), the book—as the archive of (a) time—survives as the trace of a time that is no longer. In other words, the "past" that survives, that surrounds us, is not identical to itself. It survives because it is always already divided from itself. From the moment of its inscription, the book is past, cut off from its author and readers, cut off from itself. Bolaño makes this especially clear in the context of the singular life in *Los detectives salvajes*. In the first entry of the new year in the novel's final part, "Los Desiertos de Sonora (1976)," he has Juan García Madero write, no doubt both too soon and too late, "Today I realized [*me di cuenta*] that what I wrote yesterday I really wrote today: everything from December 31 I wrote on January 1, i.e., today, and what I wrote on December 30 I wrote on the 31st, i.e., yesterday. What I write today I'm really writing tomorrow, which for me will be today and yesterday, and also, in some sense, tomorrow: an invisible day. But enough of that" (1998, 557/2007, 591). García Madero always arrives at his own life both too late and too soon, a day late and a day early. Every today is already yesterday and tomorrow. Today, here and now, the time of life, is constitutively divided between the no longer and the not yet, and no part of "today" is. García Madero is cut off, segregated, secreted from himself, from the chronology or the *cronométrica* of his life. This is the chronological abyss. The time of writing—of life-writing, of the diary or the autobiography, of any giving account of oneself to oneself (*darse cuenta*)—here and now is always anticipated and belated, prophetic and posthumous. We coincide with ourselves only virtually, in the name that is not our own, in the name that archives an identity that is no longer and not yet; in a name that, because it does not belong to us, because it is always *ex*- and *ap*-propriative, can only ever *correspond* to us. And all correspondence—no matter from how close, no matter how intimate—suffers from delay, from jet lag.

Nowhere is this clearer than in *2666*, where names are always pseudonyms. Benno von Archimboldi is only one example. Hans Reiter changes his name, he says, for his own protection. Upon completing his first novel and in the process of looking for a typewriter to rent, he decided that he would neither borrow nor rent from anyone he knew: "In other words no one who knew his name was Hans Reiter" (2004, 980/2008, 783). And when the man from whom he was to rent the machine asked him his name, "Reiter said the first thing that came into his head. . . . 'My name is Benno von Archimboldi'" (981/784). And although he reaffirms this identity when the man expresses his doubts about his "true name" (981/784), the narrator remains unconvinced, remarking that on that afternoon Reiter "perhaps, became Archimboldi" (981/784). The "perhaps" opens onto the infinite speculation of the name and identity. The question of the name returns when Archimboldi meets his editor and publisher, Mr. Bubis, who asks him for his true name and who, when told, insists that it cannot be and says that to call himself

"Benno," "in principle, is suspicious" (1012/808) because of its association with Benito Mussolini. Archimboldi counters, saying that he calls himself Benno after Benito Juárez. Mr. Bubis remarks he thought Archimboldi was going to say it was in honor of San Benito, and when Archimboldi says he does not know that saint, Bubis in fact describes three San Benitos. The name multiplies: from Mussolini to Juárez to Benedictine Benito de Aniano to Benito de Nursia (the so-called "Father of Europe") to the Franciscan Benito el Moro.

Archimboldi is not the only one whose name is "suspicious." "The Part about Fate" begins by naming Quincy Williams: "Quincy Williams was thirty when his mother died" (295/231). "'I'm Quincy, Edna Miller's son,'" he announces (295/231); yet "at work everybody called him Oscar Fate" (299/234). From this point forward, Quincy Williams disappears in and as Oscar Fate. It is not a question of hiding or of anonymity. It is how we reveal ourselves: in names that do not belong to us and yet that figure us in every way.

There are other name changes in *2666*, the cumulative effect of which is to make all names suspicious. Former FBI behavioral scientist and profiler Robert Ressler makes an appearance in the name of Albert Kessler (722/578), which effectively conflates Ressler with William F. Kessler, who along with Paul B. Weston authored *The Detection of Murder* in 1953. Ressler, however, is not the only historical personage or figure to show up under another name in *2666*. The Egyptian Omar Abdul Sharif Sharif becomes the German Klaus Haas. Ciudad Juárez becomes Santa Teresa, which in fact is a New Mexican suburb just west of El Paso, Texas, which lies just across the border from Ciudad Juárez.

The relation of history to literature and thus of literature to the world turns on the name. Indeed, the "as if" structure of the name, its constitutive virtualization or fiction, instances the world. In *2666* this is figured in (at least) three ways.

First, the names of femicide victims, of the women and girls raped, mutilated, and murdered, have been changed. All the murdered women are identified by name, but these names are pseudonyms. On the one hand, it would be a mistake to think that such nominal alteration does *more* violence either to the murdered women and girls or to the victim-survivors. Indeed, it is possible it does *less* violence to them insofar as it does not repeat the violence against them in their name, thus forcing the victim-survivors to relive that violence in the names in which they mourn their lost loved ones. On the other hand, it would be a mistake to think that such nominal alteration does *less* violence either to the murdered women and girls or to the victim-survivors.

Indeed, it is possible it does *more* violence insofar as it forgets them, registering their murders under cover of a fiction and denying the victim-survivors the opportunity to mourn them in their "real" or "true" names. What could be *more* violent than the becoming-fiction, the becoming-literature, of the murders of singular human beings, singular women and children? And yet, what could be *less* violent than mourning the murdered women and children, remembering them, in names that spare the victim-survivors the repeated trauma of remembering, that delinks their names from the violence of their violation? It is impossible to decide between the less and the more violent. It is impossible to know how to mourn the murdered, how to remember them, how to protect their names, their memories, how to spare the victim-survivors without victimizing them once more, without threatening their survival. This is so because naming instances originary, irreducible violence. It opens and closes the world. It makes singular even as it ruins singularity. In the same stroke, in the same cut, the pseudonym denies history by displacing the "real" or "true" names in which the women and children were violated and murdered; and makes history insofar as it exposes the ruse of the name, that the name does not belong, that it is always both *ex*- and *ap*-propriative: no history without such *ex*- and *ap*-propriation. No history without the violence of the name. No history that is not always already nominative and that therefore does not do a *nominal* violence, which is the violence of literature, the violence of the world.

Second, the problem of the name and its irreducible relation to mourning intensifies in the descriptions of the murders of those women and children who died anonymously, their bodies unidentified and unclaimed. Perhaps no moments in *2666* are less distinguishable from the historical record, from the public count and accounting, of these bodies of women and children who will have died in secret, in the anonymity of their being-named *sin nombre*. We remain close to the unnamed child, the anonymous girl, who died in the name of la Malinche.

Third, Sergio González's name has not been changed. Bolaño introduces him in "The Part about the Crimes": "Around this time the Mexico City newspaper *La Razón* sent Sergio González to write a story on the Penitent. Sergio González was thirty-five and recently divorced, and he was looking to make money any way he could. . . . He had been on staff at *La Razón* for four years . . . where he sometimes used a pseudonym so readers wouldn't be able to tell that all the articles were his" (2004, 470–471/2008, 376). Bolaño's Sergio González *is* (based on) Sergio González (Rodríguez), journalist for the daily newspaper *Reforma* in Mexico City and the author of, among other books, *Huesos en el desierto* (2002), *El hombre sin cabeza* (2009), and *The Femicide Machine* (2012), and most recently *Los 43 de Iguala* (2015). He died on 3 April 2017. Of interest is the decision to use González's "real" or "true" name, rather than, for instance, changing it in the way Bolaño does for Santa Teresa/Ciudad Juárez. Even if Santa Teresa cannot *not* be read *as* Ciudad Juárez, even if it is impossible not to identify—however minimally—Santa Teresa *as* Ciudad Juárez, through specific *legible* gestures or marks, namely locating Santa Teresa south of Arizona rather than New Mexico or Texas, *2666* marks their difference or distance from one another. In so doing, it *suspends* the fiction, both *sustaining* and *relieving* it, both referring to Ciudad Juárez and refusing such reference. But this is not the case—or not simply the case—with the name "Sergio González." Sergio González can only ever appear *as* Sergio González, thus taking (his) place in the interval of jet lag, in the anachronistic disjunction that opens the chance for anything to happen, for anything to be—*as* specter, *as* simulacrum, *as* fiction.

Insofar as experience takes place only in and through jet lag, spatial-temporal delay, or noncoincidence, the subject of experience is constituted belatedly. It comes after itself, which means it comes too soon and must be repeated. Sergio González *as* Sergio González means that Sergio González *is* Sergio González only in the citation, the repetition, the doubling that makes all the difference without appearing to make any difference. Such is the specularity—the speculation and virtuality—of the name and of identity. Sergio González is a fiction. We are effects of jet lag, which means we cannot *not* take ourselves on credit, on account, always already owed to a future, here and now, that cannot be amortized or deferred, that can never be paid in full.

We are *serial* subjects, exposed in and through a delay that cannot be put off. Seriality does not refer simply to one thing—one murder, for example—coming after another. In *Natural Born Celebrities: Serial Killers in American Culture*, after surveying the various attempts to denominate (and thus to recognize) the phenomenon of one person murdering several people over time, David Schmid refers to John Brophy's *The Meaning of Murder* (1966) as the key text for thinking about seriality: "'Serial murder' was a much more persuasive term, Brophy explained, because of what he described as the 'essential character' of the crime: 'repetition at intervals of time'" (2005, 71).[11] Delay—the interval of time—constitutes the seriality of murder. Every murder, each time unique, promises seriality. Moreover, this delay or jet lag haunts the first murder; it haunts *every* murder *as* the first murder. It is the anticipation—the imagination—of murder. In *The Killing Fields*,

Diana Washington Valdez quotes Robert Ressler: "Most serial killers do not start killing in their middle-age years. They usually begin in their adolescent years by fantasizing about killing, and they kill their first victim around their early adult years" (2006, 163).[12] The first murder in a series is already *more and less than one* murder, because the possibility of (accounting for) murder depends on the imagination, which means the first murder "happens" both *before* and *after*, both *too soon* and *too late*. It never coincides with itself or with the intentionality that would seem to motivate it, which nevertheless does not alleviate one's responsibility. Indeed, the asymmetry of experience opens the possibility both of murder and of responsibility. It is only because we coincide neither with ourselves nor with others that we can act against another, meaning that we must be responsible for the act that does not coincide with itself. The seriality of murder depends, therefore, not on the empirical calculation of murders accumulating one after another but on the structural delay or belatedness of murder: the jet lag of the imagination that makes murder possible in the first place.

The imagination's peculiar status as both passive and active, as an operation that happens repeatedly, spontaneously, mechanically, and secretly, without any motivation, and yet which, according to Kant, leaves a trace—its monogram—in the world, helps explain Bolaño's remark about the difference between "ordinary murderers" and "serial murderers": serial murderers leave behind a signature; they have no motive, but they do have a signature (2004, 589/2008, 470).[13] Bolaño says not that serial murderers *sign* but only that they have and leave behind a signature. A signature is left behind as a trace or mark, the remainder of an intention or motive that cannot catch up to itself. The signature is the autograph—the graphic, corporeal instance of self as corpse, as always already posthumous, dead.

SIGNING BY HAND

Bolaño's *2666* is full of signatures; the most legible and most horrible in their fatality are those left on the bodies of the murdered women in "The Part about the Crimes." The signature mutilates, cuts off the who and the what even as it realizes itself as corporeal. The signature is the becoming-corpus, the becoming-corpse, of the name. The signature always appears in one's (own) hand. In "The Part about Archimboldi," Hans Reiter remembers not the content of his mother's letters but the letters themselves, her *hand*: "All he remembered was her handwriting, shaky and sprawling, her grammar mistakes, her nakedness. Mothers should never write letters, he thought"

(2004, 925/2008, 740). No matter what we "say"—write—no matter how much we keep secret, the hand gives us away. The letter (*letra*) sends us to the other. The author of a letter is a suicide; all authors are "dead by [their] own hand" (266/208). The letter, the hand, is both the instrument of death and the chance of memory, of survival.

If it is true that a mother ought not to write letters because at the moment she does, she literally gives herself—her life—away, exposes herself to the other, to the hand or letter that kills her, it is no less true that in *2666* too many women become the surface of men's autographs. The becoming-corporeal of the name and intention—their becoming corpus and corpse in the signature or the mark—privileges the hand. We become ourselves in the hand. The hand literally gives us, hands us, (to) ourselves *as* human. Indeed, the signature marks the becoming-worldly of intentionality by realizing the relation between language and the hand, which Alfonso Reyes considered the two most essentially human attributes. In *La experiencia literaria*, Reyes quotes the French historian Henri Berr, who explains, "'The hand, language: Here I have humanity,'" and then Reyes adds, "And I hold now, that the hand also has been language and, to a certain extent, it continues to be" (1962, 26). The corporeality of the hand is not what interests Reyes. It plays a part in our humanity only insofar as its essence is language. The hand communicates. For Reyes, the hand is an extension of consciousness, of intentionality. If the hand does not sign and thus extend intentionality into the world, Reyes has no use for it, because a hand that is not essentially language—a hand that does not speak, that does not fulfill its spiritual purpose—is not a hand.

What, then, of the hands (and feet) of Marisol Camarena, whose "body had been dropped into a fifty-gallon drum of corrosive acid. Only her hands and feet remained" (Bolaño 2004, 645/2008, 516)? In the aftermath of her murder and dissolution, they will not have done her any good, useless even to identify her: "Identification was possible thanks to her silicone implants" (645/516). In this case, the hands are more "cosmetic" than breast implants. They are also less "hers" than the prostheses. The hands are useless for identification because the fingerprints (*huellas digitales*) had never been registered. What kind of hand is it that fails to name the one to whom it belongs, that fails to identify the one who manipulates it, makes it do what hands do, that fails the one who intends for it to speak?

Philosophy pays attention to the hand from the very beginning. Aristotle argued that a hand that cannot function *as* a hand (and in Reyes this means *as* language) *is not* a hand. It is a hand in name only, nominally, homonymically. Thus, it is a hand *un*worthy of the name. Aristotle's example, however, is instructive, for it opens onto the separation that has been legible all along. The hand that does not sign is cut off, removed, ruined. In the *Politics*, writing of the state, Aristotle claims:

> The state is by nature clearly prior to the family and to the individual, since the whole is of necessity prior to the part; for example, if the whole body be destroyed, there will be no foot or hand, except homonymously, as we might speak of a stone hand; for when destroyed the hand will be no better than that. But things are defined by their function and power; and we ought not to say that they are the same when they no longer have their proper quality, but only that they are homonymous. (1253a19–25)

Such would be the hand of one of the statues destroyed by the Penitent in *2666*: "The church smelled of incense and urine. The chunks of plaster scattered across the floor reminded him of a movie, but he couldn't remember which one. With the tip of his foot he nudged one of the fragments. It looked like a piece of a hand" (2004, 458/2008, 365). This is Aristotle's hand. Cut off from Aristotle by some two millennia, Hegel repeats this example in his *Elements of the Philosophy of Right.* In the long Remark to §270 Hegel contrasts the relation of particular to universal in the state and in religion. Because the ground of religion, namely God, does not exist but is rather a mere essence, religion cannot organize a world. It remains merely an immediate ground and, according to Hegel, "within its all-embracing centre, everything is merely accidental and transient" (1991, §270R:293). Were the state to have the same relation to the absolute that religion has—were it to have "the form of feeling, representational thought, and faith"—then the state would be exposed "to instability, insecurity, and disruption" (§270R:293). That the state is not so exposed depends on its organic unity in which each part is incorporated into the whole in such a way that the whole relieves the part of its essential isolation. The state, operating like the nervous system or perhaps the brain, regulates the system such that the particular appendage functions in the name of the whole. Hegel writes:

> The state is actual, and its actuality consists in the fact that the interest of the whole realizes itself through the particular ends. Actuality is always the unity of universality and particularity, the resolution of universality into particularity; the latter then appears to be self-sufficient, although it is sustained and supported by the whole. If this unity is not present, nothing can be *actual*, even if it may be assumed to have *existence*. A bad state is

one which merely exists; a sick body also exists, but it has no true reality. A hand which has been cut off still looks like a hand and exists, but it has no actuality. (1991, §270A:302)

How to tell one hand from another, how to tell a hand that merely *exists* from a hand that fully *is*? In *Metaphysics*, Aristotle is clear: "For it is not a hand in *any* state that is a part of man, but the hand which can fulfill its work, which therefore must be alive; if it is not alive it is not a part" (1036b31–32). What does it mean for a hand to be alive, to be living? A hand that cannot sign merely exists, without intention, without being, without essence. At the moment Aristotle invokes the stone hand he will have just made the distinction between the articulate sound of animals and the speech of humans.

The cutoff or homonymic hand—the equivocal hand, the hand in name only—is an accident. It looks like a hand, but it is not one. It is not animated. The possibility of homonymy is a necessary condition of language. Aristotle knew this, but so too did Heidegger, who claimed in 1931 that a language without homonymy would be dead.[14] Homonymy is an effect of referral, and referral is an effect of delay, of *spacing*, or, in the context of *2666* and of Bolaño's work more generally, of jet lag. Yet homonymy is also the figure of accidentality. Homonymy, then, is both necessary and accidental. It must always be possible for one hand to be taken for another. Every hand begins in homonymy. Both Aristotle and Hegel use the homonymic hand to figure the disfigurement of the state and of the possibility of ethical life. At bottom, the state is a stone hand, an accident. And this means that in order to sign—for this is what the sovereign does, after all—the hand must be cut off. Only a hand that is not actual, not my own, not proper, only a hand that is not attached to the sovereign and does not simply or unequivocally *live*, can sign for the sovereign, in the sovereign's name. I can *sign* only in a ruined, accidental hand, only in a hand cut off from me, from my intention to sign. Only this hand signs. When one says, "I sign in and with my hand," this is what it means: to be separated, cut off, mutilated, or ruined in the same gesture. In the same stroke (*du même coup*), one both signs "I" and divides oneself from oneself.

Edwin Johns's self-portrait, his autograph, makes this clear. The portrait is signed by hand, in the hand, with the hand. Johns inaugurates a style that would become known as "the *new decadence* or *English animalism*" (Bolaño 2004, 76/2008, 52). Although his work was not bad, he would not have had the success he enjoyed were it not for a single painting: "This painting, viewed properly (although one could never be sure of viewing it properly), was an ellipsis of self-portraits, sometimes a spiral of self-portraits (depending on the angle from which it was seen), seven feet by three and a half feet, in the center of which hung the painter's mummified right hand" (76/53). In the center of an ellipsis or spiral of self-portraits one finds Johns's hand, his "real" hand, mummified, cut off, useless as a hand, but useful aesthetically, as an element in the painting that renders Johns famous. The hand makes sense; it gives meaning or value to Johns's painting, which means, finally, the hand—cut off, mummified, incapable of doing what a hand does—nonetheless *speaks*. The destroyed hand—the hand in name only, the homonymic hand, the hand, therefore, that merely exists and that has no essence—remains *essentially* language. It could not be otherwise, because insofar as language depends on homonymy, the "essence" of language is accidental and, precisely, the ruin of language. And this means the essence of communion, of communication and community, is accidental as well and the end of community and communication.

This, in fact, is Johns's theory of chance (*casualidad*): "Coincidence . . . is total freedom, our natural destiny. Coincidence obeys no laws and if it does we don't know what they are. Coincidence, if you'll permit me the simile, is like the manifestation of God at every moment on our planet. A senseless God making senseless gestures at his senseless creatures. In that hurricane, in that osseous implosion, we find communion. The communion of coincidence and effect and the communion of effect with us" (123/90). We live in a world of non-sense, a world of chance, ruled by a god that makes no sense. What Johns calls *casualidad* must be thought according to a certain accidentality, a certain nonbeing, because here chance is not a figure for probability: it remains entirely incalculable, even if its traces remain in the world as the promise of—that is, both the chance for and the threat to—communion, to communication and community.

THE ACCIDENT OF BEING . . . MEXICAN

One way to think chance (*casualidad*)—as that which follows no rules or whose rules we cannot know—is under the rubric of magic. For instance, Boris Yeltsin, "the last philosopher of Communism," explains to Amalfitano in a dream that

> life is demand and supply, or supply and demand, that's what it all boils down to, but that's no way to live. A third leg is needed to keep the table from collapsing into the garbage pile of history, which in turn is permanently collapsing into the garbage pit of the void. So take note. This is the

> equation: supply + demand + magic. And what is magic? Magic is epic and it's also sex and Dionysian mists and play. (2004, 290–291/2008, 228)

At stake is the relation between the calculable and the incalculable, between predictable economic law (the law of supply and demand) and unpredictable, inexplicable, magic. In an interview first published posthumously in the magazine *Turia* in June 2005 and later collected in *Bolaño por sí mismo* (2011), Eliseo Álvarez asks Bolaño, "Do you owe your sentimental education to Mexico?" Bolaño responds:

> To Mexico I owe, more than anything, my intellectual formation. The sentimental education I owe to Spain, I believe. When I arrived in Spain I was twenty-three or twenty-four years old. I arrived thinking that I was a proper man, and that about sex, which for my sentimental education is almost synonymous with sexual education, I already knew everything, but in reality I didn't know anything and I realized this quickly with the first girl I was with. I knew a lot of positions, but positions are positions and sex is sex. (2011a, 38–39)

And when Álvarez clarifies, "One thing is the methodology . . . ," Bolaño remarks, "Exacto" (2011a, 39). Sex is magical in this sense. The method is calculable, determinable; but sex—what Bolaño means by sex—is alchemical. Sex names that for which the method cannot account. In this sense sex exceeds its methodological determination, the rules or procedures, the laws governing its practice. It is not, however, that sex is not without conditions (whatever they might be, however they might be defined); it is rather that those conditions—however necessary—cannot predict, do not causally determine, the event of sex, its appearing. Sex is magical for precisely this reason, but it is also accidental, without substance or essence, without being. It happens by chance, *por azar*, like literature. In an interview with Lina Meruane, Bolaño claims: "One comes to literature as to sex by chance: moved by a certain curiosity about something we do not know" (2011a, 99).[15]

In the interview with Álvarez, Bolaño points out that he arrived in Mexico at the age of fifteen: "I became Mexicanized quickly; I felt totally Mexican"; and "I never felt like a stranger in Mexico" (2011a, 36). Despite feeling completely Mexican, he affirms that what he calls his sentimental education took place not in Mexico but in Spain. Even if he was formed only intellectually in Mexico, it is nonetheless possible that he will have learned what it means to be an accident, to be without cause or substance, to be without being, hence, to be magical, in Mexico, perhaps from reading Emilio Uranga's

Análisis del ser del mexicano (1952). Uranga argues that the Mexican—or the modality of the Mexican's "being"—is accidental in the ontological sense of the word.[16] According to Uranga, if Mexicans—and not only Mexicans, but human beings more generally—are historical, that is, finite beings who make sense of their being as it manifests itself historically, temporally, always under certain conditions, then the being of the Mexican (and of all human being) is accidental rather than substantial. Or, as Uranga puts it: "All the 'existentials' or 'characteristics' of man's being are arranged under the inevitable form of being accidents" (2013, 43). Unlike substance, however, which "is plentitude or fullness of being" and which "does not imply any change," being "reposes in itself, indifferent to all mobility, alteration or decomposition" (40). Accidents are unstable; they lack the being that would allow them to rest in themselves. As accidental, the Mexican is therefore constitutively precarious, in that the accident is neither being nor nothing, but rather an "oscillation between being and nothing" (51). In other words, the accident is fragile; it is that which can always not have happened. It is unpredictable, unforeseeable. Uranga explains: "The accident's being is not 'properly' being, or simply 'being,' but rather it finds formulation in the complex expression being-in" (50–51). Being-in announces the accident's dependency or conditionality; that is, no being-in or accident lies outside the material conditions of its appearance: "The accident is pending [it is undecided], it depends on or has itself in another thing. It is not enough by itself. Its nature alludes to a reality that 'supports' or 'sustains' it and without whose support it would sink into nothingness" (51). In *Metaphysics* book V, Aristotle explains that because the accident is not "in itself" but rather always depends upon some substance, it lacks being and cannot, therefore, be the object of science or knowledge. There is no philosophy of what is not necessary, and for Aristotle the accident is not necessary.

Despite Aristotle's determination that there can be no science or philosophy of the accident, Uranga conceives *lo mexicano* as being grounded on it: "At its most extreme and radical point, the Mexican is conceived as 'accidental and in danger,' which means that he is open without defense against the human condition in his most profound strata" (2013, 60). To conceive oneself at one's "most extreme and radical point" as accidental means to be *essentially* or at bottom accidental. Consequently, rather than attempting to relieve oneself of such accidentality, which would be to relieve oneself of the possibility of oneself, the Mexican *as* Mexican ought to achieve itself in and as accidental; in short, the Mexican ought to realize itself as such *as* accidental: "*To realize oneself as accident means to maintain oneself as accident, in the horizon of possibility of the accident itself.* The inauthentic thing would be in this case to attempt to depart from the condition of accidentality and to substantialize oneself" (42).

Uranga's understanding that the accident is the essence of the Mexican *as* Mexican both does and does not exclude its universalization. That is, he dismisses the objection that "upon affirming that the being of the Mexican is accidental, we have defined with it the human condition in general in which the Mexican participates" and that "in 'truth' man is accidental and not the Mexican" (43).[17] The dismissal is direct and devastating. Uranga responds that, in the first place, "*we are not very sure of the existence of man in general and, in the second place, that what passes for man in general, generalized European humanity, does not seem to us to define itself precisely through its accidentality, but rather precisely through a boastful substantiality*" (43). Uranga's challenge to the idea of the "human in general" suggests that the human being is essentially determined in and as its conditions. The essential historicity of the human being means that the human is constitutively accidental. It follows that if "man in general" derives from a "generalized European humanity," and that this determination amounts to "a boastful substantiality," then such substantiality is, precisely, inauthentic and effectively inhuman. Indeed, Uranga writes: "If man is constitutionally accidental," then it makes sense that the Mexican is considered "authentically human when he lives in the closest proximity with the accident," which is the same as saying that "he is authentic because he lives as originarily ontological, or in the neighborhood of his being itself" (45). Ultimately, "*every interpretation of man as substantial creature seems to us inhuman*" (45).

In short, to live authentically means, on Uranga's account, to live absolutely close to—but nonetheless infinitely removed from—being *as such*, for the accident has no being that is properly its own. On the contrary, an accident is only ever *being-in*: "It lives to adhere or to attach itself. Its alteration is impregnation or priming" (52). Yet, because it does not possess its own being, because it is nothing *in itself*, the accident is always at risk of not happening: "Its adhesion to being . . . is not protected by an inalienable right, but rather whatever the form of its inheritance, it is always revocable" (51). He claims, "The accident is what suddenly appears, what is not expected" (51). Thus, Uranga defines the accident not as a *con*sisting, but as a *de*sisting or an *ex*isting (51), in sum, as that which is not, as that which oscillates between coming-to-be and passing-away. The accident, Uranga avers, "is exhausted in this relation to being" in that "it is stretched toward being" (52). The accident *tends* or *extends*—stretches—toward being; but it also *suspends*—insofar as it *distends*—being. Uranga writes: "Upon confronting the notion of substance with that of accident a 'decompression,' slackening of being is confirmed in this. Being in the accident has become distended. . . . The tense net of being has 'spaced' itself and that distention is the accident" (51). The being-*in* of the accident is not the being *of* the accident, but the accident *of* being. Accidentality loosens, slackens, diminishes being; it spaces it, distends it. There is no being without such distention, without such spacing, which, as distended or spaced, necessarily divides itself and destroys itself in its first appearing, as the impossible condition of possibility of appearing, of being *as such*. In other words, being is an accident. Being happens, arrives—being becomes being—only through the accident's pending, tending, extending, distending, suspending. Being happens—if it ever does—only through the promise of attachment, a constitutively contingent attachment. The accident promises being, *as if* (*como si*) there were being *as such*.

In positing the being-in of accidentality as the authentic modality of the human being, Uranga jeopardizes the "as such" of substance, its privilege and priority, making it an effect of accidentality, of the *as if* that neither is nor is not, that may always not be, may not have been. Uranga understood the stakes of the game: in sending off the "as such" of substance, inscribing delay (pending, tending, distending, suspending) at the heart of being, he revealed the dignity of man to be a fiction. "In the origins of our history we justly had to suffer a devaluation for not assimilating ourselves to European 'man.' With the same spiritual bias, today we return that qualification and we deny as 'human' all that construction of the European that remains in the substantiality of human 'dignity'" (45).

CHAPTER 5

SUSPENDING SUR/RENDER

Accounting for the Other

¿Quién es el extranjero?, preguntamos nosotros. . . . ¿Aquel en quien camina la palabra en lengua extraña a estas tierras para nombrar las cosas que el trabajo del hombre pone en el mundo? ¿Aquel que reniega del color oscuro de la piel, se avergüenza de su pasado y usa la palabra "indio" como insulto y descalificación?

CCRI-CG DEL EZLN, 2 OCTOBER 1994

La bandera de México, la ley suprema de la Nación, el Himno Mexicano y el Escudo Nacional estarán ahora bajo el cuidado de las fuerzas de la Resistencia hasta que la legalidad, la legitimidad y la soberanía sean restauradas en todo el territorio nacional. . . . El EZLN apoyará a la población civil en la tarea de restaurar la legalidad, el orden, la legitimidad y la soberanía nacionales, y en la lucha por la formación e instauración de un gobierno nacional de transición a la democracia.

CCRI-CG DEL EZLN, "THIRD DECLARATION FROM THE LACANDON JUNGLE," 2 JANUARY 1995

Jet lag is the law of being and identity; it is the law of inheritance in that it stipulates that one comes to oneself both too soon and too late, in and from a hand in name only, a counterfeit hand, a forged signature. We inherit in the name of what never was and bequeath it to a future that will never be.

In the wake of the Conquest, Mexico imagines itself as having been restored, rendered, and surrendered to itself. Or, as Octavio Paz put it in *Postdata*, "Mexico belonged to Cortés, not by right of conquest but because of his original property rights: he had come to recover his inheritance"

(1999, 307/1985, 311). Moctezuma greeted Cortés, Paz writes, "as the envoy of someone who was claiming his inheritance" (306/310). The Aztecs, according to post-Conquest lore, considered themselves usurpers, illegitimate rulers, bastards: "The feeling of illegitimacy, common to all barbarians and newcomers, was like a wound to the Aztecs' psyche; it was also a defect in their credentials as rulers of the world by the will of Huitzilopochtli" (305–306/309). The threat of such illegitimacy—which extended even to their gods, Huitzilopochtli being merely a tribal deity—led to the revision of their history: "The Aztec ruler Itzcóatl, with the counsel of the celebrated Tlacaélel, architect of Mexican grandeur, ordered that the ancient codices and documents be burned and that new ones be fabricated, the purpose of the latter being to 'prove' that the Aztecs were the descendants of the lords of Anáhuac" (306/310). Consequently, Paz claims, "To Moctezuma the arrival of the Spaniards meant, in a way, the paying of an old debt [*el pago de la vieja cuenta*]" (309/314). The question of inheritance, and of the rewriting necessary to it, haunts Mexico. It is always a question of how Mexico *renders account* of itself and what it *surrenders* in the account.

To inherit Mexico means to negotiate the troubled relation between "modern" (developed, European, or Americanized) Mexico and Amerindian Mexico, what Paz calls "submerged" Mexico or Mexico's "other" (289/287), which to extirpate, he claims, would require *self*-mutilation (291/291). Broadly speaking, Mexico is *rent* between two civilizations. It is divided in itself, always already cut off, self-mutilated, segregated, and separated from itself. Mexico constitutes itself mutilating itself, sending itself from itself as the condition of inheriting itself. This is the logic of the symbol, that which is separated, divided, from itself in order to recognize or return (to) itself *as* itself. All tradition, all inheritance, all identity, passes through the symbol, through the logic of symbolization. But if tradition, inheritance, identity pass through symbolization, then they also ineluctably come from the other. "Our" inheritance, tradition, and identity are always before "us"; they come both from the past (left for us by another) and from the future (what we must affirm and accept; what faces us).

This is the "false problem" that Spanish expatriate philosopher Eduardo Nicol posed in 1958, the year in which Edmundo O'Gorman's *La invención de América* was published and just one year prior to the publication of the second edition of Paz's *El laberinto de la soledad* (1959). How do "we" know that the body we encounter in the world is not merely an object but rather bears within itself the trace of intentional consciousness? How do we know that the other is a subject like us? Because the soul is invisible, Nicol asks, how does one subject know that another subject is present to it? Furthermore, if the soul is understood as autonomous—self-contained and invulnerable, immune to the world outside it, secreted from whatever it is not, from whatever is foreign to it—then communication with other subjects would not be necessary and could only be fortuitous and contingent, accidental: "This means that there would be nothing in being itself that, by its constitution itself, would permit *anticipating* its obligatory relation to a foreign being" (2009, 498). In order to communicate with another, one must anticipate the other's coming. To anticipate its coming, however, the other must be "visible"; that is, something of the other's subjectivity must appear such that another subject, another I, might respond. At stake in every communication, therefore, is an asymmetry that demands that one subject, this I, respond to another subject, another I, in anticipation of the other's appearance *as* subject. One must be open to the other, one must affirm the coming of the other, in advance of the other, in order to respond to the other. There is no communication, no community, thus no culture, without this asymmetry.

According to Nicol one recognizes the other neither through the direct appearance of its intention or soul nor through the immediate intuition of a body. Rather, the other appears in the flesh (*carne*) and, therefore, metaphorically: "Flesh is a metaphor, naturally, but a metaphor that does not induce confusion and whose meaning has been profiled and accredited in its millenarian use. As such, it can be accepted as a univocal concept of the existential order" (504). The flesh is not the body (*cuerpo*), because the body *says* nothing; it has no expression. The flesh is the site of expression. It is the *trait d'union*, the *guión* or hyphen, joining and separating *cuerpo* and *alma* (soul).[1] The conjunction of body and soul is meaning: "What gives to the human body the distinctive character of the flesh is expression. Because the flesh is not pure matter but expressively human matter, and as human it can no longer be conceived univocally as matter or as body. . . . To put it paradoxically, expression would be like the pineal gland, that mysterious point of union between the two different substances that would be body and soul" (504–505). The pineal gland as the mysterious point of union of body and soul: this is the figure of the imagination in Descartes. The flesh instances the relation of body to soul *as* expression, *as* meaningful, therefore *as* symbolic. And this means as narrative or account (*cuenta*). The flesh exposes us to the other; it puts us in touch with the world. It is that which opens us to the other and which allows us to see the other as the same as us. The possibility of symbolization makes communication and community possible. Nicol writes, "Before the other, what I perceive as foreign is its ontic individuality; what I perceive as proper is its ontological community with me. . . . The other could *alienate itself* from me existentially; but this alienation can only happen and make vital sense if the being in which it is produced is part of my own being. Communication is communion. Which means," Nicol asserts, "that communication is symbolic" (505). It is not symbolic simply because it uses expressive symbols; rather, communication is communion—and therefore is symbolic—in a much more fundamental way: "The word σγμβολον means in Greek *agreement,* that is to say, the reunion of two complementary parts, neither of which is sufficient and complete by itself alone, and each one of which acquires its proper fullness of being and of meaning only in conjunction with the other part" (506). A *convenio* is an agreement, a pact, a convention. It instances an exchange; consequently, it takes time. No symbol, no community or communication, is possible without the time it takes. There is no economy, no pact, no convention, without delay, without deferral and difference. And because time names the exposure to another that cannot be determined, the symbol is a promise, both the chance and the threat of community. The symbol only ever promises the meaning, the conjunction, of community. Accordingly, community, and not just community but every being-in-common, is constitutively "out of joint." "Ontologically," Nicol concludes, "*man is the symbol of man*" (506).

Although Nicol understands the symbol as structural in that it instances the possibility of relation such that community and communication become possible, for him, the symbol—in its metaphorical instantiation as flesh—is *meaningful.* And not only meaningful but "univocal." The meaning of the flesh—which is nothing less than the presence of the subject, of the human—never misleads or confuses. It is not subject to equivocation. The symbol makes the subject present both to itself and to another *as* unequivocal expression. It is the *as such* of the human. But as such, it is *as if,* for the economy—the temporal logic, the delay—of the symbol is such that no being can ever be present to itself. Presence is the effect of simulacrum, virtuality, fiction. Presence, then, is an effect of the *as if.* Consequently, the equivocal comes before the univocal. There will never have been an unequivocal expression, an unequivocal meaning of the subject, an unequivocal symbol. It will always have been possible to mistake the flesh of one for that of another, to confuse the living and the dead, to take an object for a subject, to take one hand for another. It will always be possible *not* to understand ourselves, *not* to know who or what we are.

The structure of the symbol determines cultural identity, tradition, and inheritance, as what is sent off and thus is always no longer and to come. Mexico identifies as a *mestizo* nation, which means, simply, that Mexican national philosophical and cultural discourse must comprehend and explain the double inheritance that informs modern, *mestizo* Mexican identity. Mexico is *rent*—it *renders* and *surrenders* itself—between (at least) two cultural legacies, the one Amerindian, the other European. And there are (at least) two accounts of the struggle to inherit Mexico that warrant tracking. The first follows the line from José Vasconcelos to Samuel Ramos to Octavio Paz.[2] The second, which no doubt could be read to begin with Paz as well, moves from Guillermo Bonfil Batalla's *México profundo* to the writings of Subcomandante Marcos and the EZLN.[3] Both lines attempt to reconcile the two legacies. In play is not only the Mexican imagination (and with it language, metaphor, the image) but also the imagination of Mexico, its future and (im)possible democratization.

THE LEAP OF SPIRIT

Inheritance "has been a particular preoccupation of Latin American writers" and, as Didier T. Jaén remarks, "especially so during the first part of the [twentieth] century" (ix). Jaén points to two works in particular "that stand out prominently even today" (ix): José Rodó's *Ariel* (1900) and José Vasconcelos's *La raza cósmica* (*The Cosmic Race*, 1925). Vasconcelos—whose *La raza cósmica* writes the history of human progress as the inexorable development toward the Aesthetic or Spiritual Age with its *mestizaje* and formation of the fifth race—figures inheritance as the displacement and return of what never was. Inheritance names the origin of civilizations. He writes: "The architectural ruins of legendary Mayans, Quechuas, and the Toltecs are testimony of civilized life previous to the oldest foundations of towns in the Orient and Europe. As research advances, more support is found for the hypothesis of Atlantis as the cradle of a civilization that flourished millions of years ago in the vanished continent and in parts of what is today America" (7/47). The interest Vasconcelos takes in Amerindian civilizations—the Mayas, the Quechuas, the Toltecs—lies not in their historical presence and present but in their legendary status as the physical ruins of a vanished civilization and a vanished continent. The remains of civilization in what is now the Americas are the material traces of a past that never will have been. Despite acknowledging that "the origins of this theory" of the genesis and development of races and civilization "remain more or less confused within a tradition as obscure as it is rich in meaning" (8/48), Vasconcelos nonetheless insists that "this profound legendary hypothesis explains the evolution of the races better than the elucubrations of geologists" (7/47).[4] Indeed, on Vasconcelos's account, "The legend still remains of a civilization born in our forests, or spread to them after a powerful growth. Traces of it are still visible in Chichén Itzá and Palenque, and in all the sites where the Atlantean mystery still prevails" (8/48). The determination that the Mayan ruins, for example, signaled the remnants of an extinct civilization unrelated to the Amerindians populating the regions surrounding those sites was not, of course, original to Vasconcelos. The gesture was already inscribed in the texts that "discovered" and described the sites in the mid-nineteenth century.[5] Put simply, we do not inherit the superiority of the Atlantean civilization from contemporary Native Americans; on the contrary, the secrets of the Atlantean world come (back) to us from Egypt. Vasconcelos speculates about "the mystery of the red men who, after dominating the world, had the precepts of their wisdom engraved on the Emerald Table, perhaps a marvelous Colombian emerald, which at the time of the telluric upheavals was taken to Egypt, where Hermes and his adepts learned and transmitted its secrets" (8/48). This movement, which is telluric rather than the effect of human migration, represents the "leap of spirit" that, for Vasconcelos, is necessary "to discover a direction, a rhythm, and a purpose" in history (8/48), one that neither "scientific" nor "empirical" historiography has been able to perceive.

> The race that we have agreed to call Atlantean prospered and declined in America. After its extraordinary flourishment, after having completed its cycle and fulfilled its particular mission, it entered into silence and went into decline until being reduced to the lesser Aztec and Inca empires, totally unworthy of the ancient and superior culture. With the decline of the Atlanteans, the intense civilization was transported to other sites and changed races: It dazzled in Egypt; it expanded in India and Greece, grafted onto new races. The Aryans mixed with the Dravidians to produce the Hindustani, and at the same time, by means of other mixtures, created Hellenic culture. (9/49)

To tell the story of the "leap" of spirit from Atlantis to Egypt, Vasconcelos has to provide "evidence" of Atlantis in America, and he has to speculate on the appearance of the spirit of Atlantis or civilization in Egypt. It is a question of *material* traces: in the Americas the ruins of the "superior" civilizations; and the Emerald Table, the inscription of Atlantis's secrets, which was tellurically displaced to Egypt where Hermes, the god of writing, deciphered it and made Egyptian civilization possible. Civilization appears only in and as such traces. The spirit of civilization cannot be thought or conceived outside its material inscription, even if this materiality is nothing more than its imagination.

La raza cósmica's remarkable opening scene determines the possibility of inheritance; yet Vasconcelos makes clear that *living* Amerindians do not inherit the "intense civilization" that will have left them behind. The spirit of civilization has abandoned—leapt over—them. Civilization is born in the inheritance of the secret of the other. Egyptian civilization inherits the spirit of Atlantean civilization, which will have "dominated the world" prior to "the foundations of the oldest towns in the Orient and Europe." Civilization encrypts—keeps, preserves, archives, but also mummifies, buries—the other. In Vasconcelos's story, the trajectory of civilization toward the Aesthetic or Spiritual Age and the fifth race charts the movement of the secret of civilization (back) to the place of its inscription, back to America, where it nonetheless will not have returned to the Amerindians, who will have been excluded at the origin. Rather, America—Hispanic America—becomes the site of the inheritance of Europe, which will have inherited America or the civilization of Atlantis via Egypt and the *mestizo* origins of Hellenic culture. In sum, there is mixing, no end of mixing, only not for Amerindians.

DEAD REPETITION

Vasconcelos's understanding of a "leap of spirit" to eastern shores, which displaces the Atlantean inheritance from Amerindians to Egyptians and to Europeans, begs the question: How does Mexico inherit Europe in order to become Mexican? This is the point of departure for Samuel Ramos's *El perfil del hombre y la cultura en México* (1934), a Jungian analysis of Mexico's constitutive inferiority complex. Ramos is clear that the possibility of developing an original Mexican culture depends on the exposure to an outside: "To believe that in Mexico an original culture can develop without relating ourselves to the foreign cultural world, it is necessary not to understand what culture is. The most vulgar idea is that culture consists in a pure knowledge. One ignores the notion that culture is a function of spirit destined to humanize reality. But certainly such a function is not spontaneously generated" (1990, 1:145). Culture, which according to Ramos is fundamentally spiritual, demands the mixing of cultures and thus a certain openness to the other.

It is a *certain* openness, because it is not just *any* other—it is not *every* other—to whom or to which we must be open. In order to become Mexicans, in order to become who we are, in order, then, as Ramos puts it, "to think like/as Mexicans [*pensar como mexicanos*]" (thereby assuming "the only just point of view in Mexico"), we must put off any relation to Indian culture, to *lo indio*, and therefore put off any *thought* of *our* indigenousness (1990, 1:176). The Indian (in us) must be sent off.

To become Mexican we must distance ourselves from—put off—Indian passivity: "We do not believe that the passivity of the Indian is exclusively a result of the slavery into which they fell upon being conquered. They let themselves be conquered, perhaps because their spirit was already disposed to passivity. Since before the conquest the indigenous were disinclined to any change, to any renewal. They lived fixed in their traditions; they were habitual and conservative. In the style of their culture remained stamped the will of the immutable" (1:107). Such passivity, which manifests itself in the simple repetition of inherited forms, is visible in indigenous art:

> In their art, for example, one notices in a clear way the propensity to repeat the same forms . . . instead of true creative activity. Still today, popular indigenous art is the invariable reproduction of the same model, which is transmitted from generation to generation. The contemporary Indian is not an artist; he is an artisan who fabricates his work by means of a skill learned by tradition. (1:107–108)

Ramos likens such artisanal repetition to the "academic procedure of artistic production" (1:107), which Kant characterized as *mechanical*, hence as mere *aping* or *imitation*.[6] But for Ramos it is perhaps worse, for in its "scarce imagination, dominated almost always by a ritual formalism," indigenous art gives "the sensation of the inexorable and static" (1:108).

Vasconcelos remarks that the Amerindian imagination is dominated by physical force in the material or warrior stage, while reason rules the second stage of humanity's development, which signals the failure of humanity to achieve the third stage of spiritual evolution, the stage of beauty or aesthetics: "Norms will be given by imagination, the supreme faculty. That is to say, life will be without norms. . . . Instead of rules, constant inspiration" (1997, 69/29).[7] Although the imagination is the highest faculty, and in its relation to the "law of sympathy" it is present at every stage of human and civilizational evolution, clearly for Vasconcelos the decadence of Amerindian civilizations, their fall away from the pinnacle of Atlantean life, bears witness to a decline in the imagination's capacity to provide the "constant inspiration" that heralds the third stage. Ramos, however, links the lack of imagination to death: "Instead of the artistic forms investing the stone with something like movement, they seem to heighten their inorganic weight. The expression of the art of the Mexican mesa is the rigidity of death, as if the hardness of the stone had defeated the fluidity of life" (1990, 1:108).

Strict imitation of tradition, immutable passivity, resistance to any change and renewal: these are signs of death, cultural rigor mortis. For Ramos indigenous culture is the culture of death. The law of indigenous culture is the law of the sepulcher. This is what Ramos calls Indian "Egyptianism," which, following Wilhelm Worringer, he characterizes as apathetic and insensitive: "Perhaps the indigenous spirit does not have that same 'apathy and insensitivity'? If the Mexican Indian seems unassimilable to civilization, it is not because it is inferior to it, but *distinct* from it. Its 'Egyptianism' makes it incompatible with a civilization whose law is the future" (1:108). The Indian cannot escape the past. He lives in the mausoleum of tradition. All Indians will ever do, Ramos argues, is repeat, imitate; Amerindians can only ape a tradition they passively, uncritically accept. Amerindian culture thus lies in state, dead. It has no future, as if the past did not come from the future, as if the past were not *before* us.

As a consequence, Ramos seeks to isolate the indigenous from the Mexican, *lo indio* from *lo mexicano*, while also pointing out that the failure of Mexican culture to develop an *adequate* sense of itself derives from its relation to *lo indio* (without, however, being *lo indio*). So, for example, Ramos writes:

> Although the Indian forms a considerable part of the Mexican population, in the contemporary life of the country it plays a passive role. The active group is the other one, the one of the mestizos and whites who live in the city. Of course, it is supposed that the Indian has influenced the soul of the other Mexican group, because it has mixed its blood with that of the other group. But its social and spiritual influence is reduced today to the mere fact of its presence. It is like a chorus that silently witnesses the drama of Mexican life. But not for being limited does its intervention cease to be important. The Indian is like those substances called "catalytic," which provoke chemical reactions simply by being present. Nothing Mexican can subtract itself from this influence, because the indigenous mass is a dense atmosphere that surrounds everything within the country. We consider, therefore, that the Indian is the *hinterland* of the Mexican. But for now it will not be the object of this study. (1:122)

Ramos makes a double gesture. On the one hand, the Indian is part of the Mexican insofar as it has mixed with the Mexican. It is represented within *lo mexicano* insofar as it is the so-called passive but catalytic element of *lo mestizo*, the active part of Mexican culture. The Indian, *qua* presence, is precisely that part or element of *lo mexicano* that is always *there*, substantial, underlying it as its potential. It is in relation to the Indian *as* passivity that the Mexican becomes—converts catalytically into—what it is. In this regard, then, the Indian is essential to *lo mexicano*. On the other hand, the Indian is sent off, excluded from Mexican culture or *lo mexicano*. Insofar as its blood is mixed into the *mestizo*, the Indian disappears; its bare presence as pure passivity marks it out as the hinterland, which lies beyond the pale, beyond the limits or borders of *lo mexicano*. Because the Indian is passive potential, it is not in itself the being or actuality of *lo mexicano*. Accordingly, the Indian is accidental to *lo mexicano*. In this double movement Ramos writes *lo indio* both into and out of of *lo mexicano*.

The double and duplicitous strategy of inclusion and exclusion of *lo indio* (as well as the double bind of its necessity and accidentality) informs *El perfil del hombre y la cultura en México* throughout. It is legible in Ramos's principal concern, which argues that the disequilibrium of desire and capacity, of will to power (*voluntad de poderío*) and the limits of one's reality, results from the double bind of the Mexican in relation to its indigenous substrate. Ramos writes that the solution to the problem of Mexico's inferiority complex, which does not signal a real or actual inferiority in relation to others but rather indicates the effect of a desire that outstrips the ability to fulfill it, hinges on adjusting want to ability: "If we adjust our desire to our ability, then the feeling of inferiority has no reason to exist" (1:159). Importantly, Ramos holds that this disjuncture (*desajuste*) results from the separation of culture from life. After insisting that "we, Americans, are Europeans by right," he holds that we have nonetheless "abused this right for an entire century, imitating Europe arbitrarily" (1:143). Further, he argues, "The original sin of Mexican Europeanism is the lack of a norm for selecting the seed of the overseas culture that would germinate in our souls and provide fruits applicable to our peculiar needs" (1:143). This is the key to Ramos's project of thinking *lo mexicano*. The future of Mexico depends on this norm and the possibility of selecting—via imitation or reproduction—from European culture that which is appropriate to Mexico.

What is the principle for selecting from Europe only that which supports Mexican cultural life, only that which will grow in Mexican soil? "That norm cannot be other than reality itself; but this was ignored, because all the interest and attention was turned toward Europe. The error of European mimeticism perhaps comes from an erroneous concept of culture that, for being too idealized, separates it [culture] from life as if heat and vital force were not indispensable for sustaining the spirit" (1:143). Mimicking Europe or European forms is deadly. It results in the mechanical reproduction of a sterile—because not lived—Europeanness as Mexican. This is what it means to say that culture is divorced, separated or severed, from reality. This is also what is at stake in Ramos's suggestion that a disjunction between desire (the desire to be European, developed, etc.) and capacity (the capacity to be European) plagues Mexico and impinges upon the development of a properly Mexican culture.

Perhaps not surprisingly, but nonetheless problematically, Ramos argues that "in order to form this 'Mexican' culture, the only path that remains to us is to continue learning European culture" (1:146). In other words, the only way to be *less* European is to be *more* European. This is so because "our race is a ramification of a European race. Our history has developed within a European frame." (Nevertheless, he confesses, "we have not succeeded in forming our own culture, because we have separated culture from life" [1:146]). So long as Mexico does not recognize the limitations of its reality, its culture will remain artificial, a simulacrum of European culture, a fiction that does not know itself as such and that suffers the consequences of the disequilibrium between its desire and its capacity: namely, the sense of inferiority that Ramos identifies. The solution, however, does not lie in turning away from Europe. On the contrary, "the good intention of examining Mexican consciousness can take a turn for the worse if we isolate it from the exterior world, closing the doors to every cultural influence that comes from outside, because then we remain in the dark" (1:145–146). In order to become who we are, in order to realize ourselves, we must turn toward Europe: "We will never be able to decipher the mysteries of our being if we do not penetrate into it enlightened by a leading idea that we can only take from Europe" (1:146). In short, Europe both inhibits and makes possible the development of a properly Mexican culture. At the same time, Europe must and must not be imitated.

Mexicans are secret to themselves; their being remains a mystery to them that can be deciphered, read, that becomes legible, only insofar as they are led by a European light, by a European idea. If a certain blind—and thus arbitrary, unguided—adherence to and imitation of Europe has resulted in the sense of inferiority, only a European enlightenment will make possible Mexican self-discovery. Mexico will render account of itself (*rendir cuenta de sí*) only by surrendering (*rendirse*) to Europe. This is the case because Mexico is a branch—a ramification—of Europe; Mexican history and culture develop within the horizon of Europe. But Ramos describes a vicious circle, for it is only "when we have obtained some clarity about the manner of being of our soul" will Mexicans "have available a norm for orienting ourselves in the complexity of European culture" (1:146). In order to examine its consciousness, in order to read the mysteries of its soul, Mexico needs a guiding idea from Europe; yet only when Mexico realizes (*se da cuenta*) who or what it is will it be able to orient itself in relation to Europe. How, then, to obtain the guiding or leading idea, the European idea that will save Mexico and guide it to itself, before it is capable of orienting itself in relation to the complexities of European culture? What is the norm or principle for determining the guiding idea prior to any possible self-orientation? What reality leads Mexico (back) to the culture that leads it to itself? What is the rule that allows for such a decision? Ramos writes:

> The best thing, in order not to be mistaken, is to consider that there exists no model of the Mexican, and to work without prejudices, attentive only to identifying the movements that are born spontaneously from inside us, in order not to confuse them with the impulses that, even when they are inside us, do not belong to us. The only norm in this case is *an accurate intuition* [*una certera intuición*] that lets us know which is the proper and which the foreign. (1:151, emphasis added)

The self-examination of Mexican culture and consciousness begins by relying on an "accurate intuition" of what is most properly one's own. Further, this intuition must be relied upon to distinguish the authentic from the inauthentic, for Mexico must not simply turn inward, away from the foreign. Indeed, what is inside Mexico may also be foreign to it. For example, as Ramos points out, Mexicans are Europeans by right and a certain relation to Europe is proper to us; hence what lies outside Mexico—what is not Mexican—nevertheless already lies inside Mexico.

Despite his contention that Mexico must discover a specifically Mexican perspective from which to observe Europe, Ramos does not consider the nationalist perspective to be properly Mexican.[8] "The danger of certain contemporary currents in Mexico is the belief that there already exists the National type, which error leads to the falsification again, the opposite sense of Europeanism, of the authentic Mexican nature" (1:150–151). Nationalism counterfeits Mexican identity. Although Ramos himself argues for Mexican education to focus on Mexico, this ostensibly nationalist orientation is intended to open onto Mexico's universality. This is the upshot of his call: we must not simply return to the European humanist tradition but instead construct a new humanism. "If the reader wants to form a clearer idea of what we mean, recall the cases of Russian art, of Spanish art, etcetera, in which precisely when the artist attempts to capture the most individual marks of his race, in that same instant his work acquires a universal transcendence. The norm of 'nationalism' should be this one: to purify our own life [*nuestra vida propia*] without failing to bring it closer to the plane of universal forms" (1:149). The failure of Mexican education to do this, means Mexicans have "falsified our destiny, and today we march disoriented, trying to find the true direction of our existence." Yet "there is a sign on the horizon," Ramos writes, "that gives us confidence in Mexico's future: its men are already conscious of the emptiness they carry in their being" (1:149).

INTUITING MEXICO

Everything comes down to the *intuition* ("*una certera intuición*") of the proper and the foreign, of what is and what is not essential to Mexican culture. The recourse to intuition, however, introduces a philosophical complication in that intuition figures the unmediated presence or the being-present of being and life. In *Más allá de la moral de Kant* (1938), Ramos follows Henri Bergson in order to think the "new emotion" that precedes representation and that lies "at the origin of great works of art, of science and civilization." This "new emotion" is "*creation and intuition*" (1990, 1:207). The decision to follow Bergson, for whom intuition is ineffable, makes clear Ramos's insistence on the present and on presence.[9] Intuition is always there, present, in the human being; it is the extension or development of instinct. Or, as Bergson puts it, "Thus human intuition, which prolongs, develops, and turns into reflection that which remains of instinct in man, is capable of embracing life more and more completely" (2011a, 144).[10] And even when intuition remains "vague," it still signals "that which can be the insertion of spirit in matter, the relation of the body to the soul" (2011b, 9). Intuition thus marks the moment in which the soul realizes itself as embodied, hence as spatially and temporally determined. All perception thus takes its point of departure from this intuition, for one can perceive only insofar as one intuits that one is embodied. The very possibility of presence to self, of being there, depends therefore on intuition, even if it cannot be said or known except through a mediating (but nonrepresentational) image. Although in *El perfil del hombre y la cultura en México* Ramos grounds the possibility of developing or discovering Mexico's own, proper culture and identity on intuition, it is in *Hacia un nuevo humanismo* (originally published in 1940) that he explains his sense of intuition. He asserts: "Definitely, ideal existence, in order to ground itself in the same source in which real existence is grounded, has to attend to intuition" (1990, 2:19), which means any dualist interpretation of existence—such as that which divides life between the spiritual and the material (2:3)—is troubled from the start. Indeed, on Ramos's account, "intuition proves indispensable as medium for returning us to direct contact with real things" (2:23). Moreover, "intuition understood as immediate evidence of certain fundamental truths must be the only criterion for discovering and selecting the *a priori* indispensable for a correct orientation of intelligence in its new journeys. Intuition must be the basis for vitalizing reason and making it reform as many times as is required by the changing circumstances in which it has to act." This is also what Ramos calls "an immediate experience of reality," which, he claims, spells out "the meaning and value that Husserl's phenomenological method has when it advises to intuit essences in a pretheoretical attitude, before emitting any judgment or making any rationalization. This is the value that 'phenomenological reduction' has" (2:23). On Ramos's account, intuition allows one to "be put in direct contact with authentic reality" (2:24).

Ramos's insistence on intuition as "direct contact with authentic reality" and as "immediate evidence" and "immediate experience" secures life in and as the present of presence to self. Such intuition instances life without delay, without jet lag. Furthermore, and importantly, such presence to self, which, according to Ramos, defines the being of the human being, is constitutively meaningful:

> Human life is not a mere existing like that of the things that surround it, but in addition, and this is very important, it is a knowing that it exists. Human existence is distinguished from all the others in that it is conscious of its existing. A stone, an insect, a tree exists, but without knowing it. Consciousness is, so to speak, a revelation of being. Now, consciousness is not an "epiphenomenon," a mere addition that accompanies existence in order to register it; it is not a reflecting plane destined to contemplation. Consciousness imprints [*imprime*] on human existence its peculiar mode of being; it is inseparable from its ontological structure. When I become aware of my existence [*al darme cuenta de mi existencia*], I not only feel it, surrounded by emptiness, but, on the contrary, I find myself situated in the middle of a group of realities that act on me and that at the same time are the object of my action. (2:29)

If I realize (*si me doy cuenta de*) my existence always and already in the world, surrounded by others both different from and like me, that both act on me and react to me, then I *am* always and only in relation to others that are able both to harm and to help me, who I am able to harm and help. It follows that if my existence (my being *qua* meaningful) is always among others, in relation to others, my existence must be temporally determined. I am historical through and through. Consequently, the mode of my existence is such that it must be open to a future that both makes it possible and threatens it. Consciousness names this relation to the future. Ramos writes:

"My consciousness is not only of my actual state, not only of the 'here' and 'now.' I also have memories and expectations. I can remember my anterior states, which have already been, and . . . anticipate myself with the representation of what still is not. In a word, I have intentions, projects, hopes. I call consciousness precisely that capacity to retain images of the past and project my imagination toward the future" (2:29–30).

Ramos undermines the claim for the constitutive temporality of human being, because the gap—difference, delay—separating past from future is illusory, the effect of the temporality or succession of language, but not of human life: "But these acts that I am separating in the exposition, because one cannot talk about everything at the same time, in fact are interwoven in the present life enriching its content and forming an uninterrupted continuity that constitutes time. Consciousness, then, gives to human existence its temporal dimension" (2:30). There is sleight of hand in play here. There is no consciousness without language; yet language corrupts consciousness insofar as it makes impossible the description (the experience)—at the same time—of the uninterrupted continuity of our existence. Human existence distinguishes itself from all other existence through its constitutive meaningfulness, yet there is no meaning without language, which means there can be no distinction between language and consciousness. Consequently, if language is successive, consciousness must be as well. This follows Aristotle's description of time as that which is divided between the past and the future, no part of which *is* (*Physics* IV); therefore, consciousness *qua* self-presence must be interrupted. Put simply, if the past were not divided from the future, there would be no time: hence the need for the present. But were the present in itself indivisible, there would be no succession, no language, and no consciousness of the meaning of our existence. There would be neither past nor future, neither memories nor expectations. The human being as meaningful would not survive.

If intuition instances *direct* contact with reality, thereby giving *immediate* evidence and making possible the *immediate* experience of reality, then it anchors human life in the present. Consciousness may provide the illusion and the sense of our temporality, but we nevertheless remain constantly and securely in touch with a reality that is present. This is Ramos's argument. If this is the case, however, then what would be the need for care? Or why even the possibility? Being-with-others, being-in-the-world, would be merely an effect of consciousness, while what really matters is what is immediately (without mediation) present to me. The present would be the horizon of the human being, who would neither have nor have any use for either the past or the future. Life would be present. It could not even be described as a succession of presents or of nows, since there would be no possible succession, which (minimally) requires that something no longer (past) be sent to or remain for what is not yet (future). In other words, for succession to happen, there must be delay, deferral, spacing. The immediacy of intuition, however, admits no delay. Yet without delay there is no identity, thus no culture, no tradition, no inheritance. There is nothing at all. The absolute life of immediate intuition is absolute death. A proper or authentic Mexican culture grounded in "an accurate intuition [*una certera intuición*]" would be dead. It would have no past, because it would have no future.

Consequently, the notion of "an accurate intuition" troubles Ramos's understanding of the way out of what he considers Mexico's cultural limitation, its perceived inferiority vis-à-vis European and North American cultures. Ramos accuses the modern, urban Mexican of being concerned only with the present, with his immediate interests, rather than inheriting culture from a past that makes it possible to anticipate a (new) future. In short, Ramos sees a certain Amerindian legacy, which will have been magically transmitted, in the urban Mexican.[11] He claims that "Mexican life gives the impression, taken as a whole, of an unreflective activity, one without any design. Every man, in Mexico, is interested only by immediate ends. . . . The future is a preoccupation that he has abolished from his consciousness. . . . Therefore, he has suppressed from life one of its most important dimensions: the future" (1990, 1:123). The implications of this are severe. The dismissal of the future costs Mexicans the possibility of thought: "In a life circumscribed to the present, nothing more than instinct can function. Intelligent reflection can intervene only when we are able to stop in our activity. It is impossible to think and work at the same time. Thought supposes that we are capable of waiting, and whoever waits is admitting the future. It is evident that a life without future cannot have norms" (1:123). It is not that there would be no norm, however; rather, the norm would be the strict and unimaginative adherence to tradition. And yet the unimaginative adherence to tradition is precisely how Ramos describes the Amerindian relation to the past. Amerindians merely repeat, imitate. For them the past is a dead weight, inert. The Amerindian is a copy machine. According to Ramos, the Indian is dead because he is incapable of change; he has no future. It is not a question of borrowing from the past with an interest in the future. It is not a question of credit or of speculation. Nothing is lost and nothing is gained. Amerindian tradition is a dead repetition that adds up to nothing.

If Amerindian cultures suffer from "Egyptianism," Ramos fears that twentieth-century Mexican culture has contracted "Indianism," its "soul empty and converted into an automaton" (1:156). Such "Indianism" signals neither a return to Amerindian cultural practices nor a sort of *indigenismo*. For Ramos it names the thoughtless, unreflective repetition of cultural forms. It therefore sounds the death knell of Mexican culture: "It would be a contradiction to live for nothing else than to destroy life, and not to foment and enrich it" (1:172).

The modern, urban Mexican is Indian because he has no future. This is Ramos's critique of Mexican culture, but it is also the necessary upshot of his determination that authentic culture is grounded in intuition. The modern, urban Mexican has no future because everything is present to him. Thus, no traces are left behind and none are inherited.

> Each authentic generation that passes leaves behind itself a perdurable trace [*una huella perdurable*] that is added to the cultural values [*acervo*, also "heap"] and contributes to forming each country's tradition. Without a certain continuity of generations, there would be no history, which is a process of accumulation over time and not a series of isolated moments, like cinematographic scenes that are precipitated one after the other without logical coherence. Life would be in this case something that ends every day, and every day it would have to begin again; then, the image of the generations would be the useless labor of Sisyphus. (1:171)

So-called authentic generations leave traces for the future. These traces, in order to be inherited, must be destroyed; that is, they must be read, deciphered, interpreted. The movement of inheritance—the leaving behind and picking up—is the synthesis of tradition and culture. It repeats in and as the performance of the same, which is always other to itself, always new. According to Ramos, the importance of Justo Sierra lay precisely in this synthetic operation: "Sierra did what every epoch should do with the material of achieved knowledge: reunite them in a synthesis in order to give them a form and meaning, which is the only way of incorporating them into the culture" (1:182). Sierra is, indeed, an excellent example. In 1910 he founded the Mexican National University (which would become the National Autonomous University of Mexico [UNAM] in 1929), and he argued from its inception for autonomy from the state. In so doing he resuscitated in a secular guise what had been the Royal and Pontifical University of Mexico—established in 1551 by decree of Carlos I of Spain—which had suffered intermittent closures during the nineteenth century and was definitively closed by Benito Juárez in 1867. In other words, the resuscitation or resurrection of the secular university instances one possible inheritance of a tradition of education (and its suppression) in Mexico.[12] And it is clear that inheritance takes time, and time is delay. Without delay, there is no inheritance, no tradition, but also no change. There is only presence, the present, and death; only (animal) instinct and (human) intuition, only the mechanical repetition of automata. Cultural values would be indistinguishable from the heap or pile (*acervo*) of traces without difference, without distinction. Life would not be the continual unfolding—the continual revelation—of meaning from one generation to the next. Life would add up to—it would count for—nothing. It would be mere existence (*existencia*) rather than being (*ser*), to recall Edmundo O'Gorman's later distinction.

Ramos understands this insofar as he claims that thought—reflection, thus delay—is necessary for human life to constitute itself: "The activity of thought is not a luxury, but before that a vital necessity for man. Thought is born from life and returns to it, in exchange, various dimensions that broaden its horizons and make it more profound" (1:174). Importantly, thought—*la actividad de pensar, el pensamiento*—opens the chance of history and the coherence of life. "Thought is the possibility of using the memory of our experiences to the benefit of the present and also, at the same time, the organ for anticipating the future" (1:174). In other words, the past makes sense only insofar as thought synthesizes the traces of experience in order to anticipate the future; thought takes up what is left behind for the future. And what is left behind is *material*, "the material of achieved thoughts" (1:182). But thought is not simply present. It is not present in or to itself, for the simple present is the unexpanded horizon of instinct and intuition. Rather, thought admits the future and in doing so, it makes possible our humanity. "Without thought," Ramos avers, "man would vegetate in the obscurity of instinctive life, and his level would barely surpass the limits of animality" (1:175). It is an Aristotelian figure, this vegetable that cannot think, but it is also the figure of a repetition without difference, without inheritance or tradition. It is not only vegetal but also Indian. Consigned to an unchanging repetition, figured as the dead weight of Mexican culture, the Amerindian names the unthinking element of modern, urban Mexico.

To be sure, Ramos recognizes the promise, which is both the chance and the threat, of thought. Thought is "above all . . . the window through which to look out at the world and put ourselves in communication with men and things." Further, thought "represents the instrument that puts us in spiritual relation with society and with the world, and it permits us to fix our position with this. Thanks to thought, we do not feel lost in our march through existence, but rather we can know which is the path that we should take" (1:174). The chance of thought is the possibility of finding ourselves, of not being lost in the world, of being with others, with men and things, of communicating with others and thus of positing ourselves in meaningful relation to others and the world. The threat is just the opposite: "But, unfortunately, the exercise of intelligence is not an easy and secure labor; on the contrary, it finds itself surrounded by difficulties and constantly exposed to error" (1:174).

If thought is "constantly exposed to error," then it is fundamentally impossible to "know which is the path that we should take." For were knowledge certain or "secure," there would be no threat, and the promise of thought would not be a promise but an actuality: thought would, in fact, be instinct, intuition, in that its horizon would be determined in advance. The promise of thought is its admission of the future: the fact that thought cannot know where it goes, where it leads. The thinking being never knows where it is. It is the promise of thought, therefore, that makes impossible Ramos's determination that "the only just point of view in Mexico is to think *as* Mexicans" (1:176, emphasis added). There is no doubt that Ramos believes thinking *as* Mexicans means to *be* Mexican. But the "as" (*como*) displaces being. It inscribes necessary or constitutive translation, which is also the unrelievable opening to fiction, to falsification, to the counterfeit. In *La letra volada*, Pablo Oyarzún explains: "The 'as' is the thesis of a commensurability, placed—but with nothing more to prop it up than our obstinate and fragile zeal—there where only slippage rules" (2009, 258). The "*como*"—the "as"—permits what Oyarzún calls a "limited confidence" that differences are comparable and therefore similar; hence to be *like* ourselves, to think *as* ourselves, is to *be* ourselves. The point, however, is that this "limited confidence" inscribes self-deception at the heart (of the possibility) of identity in the first place. One can only ever think "as," "like" (*como*) a Mexican, because one will never *be* a Mexican *as such*, for thinking ineluctably admits an uncertain future. Consequently, what Ramos calls "living thought" is already dead, because it depends on a "proper perspective," which the future violates, ruins: "Vital thought is only that of those individuals capable of seeing the world that surrounds them from a proper perspective [*una perspectiva propia*]" (1990, 1:176).[13]

Yet this perspective, which would be that of "*una certera intuición*"—an accurate, apodictic intuition—secured to and by presence, ostensibly would allow Mexico to discern the correct way forward, which means it would make it possible to decide what to inherit, what to borrow from the past for the future to come; in fact this certain intuition would make it impossible to remember the past such that the future might be anticipated. Strangely, given that for Ramos intuition is the necessary condition of possibility for an authentically Mexican culture, this perspective is that of the Amerindian. Intuitions are, at bottom, Indian: they are immediate evidence, direct contact with reality. They are present. They are *what is*, the *as such* of absolute life/absolute death. The present—and thus the presence of the present in us, the Indian in us, that which is most foreign to us in us—provides the ground for the proper path, the path that leads us to who and where we are. In stepping away from the Indian, in burying or in leaving the Indian behind, we come (back), we (re)turn to the Indian (in) ourselves. The Indian haunts Mexico from a past always to come.

THE LIVING DEAD, OR THE RETURN OF THE REPRESSED

There is a lot of Ramos in Paz. Like Ramos, Paz is concerned both with the Amerindian legacy and the Mexican tendency to follow, uncritically, European or North American cultural models. In *El laberinto de la soledad*, Paz points to Ramos from the very beginning when he writes: "We can all reach the point of knowing ourselves to be Mexicans. It is enough, for example, simply to cross the border: almost at once we begin to ask ourselves, at least vaguely, the same questions that Samuel Ramos asked in his *Profile of Man and Culture in Mexico*" (1999, 14/1985, 12). Further, it is possible to read Paz's description of the *pachuco* in Ramos's earlier description of the modern, urban Mexican, whom Ramos claims "negates without any reason, because he is negation personified" (1990, 1:123). On Paz's account, "Everything in him is negative impulse, a knot of contradiction, an enigma" (1999, 16/1985, 14). Of Mexican descent but living in the United States, *pachucos* are, Paz writes, "incapable of assimilating" to the North American society that they reject and that rejects them in turn: "The *pachuco* does not want to become a Mexican again; at the same time—at least in appearance—he does not want to blend into the life of North America" (16/14). In essence "the *pachuco* has lost his whole inheritance: language, customs, beliefs. He is left with only a body and a soul with which to confront the elements, defenseless against the stares of everyone. His disguise protects him, but at the same time it distinguishes and isolates him: it hides and exhibits him" (17/15).

The parallel between Ramos's urban Mexican and Paz's displaced *pachuco* is not what matters, however. Rather, Paz's understanding of an ostensibly sterile repetition and death locates him in the same filial line as Ramos. Paz notes: "Many of the juvenile gangs that have formed in the United States in recent years are reminiscent of the post-war *pachucos*. It could not have been otherwise: North American society is closed to the outside world, and at the same time it is inwardly petrified. Life cannot penetrate it" (16–17n2/14n2). In other words, the United States' effort to seal itself off from its "other," thus from cultural contamination, leads to the dead, uncritical, unimaginative, and unassimilative repetition of that other (the rise of gangs that remind Paz of the *pachucos*). The culture, cut off from the other, petrifies, becomes stone; it becomes Indian, which in Ramos amounts to the virtual dead weight of Mexican culture. Paz's remarks are directed at the United States, which he also believes, despite its problems, retains the capacity for criticism and self-criticism. For example, although the United States knows how "neither to listen nor to reply" (238–239/219) to its others, Paz points out that Mexico could avoid the mistake of cultural imitation if it realized that in the United States "unfolds a capacity for criticism and self-criticism that it would be vain to look for in Latin America" (239/219).

According to Paz, the failure to develop the capacity for *crítica* and *autocrítica* stems from the Spanish counter-Reformation, which closed Spain—and its empire—to intellectual and cultural developments in the rest of Europe. Consequently, neither Spain nor its colonies experienced the Enlightenment.[14] Without this influence or experience, at least according to the Paz of the mid-1950s and *El arco y la lira*, Mexico would not yet have arrived on the shores of modernity and what Paz called the liberal state ("*el Estado liberal*"), which develops "in the exercise of the critical spirit" (1967, 224). Mexico will have inherited this belatedness and all that will have been postponed on its account, not the least of which would be the failure of the imagination and, with it, of self-criticism and democratization. In *Postdata*, written in the wake of the Movimiento Estudiantil Popular (MEP), which culminated in the massacre at Tlatelolco on 2 October 1968 (and after which Paz resigned as Mexico's ambassador to India), he noted, simply, "One of the reasons for our incapacity for democratic government is our correlative incapacity for critical thinking. . . . Something similar must be said to Latin Americans: criticism of others begins with criticism of oneself" (1999, 239–240/1985, 219–220). Several years later, in *El ogro filantrópico*, Paz remarked, "The political observer who today raises his eyes towards the 'ideological heaven' of Mexico will find a desert . . . : eclipse of ideas, flight of political imagination. But it has not been critique but rather the absence of critique and, above all, of self-critique, that has transformed our political life into a wasteland" (1979, 157–158). And still later, in *Pequeña crónica de grandes días*, he complained: "How can [Mexican intellectuals] fulfill the critical function that corresponds to them if they have not been capable of critiquing themselves?" (1990, 11). Then again, pages later, "The intellectual class is the conscience of society, but in order for critique to be consistent and have authority it must begin with self-critique" (77).

Paz's insistence on *la crítica* concerns the possibility of freedom. Writing in *Postdata* of the stakes of *El laberinto de la soledad*, Paz declares, "In those days I was not interested in a definition of Mexican-ness but rather, *as now*, in criticism: that activity which consists not only in knowing ourselves but, just as much or more, in freeing ourselves. Criticism unfolds the possibility of freedom and is thus an invitation to action" (1999, 236/1985, 216). The relation of critique, freedom, and action is one of mutual implication. Simply put, there is no critique without freedom and no freedom without critique; and, since critique unfolds the possibility of liberty in that it is an invitation to action, it follows that there is no possibility or chance of action that does not imply both critique and freedom. Action realizes—literally actualizes in the world—critique and freedom.

Paz argues that critique, freedom, and action (which are separable only analytically) make possible not only democracy as a form of government but also democratization. In other words, although it ostensibly bears within itself the right—and thus, in principle, the freedom, of critique, the freedom to act—the institution of democracy does not always support this right and this freedom. Indeed, Paz points to Mexico's northern neighbor as an example of a "democracy" that nevertheless fails to listen to others, whether external or internal. But because within the United States "unfolds a capacity for criticism and self-criticism," for the first time in its history "there is a powerful current of opinion that challenges the very values and beliefs on which Anglo-American civilization has been built." Such criticism, Paz writes, is "a promise of other changes" (1999, 239/1985, 220). Hence, it is a promise of action. Clearly, then, on Paz's account, despite the United States' formal or institutional status as a democratic government, it is still—in the late 1960s, nearly two hundred years into its democratic experiment—*becoming* democratic. That is, the United States' "capacity for critique and self-critique" only promises democracy. It is this promise, Paz argues, that Mexico cannot make.

The capacity for critique—which instances both freedom and action—makes possible democracy, which is not simply a form of government but the promise of change, for better and for worse. Paz remarks that, as of 1969, democracy "has lost almost all of its magnetism in the West" (246/228), and with good reason: its problems, he acknowledges, are many and severe.[15] Nevertheless, he writes, "there can be no political life without freedom of criticism and a plurality of opinions and groups" (246/228). This holds even for countries that have no tradition of democratic government: "This is true even for nations that have inherited a high civilization and that, like ancient China, never knew democracy. The young fanatics who recite the catechism of Mao . . . commit not only an aesthetic and intellectual error but also a moral one." Critical thinking, Paz argues, "cannot be sacrificed on the altars of accelerated economic development, the revolutionary idea, the leader's prestige and infallibility, or any analogous mirage" (246/228). The slavish recitation of Mao instances the kind of "blind imitation" (*imitación ciega*) that Paz says threatens Mexico and all societies where critique, or the free act of thought, is—or would be—restricted. Such mummification announces political death. "The experiences of Russia and Mexico are conclusive: without democracy, economic development has no meaning. . . . Every dictatorship, whether of man or of party, leads to the two forms that schizophrenia loves most: the monologue and the mausoleum. Moscow and Mexico City are full of gagged people and monuments to the Revolution" (1999, 247/1985, 228–229).

The reference to mausoleums, monuments, and *mordaza* (figuratively, a gag to silence the other, precluding unwanted interruptions) makes clear that for Paz dictatorships are dead, which does not mean that they do not survive. Their discourse serves only to perpetuate the status quo; they are monological rather than dialogical. The Mexican government, Paz explains, "was neither willing nor able to examine its own conscience; but without criticism, above all without self-criticism, there is no possibility of change" (252/236). And where there is no possibility of change, Paz decides, there is only "blind imitation"—repetition without difference—of the past. This "blind imitation" manifests itself in two not unrelated ways. On the one hand, it takes the form of dead or corrupted language, what Paz calls the upper class's preferred "oratorical" style, replete with "plastic flowers" of speech, the evidence of which Paz finds in the public emissions of Mexico's "state" culture: the "barbaric syntax of the newspapers" (273/263); the reproduction in Mexico of US-produced television programs, which, he says, are "dubbed in our language by people who know neither English nor Spanish" (273–274/263); and "the daily dishonoring of the language on loudspeakers and the radio, the loathsome vulgarities of advertising." Paz calls this an "asphyxiating rhetoric" (274/265), and he contends that "when a society decays, it is language that is first to become gangrenous" (274/263). Language becomes infected and dies. All that is left is uncritical, unreflective repetition, a dubbing or doubling (*doblar*) that is duplicitous: "Every revolution that stifles criticism, that denies the freedom to contradict those in power, that prohibits the peaceful substitution of one government for another, is a revolution that defeats itself—is a fraud" (286/282). It would be a revolution *in name only*, thus it would be a revolution *unworthy of the name*, a counterfeit, a homonymic revolution. By definition, such a revolution—monumentalized, monological—would be incapable of finding democratic solutions to social problems. The result, however, will not be "the *status quo* but rather a state of enforced immobility that will end with an explosion and a return to the old cycle of anarchy and personal dictatorship" (284/276–277). In other words, the regime's resistance to change demands that it work to maintain things *as they are* against the coming of a future that cannot be determined; or, as Paz puts it, "No one knows the shape of the future. It is a secret" (285/282). The upshot of the desire to keep things the same—a desire that necessarily forecloses democracy and political and social change and that counterfeits the revolution in the name of which the regime acts—is, Paz suggests, the return of the same: the fall (back) into the cycle from anarchy to dictatorship.

In other words, the desire to remain the same provokes an explosion that leads not to something entirely new but to a fall (back) into a cycle that Paz believes Mexico knows too well. It refers to the eruption of the other Mexico, the one the ideology of progress and development has buried and that modern Mexico believes it has exorcised: "When modern progress arrived, our house, built with the rubble of the pre-Columbian world and the old stones of Spanish-Catholic civilization, was falling apart; but what we have built in its place, a lodging for only a minority of Mexicans, has been deserted by the spirit. The spirit has not gone away, however: it has gone into hiding" (1999, 288–289/1985, 286). Such occultation instances inheritance and survival. It is the figure of Mexico's past and future—what lies *before* Mexico—haunting Mexico's present. At Harvard University in 1971, Paz remarked, "In Mexico the Spanish conquest destroyed Indian civilization but . . . the cadaver *kept living*. Buried, hidden, the dead is alive" (1979, 127).

Modern Mexico's other, that which lies buried, dead-but-still-living, that which haunts modern Mexico, is not simply the culture of poverty, as Oscar Lewis calls it in *The Children of Sanchez* (an interpretation Paz calls not inexact but insufficient). For Paz, what disturbs Mexico is not visible poverty but the otherness that it secretes within itself as the condition of its *being* Mexico. The ghost or phantasm that haunts Mexico *is* Mexico: "This *otherness* eludes the notions of poverty and wealth, development or backwardness: it is a complex of unconscious attitudes and structures which, far from being survivals from an extinct world, are vital, constituent parts of our contemporary culture. The other Mexico," Paz contends, one that is "submerged and repressed, reappears in the modern Mexico: when we talk to ourselves, we talk to it, when we talk to it, we talk to ourselves" (1999, 289/1985, 287). Therefore, Mexico—the culture or civilization—sustains a dialogue with itself as the condition of possibility of its *being* a single culture. He writes, "Duality is not something added, artificial, or exterior: it is our constituent reality. Without otherness there is no unity" (289/288). If otherness is a "projection" of Mexican culture, if it is "the shadow with which we battle in our nightmares," it is also the case for Paz that "unity is a moment of otherness" (289/289). Indeed, the answer to Paz's question, "Which is the original and which the phantasm?" (289/288), is both and neither: "As with the Moebius strip, there is neither inside nor outside, and otherness is not there, beyond, but here, within" (289/288). And he continues, it is

> that moment in which we know ourselves as a body without shadow—or as a shadow without body. Neither within nor without, neither before nor after: the past reappears because it is a hidden present. I am speaking of the real past, which is not the same as "what happened": dates, persons, everything we refer to as history. What happened is indeed in the past, yet there is something that does not pass away, something that happens that does not entirely pass away, a perpetual present in rotation. (289–290/289)

These remarks reveal Paz's complex—perhaps ambiguous and confusing—understanding both of time and of Mexico's relation to its Amerindian legacy. For example, he observes: "What occurred on 2 October 1968 was simultaneously the negation of what we have wanted to be since the Revolution and an affirmation of what we have been since the Conquest and even earlier" (291/290). The "and even earlier" is troubling. Before the Conquest, "Mexico" was Amerindian. Paz attributes the violence of Tlatelolco to the sacrificial logic of Mexico's pre-Colombian heritage: "The double reality of 2 October 1968: to be a historical fact and to be a symbolic representation of our subterranean or invisible history. And I am mistaken when I call it a representation, because what unfolded before our eyes was a ritual act: a sacrifice" (291/291). The massacre at Tlatelolco actualizes what Paz calls Mexico's "perpetual present in rotation" (290/289).

Paz ignores that "rotation"—not unlike succession—does not happen without delay, which also makes possible the "return" of the "same": that is, in Paz's account, the return of the same (indigenous) violence, the same rituals. The same is an effect of the rotation or repetition that is itself possible only through delay. Paz ignores this because for him *now* (*ahora*) is the "time" that matters: "The supreme value is not the future but the present. The future is a deceitful time that always says to us, 'Not yet,' and thus denies us. The future is not the time of love: what man truly wants he wants *now*. Whoever builds a house for future happiness builds a prison for the present" (1999, 286/1985 283). Paz's preference for the present is nothing new: he insisted on the value of the present in *El arco y la lira*, where he privileged the supposed stasis of the image over the temporality of metaphor. Yet even if Paz never gives up on the present, he ultimately abandons the image (and returns to metaphor). His reason for doing so reveals the limitation of any theoretical/philosophical investment in the present as the horizon for political and social change, that is, for the possibility of democratization.

IN OTHER WORDS, AN ACT OF FAITH

Unlike Alfonso Reyes's *El deslinde*, which approaches the question of literary aesthetics from phenomenology and posits the literary entirely as an act of intention, Paz's aesthetics are existentialist through and through. *El arco y la lira* concerns the place of language (as metaphor and image) in the articulation (the [dis]jointure) of self and world. Paz asserts: "Man is inseparable from words. Without them, he is ungraspable. Man is a being of words. . . . The word is man himself" (1967, 30). From this it follows—and Paz claims to be following Reyes in this—that "the writer's first obligation is fidelity to language" (1999, 177/1985, 164). But in addition to "that radical fidelity to language that defines every writer, the Mexican has some specific obligations. The first of which consists in expressing what is properly ours—or, as Reyes put it, 'to seek the soul of our nation'" (178/164–165). For at least two reasons this is easier said than done: first, languages are historical, which means they bear the marks of the cultures that use them; second, what is properly Mexican remains undetermined. "We have no other remedy than to use a language that has already suffered the experiences of Góngora and Quevedo, of Cervantes and San Juan, in order to express a man who is not yet finished and who does not know himself" (178/165).

How to write in a language that is not your own in order to express a self that is not properly your own? For Paz, "To write implies a profession of faith" (177/164). Or, as he explains at the end of *El arco y la lira*,

> The question that the poem asks—who is the one who says this that I say and to whom does he say it?—encompasses the poet and the reader. The separation of the poet has ended: his work arises from a situation common to everyone. It is not the word of a community, but of a dispersion; it founds or establishes nothing, save its interrogation. . . . That question is not a doubt but a search. And more: it is an act of faith [*es un acto de fe*]. (1967, 283–284)

It is an act of faith because "language is man, but it is something more" (52). If language cannot be reduced to the human being, then the relation between the human being and language is structurally asymmetrical.

Something of language overflows, exceeds, the human. Rather than being an instrument of the human, language promises the human. The chance of the human is the possibility of sense. There is no human being that does not surround himself with sense: "The world of man is the world of sense" (19). This is the import of Leopoldo Zea's claim that "man is the only being that gives meaning to what surrounds him. That is, he arranges it in a way such that it is familiar to him, not foreign" (1952, 145). This fundamental relation to sense, however, means that the human being manifests herself in and as words.

If the human being is constituted of words, then he is, *by definition*, metaphor, metaphorical. The human being *makes* sense through an analogizing or metaphorizing consciousness. Paz speculates that this has been so from the very beginning: "Perhaps the first human language was imitative and magical pantomime. Governed by the laws of analogical thought, corporeal movements imitate and recreate objects and situations" (1967, 34). Later he links poetry to magic: "Both utilize the principle of analogy" (53). According to Paz, "Language and myth are vast metaphors of reality. The essence of language is symbolic because it consists in representing one element of reality through another, according to what occurs with metaphors" (34). If language is essentially symbolic because it is metaphorical, then language is fundamentally *naming*. What makes every word a metaphor, Paz notes, is "the distance between word and object—which is what obliges, precisely, every word to become a metaphor of that which it designates." Every word "is the consequence of another: as soon as man acquired self-consciousness, he was separated from the natural world and became other in his own breast. The word is not identical to the reality that it names because between man and things—and, more profoundly, between man and his being—self-consciousness intervenes" (35–36). Self-consciousness instances the moment in which the living being names himself. Naming bears witness to the difference within ourselves that we are. I am, therefore, that (which) I am: I am (what, who) I call myself. I respond to myself in my name. The name is essentially metaphorical in that it synthesizes differences *as* the same.

The operation of synthesis is possible only insofar as there is temporal deferral and spatial difference, for in the absence of such spacing there is nothing, neither consciousness nor anything else. If the human being is words, then she is delay. The human being always arrives *en retard*, posthumously. Thus Paz attests, in *El laberinto de la soledad*, that "to be oneself is, always, to become that other that we are and that we carry hidden in our interior, more than anything as promise or possibility of being" (1999,

188/1985, 175). To be human is to be alienated from oneself, to be separated and segregated, secreted in and secreted from oneself. The human makes sense; he is, in essence, language, words. The sense of language, then, is the chance of the human. And language makes sense in and through metaphor, analogy, thus through displacement, deferral, secrecy, and uncertainty. Or, as Paz notes, "The world of the 'perhaps' is that of the image through comparison of likenesses and its principal vehicle is the word 'like': this is like that" (1967, 66). This "image," whose operator is the "*como*," is the chance of the human.

Although necessary for the constitution of the sense of words, and therefore of the sense and possibility of the human, the "*como*" (as) troubles Paz. Ultimately, the "*como*" reveals a tension that can be mitigated only by rethinking the image, saving it from analogization and comparison by relieving it of the "*como*" that is nonetheless essential to it. The "*como*" constitutes and displaces in the same stroke, in the same movement, the present. The "*como*" ruins the present, divides it from itself. If the human is constituted *of* and *as* words, and if words, by definition, refer to other words, if no word is ever simply in itself or present to itself except through constitutive referral to another, then the present as the time and place of being-in-itself is ruined, divided in itself. The "*como*" marks the displacement of the present insofar as it inscribes incompletion and temporal synthesis at the heart of sense. Paz acknowledges the constitution of words *in* and *as* referral: "Every phrase possesses a reference to another, it is susceptible of being explained by another. Thanks to the mobility of signs, words can be explained by other words. . . . Every phrase means something that can be said or explained by another phrase. In consequence, sense or meaning is a *wanting to say*. In other words, a saying that can be said in another way" (1967, 109). On the one hand, meaning is understood *as* intention; on the other hand, this intention is, precisely, sent off, *in* and *as* other words. What one means ("wants to say," *querer decir*) is always deferred, delayed, put off because sent off. It is always *meant* in other words. By definition, one can only ever mean anything *in other words*. The constitutive displacement of meaning is, then, marked by the "*como*" and the "*ojalá*" (*perhaps*). Initially, Paz calls this the "image," where "image" means analogy or metaphor (carrying over, transport): "The image is the bridge [*el puente*] that desire stretches between man and reality" (66). The image "bridges"—spans and suspends—the difference, the gap, between human being and reality. It instances the desire, which is also the intention, to *touch*—to *cross over to*, to be in *contact with*—the world.

Yet because the "image" is structured according to the logic of the "as" (*como*) and the "perhaps" (*ojalá*), the present, in which touching the world would be guaranteed, is interrupted, suspended. Consequently, Paz rethinks the image without the "as," without the "perhaps," and therefore without time or temporalization, hence without metaphoricity. Indeed, he attempts to think the image without the synthesis the "as" effects. He writes: "We designate with the word image every verbal form, phrase, or group of phrases that the poet says and which united compose a poem" (1967, 98). The image—whether conceived as comparison, simile, metaphor, paranomasia or other wordplay, symbol, allegory, myth, fable—is characterized by its preservation of "the plurality of the word's meanings without breaking the syntactic unity of the phrase or the group of phrases" (98).[16] "Ambivalent being, the poetic word is fully what it is—rhythm, color, meaning—and, likewise, it is something else: image," he writes (22). But "to be something else" means to be "the 'same thing': the thing itself, those that really and primitively are" (22). The poetic word *is* image and the image *is* the thing itself. Images are words (and phrases and groups of phrases) in their *pure* form: "To purify language, the poet's task, means to return it to its original nature . . . that is to say, its possibility of signifying two or more things at the same time" (47). Paz describes not only the poetic image but also the "original nature" of language as homonymy. The image thus ostensibly threatens the principle of noncontradiction upon which, since at least Aristotle, Western notions of identity have been grounded. The image affords the possibility that, for example, stones be feathers and feathers be stones, and thus for the light to be heavy, without absolving either stones or feathers of their singularity as stones and feathers (1967, 99–100). According to Paz, "the unifying operation of science" (99) mutilates and impoverishes the singularities with which it is ostensibly concerned by reducing the singularities to abstractions. But, he explains, "the same thing does not occur with poetry's [unifying operation]. The poet names things: these are feathers, those are stones. And suddenly he affirms: stones are feathers, this is that" (99).

To say that "this" *is* "that" is to think the image beyond comparison, beyond analogy or metaphoricity, insofar as "this is that" posits identity beyond the "principal vehicle" of *homoiosis* (likeness, similarity): the "as." Rather than bridging (spanning) the gap between "this" and "that" through metaphorical or analogical synthesis, which nevertheless leaves the distance in place (suspending it between poet and the world) as the condition of the synthesis, Paz suggests the possibility of the absolute reduction of distance in the image. Or, as he puts it, "Poetry is hunger for reality. Desire always aspires to suppress distances" (66). To suppress the distance between words and things, between man and the world, but also between man and himself, Paz argues, demands a "saying" that does not determine truth *as* likeness (the *as* or *como*). "But there is another metaphor that suppresses the 'as' and says: this is that. In it desire becomes action: it neither compares nor shows similarities but rather reveals—and provokes—the ultimate identity of objects that seemed irreducible to us" (66). To say, "this is that," Paz contends, skirts metaphor, analogy. It absolutely reduces distance; it satiates hunger in and as full presence.

Instead of resolving contradictory meanings and thereby restricting or limiting the desire or hunger for reality that Paz ascribes to poetry, the poetic image *says* the *thing itself*: "The poet does not mean: *he says* [El poeta no quiere decir: dice]" (1967, 110). It is the work of the image, Paz claims, that produces "the instantaneous reconciliation between name and object, between representation and reality" (109). The image overcomes, then, the distance between name and thing. For this reason "each poem is unique, irreducible and unrepeatable" (15). Because the poem *says* what is, not according to likeness but according to being; because what the poem says *is*, what it says cannot be said in other words. The absolution of the difference between the human being and reality spells the return to the origin, to the first instance of language: "The first attitude of man before language was confidence: the sign and the object represented were the same" (1967, 29). This moment corresponds to that which, in *El laberinto de la soledad*, Paz characterizes as the childhood that precedes the consciousness that marks adolescence:

> Language, stripped of its intellectual meanings, stops being a group of signs and returns to be being a delicate organism of magical magnetism. There is no distance between the name and the thing and to pronounce a word is to put in movement a reality that it designates. The representation amounts to a true reproduction of the object, in the same way that for the primitive man the sculpture is not a representation but a double of the represented object. To speak returns to being an activity creative of realities, that is, a poetic activity. (1999, 220/1985, 203)[17]

The moment Paz decides that in the poetic enunciation "there is no distance between the name and the thing," he abandons the Aristotelian understanding that homonymy results from the difference between words and things. The gap that results from the finite number of words and the infinite number of things opens onto finite homonymy, that is, the homonymy that results from the "as" rather than the "is." In Aristotle, because words are never things, and because words are finite (thereby requiring them to refer to or to designate more than one thing), the self-identity of the word is always equivocal. It is only ever as if a word means what it says, as if an intending consciousness can be sure of what it means. This is not the case for Paz's poetic homonymy, in which words do not *want to say* (*querer decir*) but simply *say* (*decir*), and in saying they articulate the univocal identity of what is. Insofar as poetic saying says without meaning, there is no chance of equivocation. Homonymy makes no difference, because there is no difference between word and thing in the absolute present of saying. Poetry, for Paz, is equivalent to the speech of God.

Paz insists on this origin of language and on the possibility of returning to it in and through poetry. The epilogue to *El arco y la lira*, "Signos en rotación," concludes: "Man wants to be one with his creations, reunite himself with himself and with his likenesses: to be the world without ceasing to be himself. Our poetry is consciousness of the separation and [an] attempt to reunite what was separated. The poem, being, and desire to be come together for an instant. . . . Poetry, momentary reconciliation: yesterday, today, tomorrow; here and there; you, I, him, we. All is present: all will be presence [Todo está presente: será presencia]" (1967, 284).[18] In this moment of reconciliation, however, neither poem nor man nor the question the poem asks of man ("Who is the one who says this that I say and to whom is it said?" [283–284]) is any longer what Paz calls an "act" or "profession" of faith. They are no longer promises, for being—what is, the present and presence—cannot promise. A promise, and therefore an act, is possible insofar only as there is alteration and alterity, insofar as the future is admitted as undetermined, as other. The poem obviates any possible decision in its reconciliation of word and thing—as well as in its purification of language such that the word is capable of "meaning two or more things at the same time" without equivocation (47). There is no future because, as Paz says, everything is present. By evacuating temporality—metaphoricity, analogization, the "as" and the "perhaps"—the image abolishes change. The purification of language, the abolition of the distance between word and thing, however, "seems to negate the essence itself of language: meaning or sense. Poetry would be a futile business and, at the same time, a monstrous one: it dispossesses man of his most precious asset, language!" (47–48).

If the human being is meaningful, if she is essentially language, words, then the beginning of the human is the end of the human, because "language, touched by poetry, ceases immediately to be language" (111). Why would this be the case? Because where there is no chance for decision, where everything is present, where time is not divided between the no longer and the not yet, where words and things are reconciled, there is no sense, no meaning. According to Paz, "Far from enlarging itself, the distance between word and thing" in the image "becomes smaller or disappears completely: the name and the thing are thus the same. Meaning—to the extent it is nexus or bridge—also disappears: there is nothing to grasp, nothing to signal" (112). Poetry disappears meaning, sense, in its sublimation (elevation or raising up) of the bridge. If the bridge spans and suspends the gap between desire and the world such that the one touches the other and becomes meaningful, poetry suspends such suspension. It relieves—raises and cancels—the symbol (the bridge) of symbolization and, thus, of meaning. Only by means of the dissolution of sense (the removal of the bridge) and with it of language, is man able to *be*: "Man is his image: the same and the other one. Through the phrase, which is rhythm, which is image, man—that perpetual coming to be—is. Poetry is entering into being" (113). In other words, "the image is the cipher of the human condition" (98).

Nevertheless, after having privileged the image in his mid-1950s aesthetics, *El arco y la lira*, Paz dismisses it at the very end of *Postdata*, in the aftermath of the massacre at Tlatelolco and the MEP's demands for dialogue and democratization. He concludes "La crítica de la pirámide" by remarking the necessary link between critique and the imagination:

> If politics is a dimension of history, the critique of history is also political and moral critique. To the Mexico of the Zócalo, Tlatelolco and the Museum of Anthropology we must oppose not another image—all images suffer the fatal tendency to petrify—but rather critique, the acid that dissolves images. In this case (and perhaps in every case) critique is not only one of the modes of operation of the imagination, one of its manifestations. In our epoch the imagination is critique. For sure, critique is not the dream, but it teaches us to dream and to distinguish between the specters of nightmares and true visions. Critique is the apprenticeship of the imagination in its second return, the imagination cured of fantasy and determined to confront the reality of the world. Critique tells us that we should learn to dissolve the idols: learn to dissolve them in ourselves. (1999, 317–318/1985, 324–325)

Moreover, in *Postdata* Paz recalls that *El laberinto de la soledad* "was an exercise of critical imagination: a vision and, simultaneously, a revision. Something very different from an essay on the philosophy of the Mexican or a search for our supposed being" (235/215).

Paz recognizes that the image, *qua* atemporal, *qua* present, is petrified. It is stone, not unlike Hegel's understanding of the hieroglyph or Ramos's understanding of the imaginationless and stone-like Amerindian. The poetic image is silent. Because all the image ever says *is*, because there is no interval or gap between desire and being, the image cannot speculate on what may or perhaps what ought to be. Because it cannot be said *in other words*, the poetic image has no future. It is not open to dialogue, to change, to transformation and translation. The image is Mexico's tomb, its pyramid, its mausoleum. The image provides no chance for democratization, no opportunity for dialogue.

For this reason, Paz's insistence on the "supreme value" of the present even as he acknowledges both the petrification of the image and the importance of critique is disturbing. If critique dissolves images, it does so because it is *decisive*.[19] Critique is divisive, corrosive. It undermines and destabilizes.[20] Paz links *crítica* to both the imagination and freedom. This is important for two reasons. First, the imagination is not simply the faculty of subjective flights of fantasy, of fiction understood as the sovereign act of an intending subject. It is also the faculty (following Kant) that makes relation to the other possible in the first place.[21] Without the operation of the imagination, there would not even be the pure intuitions of time and space, which means there would not be the pure forms of interiority and exteriority. In short, there would be no possibility of experience. The imagination thus marks the limit of subjectivity and, with it, of any possible *inter*subjectivity. Second, there is no freedom without time. Where everything is always already present, where everything is already given and cannot be said in other words, where there is no possibility of change, alteration or alternation, there is no freedom. Freedom is conceivable only if there is a relation to the future, to the possibility of decision. The same holds for democracy and dialogue, both of which must always calculate with the incalculable, with the unknown, with what remains to come. *Crítica*, dialogue, democratization, all depend upon delay, retardation; in a word, they all depend on the future. Yet, Paz has no faith in the future, preferring instead the stability of "a perpetual present in rotation."

DIALOGUE AND DEMOCRACY

The constellation of critique, imagination, and freedom instances the promise of politics or of political life, which for Paz is necessarily democratic. But if political life is democratic, by the late 1960s Mexico had long since been dead. Paz points out, for instance, that even though Lázaro Cárdenas's slogan was "for a democracy of workers," the Partido Revolucionario Mexicano (PRM) was not "a democratic party. If there is no memory of its debates it is because there weren't any: its politics were never the product of a public deliberation" (1999, 256/1985, 241). Nor were there any debates within the party: "The Mexican party has no internal democracy" (258/243). Indeed, Paz observes, "the PRI [Partido Revolucionario Institucional] has never been an organ critical of presidential action; to the contrary, it has been an organ of unconditional support of its means and of diligent execution of its orders" (259/245). This is the Mexican mausoleum. Further, Paz points out that all the petitions of the MEP "could be summarized in a word that was the axis of the movement and the secret of its instantaneous power of seduction over the popular consciousness: *democratization*" (250/232). In short, the MEP demanded political life, hence, *public* debate and dialogue.

Paz was not the only Mexican writer to hear the call for democratization and dialogue in the wake of Tlatelolco. In *Tiempo mexicano* (1971), Carlos Fuentes writes: "Fifty years after the Madero-inspired revolution, Mexico still has no system for democratic expression" (70).[22] He notes the "radical absence of intelligent dialogue or of constructive debate" (75) and accuses the press of being "one of the principal factors in the civic death of Mexico" (75). More recently, in 1994, the year of the Zapatista uprising in Chiapas, Fuentes remarked, "Politics is dialogue" (1994, 154). Dialogue thus appears to be the minimal condition for democratization. In *Días de guardar* Carlos Monsiváis suggests that if the truth is to be set free, and with it, the country, there must be dialogue. After observing that the MEP depended only on the students' faith in their own efforts to democratize the country, he quotes the slogan, "Freedom to the truth. Dialogue!" (267). A predominantly *student* movement quickly became the Student *Popular* Movement—that is, it very quickly came to encompass the interests of a large part of the disenfranchised Mexican population rather than simply articulating the concerns of a rather privileged and, according to Paz, a somewhat artificially determined segment of society (1999, 242–243/1985, 222–223). This means, Beth Jörgensen writes, that it "embodied broad hopes for a more open, democratic society . . . and a freer dialogue between those in power and those who, fifty years after the revolution, remained powerless" (1994, 74).

The qualifier "freer," however, signals an intractable problem. What counts as dialogue is never simply given; it is determined, constituted. Dialogue must be rendered, represented. In other words, dialogue is a cipher that both sides claim, as if they knew what it was, what it meant, where to find it, and how to conduct it. There is the assumption that dialogue amounts to a transparent, face-to-face encounter, inviolable by partisan interests (which explains all the recriminations—from every side—of the other side's "bad faith"). Further, dialogue is too easily and too quickly identified with democracy, perhaps because it suggests universal participation or inclusiveness and the possibility of the determination of the "general will" of the "people," in short, of the values too quickly and too unproblematically associated with the idea of democracy.

The problem of the identification and thus of the determination of dialogue and its necessary publicness plagued the MEP. The question is always: What counts as dialogue? For example, when the students demanded public dialogue, the government responded in such a way that the circumstance of public dialogue became a question. During a meeting of the Comité Nacional de Huelga (CNH, National Strike Committee), someone asked: "Can a telephone call be considered a public dialogue?" (Poniatowska 1971, 38). It is also the case that dialogue takes place where it will not have been recognized.

> We were fools enough to believe that the government was willing to have a dialogue with us—I say that because when the granaderos hit us over the head with nightsticks and truncheons they kept saying, "Go ahead and have your dialogue, go ahead and have your dialogue!" So we thought we should be prepared to have a discussion about legal technicalities, but what happened was that they gave us an illegal and antidemocratic clubbing over the head, and the dialogue turned out to be a monologue in the form of a sixteen-year prison sentence. (62)

The mistake is to assume that torture and abuse are not democratic. In early twenty-first-century United States, we know better. The mistake is to assume that the violent suppression of demonstrations is not a "response" to demands. It clearly is. In short, the mistake is to assume that one knows what constitutes dialogue and democracy. When Jan Poniatowski Amor (Elena Poniatowska's younger brother) claims, "The PRI doesn't go in for dialogues, just monologues," the monologues are nonetheless figured as dialogues: "The government has been talking to itself for fifty years now" (Poniatowska 1971, 90, 86). Talking to oneself (monologue) is always already dialogical. It instances the opening of the secret, its impossibility. Despite its ostensible secrecy, "monologue," which always takes place between at least two, marks the necessary—constitutive—opening to the other, the necessary exposure to the outside that opens onto alterity and alteration, thus to change and a certain democratization, for better and for worse. Without the constitutive opening (or the becoming-dialogue) of monologue, there would never have been the chance or the threat (the promise) of democratization, of *alternancia*.[23]

INHERITING MEXICO

1968 haunts Mexico.[24] Paz understood 1968 as the return of Mexico's repressed past, the legacy of the violence of its Amerindian history, its ritual sacrifices and problematic inheritance. But in the wake of 1968, Mexico is no longer haunted simply by an indigenous phantom; rather, that revenant has been joined by the ghost of the MEP and its violent truncation in Tlatelolco, the Plaza de las Tres Culturas, on 2 October 1968.[25] Perhaps no early twenty-first-century Mexican text more embodies this haunting than Paco Ignacio Taibo II's memoir *68*, with its successive epilogues (1993, 2003, 2007, 2008) marking the year's incessant return. The phantom is the origin: "68 is the point of departure[;] we come from there" (2008, 136). In 1993, on the twenty-fifth anniversary of Tlatlelolco, Taibo II calls it "the mythic origin of almost everyone and of almost everything" (115/2004, 126). And, earlier, back in 1991, explaining why he would never write a *novel* of 1968, a novel that did not want to be written because it was already being lived, he remarks: "If we are all characters in a novel that is written on a damned Olivetti without ink, if we live trying to be faithful to the character that we've invented for ourselves, there's no doubt that the principal character was formed in 68, that its best gestures . . . were fabricated there, and we have lived imitating him with more or less success" (12/10–11). The year 1968, then, is the beginning, the time and place, the event, of our invention and perpetual imitation. And 1968 is what is left to us, to others, to those who will not have lived it but who want nevertheless to remember. Taibo II filled three notebooks in 1969 because he was afraid that if he didn't write down his memories of the 123-day movement, "it ran the risk of disappearing" (13/11). He explains: "I tell myself: If I die in a plane crash, my daughter has to find them; but it doesn't have to be easy for her[;] she has to find them if she makes an effort, if a tenacious curiosity brings her to look through the thousands of papers that I'm going to leave her. There, hidden" (13/11). The internal tension marking these claims is palpable. On Taibo II's account, '68 instances the historical origin, from which "we" cannot depart, which "we" imitate or repeat—for better, for worse, with more or less fortune. At the same time, 1968 determines "us" as the fiction that we cannot *not* leave behind, share. What happened in '68 is that which we are afraid will be lost (thus we write it down, preserve it, archive it), and even as we leave it to those who will not have lived it, we nonetheless bury it, make it hard to recover. It names what escapes me, what I am losing, and thus what I try to hold on to; at the same time, it names what I leave to the one who comes after me by hiding it, by burying it. That year, that date, instances "our" secret, the date "we" secrete, the year that secretes "us."

But there is more. In 1991, the year of *68*'s first publication, Taibo II suggests, "Today the 68 movement is one more Mexican ghost, one of the many unredeemed and insomniac ghosts that populate our land" (11/9–10). But he concedes that it is a rather young phantasm, one that still "enjoys good health and normally comes to the aide of our generation every time that it appeals to its presence" (11/10). A domesticated ghost, it comes when called, but it is also fading: "The ghost is losing its corporality" (16/14). Taibo II writes for this reason—to remember and share—*68*, to put some flesh back on the ghost's bones. He writes *68* to renew, restore, and recall—both summon (and thus charge [*cobrar*]) and remember—the ghost of '68. This, at least, was his intention in 1991, when he was compelled by those who had not lived '68 but who nevertheless believed that the memories of it belonged to them, that they were its heirs: "A hairy and myopic student identified me and putting his index finger on the third button of my shirt he said I had to write this book, that my memories were not mine. That there are loves that endure even for those who did not live them" (17/15). But by 1993 Taibo II acknowledges: "We tell ourselves the old story as if we hadn't lived it, as if we wanted to confirm that all that really happened" (120/131). And yet more than a decade later he attests, "Thirty-nine years have passed as if we had recorded in our DNA, 'don't forget.' And this 'don't forget' socializes. 'Don't forget' is our national patrimony" (132). Isn't it always the case that we tell ourselves (and others) our history, our story, in order to convince ourselves that we lived it, that it did happen? At the same time, we claim that history as our own, as our property, our genetic disposition such that it is unforgettable and can be passed on to those who will never have lived it but whom it nonetheless marks, informs? Which means '68—from the very beginning—is a question of inheritance. How to inherit—bequeath and accept, give and receive—1968?

Who inherits '68? In 1993 Taibo II asks and answers this question:

> Who was the heir to the movement? Without doubt the past student movement is one of the better children of 68; but we can't reject the democratic unionism of the 70s, the Cardenist electoral insurrection, the voluntary brigades that changed Mexico City working in the ruins after the earthquake of 85, the Pascual workers cooperative, the critical journalists expelled time and again from their jobs, the democratic lawyers, all those who went to Nicaragua and often left a part of themselves there; and including an important part of the Cardenista emergence against the

> PRI in 88 could lay claim to being the child of the movement. It seems, then, that it would not be just that the veterans of 68 . . . would appeal to the movement as its only child. (121–122/132)

In 2008, on the fortieth anniversary of Tlatelolco, Taibo II writes his last "epilogue" to *68* and to 1968, because, he acknowledges, "I run the risk that my memory will become the memory of memory, of reducing a part of my past to one story and not to the many that they were, of wearing out my memories" (138). And he claims, simply:

> The battles are different, the times are different. And it's true, we need to appeal to the ghosts of the past in order to survive in this corrupt and degraded present. But one must bring other histories: those of the seamstresses of Irapuato, those of the farmers' marches, those of the origins of the organization of the communities in the Valley of Mexico, that of the construction of the Zapatista free zones, those of the struggle against electoral fraud (it seems as if we Mexicans are condemned to win an election five times, *in a sort of Aztec curse*, in order that our will be recognized), that of the heroic Oaxacan resistance and hundreds more of what has been these last forty years. (138, emphasis added)

Effectively, the heirs of '68 are all those who resist oppression, resist state corruption. And because the heirs to 1968 are no longer those who will have "lived" the 123 days of resistance and protest, because the memories of those who did have become—or threaten to become—the memories of memories, because there are other histories, other stories, because time passes, Taibo II will no longer recall (summon [*cobrar*]) the ghost through additional epilogues. The ghost survives in other guises, in other stories.

Yet in the epilogue Taibo II added in 2008 to the fortieth-anniversary edition of *68*, Amerindians (the Zapatistas of Chiapas) are both *included* as heirs of 1968 and the MEP and (subtly) *excluded* as the name of the curse of electoral fraud and the dismissal of democracy, thus, of "our will." The 2008 epilogue was written just two years after Felipe Calderón's election, which was widely condemned as fraudulent and following which supporters of Partido Revolucionario Demócrata (PRD) candidate Andrés Manuel López Obrador (and he, too) occupied the Zócalo for fifty days in an effort to win a recount of the votes. It is also widely believed that Calderón's declaration of war on the drug cartels—and the subsequent unleashing of near apocalyptic violence throughout much of Mexico—was largely designed to divert attention from Calderón's allegedly fraudulent occupation of the National Palace.

Why condemn electoral corruption as an Aztec curse—a sort of Moctezuma's revenge—on Mexican democracy? Why is political corruption subtly associated with Amerindian culture? It is an odd gesture (it is a joke, in fact, or so it seems) coming from Taibo II, who not only named the Zapatista movement in Chiapas one of the heirs of 1968 but also coauthored, with Subcomandante Marcos, *Muertos incómodos (falta lo que falta)* (2006), a novel "in four hands." The *maldición azteca* (the Aztec curse) names, then, the ghost, the phantasm, that cannot be summoned, that is not domesticated. On the contrary, this ghost, "each time some one decrees it forgotten, overcome, resolved, buried, it returns" (129/140). But this is not the return of the ghost of '68, for what surfaces here is the most banal violence against the other, a violence that appears to do no harm and yet, in naming corruption and antidemocratic practices an "Aztec curse," puts the Indian in its place. Taibo II effectively accuses the Indian, the Aztec, of standing in the way of democratization. The gesture recalls the way Vasconcelos and Ramos thought Amerindians stood in the way of progress and cultural development, and the way Paz thought they figured the violence of Mexican culture.

FEELING INDIAN

Naming the obstruction of democratic voting practices an "Aztec curse"—a bad joke that is no less violent (and perhaps more so) because it goes "unnoticed" as violence—has an anthropological precedent, one ostensibly grounded in the cultural history of Amerindian societies. In *México profundo*, Guillermo Bonfil Batalla suggests that prior to the rise of the Aztec empire, Amerindian civilization was democratic, but with the defeat of the city-state Azcatpotzalco by the triple alliance of Tenochtitlán, Texcoco, and Tlacopan, and with the increasing domination of the Mexica (Tenochtitlán, the Aztecs), "democracy in Mexica society is lost" (1990, 114/1996, 71). Before Mexico, there is already a rupture in Amerindian civilization. The Aztecs are perhaps not the legitimate heirs of either the Toltecs or the Olmecs, who are "considered the bearers of Mesoamerican civilization's mother culture" (26/5). It will always have been a question of inheritance, of what it means to *be* Amerindian. Who *counts* as Amerindian? Who inherits and how is Indianness—Indian identity, Indian culture—passed on without passing away?

For Bonfil Batalla everything depends on the fundamental unity of Mesoamerican civilization. He points out that the agricultural economic base of Amerindian civilization develops over thousands of years and "gives rise to collective forms of social life that, within the diversity of their particular cultural traits, maintain common elements of civilization. Intense and prolonged contact occurred between cultures with their own historically developed profiles and between the peoples who created those cultures. Thus, different, once autonomous peoples created a unified Mesoamerican civilization" (28/7). Although "this common origin is recognized in the myths and traditions of different peoples" (28/7), it is not simply metaphorical; it is not a fiction. It is grounded in the common material practices of the different cultural units. So, on his account, it follows that "the diverse cultures that existed in the precolonial past and that, transformed, exist today as a continuation of them all have a common origin. They are the results of a unique civilizational process that gives them a unity apart from their differences and particularities" (31/9). Bonfil Batalla underlines this point: "Unity exists within diversity as a result of membership in a common civilization" (72/39). Consequently, "in all Indian cultures diversity can be observed, but within the basic unity of Mesoamerican civilization" (73/41).

This fundamental unity is preserved, moreover, through cultural transmission or inheritance. Bonfil Batalla explains, "One generation transmits to those that follow the codes that allow communication and mutual understanding. It transmits a particular language that expresses the vision of the world and the ideas created by the group throughout its history. Also transmitted are particular gestures, tones of voice, ways of looking, and attitudes *that have meaning for us, and often us alone*" (47/21, emphasis added). The fundamental unity of Amerindian civilization, which manifests itself in and as different cultural groups, is passed down from one generation to the next via a series of material signs: specific facial gestures, languages, and attitudes, all of which are meaningful, and what they mean, at bottom (which means on the surface), is Indianness. No matter what else these signs *say*, they *mean*, and thus they *intend*, Indianness: "I am Indian." Yet because this meaning is "for us, and often us alone," culture remains (a) secret. In being passed down from generation to generation, these signs are intended to remain among or between "us." Indeed, the passing down of these signs constitutes "us" *as* a culture. Passing down—inheritance, the bequest and its acceptance—instances culture by distinguishing "us," for whom such signs are meaningful, from "them," for whom they are not. Culture—which is meaningful for some ("us") but not for others ("them")—is the *sign* of culture. Culture is always in transmission, in transition; it is sent off. There is no culture without the transmission—the transference or translation—of culture from one generation to the other. And this means, simply, that culture must be left behind. Structurally, culture instances this leaving behind, this sharing but also this abandonment.

But in order to be left behind or passed on, in order for it to be meaningful among and for us, the material signs of culture must be coded. Bonfil Batalla does not think culture is transmitted without the mediation of signs. On his account, culture is a code. In "Signature Event Context," however, Derrida points out that "there is no code . . . that is structurally secret," because "the possibility of repeating, and therefore of identifying, marks is implied in every code, making of it a communicable, transmittable, decipherable grid that is iterable for a third party, and thus for any possible user in general" (1972b, 375/1982, 315). But if a code must be open to any possible user, then it follows that it cannot be tied either to the one who sends it or to the one who receives it. The code must be operative in the absence of any author or sender, auditor or receiver, whatsoever. In short, even were a code—empirically, historically—to have meaning only for us, it would nonetheless have to be decipherable, repeatable, and, it follows, imitable, by anyone. A code, then, can never be *structurally* limited to "us." In sharing the code among us, we betray ourselves to others. This is the logic of the secret. It is the condition of possibility of inheritance and of tradition, whether cultural or otherwise. There is no inheritance—no cultural transmission—that is not cut off both from the one who bequeaths it and the one who inherits it.

Consequently, the chance of cultural transmission—and with it the chance of cultural survival—is also and necessarily the risk of cultural transmission and the threat to cultural survival. In being passed on, a culture can always pass away. In leaving behind the signs of a culture, we run the risk of leaving the culture behind. No doubt the threat to cultural survival at least in part explains Bonfil Batalla's repeated claim that the unity of Mesoamerican civilization depends on neither "cultural traits" nor a shared (indigenous) language. He acknowledges that language transmission is important, and he emphasizes the role of women in passing it on, that is, preserving it, and along with it the norms and values of Amerindian cultures: "The woman's role is basic. It is her job to rear the children and pass on to her daughters all the cultural elements that will allow them to perform adequately as women. To a large extent, she is the primary link for the continuity of the language itself, and the repository of norms and values that are vital within the Mesoamerican cultural matrix" (1990, 59/1996, 29). As the principal link for the "continuity" of language from one generation to the next, as well as being the "repository of norms and values," women bear a remarkable responsibility for the survival of Amerindian cultures. But they are also, therefore, the obvious scapegoat for these cultures' demise or corruption; women are responsible for the loss of Amerindian languages and the undermining of cultural norms and values. According to Bonfil Batalla's understanding of their responsibility, women are both the chance for cultural survival and the threat to it.

Bonfil Batalla nevertheless denies that a shared language is vital to the identity and unity of Indian culture. He writes: "The Indian does not define himself in terms of a series of external cultural traits—dress, language, customs, and so on—that make him different in the eyes of outsiders" (48/21). Accordingly, a civilization "does not consist of a simple aggregate of isolated cultural traits, however complicated such an aggregate might be. Rather, it refers to a general plan for human life, which gives meaning and transcendence to human actions" (32/10). The unity of indigenous lifeways, therefore, depends not on positively determined "cultural traits" (on what Amerindians of Mesoamerican cultures *do* or *say*) but on what Amerindians *feel*. In other words, Bonfil Batalla locates the essence of Amerindian cultural identity at a level that is seemingly transmissible and immediately or properly Amerindian. He writes: "At a deeper level a spectrum of sentiments [is] also transmitted. Because they are shared, they allow us to participate, to accept, and to believe. Without them personal relations and collective effort would be impossible" (47/21). For Bonfil Batalla, cultures are fundamentally empathetic: and not just cultures but all interpersonal relations. Empathy grounds the possibility of community. The Indian "defines himself as belonging to an organized collectivity, a group, a society, a village that possesses a cultural heritage formed and transmitted through history by successive generations. In relation to one's own culture, one knows and feels oneself to be Maya, Purépecha, Seri, or Huastec" (48/21–22). How are feelings transmitted, passed between "us," without being codified? Although Bonfil Batalla claims that the unity of Amerindian cultures is not found in language and other material practices, for Indians to know or experience, to identify, what they feel (and then to identify that feeling as "Amerindian"), their feelings must be coded; they must leave a trace in the world for a future that is not yet.

Despite the need to send off and structurally dispossess culture in order to transmit feelings, Bonfil Batalla insists that culture belongs to "us," that it is our exclusive property. He writes:

> Our own culture belongs to us; it is the one to which we have exclusive access. History has defined who "we" are by specifying who belongs and who does not and when one stops belonging to the social universe that is the heir, depository, and legitimate owner of our own culture. Each group establishes the limits and norms. There are ways to join and ways to be accepted. There are also ways of losing one's membership. This is what is

> expressed in cultural identity. To know and look upon oneself as a member of a group, and to be recognized as such by other members and outsiders, means to form part of a society that has as its exclusive patrimony its own culture. (48/21)

What does it mean that a culture belongs exclusively to us if, in fact, we can be dispossessed, if there are ways both to gain the culture and to lose it? Who decides what another *feels* such that he or she may be excluded from or admitted to a determined culture? On what grounds and by what authority does one determine another's feelings? Who polices the border of culture? There is no culture without this policing, without, then, the shared gestures and practices that make apparent the feeling of belonging. These gestures and practices—police operations—*render* culture.[26] And because they are shared among us, they are our secret, one that we ought not—cannot—render to the other without betraying (surrendering) ourselves, without turning ourselves out of our culture, without dispossessing ourselves of our "common and exclusive cultural patrimony" (49/22).

Bonfil Batalla's claim that the "social universe . . . is the heir, depository, and legitimate owner of our culture" (48/21) begs the question how one does or does not become one of "us." The decision of culture always comes from the other, from elsewhere; it is never simply our own. Bonfil Batalla notes that "there are social pressure mechanisms that help enforce proper conduct," even to "the point of forcing someone to leave the community," which is what happens, for example, when someone previously identified with the Amerindian community converts to Protestantism and "refuse[s] to participate in the system of traditional government" (68–69/37). To *be* Indian, one must act *like* an Indian. Social pressure, Bonfil Batalla explains,

> is found in the fact that participation is an indispensable condition for being recognized and admitted as a member of the group. And it is the group that is the exclusive repository of the cultural patrimony that has been inherited. To gain legitimate access to the cultural patrimony and to be able to participate in decisions about it, one must be a member of the group. To be a member of the group (thus closing the circle) one must prove that he accepts the collective norms. (69/37)

For example, writing of the indigenous practice of endogamy, he admits, "On occasion endogamy is an explicit norm in customary law. Whoever violates it loses communal rights and privileges." More frequently, however, "it is an implicit norm, and compliance is achieved through social pressure. In either case endogamous marriage is a custom that contributes in an important way to the maintenance and continuity of the Indian community, insofar as it impedes the incorporation of 'the others' into the social universe of the group. It also contributes to the reproduction of community culture by guaranteeing that the new couple shares it" (60/30–31). Social pressure enforces endogamy, which is also a form of social pressure in that it enforces the perpetuation of the community through the exclusion of others. Endogamy sustains the status quo by guaranteeing the perpetuation of the community. Such a guarantee effectively excludes critical inheritance, which mandates that the community run the risk of becoming what it is (not).

But Bonfil Batalla denies this possibility. On his account, one can never let go of the "México profundo," that is, of one's indigenousness—until *it* lets *you* go. The majority of the "México profundo," which names Mexico's marginalized, subaltern majority culture, is composed of de-Indianized *mestizos*. According to Bonfil Batalla,

> Much of the mestizo Mexican population . . . is very hard to distinguish in physical appearance from the members of any community that is recognized without question as indigenous. From a genetic point of view, both are the products of mixture in which Mesoamerican traits predominate. The social differences between "Indians" and "mestizos" do not follow, then, a radically different history of racial mixture. The problem can be better understood in different terms: the mestizos are the contingent of "de-Indianized" Indians. (41–42/17)

It is not a question of affirming or denying *mestizaje*, as if there were any other biological determination of Mexico's population. It is rather a question of a certain contingency. De-Indianization results from a nonbiological cultural "ethnocide that ultimately blocks the historical continuity of a people as a culturally differentiated group" (42/17). Bonfil Batalla emphasizes: "De-Indianization is a historical process through which populations that originally possessed a particular and distinctive identity, based upon their own culture, are forced to renounce that identity" (42/17). He continues, "Separation from its cultural patrimony is the culmination of the de-Indianization process"; yet, Bonfil Batalla admits, "it does not always necessarily imply a break with cultural tradition" (42–43/18). On the one hand, the process of de-Indianization cuts off, separates, or interrupts the continuity of cultural identity, which results in the orphaning of the indigenous population. On the other hand, this caesura of cultural patrimony does not necessarily result in a break with cultural traditions.

Only an ideological ethnicide is capable of destroying—killing, murdering—a culture while, at the same time, leaving every visible sign of that culture in place. De-Indianized mestizos are virtually indistinguishable from Indians, not only biologically but also culturally: "If one looks in detail at the cultural repertoire, the way of life, of a traditional agricultural mestizo [de-Indianized] community and compares it with what happens in an Indian community, it is easy to see that the similarities are greater than the differences. . . . Even in language one can find the mark of the Indian past, since the local Spanish of a 'mestizo' community frequently includes a great number of words from the original Mesoamerican language" (42/17). Nevertheless, Bonfil Batalla remarks their difference. The de-Indianized traditional communities "have an Indian culture but have lost the sense of identity that goes with it" (77/44). He explains, "De-Indianization has been achieved when . . . the population stops considering itself Indian, even though the lifeway may continue much as before. *Such communities are now Indian without knowing they are Indian*" (80/46, emphasis added). Put simply, de-Indianized *mestizos* no longer feel or know themselves to *be* Indian. They look and act *like* Indians, but they no longer recognize (neither know nor feel) themselves to *be* Indians.

What does it mean to *be* an Indian without knowing or feeling *like* one, to be an Indian without recognizing oneself *as* Indian? If, as Bonfil Batalla repeatedly insists, Indian cultures depend on neither cultural practices nor biology (both of which constantly transform through inevitable contact, for better and for worse, with others) but rather on feeling like an Indian, how does he claim that de-Indianized mestizos—those who no longer feel like Indians and therefore cannot know themselves to be Indians—*are* Indians? Who feels their Indianness for them? In a certain way, Indians and de-Indianized mestizos are both formed from external pressures. "Indian" and "de-Indianized mestizo" are names for different responses to relations of power or "pressure." Indian culture is sustained through the pressure (of language, norms, rituals, practices, and traditions "internal" to the community, but also through resistance to what is "external" to it) that holds—forces—the community together.

But there is no "internal" pressure, no pressure that comes, simply or unequivocally, from "inside" a given culture, because cultures have no insides. Cultures are border phenomena. So-called "indigenous" or internal pressure reacts to the forces of the dominant culture, thereby "reclaiming" *as* Indian those who do not feel themselves to *be* such, identifying those who no longer identify with the community and who thus live outside it. Such indigenous pressure is also imposed upon those who live within the Indian community. Thus, the pressure of indigenous communities is doubly exterior: it is a force external both to those who do not identify as Indian and to those who do; external to those who have abdicated their cultural patrimony and to those who would claim such inheritance. Such pressure attempts to secure inheritance, to determine its legitimacy and guarantee the future of the community, of the patronym and patrimony. To do so it must counter that which makes inheritance possible in the first place: namely, imagination. "Each new generation receives [the culture] enriched by the efforts and the imagination of those who went before," he writes. "As each generation is shaped within a culture, it in turn helps enrich that culture" (21). To be sure, Bonfil Batalla's reference to the imagination is culturally loaded. For Paz, for instance, the imagination is critical, divisive and decisive. There is no inheritance without the imagination, which the Zapatistas have called "the most powerful weapon" (EZLN 1995, 2:68). Yet according to Ramos, it is the imagination that Amerindians lack, which explains why, for him, indigenous cultures are capable of only a mechanical—dead—repetition of the past.

If culture is an effect of the limit, and the limit is infinitely divisible such that it does not belong to one side or the other, such that it is crossed and crossed out at the instant of its institution, then it follows that one is never simply "shaped within a culture," as Bonfil Batalla remarks, as if the borders of a culture were determinable, as if they were unequivocally known and felt. Culture is not, which is why one never knows where one stands with respect to it. Cultures happen—take place, pass and pass away, pass over—at the limits of culture. Consequently, to say that each generation is "shaped within a culture" and that it "in turn helps enrich that culture" means, simply, that each generation *imagines*—is open to—the possibility of culture, that which is not *in itself* or *as such*, in order to leave it behind for those who are not yet. This is inheritance. It is neither passive nor active. It does not precede us such that we simply assume it, like the rightful heir to some throne. There is no culture, no cultural essence, that is not conditioned by the materiality (the practices) of culture. Rather, culture is imagined, hence simulacral, virtual. It will only ever be *as if* there were culture. Because there is no essence of culture, because culture is not, no one will ever know how it feels either to *be* or *not* to be Indian. On the contrary, it will only ever be possible to feel *like* an Indian, *as if* one were Indian.

This is not a negative determination of Indianness. It is the only possibility for appropriating any identity. And, at the same time, it is the possibility of that identity's expropriation. One can be called or named (identified *as*)

Indian or not-Indian (de-Indianized mestizo) only because one is not Indian *as such* or *in itself.* Not *being* Indian is the only chance for the survival of Indians *as* Indians.

The possibility of inheritance therefore depends on *dis*inheritance. One can inherit only what is not one's own, what is not proper to oneself, that to which one has no right or claim. To inherit one must be cut off, separated and segregated from what comes, from that which is bestowed or bequeathed. One inherits only a secret. We leave behind what is not ours to those to whom it does not belong. In a certain way, one is never equal to what one inherits. One literally has no right to it, which is precisely why rights must be established, codified, determined. A cultural patrimony—and thus the cultural patronym—is invented, appropriated, forged, counterfeited. The patronym is a fiction, a pseudonym.

AN INDIAN BY ANY OTHER NAME . . .

Cultural patrimony and the cultural patronym are inherited, imagined, invented, but they are also contested. Because an inheritance must be appropriated, it is never simply given. The name or identity that one inherits can only ever be claimed, reclaimed, and refused. Bonfil Batalla's *México profundo* announces an identity politics *in the name* of an Amerindian identity that, in theory, can be neither appropriated nor expropriated. In other words, he asserts a nonaccidental, substantial, or essential identity safe from any degradation or corruption, safe from any contamination. This is what it means to ground Indian identity not in languages and cultural practices that can be lost or transformed but in a deeper affective stratum of being. He extends this deep identity even to those who no longer feel or know themselves to be Indian. It is as if Bonfil Batalla were saying, contrary to what any Amerindian may feel or know, once an Indian always an Indian. There is no other way to be. One is *either* an Indian *or* a de-Indianized Indian who is still—unfeelingly and unknowingly, insensibly and unwittingly—Indian.

Less than ten years after the publication of *México profundo* (first published in 1987)—the subtitle of which, in the Spanish original, is *Una civilización negada* (A denied [negated] civilization)—the Zapatista insurgency announced itself in word and deed on 1 January 1994, the same day that NAFTA (known in Mexico as the Tratado de Libre Comercio [or TLC, a rather ironic instance of "tender loving care"]) became operative. When the English translation of *México profundo* was published in 1996, two years after the Chiapas uprising, the subtitle perhaps unwittingly acknowledged the stakes of the Zapatista project. While the title of the book remains the same, but without the accent (*Mexico Profundo*), the subtitle had become *Reclaiming a Civilization*. But it is not simply an Amerindian civilization that is to be reclaimed, for the Zapatistas fashion themselves the true heirs of the Mexican Revolution and the 1917 constitution, which not only promulgates land reform but guarantees it as a constitutional right in Article 27. The amendment of Article 27 in 1992—during the Salinas de Gortari *sexenio* and at the behest of the United States as a condition for NAFTA—was one of the factors in the timing of the armed insurgency. The "Second Declaration from the Lacandon Jungle" (12 June 1994) makes this explicit when, in anticipation of the Convención Nacional Democrática, it claims "the supreme government has also usurped the legality that the heroes of the Mexican Revolution bequeathed to us [*que nos heredaron*]" (EZLN 1994, 1:275). The Zapatistas do not, however, lay claim to rights (to self-determination or autonomy and inclusion in the Mexican political process) simply on account of their inheritance of Emiliano Zapata's legacy. They also claim these rights on the basis of a more millennial inheritance. More than once the Zapatistas remark their "original" status. For instance, speaking before the Mexican National Congress on 28 March 2001, Comandante David noted, "As original peoples of these lands, we have the right and freedom to live with dignity, we have the right and freedom to organize, to elect our authorities, and govern our people in agreement with the forms of thinking, of understanding, and of acting according to their laws and norms as indigenous peoples who, during centuries and until today, do not have that right" (EZLN 2003, 5:311). Comandante David is not the only one to claim such inheritance. On 12 October 1994, the 502nd anniversary of Columbus's arrival in the Americas, the Comité Clandestino Revolucionario Indígena—Comandancia General (CCRI-CG) of the EZLN addressed a message "to the Mexican people," but also "to the original inhabitants of these lands"; they claimed, "We are the original inhabitants of these lands. Everything was ours before the arrival of arrogance and money. By right everything belonged to us, and never before did we have a problem sharing it justly and reasonably" (1995, 2:101).[27] This double inheritance—the heirs of Zapata and the spirit of the Mexican Revolution on the one hand, and on the other hand the millennial proprietors of indigenous cultures—fuels the EZLN's claims against the Mexican state.[28]

At issue in this double inheritance is the name. In whose name—and in the name of what—is Mexico inherited? To whom does it pass? The question of the name is legible throughout the discourse—the thousands of pages of *comunicados* and documents—of the EZLN. Indeed, a certain politics of identification announces itself from the start, whether in the Zapatistas' address to "the Mexican people" and to their "Mexican Brothers" in the first

"Declaration from the Lacandon Jungle" (EZLN 1994, 1:33), or in their address to those who are "like us," who are "humble and simple people," a claim that is repeated several times in the "Sixth Declaration from the Lacandon Jungle" (Marcos 2006, 60, 62, 64, 66, 126). Identification—who is named what by whom or what?—is always complicated, always violent.

What does it mean, for example, to name oneself? It is always a gesture of *propriation*, of *ap*propriation, whether by oneself or by another, and therefore of *ex*propriation. On 1 January 1994 the Zapatistas named themselves before others had a chance to do so. "TODAY WE SAY 'ENOUGH!,' we are the heirs of the true forgers [*forjadores*] of our nationality. . . . We have the Mexican people on our side, we have the homeland and the tricolor Flag is loved and respected by the INSURGENT combatants, we use the colors red and black in our uniform, symbols of the working people in their struggles, our flag bears the letters 'EZLN,' ZAPATISTA NATIONAL LIBERATION ARMY, and with it we will always go into combat" (1994, 1:33–34). And just after this act of self-nomination comes the refusal of any other name: "We reject beforehand any attempt to detract from the just cause of our struggle by accusing it of narcotrafficking, narcowar, banditry or any other qualifier that our enemies could use" (1:34). This is an anticipatory gesture to indemnify their good name. But it is not simply their name that annoys the police and those charged with maintaining the status quo. Rather, it is the fact that Zapatistas name themselves. Nothing seems as pejorative as Mario Vargas Llosa's remark—reprinted in the Mexican daily *Unomásuno* on 16 January 1994—concerning the "rebellion in Chiapas of the self-proclaimed Zapatista National Liberation Army," which he claims had already been largely "crushed" by the military forces of the federal government.[29]

How do we know that the designation "*autoproclamado*" (self-proclaimed) is pejorative? Because the Zapatistas accuse President Salinas de Gortari of the same gesture. On 10 April 1994, the CCRI-CG accused "the usurper Salinas de Gortari, who designated himself 'president of the Mexican Republic,'" of lying "to the people of Mexico saying that the reforms to constitutional Article 27 reflect the spirit of General Zapata" (EZLN 1994, 1:208). Later that same year, on 10 July 1994, Marcos referred to "the self-determined MPs of the (who doubts it?) PRI, Ramón Mota and Cuauhtémoc Sánchez" (1:288). And five years later, the Zapatistas note that "on Wednesday, 7 April 1999, in the morning hours, armed forces of the self-named 'Chiapas State Security Police' took by assault the presidency of the municipality of San Andrés Sacamch'en of the Poor, the place where the autonomous municipal council (democratically elected in accordance with the practices and customs of the indigenous communities) [meets], and the seat of the San Andrés dialogues between the federal government and the EZLN" (2003, 4:300). The accusation of self-nomination is always the accusation of fraud, of counterfeit, that one is not who or what one claims to be.[30]

Legible in such accusations of self-nomination is the politics of the name and, therefore, of politics writ large, for there is no politics that is not *of the name*: no politics without the name, without naming and being-named, without giving and withholding the name. There is no politics that is not invested in the name. The politics of the name can be read in the Zapatistas' routine self-identification as "the voice of the unnameables [*los innombrables*]" and the ones who are "without name, without face [*sin nombre, sin rostro*]" (1995, 2:123).[31] And it is why, on 12 March 1995, they claim that another "voice" (*voz*, also "word"), a voice and word of life, having arrived from other lands and other hearts, from other hopes, gave them a name, which is the

> name that voice gives us. We are no longer the unnameables. Name we have, the forgotten ones. Our flag can now cover, without hiding, our dead and our history. We already have a place in the heart of our brothers, you, and a small corner in the history that truly counts: the one that is contested. Already having a collective name, we discover that death shrinks and becomes small to us. The worst death, that of being forgotten, flees in order that the memory of our dead will never again be buried together with their bones. We now have a collective name and our pain has shelter. We are now greater than death. . . . No longer will we die. We are named. (EZLN 1995, 2:276–277)

Having a name means they survive. They count (*cuentan*) because the name makes possible their account (*cuenta*), their story (*cuento*). Because they are named, they live on in Mexican history and do not suffer the absolute death of the nameless. Without a name, one's memory is buried with one's bones. It is hard—impossible—to mourn the unnamed.

Thus the struggle for the name, for the "right" to determine oneself and the other. This was the Zedillo administration's strategy regarding Subcomandante Insurgente Marcos in early 1995 when it announced that Marcos was, *in fact*, Rafael Sebastián Guillén Vicente.[32] The gesture was intended to delegitimize the EZLN in a way similar to the government's claim, in 1968, that the MEP was not Mexican but rather fomented by foreign agents and agitators. In 1995 the government suggested that Amerindians by themselves were incapable of demanding—as they so often do in the salutation to their communications—democracy, freedom, and justice. Only a non-Indian—an outsider, a "foreigner" of sorts, a disaffected philosophy professor, a leftist militant educated at UNAM in the late 1970s (and the winner of the Gabino Barreda Medal as the highest ranked student in his class), reader of Althusser and Foucault—could foment a self-proclaimed, autonominated (counterfeit) Indian revolution in Chiapas. This is the argument that Italian journalist Gianni Minà put directly to Marcos: "Do you realize that its dangerous that people will think the Indigenous cannot act for himself, if he doesn't have a white intellectual advisor?" (quoted in Volpi 2004, 131). Marcos's response is long and multifaceted; he makes a distinction between the earliest days of the Zapatista revolution, when he was considered "a perverse agent," and his later transformation into a sort of Robin Hood or Zorro, but he also observes that the cult of Marcos is media-driven: "The later image of Marcos was constructed when the media began to notice that behind the ski mask was an organized people, an indigenous people, and that the strongest word[s] of the EZLN had indigenous roots; and it is actually what attracts the most attention in Europe. . . . The roots of the discourses and communications are properly indigenous" (quoted in Volpi 2004, 131). Two things are in play here: on the one hand, the obsession with Marcos as the name of the EZLN; on the other hand, the insistence on the properly indigenous "roots" of the EZLN.

The obsession with Marcos is evident in the interview conducted by Julio Scherer García on 10 March 2001, which was originally published in the Mexican weekly magazine *Proceso* and broadcast by Televisa. Scherer García's first questions are focused entirely on Marcos, his charisma and personality (EZLN 2003, 5:339–359). Carlos Monsiváis also participates in the Marcos obsession in his *crónica* of the National Democratic Convention, "Crónica de una convención (que no lo fue tanto) y de un acontecimiento muy significativo" (Chronicle of a convention [which wasn't so much one] and of a very significant event). When Marcos offers to unmask, Monsiváis and the other journalists reject the idea. He concludes: "Marcos without the ski mask is not admissible, he is not photographable, he is not the living legend" (EZLN 1994, 1:323).[33]

In *Thresholds of Illiteracy: Theory, Latin America, and the Crisis of Resistance*, Abraham Acosta signals this same cult of Marcos when he remarks that, despite his interest in "the ways the EZLN conceives and deploys a language of radical political equality within Mexican constitutionality," his study has "very little to do with [Marcos] specifically" (2014, 168, 169). As a consequence he ignores the signature of the EZLN's principal voice (*voz*) and thus the principal purveyor of its word (*voz*). He does this, he explains, because

> unfortunately, and contrary to what a number of studies devoted to Marcos would seem to suggest, all the emphasis on him simply confirms the public's curiosity about a Western man interested in indigenous issues, not the indigenous issues or indigenous people themselves. In other words, this investment in Subcomandante Marcos ultimately (and again, lamentably) reproduces the trope . . . that non-Western peoples simply cannot be understood without cultural mediation. (169)

Acosta is right to avoid the cult of and fascination with Marcos and the trope that only non-Western peoples can speak without mediation. At the same time, however, to ignore the signature "Marcos," as if Marcos did not sign the majority of the EZLN communiqués (that is, the majority have appeared in that name, under the auspices of that signature), is to make the same mistake—but in reverse—that Acosta argues Brian Gollnick makes when he goes "so far as to admit what many critics might have wanted to say all along: 'To avoid putting too fine a point on this issue, my own sense is that Marcos is the author of all of the Zapatista communiqués, both literally in terms of writing the final language in them and even more importantly as the authorial signature whose connection to a style authenticates EZLN discourse for dissemination'" (2014, 170). Gollnick's decision *not* to read the various signatures of EZLN communiqués in order to read them all *in the name* of "Marcos," allows him to ignore the tension within the EZLN, as if the multiple voices simply masked one—undivided and indivisible—voice.[34] Underneath the different *pasamontañas*, finally, everyone is the same: *todos somos Marcos*. Acosta's position is structurally no different: he too ignores the particular signatures, reading every communiqué as if it were signed simply "EZLN," as if the different signatures made no difference, as if no one was Marcos. Both Gollnick and Acosta manufacture a hegemony that never will have existed. Both elide the tensions legible *within* Zapatista discourse; both ignore the singularity of the signature. In Acosta's case this is perhaps more unfortunate for two reasons. First, the insistence on the absolute equality of human speech ("Human speech is either always already speech or it is not" [2014, 170]) ignores the materiality of speech; that is, it is always a singular being in singular circumstances who speaks, which means speech is materially determined, "accented," in a certain way. Second, the signature is both singular and repeatable; because iterability belongs to the signature, it instances the mediation against which Acosta writes. In other words, by ignoring the signature—the various signatures, including that or those of Marcos—Acosta ineluctably creates a single, unified, and *unmediated* Zapatista discourse, as if the Zapatistas spoke in one voice, as if they wrote in one hand.

Yet the Zapatistas sought mediation. In the "Fifth Declaration from the Lacandon Jungle" (17 July 1998), which was not signed by Marcos but rather by the CCRI-CG del EZLN, "the absence of mediation" is understood as one of the "enemies" of dialogue and negotiation (EZLN 2003, 4:231). It declares, "Mediation in the negotiation of a conflict is unavoidable [*imprescindible*], [for] without it, it would be impossible for a dialogue between the two opposed parties to exist. When the government destroyed the National Commission of Intermediation [CONAI] with its war, it destroyed the only bridge there was for dialogue; it got rid of an important obstacle to violence and provoked the uprising of a question: national or international mediation?" (4:231–232). For the EZLN there is no possible dialogue, no possible negotiation, without mediation, without a "bridge" that spans and suspends the relation between (at least) two sides. The condition of possibility, then, for the equality of speech is its suspension: the spanning/suspending (the bridging) of singularities, of speaking beings that are cut off, separated and secret, from one another. Such bridging is one of the legacies of the Zapatista movement:

> The Zapatistas have extended a bridge [*hemos tendido un puente*] to other social and political organizations and to thousands of people without party; from everyone we have received respect and we've corresponded with everyone. Moreover, we have, together with others, extended a bridge to everyone [*tendido puentes a todo el mundo*] and we have contributed to creating . . . a large network that struggles, by peaceful means, against neoliberalism and resists, fighting for a new and better world. (4:232–233)

In fact, according to Marcos, all the Zapatista communiqués (regardless of signature) have the structure of the bridge. On 12 October 1998—the 506th anniversary of Columbus's communication between Europe and what would become known as the Americas and more than a month after the EZLN's response to the proposal for a meeting or encounter between the EZLN and the "*sociedad civil*" (see the communiqué of 7 September 1998) and during the preparations for that encounter—Marcos claims "While we are meeting, we will continue using these letters that some call 'communications' and that are no more than bridges to overcome [*salvar*: save] distances and differences" (4:246). Letters, then, are "bridges" for overcoming, "saving"—spanning and suspending, crossing over—distances and differences. But Marcos says it is not so easy to bridge differences and distances without, finally, saving differences and distances, that is, without their imposing themselves and destroying the bridge.[35]

> You read these letters [*letras*] and, with a little luck, come to understand what they say. And to you it seems easy, the letters are already there, arranged in a form that may or may not please you, but comprehensible and, in any case, the work is yours, because you have to make the letters group themselves and produce that which some call words, and get them to acquire a meaning. But don't believe it; to convoke all these letters was very difficult, to get them to be calm required whips with seven tails, threats of every kind, punishments, begging and promises. Later came the nightmare, to attempt time and time again to put together the puzzle in a way that it approximated, if only more or less, the other puzzle that we have in our head. Then, and only then, come the science and the technological development to help us and we opt then for the very efficient and efficacious mechanism that consists in making a small paper boat, painting on it a little flag with ferocious skull supported by two crossed shin bones, putting on top of it a little rubber monkey that the sea gave to me and who didn't know (the little monkey) that his future would be that of a sailor on such a fragile embarkation. (EZLN 2003, 4:247)

At stake in this letter (*carta*) or communiqué, this missive, is the necessity and fragility of mediation, of a *puente* or bridge spanning and suspending, *saving*, distances and differences. But importantly, such mediation goes all the way down: it begins with the discipline to pull together the "puzzle" (*rompecabezas*) in the head and continues in the effort to make the puzzle (the written letters that, disciplined, become recognizable by some as words) outside match the one inside. In every case there is mediation, which means a bridge or a bridging that spans/suspends/saves distance and difference. There is in every case, in every instant and instance, a sending, an embarkation that suspends, and there is drift. The bridge is also a boat (a *barquito*), which means it is cut off on both sides, adrift.[36] There is delay: "And then it follows to wait for the rain, which in these times has neither pity nor consideration, and here comes a little stream with little branches and mud and then in a little bit the little stream becomes clear and it follows to put the little paper boat in the stream in the direction of the West and downhill, and hours later . . . the little paper boat appears already destroyed in the middle of your newspaper or on your computer screen" (4:247).

If mediation goes all the way down, then not only—as *el viejo* Antonio says—is dialogue structured like a puzzle and sent off down the creek in a little boat to see where it might be taken apart, but thought, too, is like this. That is, thought is not identical to itself; it is not one or unified or hegemonic. It does not necessarily know where it is going or what it says. It has to be disciplined, and even then it can always go astray, not arrive at its destination. The Zapatistas know this. On more than one occasion they acknowledge their lack of self-understanding. On 19 November 1994, the anniversary of the formation of the EZLN, they write: "Our clumsiness has caused, more than a few times, that in place of unity and clarity, confusion is promoted and grudges and resentments, which by themselves abound among the democratizing forces in Mexico, are encouraged" (1995, 2:136). As Marcos puts it in the interview with Scherer García: "Well, at times, we don't understand ourselves either" (2003, 5:347). This is what it means to say that the bridge spans/suspends/saves distance and difference. But it also means that Acosta's dream of an unmediated human speech, a human speech, therefore, that simply is or is not, is impossible. Without mediation, without the bridge that both separates and divides, that *saves* (overcomes and preserves) distance and difference, without, therefore, constitutive delay, jet lag, there is no speech—either monological or dialogical—and therefore no democracy. But because delay is constitutive, it is also impossible that there *be* speech and democracy, that there *be* a single origin of speech and democracy. It is always too soon and too late for speech and democracy, too soon and too late to say that *there is* speech and democracy.

In every case, in every instance, a signature is a matter of style. Whether one reads every signature as "Marcos" or one refuses to read any signature as "Marcos," one effectively ignores style and the *matter* of the name. That is, in every signature, something singular remains. Whenever anyone claims "through my voice speaks the voice of the EZLN," something of the singularity of the voice remains. No doubt this explains the tension legible within the EZLN and the need, at certain moments, to silence the only "valid" voice of the Zapatistas.[37] To refuse to insist on the singularity of the signature abolishes difference in the name of an empty equality. By singling out "Marcos" and by "unmasking" him as a literary conceit, a *nom de plume*, the Zedillo administration sought to undermine both the signature and the style, which is to say, the "matter" (but not the "substance") of Marcos. The federal government effectively tells the people "Marcos" is not who you think he is: he is a fiction. In response, in a series of postscripts, Marcos plays with the federal government's (the police's) determination of his identity.

> P.S. that applauds tremendously the new "success" of the governmental police. I heard that they already discovered another Marcos and that he is Tampiqueño. That doesn't sound bad. The Port is pretty. . . .
>
> P.S. that does not abandon, despite the circumstances, its narcissism. Good, and to all that, that new *subcomandante Marcos* is he handsome? It's that lately they identify me with very ugly people and it ruins the female correspondence. (1995, 2:218)

It is clear, however, that Marcos understands that the matter of "Marcos" is nothing more, but also nothing less, than a certain style: a syntactic resistance within a hegemonic network of symbolization. In a *postdata* to a communiqué dated 28 May 1994, which was devoted to the question of his sexual orientation, he remarks, channeling Tom Joad in John Steinbeck's *The Grapes of Wrath*:

> P.S. Majority that disguises itself as intolerable minority. About all that of whether Marcos is homosexual: Marcos is gay in San Francisco, black in South Africa, Asian in Europe, Chicano in San Isidro, anarchist in Spain, Palestinian in Israel, Indian on the streets of San Cristóbal . . . informed and dissident student in neoliberalism, writer without books or readers, and, for sure, Zapatista in southeastern Mexico. In sum, Marcos is a human being, anyone, in this world. Marcos is all the untolerated, oppressed minorities who are resisting, exploding, saying, "Enough!" All the minorities at the time of speaking and the majorities at the time of being quiet and waiting. All the untolerated searching for a word, their word, which will return the majority to the eternally fragmented "us." Everything that makes power and the good consciences uncomfortable, this is Marcos. (1994, 1:243)

"Marcos" names all majorities disguised as minorities and all minorities that threaten the majority. "Marcos" is therefore the name of all who resist, of all who search for the word that will make them whole, the dream of finding the word that would put them back together again, that would, then, restore them to their unified, whole selves.

If resistance designates or determines Marcos, and, by extension, Zapatistas, and if one puts these claims in relation to Bonfil Batalla's understanding that Indians are those who, since 1492, *resist*, then Zapatista identity coincides *without remainder* with Indian identity. It is not that Zapatistas are 100 percent Indian (or almost 100 percent Indian according to their 2006 census). Rather, Indians are 100 percent Zapatistas. *Todos somos Zapatistas. Todos somos Marcos.* The failure to resist, the cessation of resistance, the decision *not* to resist, terminates or absolves Indian identity. It is impossible for an Indian *not* to resist. No Indian, then, could decide not to resist. But this interdiction of decision means, simply, that no Indian is free to decide. No Indian is free. The price of Indian identity is freedom. That's the upshot. The moment of decision *suspends* Indian identity.

It is worth remembering that the impossibility of Amerindian decision—the dead repetition of unvarying traditional forms, the lack of imagination—marks the thought of Vasconcelos, Ramos, and Paz. In their accounts, an all-too-Amerindian imitation of the past (rather than its critical inheritance) informs Mexican cultural and political stagnation. And in Paco Ignacio Taibo II's bad joke, a certain Amerindian (Aztec) curse determines Mexico's lack of democracy and its political corruption. In other words, on all accounts, whether those who seek to overcome Mexico's Indian legacy or those who believe there is no Mexico without this legacy, the Indian is incapable of decision.[38] She is not free to decide. Importantly, decision is the condition for democracy. There is no democracy where there is no possibility of decision. And there is no decision where there is no temporal disjunction, where there is no delay. The dream of a unique word to make "Marcos" (the oppressed majorities and minorities of the world, including Indian communities) whole is the dream of absolute identity and the absolution of delay, the absolution of violence. Where word and being are one, where there is no fragmentation, there is no symbolization, thus no promise, no future, no life.

SUR/RENDER

Throughout the more than two thousand pages of documents and communiqués, the Zapatistas refer to themselves as people who do not surrender. In the "Sixth Declaration from the Lacandon Jungle," they write: "And us running around and fighting, fighting and running, like our ancestors did. Without turning ourselves in, without surrendering, without being defeated" (Marcos 2006, 64). Like our ancestors did. This is the Zapatista/Indian inheritance. The legacy of not surrendering, of resistance, goes all the way back to the moment of becoming-Indian.

> They, our ancestors, taught us that a people with shame [*un pueblo con vergüenza*] are a people that do not surrender [*un pueblo que no se rinde*], that resist, which is worthy. They taught us to be proud of the color of our skin, of our language, of our culture. More than five hundred years

> of exploitation and persecution have not been able to exterminate us. We have resisted since then because history is made over our blood. The noble Mexican nation rests on our bones. If they destroy us, the entire country will fall and will begin to wander aimlessly and rootlessly. Prisoner of shadows, Mexico would deny its tomorrow denying its yesterday. (1997, 3:37)

The last sentence adheres to the inarguable logic that governs Mexican history, indeed, all history: Mexico is unrelievably haunted by the past. For Mexico there is no future without the ghost of the past. The future comes from the past, which comes from the future. The past is *before* us. This is the logic—the (dis)jointure—of inheritance and no accounting for the past will ever set it right, will ever put it behind us.

What is most interesting about the Zapatistas' claims—which were made on the 503rd anniversary of 12 October 1492—and what makes them specifically Mexican, however, is that without Columbus there would be no Indians, for the essence of Indian identity is resistance, which the Zapatistas indicate has a historical/material origin, namely, 1492. Columbus leaves the Indians behind. That is, Indians become Indians only in the wake of Columbus's arrival and the devastating effects of Spanish colonialism, because it is only in relation to "Columbus" that the essence of Indian identity forms—and can become the "roots" (*raíces*) of Mexico—around the notion of resistance. It is precisely this "indigenous essence" that the EZLN sought to demonstrate on 1 January 1994 (1995, 2:190). Because the essence of Indian identity is historically/materially determined, it must be, by definition and as a condition of its ideality, subject to the exigencies of time and space. On the one hand, insofar as it is historically determined, the essence of Indian identity is accidental, contingent; on the other hand, because its *essence* is accidental, Indian identity has no *being*, because being is not accidental but, rather, necessary.

The condition of accidentality is the difference and distance—the temporal/spatial gap or delay—between appearance and thing, between thing and word, between body (*cuerpo*) and flesh (*carne*), between matter (*hylē*) and form (*morphē*). Being-*qua*-presence, another name for "essence," demands the in-itselfness of what is, hence, the "as such." Accidentality is marked by the "as if," thus by virtuality, fiction, symbolization.

Yet despite the historical and thus empirical origin of Indian identity as resistance and nonsurrender, an origin dated to 1492, the Zapatistas nonetheless claim an absolute, thus universal, identity grounded in the absence of a single word. The lack of the word for surrender makes them whole. In the second postscript to the communiqué dated 10 June 1994, Marcos writes:

> P.S. In the committee we argued all afternoon. We looked for the word in [our] language to say "surrender" [*rendir*] and we didn't find it. It doesn't have a translation in Tzotzil or in Tzeltal, no one remembers that this word exists in Tojolabal or in Chol. They've been looking for equivalents for hours. . . . . In silence old Antonio approaches me, coughing with tuberculosis, and he whispers in my ear, "That word doesn't exist in the true language, thus ours never surrender [*nunca se rinden*] and they would rather die, because our dead order that words that don't walk shouldn't be lived." Then he goes toward the fire to scare off the cold and the fear. I recount this to Ana María; she looks at me tenderly and reminds me that old Antonio is dead.
>
> . . . Someone arrives, his hat and rifle dripping water. "There's coffee," he tells us. The committee, as is customary in these lands, takes a vote to see if they drink coffee or keep looking for the equivalent of "surrender" in the true language. Coffee wins unanimously. No one surrenders [*Nadie se rinde*]. (1994, 1:268)

This postscript follows a communiqué addressed to various national periodicals (*Proceso*, *La Jornada*, *El Financiero*) as well as to the local Chiapas newspaper (*Tiempo*). Marcos (though his voice in this instance does *not* speak the voice of the EZLN or the CCRI-CG of the EZLN) dispatches a telegram to his addressees advising them to hurry and inform numerous Amerindian communities—the *ceuístas*, workers, farmers (*campesinos*), housewives, teachers, and students, all Mexicans currently outside Mexico, but also the bankers and the "dinosaurios de Atlacomulco," and even the Mapuches of Chile—that "*the Zapatistas. Stop. ¡Do not surrender! Stop*" (1994, 1:268). The postscript affirms that Zapatista surrender is impossible. No Zapatista can say, "I surrender," without translating him- or herself out of not only the EZLN but Indian communities as well. "I surrender" cannot be said in any historical Indian language: not in Tzotzil, Tzeltal, Tojolabal, or Chol, and by extension also not in Quiché or Chontal Maya or Náhuatl, or any of the other fifty-plus indigenous languages in Mexico, which means, simply, that one cannot surrender *as* an Indian. Nor can "surrender" be said in what Old Antonio calls the "true language," the language of Indian ancestors, the language of Indianness more generally. (It is fair to ask, however, why not? If resistance and the refusal to surrender [*rendirse*] are effects of Amerindian contact with European colonization, why would languages that predate that historical, empirical moment not be able to say "surrender," which Amerindian cultures or groups clearly did when the occasion demanded before the arrival of Spaniards? There were inter-Amerindian conflicts prior to the arrival of Europeans; there were sacrifices and bloody battles; there were victors and victims and the defeated who will have surrendered.[39])

According to Marcos, then, what one inherits as the essence of Indian identity is the inability to say—and this would also mean to think—"surrender" (*me rindo, se rinde, nos rendimos*) *as an Indian*. Even so, and this is the aporia of Indian identity and perhaps of all identity in general, in order to inherit Indianness, in order to *be* Indian, that is, in order to give or render account of oneself (*rendir cuenta de sí mismo*) *as* Indian, one must surrender (*rendirse*) to that identity, to that nomination. All Indian identity takes place within the horizon of this aporia. If Indian identity depends upon not surrendering, not doing so nevertheless depends upon *rendering account* of oneself. In order to render account (*rendir cuenta*), which is also to settle accounts, one must be aware of oneself, one must realize, accomplish or achieve, recognize oneself (*darse cuenta de sí mismo*). It is impossible either to surrender or not to surrender *oneself* (*rendirse*) without giving or rendering account of oneself to oneself (*dar cuenta de sí mismo a sí mismo, rendir cuenta de sí mismo a sí mismo*). In order either to surrender or to resist, one must render account of oneself. Thus, one surrenders. It is impossible *not* to surrender. Not surrendering, we surrender.

The logic of *rendirse* and *rendir cuenta* means Indians will always already have surrendered as the condition of inheritance. Indian identity is passed on *as* a *cuenta* (an "account," but also a "bill" and thus a debt or obligation). Indianness is rendered, given, passed on, or left from one generation to the next. There is no Indian identity without the possibility of rendering account, *rendir cuenta*, thus without a certain calculation, an accounting; but there is also no Indian identity without narrative (*cuenta*), without stories (*cuentos*), hence without the possibility of fiction, of lie, subterfuge, secret, in short, deceit and deception. A certain double agency structures identity and inheritance. In accounting for ourselves, in becoming aware of ourselves, we necessarily surrender ourselves to ourselves and to others. Consequently, we (Indians, say) surrender ourselves to ourselves and others in *not* surrendering to others. We cannot *not* surrender in order to resist, and we cannot *not* resist in the very act of surrendering. In order to resist, in order *not* to surrender (*para no rendir y para no rendirse*), we must *rendir cuenta*, we must give—render—account, calculate, pass on or leave behind our "identity," that is, myths and traditions, stories and secrets. In doing so, we cannot *not* surrender (*rendirnos*); we must open ourselves to the other in order to leave (an account of) ourselves to ourselves and to others. We must appropriate and name ourselves even as we expose ourselves—through the same rendering or rendition (*rendición*)—to expropriation. In order to save ourselves and our culture, in order to preserve "our" identity, we must expose "ourselves" to the other and this means we must surrender.

Sur/rendering names the logic and structure of cultural identity and instances the impossible condition of cultural inheritance. Culture survives only insofar as it is left behind; it names the promise of passing on, passing away. For better and for worse, it is a fiction, *un cuento*, a phantasm, a figure of imagination, what the Zapatistas call the most powerful weapon, but one which nevertheless has no aim or (which is to say the same thing) always backfires.

THE PROMISE OF ZAPATISTA DEMOCRACY

The aporetic logic of sur/render—namely, the ineluctable slippage between *rendir cuenta* and *rendirse*—makes it impossible to know, with what Ramos called "an accurate intuition," one's intentions. This has implications for what the postscript to the communiqué dated 10 June 1994 (quoted above) suggests is the Zapatistas' normal democratic practice. One's interests and intentions remain secret. Thus the secret ballot of democracy is always doubly secret: one knows neither the other's intentions nor one's own. One literally knows neither *for whom* nor *for what* one votes. This is so because the "puzzle" that is one's discourse—one's words, one's vote—only ever approximates the puzzle in one's head. The one is necessarily sent off to and from the other in an always precarious boat that must be "*desarmado*," taken apart in order to be put back together. But it is an *unarmed* boat, always in jeopardy, at risk of destruction. The promise of democracy is this risk. In other words, what makes democracy possible is the structural delay or jet lag, *envío*, that promises decision, that makes it possible and also threatens it.

The Zapatistas practice what the Mexican philosopher Luis Villoro calls a "communitarian democracy" (2007, 119); that is, they "command obeying [*mandar obedeciendo*]" instead of "command commanding [*mandar mandando*]." Villoro writes: "The Zapatista movement . . . has made a permanent call to 'civil society' to establish a 'democracy with justice and dignity.' They do not push for a subversion of representative democracy, but for its full realization, in forms that attempt to eliminate the exclusion of the unequal. Through it they have succeeded in attracting the associations that represent the old Indian peoples and important sectors of national public opinion" (118–119). Previously he had remarked that "the rebellion of the Indian communities of Chiapas . . . can be interpreted . . . as a call for the recuperation of the values of the community within the breast of modern society" (1997, 373). According to Villoro, the Zapatista movement "is tied to the restoration of forms of originary life." He notes, "Before the European conquest, that political system [communitarian democracy] maintained itself in the local areas, beneath the dominant structure of the great theocratic and military states. If it is true that at the summit dominated a priest and warrior caste, on the bottom remained communities with egalitarian forms of association" (2007, 119). What Villoro means when he claims that the Zapatista movement is tied to the restoration of "originary forms of life" remains unclear, although it would seem that he thinks indigenous lifeways are more "originary" than European ones, as if time will have made no difference, and this despite the EZLN's emphasis that the very essence of Indianness will have changed on 12 October 1492. What is clear, however, is that he believes an originary and perhaps pure form of democracy was to be found in the indigenous Americas prior to the European conquest. Bonfil Batalla shares this notion but points out that, with the triple alliance's (Tenochtitlán, Texcoco, and Tlacopan) defeat of the city-state Azcatpotzalco and the increasing domination of the Mexica (Tenochtitlán), "democracy in Mexica society is lost" (1990, 114/1996, 71). In other words, if there was democracy in the Americas (and no doubt there was democracy or the trace of democracy in the Americas) prior to contact, it was not pure. Democracy is never pure. Aristotle himself called democracy a perversion (*Politics* 1279b5–6). It is always a question of the more or less democratic, and it will never be possible to decide whether one form of democracy is more or less democratic than another.

Despite this, and despite his recognition that cultural and political domination was not absent from the precolonial Americas, Bonfil Batalla nonetheless thinks that a return to Indian democracy—a return, then, to the lifeways of the *México profundo*—would be to find "the path to a better future" (1990, 17/1996, xxi).[40] He claims this would be "not the formal, docile, and awkwardly traced democracy of the West, but a real democracy derived from our history and responding to the rich and varied composition of Mexican society" (15/xix). Bonfil Batalla is not the only one to think so. In Indian "communitarian democracy" Luis Villoro recognizes "an ideal of association" in which "ultimate power resides in the assembly, in which all adult men participate equally" (2007, 119). Moreover, he argues that "in the contemporary Zapatista movement the ancestral division is rectified and the equal participation of women is guaranteed" (119). Villoro signals the similarity between the traditional indigenous forms of democracy in the precolonial Americas and those that appeared in precolonial Africa, which, citing Kwasi Wiredu, he calls "consensual democracy" (120).[41]

Villoro's description of noncolonial democracy, however, absolves democracy of calculation:

> Consensual democracy is based in reasoned dialogue that takes place between all the members of the community. In place of the imposition of a quantifiable majority, the dialogue always comes close to a reasoned consensus. No decision is taken without a collective agreement. The elders of the tribe receive from the community their orders and, following the agreements, annul disputes. In the final decisions everyone has participated; no one is excluded from being heard. Everyone remains equally obligated to community tasks. The consensus manifests the solidarity of everyone. (2007, 120)

On Villoro's account, consensual or communitarian democracy grounds itself in an inclusivity that forecloses the necessity of calculation. In such democracy no one counts; that is, communitarian democracy does not render account (*rendir cuenta*) for two reasons. First, there is no reason for calculation because such democracy is absolutely inclusive and "always comes close to a reasoned consensus." According to Villoro, the four principles of communitarian democracy "avoid exclusion" (121). Second, there is no need for calculation because consensual or communitarian democracy is reciprocal. Villoro writes: "It doesn't want power for itself, but for everyone. 'Everything for everyone, nothing for us' is its slogan. It proposes to advance toward a new society, where the values of the community are freely assumed. It would be an association where fraternal cooperation, based in reciprocal service, would be the common goal; an association where power would be controlled by the community; where all authority 'orders obeying'" (1997, 374).

"To order obeying [*mandar obedeciendo*]," which is the minimal definition of Zapatista democracy, suggests the possibility—excluded in Aristotle—that one can rule or order and obey simultaneously and thus absolve the distinction or difference between sovereign and subject, between sovereignty and subjection. In other words, this conception of democracy would ostensibly have no need for mediation, for translation, or for the bridge (*puente*) and boat (*barquito*) that *saves*—both overcomes and preserves—difference and distance. The Zapatistas believe that "true" democracy, or the full realization of democracy, is not concerned with taking or occupying power; that such democracy does not actualize power. In the "Fourth Declaration from the Lacandon Jungle," dated 1 January 1996, the Zapatistas affirm, "We want not power but democracy, freedom, and justice for ourselves and our children" (EZLN 1997, 3:87). Further, they remark that the EZLN instances "a political force that does not struggle to take political power" but instead seeks "the democracy in which the one who orders, orders obeying [Una fuerza política que no luche por la toma del poder político sino por la democracia de que el que mande, mande obedeciendo]" (3:88). Indeed, they assert, "there is no place for us in the world of power" (3:81). In a communiqué dated 29 August 1996, in which they reject the help and support of the Revolutionary Popular Army (EPR), Marcos writes: "You struggle for power. We for democracy, freedom, and justice. It is not the same thing. Even if you are successful and conquer power, we will keep struggling for democracy, freedom, and justice. It doesn't matter who is in power, the Zapatistas are and will continue fighting for democracy, freedom, and justice" (3:369). The Zapatistas explicitly oppose a power that could be possessed, occupied. They oppose a power that *is*, that is thought to *be* substantial. They fight against the powers that *be* and thus against a given or present power, a power that can be taken. Earlier in the same text, Marcos rejects the EPR's support in the name of everyone who supports and who forms part of the EZLN; he accuses the EPR of wanting to "take power" (*tomar el poder*) and explains, "What we are looking for, what we need and want, is that all the people without party or organization can come to agreement about what they do not want and what they want and organize themselves to obtain it . . . not in order to take power but in order to exercise it" (3:367). The Zapatistas have never been against sovereignty, which is to say, against the exercise of power. Rather, they oppose the substantialization of power in and through the state form (i.e., its party system and investment in the figure of the president), but they do not dissent or subtract themselves from the nation, not least because they conceive their desired autonomy—which is precisely to claim a certain sovereignty—not as a way to separate from the nation but as a means to integrate Mexico's indigenous population into it in a meaningful (representative) way. Further, they sought to preserve (as the second epigraph to this chapter shows) the symbols of the Mexican nation. The Zapatistas seek a State of Revolution, which is already heralded and guaranteed by Article 39 of the Mexican constitution, which states, simply, "National sovereignty is bestowed essentially and originally upon the people. Every public power derives from the people and is instituted for their benefit. The people possess, at all times, the inalienable right to alter or change their form of government." This is what, in the "Second Declaration from the Lacandon Jungle" (12 June 1994), they call not a new world but merely "the waiting room of the new Mexico" (1994, 1:273).

Yet insofar as the Zapatistas seek to exercise power, even if only to "institute" a State of Revolution that would continuously ruin itself,[42] they necessarily require sovereignty, that is, the possibility of acting, of deciding, of ordering and obeying. Only a sovereign being can decide to obey. And sovereignty is by definition exceptional, thus beyond the law that would demand obedience to it. And, at the same time, this sovereignty is conditioned by the future that it cannot know, the future that ruins every decision in advance. This is the tension that the Zapatistas cannot resolve; it is the tension ignored by those who find in "the waiting room of the new Mexico" no room for sovereignty. They find in the absolute coincidence of ordering and obeying (*mandar obedeciendo*) an idealized and absolute reciprocity, one that abolishes the "in turn" and thus the *alternation* (and with it the delay or jet lag) of power outlined in Aristotle's understanding of democracy. The new Mexico would be the place of an absolutely reciprocal democracy, where ordering is obeying and obeying is ordering. In this waiting room, on this side of the door to the new Mexico, there will be no mediation, no translation or transition, no bridge, saving (thus overcoming and preserving) the distance and the difference between sovereign and subject.

Reciprocity, then, is a key tenet of Indian or Zapatista democracy, invoked as much by Villoro as by Bonfil Batalla and the Zapatistas themselves. Nevertheless, the promise of reciprocity necessarily entails the threat of its failure. An absolutely guaranteed reciprocation is possible only noumenally, Kant would say, unconditional and abstracted from the conditions of space and time.[43] But such abstraction in fact obviates the need for reciprocity in the first place. Reciprocation is by definition conditioned, conditional. In any reciprocal relation one party must always perform before the other. Reciprocity implies alternation, which itself requires delay. As a consequence, there is always the chance—the possibility of reciprocity depends upon it—that the other will *not* reciprocate. There is no reciprocity without this threat. Hence, it is necessary in every reciprocal relation that an account be kept. There is always a *cuenta*. Bonfil Batalla recognized as much: "Cooperation is always based on reciprocity—today for you, tomorrow for me. In many cases each person keeps an exact record [*una cuenta exacta*] of what he has given to other members of the lineage and what he in turn has received from each of them" (1990, 60/1996, 30). Structurally, the logic of reciprocation is no different from contract or promissory theories of community. It is the temporal interval—delay, jet lag, disjunction—that makes reciprocity necessary and possible, but that interval also threatens it. For this reason, one keeps accounts, one keeps count. Democracy—even communitarian democracy—*counts*. There is no democracy without counting and accounting, without rendering accounts, without calculation. Consequently, there is no democracy that does not sur/render democracy.

POSTSCRIPT

Fear of Democracy

On Saturday, 31 July 1999, in Mexicali, Baja California, Mexico, Paulina was raped and impregnated by a heroin addict with a lengthy record of incarceration, Julio César Cedeño Márquez. At the time, all thirty-one states in Mexico permitted the legal termination of pregnancies resulting from rape. Paulina pursued this option, strictly adhering to the procedures established by the state, but she would never have the abortion. She would carry the unwanted child to term, give birth to him, and name him Isaac. Another Isaac, another crucible of faith; Mexico, another Mount Moriah. Paulina, a mother at fourteen to a child she did not want, forced upon her by a man she did not choose. And there is not just one Paulina. Poniatowska insists on this:

> Not only is Mexicali, Mexico, full of Paulinas. Ramón Esteban Jiménez, director of the Clinic for the Care and Prevention of Violence at UNAM, declares that 90 percent of the victims of intrafamilial violence are women. Generally it is the father who attacks the wife and the children. Ruth González Serratos, director of the Program for the Integral Care for Victims and Survivors of Sexual Aggression in the School of Psychology at

> UNAM, declared: "It is a prerogative of all men to use women for their service, for their pleasure. It is a system of roles perfectly organized in the law, school, religion, the media, that is, there is always a situation of power over woman, of conquest, where submission and service in every sense is expected of women." (2007, 65–66)

Paulina, then, stands for all Mexican women; her wound is every woman's wound, as if women marked the border between men, the border that is "an immense wound that has no cure" (26).

Why did Paulina not abort the unwanted fetus? Despite living in a democracy in which a woman's right to an abortion in the case of rape is constitutionally protected, Paulina was unable to secure the services of medical staff at a state-operated hospital. Doctors refused to perform the abortion, and the state attorney general not only refused to insist that they do so but also applied pressure on Paulina and her mother, María Elena, in an attempt to force them to desist in their efforts to compel the state to honor its own law protecting women. For nearly two months they persevered in the demand for justice in the form of a legal abortion. They bore the pressure of the medical staff, of the clergy, of the state attorney general's office, of anti-abortion advocates who violated her privacy by entering her hospital room uninvited and offering her unsolicited advice and information. Only when María Elena was misled to believe that an abortion was more dangerous for Paulina than her pregnancy did she give up her pursuit of a legally sanctioned, authorized abortion for her daughter.

The medical staff refused to perform the operation despite its legality and despite an order from the Public Ministry authorizing it, claiming, simply, that if it were a matter of law, then the ministry should perform the operation rather than involve the Hospital General de Mexicali: "Why does the General Hospital of Mexicali have to resolve these cases for the Public Ministry? The Public Ministry is supposed to help its constituents in private hospitals" (44). In short, the state-run hospital refused to fulfill state law, suggesting instead that the Public Ministry pay private hospitals to resolve such cases.

State Attorney General Juan Manuel Salazar Pimentel called Paulina and her mother into his office and, according to María Elena, told her, "But, madam, this is a crime because it is already a living being" (57). María Elena disagrees with Salazar Pimentel, claiming that the fetus is not yet a "criatura" but agrees that "it is already beginning to live" (57), which is why they must interrupt the pregnancy without further delay. Salazar Pimentel asks her to take more time to think it over, saying, "Think about it, madam; this is a crime" (58). María Elena responds, "It is already decided and I don't have anything to think about. I want this to be done." Salazar Pimentel then asks, "Madam, are you a Catholic?" (57). The attorney general of a secular state asks the mother of a child pregnant via rape about her religious affiliation. He accuses her of suborning a crime if she persists in seeking an abortion for her pregnant daughter, despite his knowing that her pregnancy results from a violent crime.

In a gesture that ought to have been illegal and unthinkable for a government official of a secular state, Salazar Pimentel explains that he wants to take María Elena and Paulina to see a priest, who first asks María Elena to explain what happened and then tells her, when she asserts her daughter's right to an abortion, "It is a crime. Think about it, madam, because it is a murder" (58). It is a crime, a murder, to have an abortion the state itself sanctions and the right to which the constitution of Baja California guarantees to every woman whose pregnancy is the result of rape or incest.

What does it mean for an attorney general of a secular state and a priest to tell a girl and her mother that a constitutionally protected right to an abortion is a crime, a murder? What is murder? But also, and no less important, what is the law when a constitutionally protected right—according to the attorney general charged to protect such rights—is called a crime, a murder? A right by any other name is a crime. And when this law results from a democratic process? How to think about the relation between rights, crimes, and democracy? According to Poniatowska, Isabel Vericat, an attorney who works for the Grupo de Información en Reproducción Elegida (GIRE) in Mexico City, "insists on the urgency of finding much more efficient and expeditious mechanisms for fulfilling the law. The law is not enough. Paulina's case demonstrates that. While Provida [an anti-abortion group] and the Catholic Church (or whomever) argue in defense of life, they conveniently leave the responsibility for the maintenance of the baby to Paulina and her family. The defense of life is pure fiction, it's a bluff, hypocrisy" (2007, 55).

There are two issues. The first is a question of the laws that protect a woman's right to an abortion in the case of rape and their right to privacy—in short, the laws that ought to protect women from the unwanted results of two different violent crimes: the violation of their bodies and of their privacy. The second issue concerns the responsibility for the maintenance of children who are the undesired products of rape. To be sure, groups like Provida and the Catholic Church argue against abortion (thus arguing in favor of a *certain* life), but they also refuse the financial responsibility for the children who result from rape. They are hypocrites. "Pro-life" becomes another name for abuse, for the violation of women whose lives are irreparably altered, who often suffer a form of social death. However, the law—as law—is not enough.

The law, in principle, asserts women's right to an abortion in the case of rape. Even if one thinks the law ought to be broader, protecting all women's right to an abortion in every case, regardless of the circumstances, what is lacking is not the law. What is lacking is justice.

While in the broadest sense it is unjust that private organizations like Provida and the Catholic Church argue in favor of life yet do nothing to support the life they seek to save, often consigning the living being whose "life" they "save" to misery, a democratic state cannot constrain private organizations (like Provida and the Catholic Church) to pay for their right to free speech. Like any other organization, Provida and the Catholic Church ought to have the right to speak freely without having to bear the cost of the lives they seek to bring into the world. While it may be *unjust* not to bear those costs, it cannot be *illegal* not to do so. At the same time, however, Poniatowska sees abortion as a problem rather than as a solution: "Like many feminists, I'm not in favor of abortion" (9). But her suggested solution to the problem of abortion is itself unjust.[1] "If the Mexican State were to say, like in Brazil, that the children resulting from violation enjoyed a minimum salary until twenty-one years of age, it would be magnificent and it would disable the petition to legalize abortion, but as this has not happened, for thousands of children life is a bad dream" (60).

Economic support for the children of rape may well be "magnificent," but it does not obviate the need for the legalization of abortion in cases of rape or in any other case. In effect, by denying the right to abortion the state consigns the mother to carry to term and give birth to a foreign invader that is itself, and not only for the nine months of pregnancy, the trace and thus the reminder, the remainder, of her violation. There's no justice in this. Abortion does not simply solve the problem of the population of unwanted children, for whom life may be, as Poniatowska suggests, "a bad dream"; rather, abortion also saves mothers from unwanted physical changes and long-term, if not permanent, disruptions to and violations of their lives. Moreover, it is hard to imagine that a nine-month pregnancy followed by the experience of giving birth to a child resulting from rape could possibly facilitate the mother's recovery from the trauma of her violation. Or, as Poniatowska asks, "Is Paulina the child only an apparatus for reproduction? Does Paulina not have a right to pleasure, rather than only to violence?" (73).

Even if it is necessary to recognize the state's biopolitical interest in protecting (certain) lives—and thus the state's competing interest in the woman's body, which interest has resulted in restricting abortions following the first trimester—a woman's right to abortion ought (at the very least) to be absolute within the first trimester. Yet importantly, and not only in

Poniatowska's *La herida de Paulina*, decisions concerning abortions and the state's interest in life turn not only on the question of life but also on the threshold of personhood. As Poniatowska herself remarks:

> I'm petrified. If I myself, already living and fishtailing, have never known when my life started to be my life, if I truly did what I wanted to do, how am I going to know when the life of an embryo begins? If I don't even know what the soul is and I confuse it with spirit, brain, consciousness and psyche (Indians don't have a soul, according to the statement of the University of Salamanca; we weren't rational people, according to the conquerors), what am I going to do faced with a similar dilemma? Marta Lamas . . . told me once that the embryo does not have neurological development in the first trimester. This only occurs after the fourth month. Thus, an abortion performed in the first three months means removing a tissue that neither feels nor suffers. (73)

Does neurological development—sensitivity to pain—mark the beginning of life? Or does life exist from conception? Poniatowska quotes Mexican philosopher Luis Villoro, who observes: "There is no sure criterion, grounded in science, to determine when a human person begins to exist" (2007, 73). The beginning of life and the beginning of the human person, however, are different issues. According to Poniatowska, at the time she wrote *La herida de Paulina* Article 329 of the Penal Code of the Federal District (Mexico City) stipulated that "abortion is the death of the product of conception in any moment of pregnancy" (2007, 73–74).

To be sure, things have changed. The Federal District is the only governmental body in Mexico to decriminalize voluntary abortions performed within the first trimester. The thirty-one Mexican states continue to interdict and criminalize a woman's access to legal abortion services at any time (with certain exceptions, one of which concerns the case of pregnancies that result from rape). Indeed, GIRE calculates that from 2009–2011 some 679 women were reported or sentenced for the "crime" of abortion.[2] The discrepancy between the state constitutions and the constitution that governs the Federal District is legible in the tension that results from the federal constitution's explicit protection of human rights and its respect for international law, both of which consider women under the aegis of reproductive subjects. The laws of thirty-one Mexican states, however, consider them criminals.

How to think of the limit between two laws of abortion: one that protects the right to an abortion in the case of pregnancy resulting from rape, the other that interdicts any abortion whatsoever? How to protect as a right according to one constitution an act that, according to another constitution, constitutes murder? And yet in not protecting that right, the state effectively sanctions the abuse and violation of women, effectively saying that a woman's body is not hers under any circumstance. Only thirteen of Mexico's thirty-one states permit abortion in cases in which the mother's life is in jeopardy. A woman's body is not her own because it shelters another life, that of a fetus, which despite being unborn has (state) constitutional rights from the moment of conception in more than half of the Mexican states (since 2012), including Baja California (since 2008). Consequently, the life of the fetus is worth more than that of the woman who bears that life. How to calculate the value of these two "lives," as if the one were the same as the other, as if that of the one who is not born is worth more than that of the one who carries it? How to calculate the effects of the denial of the right to choose, which is neither more nor less than the right and the duty to give account?

But this is not the tyranny of the unborn. It is the democratic tyranny of men over the right of women to their bodies. We are back at the problematic schematized by Sergio González Rodríguez as "body/person of . . . ," where all the violence of the world turns on how we read the slash (/) and the possessive (*de*, of). Whose body? Whose person? Is it possible to be a person without the right to decide about one's body? *La herida de Paulina* describes one more instance of the trafficking of women—of their bodies, as if women were counted only as bodies—between men. It is the democratic tyranny of class and sex. Poniatowska asks, "About what democracy are we speaking, if Mexican women, according to their social class and the state in which they live, have different access to public health?" (107). Furthermore, she notes that the poor—and particularly poor women, poor girls—have less access to information and knowledge. This, too, is a problem of democracy. But it will not do to say this is not democracy or that it is the perversion of democracy, as if there were a pure democracy, one that had already solved the problem of equality and freedom. Democracy has never been anything but this perversion. On Aristotle's account, for instance, democracy is the perversion of timocracy, in which the ruling class is constituted of property owners. The perversion that is democracy allows for the greatest participation in that it instances rule by the people (or citizens) without further criteria for exclusion. It was precisely this perversion—that it includes too many—that made Aristotle nervous and led him to limit the nefarious effects of the "too many," that is, of the *demos*. The perversion of democracy, however, makes the concern in Mexico for a more authentic or genuine form of democracy both troubling (how to make what is defined as a perversion "pure"?) and symptomatic (because the same concern is legible everywhere there is democracy).

Three short books by major Mexican thinkers mark the *alternancia*, or transitional years from the PRI to the PAN (and subsequently back to the PRI in 2012). In Héctor Aguilar Camín and Jorge Castañeda's *Un futuro para México* (2009), Guillermo Hurtado's *México sin sentido* (2011), and Roger Bartra's *La sombra del futuro: Reflexiones sobre la transición mexicana* (2012) everything turns on a democratic renewal of politics or a renewal of democracy that frees Mexico for a future that is not a prisoner to the past.

This is explicitly Aguilar Camín's and Castañeda's concern at the outset of *Un futuro para México*: "Mexico is prisoner to its history. Inherited ideas, sentiments, and interests impede it from moving rapidly to the place its citizens long for. The history accumulated in the head and in the sentiments of the nation—in its laws, in its institutions, in its customs and fantasies—obstructs its road to the future" (13). We have heard this before: it was Vasconcelos's and Ramos's complaints about indigenous culture. The revolution was meant to change all that, but in the early twenty-first century, Mexico remains indentured to its past. The revolution, the institutionalized revolution, has become indigenous; Mexican culture is enslaved to the past, dead. On Aguilar Camín and Castañeda's account, Mexico has lost its way, its step, and with it, its sense or meaning, its rhythm or tone: "Mexico has lost its way: it walks slowly, above all in the presidential palace. It seems a country of weak institutions, unclear in its international identity: a sleeping giant that suddenly stirs without being able to move. Countries, like persons, need an identity and purpose, a desirable destination: future music. Mexico has lost the tone of the revolution that gave it symbolic meaning and national cohesion for decades" (14–15).

This is not nostalgia for the PRI; rather, Aguilar Camín and Castañeda share with Guillermo Hurtado the understanding that Mexico needs a common "sense" (*sentido*) to unify the country, to give it direction and purpose. Hurtado writes, "Mexico's crisis cannot be reduced to the set of its grave political, social, or economic problems—like poverty, ignorance, violence, and the destruction of the environment. Underlying those problems, our crisis has a dimension perhaps more profound and disturbing. Put simply, we have lost the sense of our collective existence" (2011, 13).

What does it mean that Mexicans have lost the sense (both meaning and direction) of their collective existence? "When I sustain that we have lost the sense of our collective existence, what I mean is that we have lost cohesion, direction and confidence. When a collectivity lacks sense, it has lost its reason for being, it has forgotten what it ought to respect, [and] it has lost its direction" (13–14). Hurtado understands, however, that it would be easy enough to object: "To suppose that there can be a collective sense of the existence of Mexicans is to fall into the same error as the philosophers of *lo mexicano* who looked for the essence of the Mexican" (17). We know who these philosophers and critics were: Ramos, Zea, Uranga, Paz. Hurtado, however, has something else in mind: "My response is that the collective sense about which I speak is not a specific attribute of each of the members of a collective taken as a unitary whole, but rather an *integrative function that affects the orientation of the practices of the majority of the members of said collectivity*" (17). Collective sense or collective meaning grounds democracy insofar as it informs and impacts the way the majority acts. And yet it also depends on the sense of democracy, because the collective sense, although it determines how the majority acts, is collective only insofar as the majority acts in a certain way. Consequently, the collective sense depends upon the democracy (the acts of the majority) that it informs.

On the one hand, then, Mexico needs a collective sense of itself to establish a majority that acts cohesively and democratically; on the other hand, Mexico needs democracy in order to establish the collective sense that makes it cohesive. The one comes before the other that comes before the other. For example, according to Hurtado, Mexico's democracy is fragile and its fragility depends at least in part on its lack of an integrative vision:

> Another factor that has to be taken into account is the crisis of Mexico's tender democracy. The defects of our democracy are well known. One of them is that it is an electoral democracy and, therefore, its gaze is short-term. Another defect is that the Mexican democracy lacks an integrative vision; the struggle between parties fragments it completely into a cacophony of disconnected proposals. . . . It shouldn't surprise us that a democracy like ours is incapable of solving the big national problems, like violence or poverty, which require, in order to be approached efficaciously, a long-term national project, a higher vision, and, above all, the participation of the right people for solving them. (22–23)

Hurtado ranks the weakness of Mexico's democracy with two other major problems troubling Mexico's future: first, fear stemming from rampant violence and criminal impunity; and second, "economic stagnation [*estancamiento económico*]" (21), that is, poverty, unemployment, and inequality.

Clearly "the failure of democracy" (21), specifically its shortsightedness and unpredictability, is the most serious concern, not least because it conditions Mexico's failure to solve the other two problems.

It should be easy to see the problem. On the one hand, Hurtado signals the need for a stronger democracy; on the other hand, he is reluctant to invest too heavily in the vote. What democracy, worthy of the name, is not electoral? And what electoral democracy does not suffer from a sort of structural shortsightedness resulting from the necessity of elections that occur often enough for the electorate—the "people"—to retain and to exercise its sovereignty? In other words, the strength of democracy is its fragility. There is no democracy without elections, without some form of alternation decided by the "people." This is democracy's strength. But elections are also democracy's weakness in that they are subject to suspension, to fraud, but also to the "people" who vote and do not vote.

How to guarantee, then, that the people capable of solving—or even of articulating—the problems facing a nation will participate in a government committed to recognizing and solving those problems? In democracy there can be no such guarantee. Rather, those who are elected and those the elected appoint determine—often according to the implied interests of the majority that elected them, but not always—what problems face the nation and who the appropriate people are to solve them. According to Hurtado, the action of this majority—the problems it articulates and the solutions it seeks—is informed by the collective sense of the nation. Yet the collective sense of the nation is nothing more and nothing less than the action of the majority, which defines the success and failure of every democracy, thus, of democracy as a form of government. Consequently, the collective sense is both the chance and the threat of democracy. It is the promise of democracy.

We know that in 2012, after twelve years of administration by the Partido Acción Nacional (PAN), the PRI returned to the presidency. We know that Roger Bartra, in *La sombra del futuro*, thought the return of the PRI would indicate the failure of Mexican democracy. In January 2012 he wrote, "I wonder if the rise of the PRI is not the strange syndrome of abstinence in a society that requires a dose of the old drug that kept it calm. It would be the symptom of a society full of fear that, as I see it, resists abandoning the old political culture, resists renouncing deeply ingrained habits" (78). An addict in withdrawal, Mexico needs a fix. But the fix will already have left it in ruins: "Thanks to the culture of corruption that they were fed by the PRI for many years, today many people distrust all politicians and all elections" (78). There is no democracy without the fear of elections. Such fear was lacking in Mexico for the better part of the twentieth century because the outcome of elections was largely known in advance, but "in those places in which the PRI has been broken, and where therefore it has lost elections, ruptures of democratic civic culture appear" (75). Yet, despite such democratization, Bartra agrees with Hurtado that Mexico's democratic culture is fragile:

> I would say that we are faced with a precarious and fragmented democratic culture. It has not impetuously expanded a new civility that obliges the political parties to adopt a behavior that is tolerant and responsible. It has not developed with sufficient vigor a culture of dignity or a democratic pride. In contrast, the enormous weight of the old authoritarian political culture, which is profoundly inscribed in Mexican society, still oppresses us. It is the rancid culture of the PRI that, although it has retreated in many areas, has extended outside the party that feeds it and has invaded the PAN, the PRD and the political elites. (64)

The fear of democracy is provoked by the failure to consolidate a stronger, more vigorous culture of democracy capable of supplanting the remnants of the authoritarian culture sown by the PRI during some seventy years of rule. Hurtado, for instance, insists that "the idea of democracy that I defend is one form of life-in-common based on a certain kind of values and ideals" (2011, 10); further, he argues that "in order to achieve this form of life, we have to undertake a new transition that carries the practices and values of democracy to all the corners of our public space" (10). If this does not happen, "if our young democracy does not advance," Hurtado avers, "there exists the real danger that it will retreat" (33). Such an advance will require, he claims, "a profound moral reform of society" (11). As a consequence, he argues, what is necessary is not only "a philosophy *of* democracy" but also "a philosophy *for* democracy whose space of action would be the educational system" (11). This is so because "in order to form the future citizens of the democracy that we want, education [*la escuela*] has to offer them a horizon of reasons, values, and ideals, and this is work that philosophy can realize in an optimal way" (11). To be sure, no institution is more important to the vitality of democracy than universally accessible education. At the same time, however, democracy cannot wait for the formation of those "future citizens of the democracy we want," whatever these citizens and this democracy—thus this future—may appear (to us) to be. We cannot put off democracy in the name of the future, not least because democracy is constitutively open to the future, to the undetermined and undeterminable *à-venir*. For this reason, democracy cannot be put off in the name of a future we believe we can see coming. Democracy instances the *here and now* of the future, its irruptive force.

Because democracy is an irruptive force, it cannot be limited to its austere definition as a form of government; but neither can it be limited, as Hurtado suggests, to its substantive definition as "a form of life in community" (37; see also 40). Democracy as a form of life-in-common is what Hurtado calls "more democracy" rather than less democracy. To make this "more" democracy effective or operative, Hurtado calls for the reform of Mexican morals, but he makes clear that "morals" does not refer to the private lives of Mexicans but rather to their public practices or "*costumbres*" (habits, customs). In other words, for Hurtado democracy as a form of government is limited to electoral politics, that is, to the vote and a certain calculus, whereas democracy as a form of life-in-common is more than this in that it requires a moral reform that would "take us from a conception of morality as something imposed, something suffered, to another in which morality is seen as part of the fiber that forms our person and grants us dignity" (46). Hurtado treads the ground Kant walked in *The Metaphysics of Morals*, in which Kant separates the doctrine of right, which entails the public reform of morals (the practices that the law—or an external power—can limit and punish) from the doctrine of ethics (the inner realm of freedom and dignity, which no external power can control, for which there can be no positive law but rather only the moral law). Hurtado seeks to make right derive from ethics. Rather than seeing our customs (or morals) as being imposed upon us, as something we suffer passively, Hurtado wants us to understand them as stemming from the "fiber" (*fibra*) that shapes our person (*persona*, and what perhaps he calls citizenship, *ciudadanía*) and grants us dignity. What is dignity? And what is the "fiber" that both shapes our "person" and grants us dignity?

According to Scott Cutler Shershow, since the term's introduction in the West by Panaetius of Rhodes in the second century BCE, dignity has referred *both* to the unconditional essence *and* to a conditional effect of human being (2014, 53–84) On the one hand, as Kant makes clear in *The Metaphysics of Morals*, dignity, *qua* the essence of the human being, names that which is immanent to the human being and beyond any possible—that is, calculable—value. Dignity's absolute value means, simply, that it is without what Kant calls "market price." Hence, it is incalculable. On the other hand, dignity refers to decorum and to decoration, thus to a certain appearance or seeming, a certain artifice, a certain standing or rank. Dignity in this sense is necessarily economical. It has a relative value. Hence it is calculable. It is important to note that these two notions of dignity are not simply opposed to one another. They are, rather, heterogeneous yet indissociable in that they derive from the same "fiber," namely, freedom. Freedom instances the essence of the human being; yet such freedom, which is beyond all economization, essentially manifests itself as the possibility of deception. Consequently, the dignity of man is, precisely, his dishonor, his immorality; the truth of man is his capacity to lie, to deceive. The absolute value of the human being is that which destroys all value by corrupting it, by making it worthless.

If the essence of the human being cannot be disentangled from the artifice of the human being, what does it mean, finally, to call for a more genuine, stronger, more vigorous democracy—not as a form of government but as a form of shared life that would depend upon and also inculcate a culture of dignity? If unconditional and incalculable dignity is at bottom entangled with conditional and calculable dignity, how to think a democracy, *qua* irruptive force of freedom, as "genuine," that is, as not constitutively marked by calculation, ruse, deception? How to distinguish democracy as a form of life from democracy as a form of government? How to think democracy before or beyond the count if calculation is inextricably intertwined with incalculability? How to think an unconditional form of democracy (*qua* form of life) that is not always subject to the conditions of democracy (*qua* form of government)—thus to fraud, deception, deceit, subterfuge, artifice, in a word, representation. How, then, to make a calculation—even of one's own intention—that is not always necessarily a miscalculation?

How are we to know, for instance, that in educating ourselves and our children for the democracy and the future we want to have, that we are not, in fact, deceiving ourselves and our children, thereby closing off the future for all of us? How do we know that the culture of dignity we aspire to form is not, at the same time, a culture of deception? How could this not be the case? In other words, is a better, more vigorous, stronger democracy not also and always a worse, more moribund, weaker democracy? This is the promise—the chance and the threat—of democracy. This promise provokes the fear of democracy. It is this promise that will have made it possible, during the *alternancia*—that is, during the time of *more* democracy in Mexico—that women's right to abortion would be more restricted and that women who sought or performed abortions would be more frequently prosecuted. Because a stronger democracy, one that ought to protect the autonomy, the freedom, of all citizens, cannot be divorced from calculation and necessarily runs the risk of denying certain classes of persons their rights and protections. In rendering itself *more* democratic, Mexico cannot not surrender itself to calculation, thus to exclusion. Consequently, it becomes *less* democratic and the violations that ensue too often target women and minorities.

Although the violence of the name is constitutive, irreducible, the violation that follows is not ineluctable, inevitable, which is why it is necessary to remain vigilant, to track the play of nomination, to bear witness to its implications, for better and for worse. The autoimmunity of the name, its constitutive violence, means there is no silver bullet that protects bodies and persons without always at the same time threatening to harm them. There is no guarantee that democracy—whether more or less democracy, communitarian or republican, indigenous or European, or any other ostensibly emancipatory political form—will be able to protect us once and for all against violence and violation. On the contrary, in every case and at every turn, we must testify against violence, against violation; we must render account even if it means surrendering to the violence of the name in order to protect ourselves from violation in the name of democracy, in the name of community, in the name of culture. We must recognize that more democracy can be less democracy and less democracy can be more democracy (and we can do so only insofar as we name what comes both in order to protect its coming and in order to protect ourselves from its potentially unwanted arrival). This is what is at stake in any *account* of a democracy that *counts*. And democracy counts. Yet because democracy depends upon a calculus that takes place always and only *in the name of* democracy, in the name, then, of that which is not, of that which is always both too much and too little, too strong and too weak, which comes both too soon and too late, democracy remains incalculable. It will only ever be *as if* there was democracy. This is its chance and its threat, its promise: the incalculable calculation of democracy—the count that can only ever be an account (*cuenta*), a story (*cuento*), a fiction—that inscribes the name of justice in the violence of injustice.

NOTES

INTRODUCTION

1. Whenever possible I cite the page number references for both the original text and its English translation. In such cases the first parenthetical reference is to the original, the second to the translation. Where there is only the page reference to the original, the translation is my own.
2. These are the names: Abel García Hernández, Abelardo Vázquez Peniten, Adán Abrajan de la Cruz, Alexander Mora Venancio, Antonio Santana Maestro, Benjamín Ascencio Bautista, Bernardo Flores Alcaráz, Carlos Iván Ramírez Villarreal, Carlos Lorenzo Hernández Muñoz, César Manuel González Hernández, Christian Alfonso, Rodríguez Telumbre, Christian Tomás Colón Garnica, Cutberto Ortiz Ramos, Doriam González Parral, Emiliano Alen Gaspar de la Cruz, Everardo Rodríguez Bello, Felipe Arnulfo Rosa, Giovanni Galindes Guerrero, Israel Caballero Sánchez, Israel Jacinto Lugardo, Jesús Jovany Rodríguez Tlatempa, Jonás Trujillo Gonzáles, Jorge Álvarez Nava, Jorge Aníbal Cruz Mendoza, Jorge Antonio Tizapa Legideño, Jorge Luis González Parral, José Ángel Campos Cantor, José Ángel Navarrete González, José Eduardo Bartolo Tlatempa, José Luis Luna Torres, Joshivani Guerrero de la Cruz, Julio César López Patolzín, Leonel Castro Abarca, Luis Ángel Abarca Carrillo, Luis Ángel Francisco Arzola, Magdaleno Rubén Lauro Villegas, Marcial Pablo Baranda,

Marco Antonio Gómez Molina, Martín Getsemany Sánchez García, Mauricio Ortega Valerio, Miguel Ángel Hernández Martínez, Miguel Ángel Mendoza Zacarías, Saúl Bruno García.

3. For another account of the disappearing of the forty-three students, one that is both intelligent and perhaps exaggerated in its desire to read in the "event" of Ayotzinapa the end of the state, see Dove 2014. In the rise of narcoviolence Dove reads the withdrawal or retreat of the modern form of state sovereignty, and he sees the traces of this withdrawal in the tortured, mutilated, murdered/executed bodies strewn and hung all over Mexico. No doubt he is correct, but it is worth remembering that tortured, mutilated, murdered/executed bodies have always *also* been the sign of state sovereignty.

4. It is worth noting the difference between what is at stake in this work and in Sergio Villalobos-Ruminott's *Soberanías en suspenso: Imaginación y violencia en América Latina* (Sovereinties in suspense: imagination and violence in Latin America), a difference that hinges on the problem of language and "propriation." Villalobos-Ruminott argues, "Beyond the vulgar or bourgeois (mercantil, communicative, fall [into] circulation and value) understanding of language, are the 'philosophies of the name' (Rosenzweig, Heidegger, Benjamin, Levinas, Derrida), for which language is thought as gift and excess with respect to its merely communicative function; a gift, however, that cannot be *appropriated*, this lack of properness [*propiedad*: property] being what would allow us to understand as much its excessive condition as its uncapitalizable character" (169). I will construe language's lack of "properness" (what Villalobos-Ruminott calls its *propiedad*, thus also "property") differently. Contrary to what Villalobos-Ruminott argues, because language has no propriateness, because no language is ever properly one's own, language must always be appropriated. We appropriate the language we use. But because no language is ever one's own, languages can be lost, taken away, expropriated; and languages can be imposed. The lack of *propiedad* makes it possible for language—through propriation, whether appropriation or expropriation—to do the work of both colonization and decolonization. Language both enslaves and emancipates. This is what Derrida means when he claims that every instance of language is a promise. Every instance of language opens both the chance for and the threat of the future. Every instance of language both institutes and suspends sovereignty. The dream of a language beyond representation—a language that would make possible a move simply and absolutely beyond sovereignty, as if this were desirable—necessarily remains tied to the language of representation and sovereignty. It is worth wondering what is at stake in Villalobos-Ruminott's claim that "the question of the gift of language (and of language as gift) as impropriety [*impropiedad*] and interruption is already a deactivation of the general problematic of judgment" (170). This "deactivation" of judgment or of the "general problematic of judgment" becomes effective, apparently, through the "subtraction of the name from circulation" (170). Simply put, what would be a name that did not circulate? What would be a name that was not in circulation, in exchange, as the possibility of circulation

and exchange? What would be a name that did not pass between us? A name is a name only insofar as it circulates, insofar as it operates within (and is the operator of) an economy of sense. Moreover, it is hard to understand why Villalobos-Ruminott seeks in poetry the "deactivation" of judgment, as if all judgment was already inscribed within what he calls the "figure of capital [*guarismo del capital*]" (170). In a completely different attempt to conceive the (in)communicability of language, in this case through a reading of Julio Cortázar's understanding of the *cuento*, David Kelman writes: "For Cortázar, the cuento is a more general structure of 'communication,' taking that word not only in the sense of sending and receiving messages, but also and more generally in the sense of a passage or relay (as when we say that one room communicates with another)" (38). According to Kelman, "Cortázar's idiosyncratic theorization of the cuento" results in "a communicative structure that never presents this communication as such, a structure that presents a passageway to the outside without ever presenting that outside" (38). Importantly, this (in)communication, takes time: "Even when this conversation does manage to get transmitted across boundaries or limits, there is nevertheless a crucial delay that marks that passage. The passage through the boundary produces a passing away" (39). This delay, which I theorize under the heading "jet lag," instances the originary violence of the name. It is what makes communication possible *as* impossible. In "The Jew or Patriarchy (or Worse)," Brett Levinson also addresses the problem of communication. While it is difficult to credit Levinson's claim that "the name, the signifier, lack, signification, are not essential, not even to language" (74), his arguments that "because repetition, mechanicity, is the condition of communication, communication does not obey the will of 'human lives'" and, furthermore, that the "communication of 'meaning' is never not the communication of 'disease'" (75) are unassailable.

5. Take, for instance, Patrick Dove's excellent reading of *2666* in *Literature and "Interregnum"* (2016). In thinking about Santa Teresa, the setting for a substantial portion of *2666*, Dove writes:

> Although the Santa Teresa of *2666* is located in the state of Sonora and not Chihuahua it displays many if not all of what have become the most recognizable traits of Juárez: a sprawling border town with a thriving transnational *maquila* industry together with abundant sex and entertainment industries; a major destination for migrants seeking employment as well as a nexus for illegal international trafficking of people and narcotics; and, of course, the unresolved brutal murder of women, many of whom were employed in the *maquila* or sex industries. (218)

This is a reasonable description of both Bolaño's Santa Teresa and the historical Ciudad Juárez. Dove then explains: "For the time being I am going to pass over the distinction between Santa Teresa and Ciudad Juárez, treating them as if they were two names for the same thing. Later on, I will look more closely at what is at stake in the composition of Santa Teresa as literary space" (218). What is at stake in this decision to read Santa Teresa and Juárez as two names for the same thing? Dove writes: "The question I am pursuing here is . . . how the reality of Juárez might oblige us to reconsider our accustomed belief in the self-reflexive totality that we call 'world'" (218). Later, Dove remarks: "Santa Teresa/Ciudad Juárez is at one and the same time the spatialized synecdoche of unregulated global flows . . . and a killing field that attests to the violent inscription of a new 'paralegal' pseudo-order alongside the order of legitimacy represented by the state. One of the novel's most significant contributions to Latin Americanist debates about literature and critical thought is to have placed in question the adequacy of traditional epistemological tools for understanding what is happening in our world today" (224). On Dove's account, then, "the literary appearance of Santa Teresa in *2666* both discloses a world to us and raises the possibility of its unworlding. What I have elsewhere referred to as *the secret of literature*—a fold where form and content, reference and self-reference, presentation and withdrawal become undecidable—here proves to be formally indistinguishable from *the secret of the world*, or the site of a breakdown in the global circuitry that at once calls attention to the fact that there is (*es gibt*) a world while simultaneously illuminating the terrible specter of the end of the world (as we know it)" (224–225). Although later Dove will write, "Until now, I have been treating Santa Teresa and Ciudad Juárez as if they were two names for the same thing. I now turn to take a closer look at the question of the literary in *2666*, focusing on how literary figuration and innovation emerge as concerns for the novel" (236). The full stop between these two sentences is instructive. Given his earlier determination to treat Santa Teresa and Ciudad Juárez as two names for the same thing, a decision that allows Dove to consider only Ciudad Juárez in what is, effectively, a sociological/philosophical account of the effects of globalization in the borderlands, it would be reasonable to think that at some point he would show how literature (*2666*) displaces the privileging of Juárez in the name of Santa Teresa. In other words, Dove might have shown how they are not the same thing and that, in fact, to privilege Juárez (its historical reality) over Santa Teresa betrays literature by subordinating it to—by deriving its fiction from—history. But he nowhere does this. He takes up, instead, Amalfitano's experiments with Diesti's geometry book (which allows an excursion through Duchamp's ready-made) and, briefly, treats his notion of jet lag (255–256). The upshot is that literature can only respond to history (in this case, to the nefarious effects of globalization), which means literature is derived from history and exhausted by it. All literature can do is respond to history.

6. Numerous critical-theoretical texts account for this function of literature. For a classic account of the violence and politics in and of Latin American literature, see Kohut 2002.
7. For a discussion of the conditions of critique, see Foucault 2015, *Qu'est-ce que la critique?* On the limitations of any theorization of "thinking from" and "thinking about" Latin America, see Johnson 2007.

CHAPTER 1: *DAR(SE) CUENTA*

Epigraph translations:
"The action of men in time is history, on the condition that someone remains to realize what has happened. This 'realize,' for its part, is precisely the action of history on men. Through this 'realize' we are able to put ourselves in an attitude to receive or to reject the past" (Uslar Pietri, *La invención de América Mestiza*).

"The secret . . . burns—the hands and the tongues—it cannot be kept, q.e.d. It remains secret, what it is, but must immediately circulate, like the most hermetic and most fascinating of anonymous—and open—letters" (Derrida, *The Postcard: From Socrates to Freud and Beyond*, trans. Alan Bass).

1. Bartra writes: "To many intellectuals a world in which men have no fear of death has seemed fascinating. And why not fear it? Behind this mask—if it is that it is a mask—there must be an old secret, a lost ancestral truth. Death, then, makes sense: it hides something that it is necessary to decipher. It hides the mystery of the Other. . . . Thus, then, 'the indifference to death' of the Mexican is an invention of modern culture" (1987, 91).
2. This is not what Michael Taussig calls a "public secret." The public secret, according to Taussig, "can be defined as *that which is generally known, but cannot be articulated*" (1999, 5).
3. Sahagún's *Historia* is not the first place that the secret reveals itself as the interest of discovery and conquest. On Hernán Cortés's investment in the secret, see Villoro 1996 [1950], 21–35.
4. See Michaelsen and Shershow 2005 on the ambiguous structure of the *plus d'un* of the secret. *Plus d'un* in French means both "no more" and "one more" or "more than one." This is the logic of the secret, although Michaelsen and Shershow emphasize only the first sense of *plus d'un*, which insists on the limit of the secret: the secret passes between us and no one else. But inasmuch as the secret passes—in order to be a secret—structurally it must be open to more than one. Michaelsen and Shershow link the second meaning to the logic of democracy.
5. Contrary to Paul de Man's claim that Hegel does not value the sign over the symbol (1996, 96), he in fact considers the sign "the most appropriate medium of intellectual representation" (Hegel 1971, §458:213), which "must be regarded as a great advance on the symbol" (§457z:212). On Hegel's semiology, see Derrida (1972b, 79–127/1982, 69–108). On Hegel's inability to maintain the distinction between sign and symbol, see de Man 1996, 91–104.
6. Derrida points out that although Hegel acknowledges that hieroglyphs have phonetic elements, "he reproaches [the Egyptian model] above all for being too 'symbolic'" (1972b, 113/1982, 97).
7. Hénaff writes: "This symbolic level constitutes as well . . . a mechanism of *communication*. Insofar as it puts in place differential elements, it forms a code interior to language, which grounds the possibility of 'speaking to,' anterior condition to that of 'speaking about'" (2012, 292).

8. On the right of the dead to last rites, see Irlam 2009.
9. It is supposed that her name was Malinali or Malinal; see Cypess 1991, 2.
10. About this son Cortés confessed in a letter to Francisco Núñez that “I don’t love him less than the one God gave me with the marquise” (Cortés 1992, 4:40). The letter is dated 20 June 1533.
11. Malinche is not the only “virgin” who passes between men and between cultures. In a brilliant interpretation of the scene of exchange, Bartra outlines the symmetry between the Spanish violation of Malinche and the Mexica violation of the Virgin Mary. What Bartra describes, without saying it like this, is precisely what I will call the becoming-Spanish of the Indian Virgin and the becoming-Indian of the Spanish virgin. See Bartra 1987, 205–224.
12. In his declarations against Cortés, Gerónimo de Aguilar attempted to disappear Malinche; see Cortés 1990–1992, 2:67–68.
13. See Johnson 1992. In the *cartas de relación*—which were addressed to Carlos V but were more or less public because they were disseminated rapidly throughout Europe—Cortés referred to Malinche by her name only once (calling her Marina). Typically he referred to the translator as his “*lengua*.” Nevertheless, in the more private correspondence that Cortés addressed to Carlos V (in the “*carta reservada*,” for instance), as well as in many other documents, Cortés named her much more frequently.
14. Todorov affirms: “Malinche” is the nickname (*le sobriquet*) that the Mexica gave to Cortés, and parenthetically he comments, “For once, it is not the woman who takes the man’s name” (1982, 107).
15. Zamora claims that “Christoferens” is “the name with which Colón signed his writings from 1501 forward” (1993, 97).
16. Morison noted that the meaning of his signature “was a secret that Columbus carried to his grave” (1942, 357).
17. Todorov writes, “We are all the direct descendants of Columbus” (1984, 5). Writing of Columbus’s first voyage, Uslar Pietri makes a similar claim: “Three ships, eighty-eight crewmen, and that visionary man who brought along behind him, without knowing it, the destiny of the world” (1996, 205).
18. In *The Morals of History*, referring to 12 October 1492, Todorov affirms, “Our modern history also begins on that day” (1995, 17).

CHAPTER 2: MURDER AND SYMBOL

Epigraph translations:
“They are the remains of the remains” (Guzmán, *Nostalgia de la luz*).

“But one should never speak of the assassination of a man as a figure, not even an exemplary figure in the logic of an emblem, a rhetoric of the flag or of martyrdom. A man’s life, as unique as his death, will always be more than a paradigm and something other than a symbol. And this is precisely what a proper name should always name” (Derrida, *Specters of Marx*, trans. Peggy Kamuf).

1. José Santos-Herceg writes of the "discovery" of the "Americas" and Europe's nominal conquest:

> Indies, America, New World, together with the list of proposed names that don't fructify, all disrespectful, overwhelming, appropriating, invading, fruit of a naming that ignores and passes over the history of preexisting names. The indigenous names remain forgotten and are thoughtlessly replaced. . . . History of names imposed from the outside, of names with the intention to appropriate and dominate, of names born of hegemonic interests. . . . As a corollary, the name of the continent has been lost. The original, the true name, if there was one, was enchained, muted and has been forgotten. America is, in the words of Pablo Neruda, a land "without names, without America." It is a world from which, as Uslar Pietri says, "the name has been taken." (2011, 46–47)

Santos-Herceg here quotes Arturo Uslar Pietri's essay, "La otra América," the first sentence of which reads: "That which many call Latin America is, in a very significant way, the world from which the name has been taken" (Uslar Pietri 1996, 262). Of what we call America, Uslar Pietri claims, "it has always been a metaphor or a misunderstanding, or a reasonable nonconformity about its name" (262). Santos-Herceg's "if there was one" and Uslar Pietri's "always" must be read strongly. There was never an original or true name, a given name; and there is *always* something metaphorical or equivocal, some reasonable discomfort and nonconformity about the name, any name. Uslar Pietri notes, however, "The fact that the name does not correspond exactly to the thing is not what's important. No name corresponds exactly to the thing it designates. Arbitrary and capricious in their origin, they were no less designations than Asia, Africa, or Europe, to say nothing of Italy or even of Spain" (262). For Uslar Pietri, the problem does not concern the name so much as "the lack of a sufficient and secure identity" (262). Yet, the lack of a sufficient and secure identity is indissociable from the problem of the name: "Difficult, inconclusive, and four centuries long is the search for identity of the children of the other America, of that which is still called by so many objectionable and provisional names like Hispanic America, Latin America, Iberian America, and even Indian America" (262). Identities are provisional because they are irreducibly linked to the names by which we call and institute them.

2. Todorov quotes from the *Carta a Santángel*: "To the first [island] I came upon, I gave the name of *San Salvador*, in homage to His Heavenly Majesty who has wondrously given us all this. The Indians call this island Guanahani. I named the second island *Santa María de Concepción*, the third *Fernandina*, the fourth *Isabella*, the fifth *Juana*, and so to each of them I gave a new name" (Colón 1992, 220; also see Todorov 1982, 27).

3. For the play on *'adam* (human being) and *'adamah* ("humus" or ground), see *The New Oxford Annotated Bible*, Genesis, the notes to 2:7 and 2:21–23. Alter identifies this as a Hebrew "etymological pun."

4. This chapter focuses on the feminicide in northern Mexico, but, as Jean Franco writes, such serial murders are not unique to the region:

> The feminicides in Juárez, although the most publicized, are not unique. The Spanish newspaper *El País*, reporting on a meeting in Madrid titled Iberoamérica Frente al Feminicidio: El Fin de la Impunidad (Iberoamerica Confronting Feminicide: The End of Impunity), organized by Casamérica, gave some startling statistics: in El Salvador, where violence against women increased by 197 percent during the last decade, there were 477 murders between January and October of 2010. In Guatemala 5,300 were killed between 2001 and 2010, and in Honduras during the same period 1,464 women were killed, 44 percent being young women between fifteen and twenty-nine years old. There is no telling how many of these deaths could be attributed to "domestic violence." (2013, 22)

On the Latin American feminicides, see also Fregoso and Bejarano 2010b, 11–15.

5. See Monárrez 2009, 97. Monárrez insists on the difference between "femicide," which describes the murder of women by men; and "feminicide," which operates as a feminist analytical concept that considers economic and social status, race, and includes both "private" and "public" murders. So-called crimes of passion and murders resulting from domestic violence, rather than being excluded from the category of feminicide, in fact stem from the same underlying factors: in particular, the social, political, and economic power that men exercise over women, the structural inequality of their relation. In a certain way, then, every murder of a woman by a man must be analyzed within the compass of feminicide and is feminicidal. Moreover, systemic sexual feminicide does not just include cases where women are murdered after being "sexually" assaulted (raped). Rather, feminicide includes cases not only of torture and mutilation but also sequestration and verbal abuse—in short, any abuse that stems from the fact that the victim is a woman. Indeed, Monárrez points out that to refer to the results of feminicide, that is, to the victims of misogyny, as merely "murders" or "homicides" is to make the victims invisible—to disappear them once again—insofar as these more neutral terms ("homicide," "murder") ignore the role of gender in the violence perpetrated against the victims because they are women (2009, 85). On the difference between "femicide" and "feminicide," see Fregoso and Bejarano 2010b, 3–5; and Bueno-Hansen 2010, 290–311.

6. The feminicide in northern Mexico is generally believed to have begun in 1992 (the five-hundredth anniversary of Columbus's "discovery" of the Americas) or 1993 in and around Ciudad Juárez, Chihuahua. It is often thought to have been precipitated by the development of NAFTA (known in Mexico as the Tratado de Libre Comercio [TLC]) and the rise of Mexico's narcoculture and narcoeconomy, which saw the wholesale infiltration of drug money (and therefore the cartels themselves) into every aspect of Mexican life: most prominently the political apparatus, the judiciary, and the economy. Alicia Schmidt Camacho, however, explains that "decades before the passage of the North American Free Trade Agreement [1994], Mexico experimented with political projects that would

suspend national sovereignty in the border space in favor of attracting foreign exchange" (2005, 256). In the 1960s Mexico's federal government promulgated the "National Border (1961) and the Border Industrialization (1965) plans" (González Rodríguez 2012, 18), which eventually established Ciudad Juárez as the *maquiladora* capital of Mexico. Consequently, for at least the last fifty years, Mexico has opened itself to other sovereign entities in a gesture of hospitality that has complicated its national sovereignty, making itself the hostage of its invited guests in the name of (economic) salvation. More recently, two strategies or politico-economical configurations have explicitly opened Mexico (and not only Mexico) to exploitation, both internal and external: on the one hand, the United States's off-shoring of its drug problem, the so-called "war on drugs"; and, on the other hand, neoliberalism, the economic program of state-sponsored privatization coupled with the ideology of development and progress. The results have been disastrous. The drug war that marred the Calderón administration (2006–2012) resulted in the murder of thousands of Mexicans and foreigners. But the drug war has to be seen in the context of ingrained political corruption that impacts the entire state police (the legislature, judiciary, police, and military) apparatus, which in turn has resulted in generalized lawlessness. González Rodríguez reports "a 99 percent rate of impunity from prosecution by all criminals nationwide" (2012, 46). Mexican novelist, historian, and political commentator Héctor Águilar Camín makes a similar point, although he targets state governments rather than the federal one. (No doubt both are complicit and culpable.) Writing of the deleterious consequences of the post-2000 (thus post-PRI) autonomy of state governments, Águilar Camín accuses the states of failing to fulfill two important tasks, one of which concerns the failure of the rule of law: "They don't apply the law or guarantee the security of their citizens. The state governments are responsible, for example, for the fact that in Mexico on average only five of every one hundred voluntary homicides are punished" (2012, 463); for more on Aguilar Camín, see the postscript in this volume. On the northern border, the upshot of the failure of the rule of law is that women are murdered with impunity and the persons who investigate, report, and protest the murders are threatened and are themselves too-often murdered. See Franco 2013, 217, 232; González Rodríguez 2006, 274–279; Segato 2010, 70–71.

7. It would be a mistake to read in this assertion of the primacy of symbolic violence a forgetting of the material damage that so-called nonsymbolic (or historical, real) violence does. The symbol and symbolization are necessarily material, embodied. It is impossible for a symbol, *qua* material, not to affect and be affected by and as a body. There is no symbol and no symbolization without embodiment, without incorporation. Consequently, there is no symbol without remainder, without a corpse, without ashes.
8. This is the total that Diana Washington Valdez gives in *The Killing Fields: Harvest of Women* (2006). Alicia Gaspar de Alba cautions that ascertaining the number of murder victims is not easy. In her introduction to the edited volume *Making a Killing: Femicide, Free Trade, and La Frontera*, she writes:

> Readers will note that the numbers do not match in any of the essays in this book; the body count is always different. Indeed, that is one of the major issues with these crimes. There has been no systematic accounting of the victims or accountability by the authorities, which results in only more confusion, more impunity for the perpetrators, and less chance of resolution. Despite the discrepancy in the numbers, however, the contributors all agree with the activists and the NGOs that have been working on these cases that the numbers given by "official" channels are much lower than the actual body count. (2010b, 10)

At the time of the publication of Washington Valdez's *The Killing Fields*, the United Nations counted some 328 murdered women and girls. Relying on Amnesty International, Alicia Schmidt Camacho gives different, less precise totals: "Since 1993, *some* 370 women have been murdered in Chihuahua City and Ciudad Juárez, of which *approximately* 137 were sexually assaulted. . . . Of these, 100 fit a pattern of serial killings. *At least* 75 of the bodies have not been identified or claimed" (2005, 259, emphases added). In *Trama de una injusticia*, for the same eleven-year period (1993–2004), Julia Monárrez counts 382 feminicides, 144 of which she considers the victims part of a "systemic sexual feminicide [*feminicidio sexual sistémico*]" (2009, 89–108). Elsewhere, Monárrez and Cynthia Bejarano expand both the temporal frame (from 1993 to 2008) and the geographical horizons (from Ciudad Juárez to the Paso del Norte region, including El Paso, Texas, and Las Cruces, New Mexico) and count 571 feminicides (2010, 43).

On the difficulty of determining the number of victims, see Washington Valdez 2006, 65–66. The author rightly notes, "To reduce the number of victims, as the authorities had done casually over the years, would be to commit a further injustice to the slain women and their families" (66).

9. See Irlam 2009, which makes this argument in the context of the Rwandan genocide. On the problem of bodies without names and names without bodies, and on the Colombian "economy" of mourning bodies in the name of others whose bodies are lost, see M. Acosta 2012. On mourning, the name, and the body, see Naas 2008, 167–186.

10. In *Dying for Time*, with reference to Derrida's nomination of "the necessity of mediation" as murder, Martin Hägglund writes:

> To describe this necessity of mediation as a "murder" may seem to presuppose a metaphysics of immediacy, where existence is an absolute singularity that is "killed" by the generality of language, a wholly unique and ineffable other who is betrayed by the repeatability of linguistic signs. The logic of Derrida's writing, however, undermines such a metaphysics of immediacy. There is no one and no thing that exists immediately in itself. Rather, because the singular is temporal in itself, it begins to pass away as soon as it comes to be and must rely on mediation to live on—to survive—in the first place. (2012, 163–164)

11. According to Monárrez,

> The *I* that sees the suffering of the *other* (*la otra*) and consciously or unconsciously makes use of this suffering burst onto the scene in January 2004 in the offices of the Instituto Chihuahuense de la Mujer (Chihuahua Women's Institute), in a symposium organized by then-director Victoria Caraveo Vallina. Also in attendance were the state's attorney general, José Jesús Solís Silva (2001–2004); the governor's representative, Patricio Martínez; Álvaro Navarro Gárate; and thirty-two of the victims' mothers. The mothers' petitions focused on "asking judicial representatives to force nongovernmental organizations (NGOs) to stop profiting from their daughters' deaths." Rosario Montanés, a victim's mother, demanded, "I want this woman, Esther Chávez Cano [founder of Casa Amiga, and according to Monárrez one of the women responsible for bringing the Juárez feminicides to the international media's attention], to listen to me. I ask her, are you a mother? How many children do you have? What do you know of the pain of losing a child? Because I do feel pain for my daughter." She also denounced a group of Chihuahua activists—Las Mujeres de Negro (Women in Black)—whom she asked, "With what morality do you go to the streets protesting the homicides when you have not been able to understand the pain that mothers feel at these losses?" (Monárrez 2010a, 188)

12. In a conversation after a session at the 2012 annual meeting of the Latin American Studies Association in San Francisco, a friend and colleague, Justin Read, suggested that Roberto Bolaño had written *2666* to capitalize on the feminicide and that in particular "The Part of the Crimes," which recounts the murders and "names"—with pseudonyms—the victims, was particularly egregious in violating the "real," "historical" victims. He may be right. But it is also the case that the only way to mourn the victims of the Juárez feminicide is to name them and, perhaps, the only way to name them, to account for them, without violating the mothers' right to their daughters' names, is to do so in and with names that are not their own, pseudonomynously, a gesture of reinscription that both preserves the victim-survivors' privacy, safeguards the dignity of their mourning, and, obliquely, makes clear that names can and are routinely changed, for better and for worse. The only proper name is one that is not proper. See chapter 4 for more on the problem of the name and *2666*.
13. Consider, for example, the case of Elizabeth Ontiveros, who was supposedly murdered by the Egyptian chemist Abdel Latif Sharif Sharif. Sharif was arrested in 1995 and charged with eighteen homicides. In 1999 he was cleared of these charges, but he was not released from prison. Instead, he was charged with the 1995 murder of Elizabeth Castro and sentenced to thirty years. This conviction was overturned on appeal, only to have the revocation overturned on appeal by the state. Subsequently, he was also charged with the 1995 murder of Silvia Rivera Morales (Washington Valdez 2006, 146). Diana Washington Valdez calls Sharif one of the principal scapegoats for the feminicide (140). Sharif was the perfect suspect: "He was a stranger who did not speak Spanish, had no support network in Juárez, and had the right kind of criminal record" (142). He was "a victim of politics, of the pressure the authorities were under to solve the

murders" (142). He was such a good suspect that he was accused of murders that never happened. One of his victims, Elizabeth Ontiveros, "reported in person to the Chihuahua State Police office to prove that she was very much alive. The body that had been identified as hers was then exhumed" and identified as "the remains of seventeen-year-old Silvia Rivera Salas, a 1996 victim unrelated to Sharif's case" (144–145).

14. The misidentification and obfuscation of the bodies is endemic in the investigation of the Juárez feminicide. Of the cotton field murders, Washington Valdez writes:

> The authorities had not notified the families of the young victims they identified at the press conference. Most of the families heard it from the news media. . . . Some were shown clothing worn by the victims, but not the bodies. Benita Monárrez, mother of Laura Berenice Ramos Monárrez, said she never got to see the actual body "because they told me I wouldn't be able to handle it." Benita was not the only mother who wondered later whether the body she signed for was really her daughter. (2006, 68–69)

15. In the first session of his 1999–2000 seminar on the death penalty, Derrida takes up "the *disappearance* of [Jesus's] unburied body":

> Not only has Jesus died; this one who has been condemned to death is first of all one who has *disappeared*, his corpse has disappeared (which is the first meaning of the untied bandages). The one condemned to death has not only been executed, the deceased has disappeared, without burial place, and the sorrow is worse, more inconsolable; it is the sorrow of the woman unable to weep over the body of the beloved, unable to do, as one says, her work of mourning. A little like Antigone . . . who weeps less for the death . . . of her father rather than her son, than for the absence of a localizable burial place—and who thus weeps for not being able to weep her mourning in front of a body, a present corpse. . . . At that moment, when Mary complains to the angels while standing before the bandages that she no longer knows where "they laid" the body of Jesus, one could say, without too much pathos, that she prefigures the misfortune and complaint and the anger of all the women, mothers, daughters, and sisters of the "disappeared" of our time who, whether in the streets of Chile, Argentina, or in South Africa, also accuse and denounce those who did worse than torture and kill their men, because they also made them *disappear*, a disappearance that sometimes seems worse than death. (2012, 66/2014, 35–36)

The streets of Mexico can be added to this list.

16. González Rodríguez remarks that "in many cases the victims' clothes and identification cards were interchanged in a kind of perverse game" (2012, 72) to mislead authorities and, no doubt, provoke even more uncertainty and pain in the surviving victims. The effect is to render every identity suspicious and every identification doubtful.

17. According to Segato, however, no violent act can be devoid of meaning:

> It is necessary yet to understand that all violence, including that in which the instrumental function prevails, somewhat exceeds instrumentality and contains an expressive dimension. In this sense, one can say what every detective knows: Every act of violence, as a discursive gesture, has a signature. It is in this signature that a subject's reiterative presence can be seen through an act. Any detective knows that if we recognize what is common to a number of crimes, we can identify that signature, the profile, the presence of an identifiable subject behind an act. An aggressor's modus operandi is nothing more and nothing less than the mark of a style across various speeches. Identifying the style of a violent act the way we identify the style of a text will take us to the perpetrator in his or her role as author. In this sense, the signature is not a result of deliberation, of will. It is instead a consequence of the enunciation's own automatism—the recognizable trace of the subject, his position and interests, in what he says, in what he expresses by word or deed. (2010, 75)

This is seductive but problematic. Although the signature is automatic (hence Segato is correct that the signature "is not a result of deliberation" or at least not simply), it is not unequivocally "expressive" of the intentions of a subject. Were it so, forgery (and thus copycat violence) would be impossible, as would perjury. The "automatism" of the signature precludes its simple identification with the intention of a subject. On the contrary, the necessity of the signature divides intentionality, making possible the intention of a subject at the same time that it opens that intention to a future that no amount of deliberation can determine and delimit. The history of mistaken identity and bad judgments resulting in the incarceration of the wrong people can be read in what Segato claims "every detective knows." Indeed, what every detective ought to know, but clearly does not, is that although there may always be a signature, that signature does not necessarily reveal the subject's intentions, "his position and interests." Not always and not necessarily, which is not to say that a signature cannot be read. On the contrary, a signature is a signature only insofar as it is "legible," that is, repeatable, idealizable.

18. See also González Rodríguez 2006, 46.
19. Grant Farred thematizes the problem of the time of death in Roberto Bolaño's *2666*, the fourth part of which forensically narrates—counts and recounts—the murders in northern Mexico (2010). Farred does not take up the question of temporal delay, but Henry Sussman does in his suggestive essay on jet lag in the works of Kafka and Bolaño. Sussman's essay, "The Phenomenology of Jetlag" (2009), first alerted me to the problem of temporal delay in Bolaño's *2666*. See also Dove 2016, 255–256. Both González Rodríguez (2006, 59–60) and Washington Valdez (2006, 14) report cases in which the victim's neck is broken during rape: the convulsions of the dying victim apparently heighten the pleasure of the rapist-murderer.
20. Patrick Dove writes:

> *2666* could be read as a literary meditation on the possibility that neoliberal globalization generates a new form of enclosure within which infinity, alterity, and heterogeneity are all too easily captured: a world that has been entirely produced and whose horizon has been subsumed within a calculative logic that forecloses any possibility of the event. If the "secret of the world" lies concealed in the crimes of Santa Teresa, as one of Bolaño's characters asserts, this may be because those crimes illustrate a mortal danger that accompanies globalization: that the unification of the globe does not yield "One World" but instead unleashes an unworlding through which life is tendentially reduced to the status of detritus and disposability. (2016, 221)

21. The case of Lilia Alejandra was highlighted as well in the documentary *Bajo Juárez: La ciudad devorando a sus hijas* (2008, directed by Sánchez Orozco; screenplay by Alejandra Sánchez and José Antonio Cordero). Franco's account of the film names Lilia Alejandra, "Lila Alejandra," and focuses on the film's representation of her *quinceañera*, the celebration of a girl's fifteenth birthday and entry into womanhood (2013, 220). Although Franco doesn't say so, these parties often look like dress rehearsals for wedding celebrations, with the girls wearing mock wedding dresses and young boys in tuxedos. The girl has "bridesmaids" and her date (the pseudo-groom) has his "best men." In short, the *quinceañera* marks the girl's introduction into Mexican society by anticipating her move from her father's house to her husband's. Despite its celebration of a girl's putative maturity, the *quinceañera* is wholly of a piece with the culture that also produces the misogynistic jokes recorded in Bolaño's *2666* (689–692) and that Franco notes in *Cruel Modernity* (241–242).
22. See also Monárrez 2009, 132–133, for testimony concerning the case of María Sagrario González Flores, who disappeared 16 April 1998.
23. For examples, see Monárrez 2009, 156–157, 162–164, 167–168.
24. Elvia Arriola writes:

> Even the corporations that own the maquiladoras see their employees as mere cogs. Therefore, when Lear Corporation representatives were asked by a reporter from *Salon* magazine about the lack of security for workers like Claudia (who was sent home and later found murdered), they responded, "The murder didn't happen on company property." Technically, it had not, but a policy of fatal indifference to her safety and that of other similarly situated workers was already in place and enforced on the day of her disappearance. Legally, the company might not have been directly responsible for the abduction or murder, but morally? (2010, 39)

For her part, Segato is "convinced that the victim is the waste product of the process, a discardable piece" (2010, 77). Importantly, Segato also argues that impunity is not the *cause* of the feminicide(s) but rather a *product* of them; that is, the murdering of women results in the production of impunity through blood pacts—signed, Segato notes, in the blood of the victims—which effectively guarantee (she argues) silence (76–79).

25. In their introduction to the edited collection *Terrorizing Women: Feminicide in the Américas*, Rosa-Linda Fregoso and Cynthia Bejarano remark that women's bodies in the Americas instance both the site of and object of "low-intensity warfare" (2010b, 1).

26. Hägglund explains the constitution of the "now" or the "present" by following the logic of Derrida's reading of Aristotle's *Physics*, book IV: "The now cannot *first* be present in itself and *then* be affected by its own disappearance, since this would require that the now began to pass away after it had ceased to be. Rather, the now must disappear *in its very event*. The succession of time requires not only that each now is superseded by another now, but also that this alteration is at work from the beginning" (2008, 16). It follows, therefore, that nothing that *is* can reside in itself. Accordingly, being must be thought as constitutive virtuality. See also Derrida 1972b, 13/1982, 13.

27. Monárrez, in fact, is one of those who think—despite all the evidence of the corruption and fatal indifference of the state—that it remains responsible for its citizens. At the conclusion of "The Victims of the Ciudad Juárez Feminicide," she remarks: "It is only when the State, as the guarantor of justice, recognizes these omissions that they will become crimes against humanity and the logic of justice, though late, will be reestablished. It is at that moment that victims and their families will have justice" (2010b, 69). Monárrez here deploys a positivist notion of justice, one that would permit it to be "had" or "attained," as if justice were substantial, a present-being. Justice is not.

28. The question of the autoimmunity of the Mexican state is central to Gareth Williams's *The Mexican Exception: Sovereignty, Police, and Democracy*. On Williams's account "autoimmunity" refers to procedures that are "designed to avoid the conditions of violence, or the forces of disorder," but can "only do so partially at any given instance" (2011, 65–66). Having quoted Derrida's claim that democracy, in "its constitutive autoimmunity" (2003c, 95/2005a, 63), is always marked by the mutually exclusive gestures of hospitality and exclusion, Williams claims that "democratic autoimmunity is a name for the techniques that the social body establishes in order to immunize itself (and therefore save itself) from the disorder and violence that it itself installs and perpetuates" (2011, 66). The problem is that insofar as the state (formally democratic or not) is *constitutively* autoimmune, autoimmunity cannot be a technique *of* the state. Autoimmunity, rather, happens as the effect of an immunitary process or technique that, ultimately, targets the state that seeks to preserve itself. So, for instance, autoimmunity happens the moment that (in order to save democracy and thus to save itself) the state suspends democratic institutions (the right to vote or the calculation of votes already cast, freedom of speech, freedom of the press, etc.) and thereby destroys itself. The state does not control the autoimmunity that makes it possible. The state establishes strategies of immunization, of protection, always directed at an other (domestic or foreign); these strategies

cannot be limited and ultimately turn on the state itself: the state thus immunizes itself against itself. Autoimmunity names the condition in which the state, while attempting to immunize itself against some perceived threat (domestic or foreign), ineluctably targets and destroys itself. If this is a constitutive condition, then, there is no democratic state (or any other for that matter) that is not *from the start* ruined in its very constitution. Autoimmunity cannot *not* happen, which is why Williams's claim that autoimmunity refers to "procedures" that "are designed to avoid the conditions of violence" makes little sense. Autoimmunity names and instances constitutive violence. Indeed, on Derrida's account, without autoimmunity nothing would ever happen: "*Without autoimmunity*, with absolute immunity, nothing would ever happen or arrive; we would no longer wait, await, or expect, no longer expect one another, or expect any event" (2003c 210/2005a 152, emphasis added). Where there is no autoimmunity, the forces of immunity (and thus an absolute sovereignty) would reign and destroy the possibility of any possible future, that is, of the coming of the event *as* impossible and with it the chance for anything to happen, including sovereignty, democratic sovereignty, revolution, social change, tyranny, etc. This means, simply, that it cannot be correct that "the task of democratic thought is to suggest the possibility of a time for the people in which the political is not neutralized or immunized; in which something other than populist autoimmunity can happen; a time that contains an internal necessity that signals a coming event" (Williams 2011, 86). What would be the possibility of a democratic thought beyond or without the chance opened in and by autoimmunity? If autoimmunity is constitutive of democracy (and of sovereignty more generally), then whatever chance *there is* for or of democracy depends on autoimmunity, hence on the *impossibility* of the event. *As such*, that is, *as the impossible*, it is only ever *as if* there were democracy; democracy is only ever promised:

> At stake here is the very concept of democracy as concept of a promise that can only arise in such a *diastema* (failure, inadequation, disjunction, disadjustment, being "out of joint"). That is why we always propose to speak of a democracy *to come*, not of a *future* democracy in the future present, not even of a regulating idea, in the Kantian sense, or of a utopia—at least to the extent that their inaccessibility would still retain the temporal form of a *future present*, of a future modality of the *living present*. (Derrida 1993b, 110/1994b, 64–65)

29. The "concept" of "terrorism" derives largely from the Terror of 1793–1794, which occurred after the beginning of the French Revolution and the overthrow of the French monarchy; consequently, it was the effect of the institution of a (more or less, more and less) democratic regime. Implicit in the concept is its repeatability, that one anticipates always and everywhere that acts of terror will repeat themselves; yet, despite this anticipation, terror always takes one by surprise. We can never be sufficiently prepared, vigilant, for terror, that is, protect ourselves all we want; we are always exposed to the violence of terror. And this violence is as much in the anticipation of terror as in its execution, not

least because we will never know what terrorism is, if there is any. In a certain way, then, we can only ever say that *there is* (no) terrorism: we will never know *what* terrorism *is*, as if it will ever have been just what we say it is. While it is imperative to condemn the violent acts that have taken place in Paris, in Nice, in Madrid, in New York City, in Oklahoma City, in Mumbai, in Orlando, in Baghdad, in Manchester, in Boston, in London, in Teheran . . . in Iguala—in every possible "elsewhere," in every possible "here" and "there," whenever and wherever such acts occur, and they occur always and everywhere, *here and now*—it is no less important to be wary of our nominal certainty. *Who* calls "terrorism" by its name? Who and what *counts* in this nomination? Do those who believe they have no other recourse, no other future, call what they do "terrorism"? As Jacob Rogozinski writes: "No movement has ever defined itself as 'terrorist.' Even when some have the explicit goal to terrify their enemies—and this is the case of the jihadists—they continue to figure themselves otherwise, as combatants, partisans, resistance fighters, militant revolutionaries or 'soldiers of the Caliphat.' In short, the 'terrorist' is always the other, the enemy that we combat. This pseudo-concept has a purely polemical function; it does not have the goal of explaining, but only of denouncing—but what is the value of a term so equivocal that it can be applied as easily to bin Laden as to Jean Moulin and Nelson Mandela" (2017, 30). In short, a terrorist *by any other name* is not a terrorist. Terrorism as such exists *in name only*, as if there were terrorism, as if terrorism was not always already *not*-terrorism. And if so-called "terrorists" do not respond to that name, in what name, in whose name, do they respond? What does "terrorism" mean to them? What does "terrorism" mean to us? The FBI defines terrorism as international and domestic. International terrorism is "perpetrated by individuals and/or groups inspired by or associated with designated foreign terrorist organizations or nations (state-sponsored)." Domestic terrorism is "perpetrated by individuals and/or groups inspired by or associated with primarily U.S.-based movements that espouse extremist ideologies of a political, religious, social, racial, or environmental nature" (accessed 7 April 2018, www.fbi.gov/investigate/terrorism). The US Code of Federal Regulations defines terrorism as "the unlawful use of force and violence against persons or property to intimidate or coerce a government, the civilian population, or any segment thereof, in furtherance of political or social objectives" (accessed 7 April 2018, www.cnn.com/2017/04/19/us/hate-crime-or-terrorism-definition-trnd/index.html). Why do we, in the United States, call the 1994 bombing of the Murrah Building in Oklahoma City an act of terror, terrorism? ("Domestic terrorism," we say, as if it were less extreme, less violent, more tame, than, say, "terrorism" or "international terrorism," as if we knew where to the draw the line between the inside and the outside, between the national and the international.) Why do we not use the term for the lynching of thousands of African-Americans by white Americans or for the murders on 7 June 2015 of nine African Americans in a Charleston, South Carolina, church by white supremacist Dylann Roof? What about the 2016 Halloween "decoration" of effigies of black men hung from a tree in Kendall, Florida? Why do we not call the death penalty state-sponsored (domestic) terrorism? Why do we not call "terrorism" the entire police apparatus, which largely puts white males in the position of surveillance and of disciplining African American people or, more generally, people of color? Isn't this what ought to be called an *unjust* justice and a just *in*justice? Isn't it the promise of terrorism? And if it is the promise of terrorism, then isn't it also the promise of democracy? See Derrida 2003e, 100–106; see also Johnson 2018, from which this note derives.

30. On Hobbes and fear, see Johnson 2014. Hobbes does not simply claim that men—always men—fear death; rather, they fear a violent death.

31. And Franco is not the only academic who does so. Tabuenca Córdova, for instance, writes, "The women whom the Municipal Police propaganda is addressing are those who have transgressed men's spaces and good social and moral values. They are working-class women who are violated both in their everyday life—facing exploitation in the factory and the home—and, symbolically, in these representations of them" (2010, 106). Silvia Giletti Benso explains, "These bodies have been transformed symbolically into the mirror of the indifference of Mexican institutions toward the violent death of a woman and more so being of humble origins" (2014, 2). See also Monárrez 2009, 2010a, 2010b, who consistently recurs to symbolization to explain the feminicides and the culture that sustains them.

32. On the infinite substitutability of the symbol, see Gasché 2012, 136.

33. Insofar as narcoviolence and terrorism are instances of what she calls "difuse" violence—that is, unforeseeable and unanticipatable violence, the violence of fantasmatic entities (for example, the "narco machine")—Rossana Reguillo notes that they are unsymbolizable forms of violence. Contrasting the narco machine to what might be called the Nazi machine, she writes,

> While Nazi power installs buildings, and its creations are clearly perceptible and sustain a localization for the realization of its work of violence, the narco is dislocated; its power appeals precisely to the densest dimension of the meaning [*el sentido*] of the machine; its unlocalizable ubquity, which acts silently but efficiently; its presence is phantasmagorical. The narco machine is a phantasm. Its dominance derives from ocupying an unsymbolizable (in the Freudian sense) dislocalized space, which appeals to and awakens the deepest fissures between what we conceive as real and the fears that are dislocating. The impossibility of symbolization works in the imaginary, in the obturation of any possible meaning. (2011, n.p.)

In other words, because the violence of the narco or terror machine cannot be anticipated and, no less important, because it escapes comprehension, which means it results from phantasmagoric entities, Reguillo argues that such violence "works in the imaginary" to trouble the line between what we accept or posit as reality and the fear that displaces it. Such phantasmatic violence is unsymbolizable because it cannot be named; language exhausts itself in the effort: "Facing these violences, language sinks, it exhausts itself in the same act of trying to produce an explication, a reason; the violences in the country make our interpretive systems collapse" (2011, n.p.). Nevertheless, she notes, "But at the same time, these broken bodies, violated, destroyed with fury, are converted into a clear message: shut up and submit" (n.p.). The "but [*pero*]" marks the double bind: at once unsymbolizable and symbolizable, thus meaningless and meaningful. Violence is a message, a letter at once illegible and legible, uninterpretable and interpretable. There is no symbol; there are only symbols.

34. Jean Franco cites this "much quoted sentence" (2013, 238), as do, for example, Espinosa, Farred, Moreiras, and Volpi. Moreover, in *La guerra de los Zetas*, after having noted that "since 2007 the necessity of narrating, more than of registering what happened according to a predetermined form, became imperative," Diego Enrique Osorno remarks, "Another recent, fictional reading, *2666*, by the spiritual piedpiper Roberto Bolaño, ended up by making the reporter I am capture the value of a certain inexhaustive, even marathonic, narrative, when it does what in appearance is impossible: speak of narcotrafficking without showing narcotraffickers" (2012, 33–34). The reading of Bolaño's *2666* helps Osorno recognize "that Mexican violence demands a total personal implication" (34). This recognition, moreover, demands that he assume "a pact with narrative journalism," which he sometimes calls "*periodismo infrarrealista*" (34), in homage to Bolaño.
35. I thank Sergio Waisman for insisting on this in a conversation following a panel presentation at the Latin American Studies Association annual meeting in San Francisco, California, on 26 May 2012.
36. See Shell 1993, 49.
37. See also Élmer Mendoza's *Balas de plata* (2008), which concerns narcoviolence and in which the protagonist, the detective Edgar "el Zurdo" Mendieta, proposes, "We are all guilty until the contrary is proven" (47).
38. On the necessity of care, see Hägglund 2012.

CHAPTER 3: AS IF . . . LITERATURE BEFORE THE WORLD

Epigraph translations:
"What matters to us is the intention, the direction of the flow" (Reyes, *La experiencia literaria*).

"The idea of fiction . . . lies completely in that pedestrian and disconcerting *as if*. The *as if* that our brain applies daily in order for our body to move reasonably through the world, in order to discover new sources of energy and to enable us to protect ourselves from predators and enemies. The *as if* that keeps us from tripping at every instant, that maintains us in equilibrium and impedes us from crashing against a window or falling down the stairs. The *as if* that permits us to relate to the ambulant ghosts of others" (Volpi, *Leer la mente*).

"The possibility of fiction cannot be derived" (Derrida, *Limited Inc*, trans. Samuel Weber).

1. Two instances of such questioning are Roger Bartra, *Antropología del cerebro: La conciencia y los sistemas simbólicos* (2007), and Jorge Volpi, *Leer la mente: El cerebro y el arte de la ficción* (2011). Both Bartra and Volpi argue, by way of neuro- and cognitive sciences, that far from being a phenomenon of interiority, indemnified against the vagaries of the world that it "creates," consciousness is formed "outside" itself in and through the world that "creates" it. Moreover, in both Bartra and Volpi, fiction or narrative is essential to consciousness. Consciousness realizes itself—accomplishes itself in becoming aware of itself—in the demand for narrative, in the becoming-fiction of the world that will have provided the context (the community) necessary for fiction or narrative in the first place. Here the question is not whether Bartra's and Volpi's adventures in the neuro- and cognitive sciences are rigorous enough to bear the scrutiny of experts in those fields; what matters is the investment and interest in the thesis that "literature"—or something like literature, "fiction" or narrative, thus symbolization—figures consciousness and does so only insofar as it is the effect of an originary exposure to the world, whatever the world may be.
2. In 1909 Antonio Caso gave a series of lectures on positivism at the Escuela Nacional Preparatoria. In "Pasado inmediato" Reyes claims that "Mexican positivist philosophy, which received its first attacks from Gómez Robelo, had to disappear under the eloquent words of Antonio Caso" (1960b, 205) and that Caso's lectures on positivism ultimately defined "the attitude of young people toward the official doctrine" (209). Reyes located the theoretical origins of the Mexican Revolution in the 1908 demonstration in honor of Gabino Barreda that "resulted in . . . something like the expression of a new political sentiment. It was the first clear signal of a public consciousness emancipated from the regime" (208–209). With respect to Caso's lectures, however, in two consecutive numbers of *Revista moderna de México* (July and August 1909), Pedro Henríquez Ureña signaled his disappointment with Caso's explanation of positivism, not least because he had expected a more devastating critique, which he himself provides in the two review-essays. See Henríquez Ureña, "Conferencias sobre el positivismo" and "El positivismo independiente" in Caso et al., 2000, 305–325. For the engagement with Husserlian phenomenology, the best source is Zirión Quijano 2009. The two most important assessments of Husserl in Mexico prior to Alfonso Reyes's *El deslinde* (which is not about Husserl but which nevertheless depends on the introduction of phenomenology in Mexico) are Adalberto García de Mendoza, *Filosofía moderna: Husserl, Scheler, Heidegger: Conferencias de 1933* (Morelia, Mexico: Jitanjáfora, 2004); and Antonio Caso, *La filosofía de Husserl* (1972 [1934]).
3. *La experiencia literaria* was first published in 1941. For an important reading of Reyes's humanist politics and of the way his texts operate as a police action in relation to the possibility of a democratic Mexican future, in particular with regard to two essays from 1939, "Pasado inmediato" and "Justo Sierra y la historia patria," see Williams 2011, 87–115.
4. Reyes writes:

> The whirlwind of fiction, animated by literary intention . . . turns and ascends, from the adjustment with the more singular and contingent real event to the heroic maladjustment of the imagination. But at none of its levels, nor at this last one, could literature escape: first philosophical truth or universality in the Aristotelian sense . . . ; second psychological truth or the expression of subjective representations, of which the poet gave us examples at twilight . . . ; and third the minimum of the real event, practical truth, which every operation of our mind necessarily carries within itself. Fiction flies, yes; but, like the comet, attached to a thread of resistance: it doesn't leave the universe, it does not leave the I, nor does it leave physical nature no matter how much it makes it thinner. (1963a, 196)

5. One can read more or less the same understanding of literature in Jorge Gracia's conception of the relation between text and work in literature and literature's consequent untranslatability; see Gracia 2002. For a discussion of why Gracia's understanding is untenable, see Johnson 2011, 1–24.
6. Although Reyes's analysis of the constitution of literature seems dated, his understanding of it as a "practical lie" and as a "suspect truth" remains operative. For a Mexican example, see Jorge Volpi, *Mentiras contagiosas* (2008). For an Anglo-American philosophical analysis of literature's relation to the world, see Gibson 2007.
7. In "Pasado inmediato," Reyes's survey of the condition of pedagogy at the Escuela Nacional Preparatoria at the end of the nineteenth and beginning of the twentieth centuries, that is, during the Diaz regime's sponsorship of positivism as the official doctrine of Mexican education, Reyes writes that Porfirio Parra, "direct disciple of [Gabino] Barreda, respectable memory in many ways, no longer did anything more than repeat his treatise on Logic, where unfortunately it was shown that, with the exception of the positivists, all philosophers bore on their foreheads the dark stigma of sophism; and in no way did he want to know about new things, neither to let himself be convinced even by the Hamiltonian 'quantification of the predicate,' hint of the future Logistics" (1960b, 190).
8. For a summary of the debate concerning the status of the noema, see Zahavi 2004, perhaps especially 47–48; but see as well Føllesdal 1969; Holmes 1975; Smith and McIntyre 1975; Dreyfus 1982; Bernet 1991; Drummond 1992; and Kosowski 2012.
9. According to Husserl, "Intentionality is an essential peculiarity of the sphere of mental processes taken universally in so far as all mental processes in some manner or other share in it. . . . Intentionality is what characterizes *consciousness* in the pregnant sense and which, at the same time, justifies designating the whole stream of mental processes as the stream of consciousness and as the unity of *one* consciousness" (1983, §84:168).
10. Courtine writes:

> What interests us here is precisely that the *appearing* object—it comes from the essence of the appearing—is always determined "like this and like this," is

> targeted or targeted presumptively "as" such and such ("the object of such and such side," as the course *On the Theory of Meaning* names it). The "so and so" and the "as" belong to the essence of the "perceived life" [*vécu perceptif*] and through it more generally to the "intentional life" [*vécu intentionnel*], which does not orient itself on the object taken purely and simply, the "absolute object" [*Gegenstand schlechthin*], which . . . targets it from the start *as* such and such, i. e., as well, as one and the same within the diversity of its ways or its modes of appearance. . . . It is to this analysis that Husserl remains faithful. (2007, 86)

11. See also Husserl 1983, §53:103–104, on the insertion of consciousness, via its embodiment, in the world.
12. Rodolphe Gasché suggests just this in his discussion of Derrida's understanding of the "general text" and its deconstruction of intentionality:

> If the text is characterized by reference, and if no extra-text (the existence of which is not being put into question) can ever hope to saturate the text's referring function, then it represents, phenomenologically speaking, an intentionality without an intentum. *Such a decapitated or beheaded intentionality*, because it lacks a decidable intentum, cannot be fulfilled by a corresponding extraintentional referent. The text, as defined by Derrida, does not do away with the phenomenological idea of intentionality. On the contrary, it inscribes and displaces the intentionality of consciousness with its corresponding intentum and its possibly fulfilling object. From a grounding perspective, the text as an intentionality without intentum is of a greater power of formalization than phenomenological intentionality, since the unsaturatable relation to Otherness that characterizes it can serve as the matrix to account for the possibility of phenomenological intentionality, and thus of the principle of all principles, evidence, as a necessary effect. As such it can serve to account also for the structural impossibility of a final coincidence of intention and its intentum. (1986, 281, emphasis added)

13. This is in fact Caso's assessment of Husserl's phenomenology. In a brief essay published in *El Universal*, "¿Qué es la conciencia? (El descubrimiento de Brentano)" (5 August 1938), Caso claims that "Brentano's psychology agrees with Platonic and Aristotelian thought, as well as with one of the most ilustrious directions of contemporary philosophical thought," that is, phenomenology, and he asserts that the "great psychological discovery has been the basis on which Husserl founded the edifice of phenomenology" (1972, 7:180). And, in *La filosofía de Husserl*, he explains: "But if by antipsychologist is understood the negation of all psychological foundation of logic, Husserl is not, then, antipsychologist in any way. The inductive methods, which only reach probability, an asertoric and not apodictic certainty, are founded, according to Husserl, in psychology, and not only in pure logic. . . . Therefore, without psychology, without the science of the processes of the human psyche, *a part* of logic cannot be founded" (1972, 7:36).
14. "Whether everywhere and necessarily such sensuous mental processes in the stream of mental processes bear some 'animating construing' or other . . .

whether . . . they always have intentive functions, is not to be decided here. . . . We likewise leave it undecided at first if the characteristics essentially making up intentionality can have concreteness without having sensuous foundations" (Husserl 1983, §85:172).

15. This solution, Derrida writes, "clearly indicates that at this level he remains a prisoner of an *already constituted* noetico-noematic correlation" (1990a, 156/2003d, 88).
16. On the passivity and activity of *hylē*, see Marrati 2005, 10–14, 202n39; and Rabanaque 2005.
17. The "intentional object" is not simply the noema, but there is no intentional object without the noematic structure or, simply, without a correlative noema. Husserl writes: "Like perception, every intentive mental process—just this makes up the fundamental part of intentionality—has its 'intentional Object,' i.e., its objective sense. Or, in other words: to have sense or 'to intend to,' something [*etwas 'im Sinne zu haben'*], is the fundamental characteristic of all consciousness which, therefore, is not just any mental living [*Erlebnis*] whatever, but is rather a <mental living> having sense, which is 'noetic'" (1983, §90:185). The ontological difference between intentional object and noema is not entirely clear; see Kosowski 2012.
18. In a notably clear passage, Husserl explains that although it may be tempting to conceive of intention as immanent to the intentional object, which would mean that the intentional object is inherent in intentionality, in fact, this cannot be so:

> If, in this way, we try to separate the actual Object (in the case of perception of something external, the perceived physical thing pertaining to Nature) and the intentional Object, including the latter <as> really inherently in the mental process as "immanent" to the perception, we fall into the difficulty that now two realities ought to stand over against one another while only *one* <reality> is found to be present and even possible. I perceive the physical thing, the Object belonging to Nature, the tree there in the garden; that and nothing else is the actual Object of the perceptual "intention." A second immanental tree, or even an "internal image" of the actual tree standing out there before me, is in no way given, and to suppose that hypothetically leads to an absurdity. The image as a really inherent component in the psychologically real perception would be again something real—something real which would *function* as a depicturing of another something real. But that can only be by virtue of a depicturing consciousness in which something first appears—with which we would have a first intentionality—and this would function again in consciousness as a "picture Object" representing another "picture Object"—for which a second intentionality founded in the first intentionality would be necessary. It is no less evident that each particular one of these modes of consciousness already requires the distinction between the immanental and actual object, thus comprising the same problem which should have been resolved by the construction. Over and above this, in the case of perception, the construction is subject to the objection which we have discussed earlier: to include depictive functions in the

> perception of something physical signifies ascribing to it a picture-consciousness which, descriptively considered, is something of an essentially different kind of constitution. Nevertheless, the main point here is that perception and, then consequently, every mental process, requires a depictive function, unavoidably . . . leads to an infinite regress. (1983, §90:186; see also §43:78–79)

19. In the fourth of the *Cartesian Meditations*, Husserl writes: "Each object that the ego ever means, thinks of, values, deals with, likewise each that he ever phantasies or can phantasy, indicates its correlative system and exists only as itself the correlate of its system" (1999, §30:100).
20. The "as-structure" of the noema also includes, for instance, assent and dissent, affirmation and negation. See Husserl 1983, §106:218–219.
21. See Husserl 1983, §108:220–222.
22. Elsewhere Derrida writes: "No exposition [*énoncé*], no discursive form is intrinsically or essentially literary before and outside of the function it is assigned or recognized by a right, that is, a specific intentionality inscribed directly on the social body. The same exposition may be taken to be literary here, in one situation or according to given conventions, and non-literary there" (1998a, 29/2000, 28).
23. "Literature seemed to me," Derrida writes, "to be the institution which allows one to *say everything* in *every way*. The space of literature is not only that of an instituted *fiction* but also a *fictive institution* which in principle allows one to say everything" (1992, 36). According to Derrida, literature shares this right with the modern university and with "the modern idea of democracy," but not, he emphasizes, with any democratic government already in place; rather, he explains, the right to say everything "seems inseparable . . . from what calls forth a democracy, in the most open (and doubtless itself to come) sense of democracy" (37). Derrida claims that the right and the freedom to say everything can be a "powerful political weapon," but it can also "let itself be neutralized as a fiction" (38).
24. See Derrida 1972b, 383–384/1982, 322–323.
25. The relation between intentional consciousness and interest, however, is not simple. According to Jean-François Lyotard, the world of (empirical) interest is the price of phenomenological reduction. Hence, it is the disinterestedness of the transcendental I that permits it to take an interest in the world *as world*, that is, in the question and origin of the world. Yet, the transcendental I's disinterested interest in the world owes itself to the empirical I's interested disinterest in the I as such; that is, the transcendental I owes itself to the empirical I's concrete determination. In other words, what is at stake is the possibility of the empirical I that is in the world distinguishing itself from the world such that the world becomes an object for it (and that it itself becomes an object in the world, one object among others); this movement of difference or differentiation is the phenomenological reduction, which results in the positing of the world as "*existence réelle*" outside or beyond the I that targets it. The movement from the empirical I in the world (for which the world is transcendent) to the transcendental I that

envelopes the world requires an operation that is neither *of* the world *nor* beyond it. See Lyotard 1954, 31–33.

26. The insistence upon *literature*, with its etymological relation to the letter, is not unimportant in that the letter has a material support that inscribes it *in* the world, forcing it to pass into exteriority. Derrida claims that "the system of 'hearing (understanding)-oneself-speak' through the phonic substance—which *presents itself* as the nonexterior, nonmudane, therefore nonempiricial or noncontingent signifier—has necessarily dominated the history of the world during an entire epoch and has even produced the idea of the world from the difference between the mundane and the nonmundane" (1967a, 17/1974, 7–8). Following this, Sean Gaston writes: "The phonocentric tradition casts language not *in* the world (the exterior, mundane, empirical, and contingent), but as the origin *of* the world. Language is the transcendental possibility of the world. It is itself entirely free of the world: intelligible, necessary, and universal. Without the ideality of the *phonē* and the logos, there would be no 'idea of the world'" (2011, 503).
27. Derrida recognizes this proximity; see 1962, 58n1/1978a, 67n62.
28. Derrida never gives up on the importance of this claim of spontaneous reduction or annihilation effected in the name; see, among other examples, 1967a, 152–168/1974, 107–118; and 2012, 165/2014, 112.
29. Husserl writes: "The *tree simpliciter*, the physical thing belonging to Nature, is nothing less than this *perceived tree as perceived*, which, as perceptual sense, inseparably belongs to the perception. The tree simpliciter can burn up, be resolved into its chemical elements, etc. But the sense—the sense of *this* perception, something belonging necessarily to its essence—cannot burn up; it has no chemical elements, no forces, no real properties" (1983, §89:184). Simply put, the noema "is not touched by excluding the actuality of the tree and that of the whole world" (§97:202).
30. Derrida writes: "But the word's degree of ideal objectivity is only, we could say, primary. It is within a facto-historical language that the noun [*nom*: "name"] '*Löwe*' is free, therefore ideal, with regard to its sensible, phonetic, or graphic incarnations. But it remains essentially linked, as a German word, to a real spatiotemporality; it remains in solidarity, in its very ideal objectivity, with the de facto existence of a given language, thus with the factual subjectivity of a certain speaking community" (1962, 62/1978a, 70).
31. Despite the necessity for Husserl that such ideality be free, Derrida insists upon the constitutive enchainment or contextualization—hence valuation and limitation—of so-called "free" idealities; see 1962, 65–66/1978a, 73.
32. The necessity of "retention" for transmission and inheritance—and for thought in general—marks the place where the analysis of the noema (or the objective, ostensibly passive side of intentionality) ineluctably comes into contact with its correlate, the noetic act (or the subjective, ostensibly active side of intentionality). For a decisive account of the necessary "trace-structure" of the intentional act or of noetic activity, see Hägglund 2008, 50–75. Against Husserl's claims that the noetic (or intentional) act is ultimately grounded in an "internal conscious-

ness" or "prereflexive self-awareness of the absolute flow" (63), which is defined by the simultaneity of perception and perceived (62), Hägglund demonstrates that Husserl's own account acknowledges the noncoincidence of constituting and constituted (68–69). Such noncoincidence is necessarily temporal and therefore marked by the delay and deferral of retention and protention. Taking issue with the notion of a pure auto-affection, which would precede reflection, Hägglund writes: "What precedes reflection is not a prereflexive unity or immediate sensation of self. On the contrary, it is the deferral and delay of *différance*. *Différance* makes reflection possible but at the same time makes it impossible for it ever to close upon itself. Consequently, heteroaffection inhabits even the most immediate autoaffection, since its very structure hinges on the difference between the affecting and the affected" (67). The upshot, Hägglund writes, is that "Husserl's idea that the subject *constitutes* time is thus untenable. The subject does not constitute time but is rather *constituted by* the movement of temporalization" (70). Furthermore, on Hägglund's account, the moment it becomes clear that no recourse to a nontemporal instance can be sustained, "the necessity of arche-writing makes itself felt" in that it "allows us to think the necessary synthesis of time without grounding it in a nontemporal unity" (71). Hägglund thus concludes, "The primal impression is . . . a *primal inscription* that enables repetition across the gap in time and exhibits the general structure of re-presentation. Without such inscription there would be nothing to retain or protend, no mediation between past and future, and consequently no perception of self-awareness at all" (71). See also Rodolphe Gasché's analysis of what he calls "the general theory of doubling" (1986, 225–239). Gasché writes: "Most generally, the structure of auto-affection requires a minimal division of the same in order for this same to constitute itself *as* itself. This minimal division takes on manifold shapes. It explains why auto-affection is possible only through an immediate exiting from interiority and why the same *as* the same . . . must affect itself by Otherness" (232).

33. Derrida develops Husserl's insight most extensively in 1972b, 365–393/1982, 307–330, and in 1990b/1988, *passim*.

34. Husserl will already have accounted for the threat of such noncoincidence, which, according to his own argument, is nonetheless necessary, by making *logos* the beginning and the end of sense. Husserl writes: "Every act, or every act-correlate [hence noematic sense], *includes in itself, implicitly or explicitly, something 'logical'*" (1983, §117:282). This means that noematic sense (the meant as meant)—which is not expressive in itself, although Husserl claims it attains the level of *logos* only through expression—always already bears within itself "something logical" and thus the possibility of expression and of logos. Consequently, superstructure—*logos*, language, expression—underlies the substratum or noematic sense. This allows Husserl to have it both ways: on the one hand, he can claim that the ideality of language makes it impossible for expression to coincide absolutely with the noematic sense; on the other hand, it affords just such underlying coincidence by positing *logos* (reason, language) as the element or ground of noematic sense.

35. See Derrida 2004, 30–31. The irreducible—thus undecidable—homonymy of *et* (and) and *est* (third-person singular of "to be"), between the beast *et/est* and the sovereign, thus the becoming-beast of the sovereign and the becoming-sovereign of the beast, is what he calls "the passage from one to the other, the analogy, the resemblance, the alliance." Derrida remarks, "That's our first impetus, the nerve of our *et/est* analogy. Our *eh eh*, undecided or even undecidable" (2008b, 60/2009, 33).
36. Husserl writes:

> It then becomes evident that *while the being of consciousness*, of any stream of mental processes whatever, *would indeed be necessarily modified by an annihilation of the world of physical things[,] its own existence would not be touched.* Modified, to be sure. For an annihilation of the world means, correlatively, nothing else but that in each stream of mental processes (the full stream—the total stream, taken as endless in both directions, which comprises the mental processes of an Ego), certain ordered concatenations of experience and therefore certain complexes of theorizing reason oriented according to those concatenations of experience, would be excluded. But that does not mean that other mental processes and concatenations of mental processes would be excluded. Consequently no real being, no being which is presented and legitimated in consciousness by appearances, is necessary to the being of consciousness itself (in the broadest sense, the stream of mental processes). (1983, §49:110)

37. On the necessity and threat of homonymy, see Aristotle 1a1–5, 16a4–9, 165a6–14, and 1006b7–10. On the problem of homonymy in Aristotle, see Aubenque 2013, 172–198; Cassin 1995; Courtine 2005, 153–229. The most comprehensive treatment of homonymy from an analytical perspective is Christopher Shields, *Order in Multiplicity* (Oxford: Clarendon Press, 1999). Courtine points out that the distinction instituted by Aristotle's ancient commentators (Porphyre and Simplicius, in particular) between accidental and intentional homonymy is not, in any strict sense, Aristotelian; see Courtine 2005, 177. The problem of homonymy is particularly vexing for the question of being. Aubenque concludes:

> The proper character of the homonymy of being is to be at the same time irrational (like all homonymy) and inevitable (precisely because the *pollachos* [many] is here a *pros hen* [toward one]): in this way, homonymy is the problem that has never finished posing itself to philosophy and that, following the expression of Book Z, is always "a subject of research and embarrassment." In effect, if homonymy is at once that which ought to be reduced (if we want our discourse to have a sense) and that which, in the case of being, is nevertheless irreducible, we can ask ourselves whether ontology . . . will not be in its entirety the properly human effort to supply, by a necessarily infinite investigation, the radical homonymy of being. (198)

For her part, Cassin remarks: "Aristotle's diagnostic made of homonymy something like the radical evil inherent to the finitude of language, set off from the infinity of the real" (340). In addition, see Johnson 2015.

38. In *Of Grammatology*, for instance, Derrida explains that spacing "is always the unperceived, the nonpresent, and the nonconscious. As such, if one can still use that expression in a nonphenomenological way; for here we pass the very limits of phenomenology. Arche-writing as spacing cannot occur as such within the phenomenological experience of a *presence*" (1967a, 95/1974, 68). Derrida's most extended engagement with the *comme tel* and the *comme si* occurs in his last seminar, *La bête et le souverain II (2002–2003).*
39. In "La double séance" Derrida refers to "a tropic movement," which parenthetically he qualifies as "analogie, métaphore, métonymie" (1972a, 307/1981, 251). In "La mythologie blanche," however, he distinguishes "tropic" movements from "metaphorical language": "The constitution of the fundamental oppositions of the metaphorology (*physis/tekhnē*, *physis/nomos*, *sensible/intelligible*; space/time, signifier/signified, etc.) has occurred by means of the history of metaphorical language, or rather by means of 'tropic' movements which, no longer capable of being called by a philosophical name—i.e., metaphors—nevertheless, and for the same reason, do not make up a 'proper' language" (1972b, 272–273/1982, 228–229).
40. Derrida claims, "In the end, the critico-political function of literature, in the West, remains very ambiguous. The freedom to say everything is a very powerful political weapon, but one which might let itself be neutralized as a fiction" (1992, 38).
41. Derrida repeats this in *Béliers*, which he suggests could serve as a "veritable introduction" (2003a, 11) to *Chaque fois unique*.

> For each time, and each time singularly, each time irreplaceably, each time infinitely, death is nothing less than an end of *the* world. Not *only one* end among others, the end of someone or of something *in the world*, the end of a life or of a living being. Death puts an end neither to someone in the world nor to *one* world among others. Death marks each time, each time in defiance of arithmetic, the absolute end of the one and only world, the end of the unique world, of that which each opens as a one and only world, the end of the unique world, the end of the totality of what is or can be presented as the origin of the world for any unique living being, be it human or not. (2003b, 23/2005b, 140)

42. This remark takes place within the context of sentences that challenge the phenomenological *comme tel*: "*Spacing* . . . is always the unperceived, the nonpresent, and the nonconscious. *As such*, if one can still use that expression in a non-phenomenological way; for here we pass the very limits of phenomenology. Arche-writing as spacing cannot occur *as such* within the phenomenological experience of a *presence*" (1967a, 95/1974, 68).
43. Derrida's calculation that there is world neither with nor without death adds up to a critique of the thought of resurrection, whether in the classical sense

or in that of Jean-Luc Nancy in *Noli me tangere*: "This book is a book of *adieu.* A salutation, no more salutation [*plus d'un salut*]. Each time unique. But it is the adieu of a salutation that resigns itself to salute, as I believe every salutation worthy of the name is held to do, the possibility always open, indeed the necessity of the possible non-return, of the end of the world as end of all resurrection" (Derrida 2003a, 11). For Derrida this includes Nancy's notion of *anastasis*: "No matter how different it is from the classic resurrection, *anastasis* continues, with the rigor of some cruelty, to console. It posits both the existence of some God and that the end of *a* world would not be . . . the end of *the* world" (11). "God" thus names the desire that death *not* put an end to *the* world, but rather that one world replace another, that one world survive another; that there be more than one world, thus not one world (*plus d'un monde*). That there be (the) world without death, (the) world without end.

44. See Derrida 1972b, 16/1982, 15.
45. In *Langues sans demeure*, Marc Crépon remarks:

> The maternal lanaguage is, as its name also indicates, the language within which each person does his apprenticeship to authority—most often, to parental authority. It is the language in which the law makes itself known and demands to be respected. Language that commands that one obeys, language that threatens, language that punishes. Double authority, in reality, by language and in language, since its rules, orthography, grammatical correctness, also are the object of an apprenticeship that, as everyone has experienced, at school or elsewhere, is not exempt from threats and sanctions. Language . . . is at the same time the support of the law and the object of a law. (2005, 23)

See also Crépon 2014, 8–22.

CHAPTER 4: KILLING TIME

Epigraph translations:
"The serial killer leaves his signature, you see? He doesn't have a motive but he does have a signature" (Bolaño, *2666*, trans. Natasha Wimmer).

"I am completely elsewhere" (Derrida, *The Postcard*, trans. Alan Bass).

1. On auto-affection, life, and touch, see Johnson 2015.
2. Recall Husserl's claim that "*while the being of consciousness*, of any stream of mental processes whatever, *would indeed be necessarily modified by an annihilation of the world of physical things its own existence would not be touched.* . . . *Consequently no real being*, no being which is presented and legitimated in consciousness by appearances, *is necessary to the being of consciousness itself*" (1983, §49:91–92).
3. Reyes writes: "The year of the Centenary [1910] is already far off. One remembers it already with effort. Perhaps it would like to be forgotten" (1960b, 216).

4. In *On Interpretation* Aristotle explains: "Words spoken are symbols or signs of affections or impressions of the soul; written words are the signs of words spoken. As writing, so also is speech not the same for all races of men. But the mental affections themselves, of which these words are primarily signs, are the same for the whole of mankind, as are also the objects of which those affections are representations or likenesses, images, copies" (16a4–9).
5. This is not an argument, however, that agrees with Alberto Moreiras's claim that the infrapolitical dimension of the thriller "also gives us a possible form to think about the ethico-political, and thus to understand the possibility of a *properly democratic literature, a literature thoroughly invested by and in ethical universalism*" (2007, 164, emphasis added). Democracy's mutually exclusive demand for equality and freedom for all complicates this claim. It remains unclear, moreover, what a literature "thoroughly invested by and in ethical universalism" would be. On the one hand, an ethical universalism must necessarily be impossible insofar as ethics is predicated upon a decision, and every decision does violence to the other. Moreiras, however, argues against the decision—or what he calls the calculative decision—in the name of democracy or of democratic literature, as if democracy were beyond calculation. According to Moreiras, literature has an "undeniable privilege as a means of thinking about democracy, which is also, or above all, a means of imagining the possibility of a decision outside calculative reason" (2007, 164). Literature's "undeniable privilege" is hard to understand, not least because literature—the modern institution of literature—arises alongside the great modern democratic experiments. The question, however, is rather simple: What would a democracy beyond calculation look like? What would be the chance for a democracy that does not count? What would be a decision that does not calculate, that would take place "outside calculative reason"? A decision that does not count? As if the calculable and the incalculable were simply opposed, when, in fact, every decision—every *just* decision—calculates *with* (not against or outside or beyond) the incalculable. Moreiras claims that what interests him is "the regional question of the relation between literature and crime, and its relation with the ethical secret of the world" (171). He argues, moreover, that "to recognize, to unconceal, to show the secret of the world, if that is the essence of the literary, is an extraliterary essence. The relation between literature and murder seems to posit that the essence of the literary is not itself literary, that the literary apparatus deploys its potentiality at the service of something other than itself. That something other—the secret of the world—determines the structure of the literary apparatus" (165). The question, I think, is the following: Even if, as Moreiras argues, literature is necessarily invested in and by ethical universalism and even if the essence of literature is extraliterary, does it necessarily follow that the "secret of the world" must be ethical? Moreiras's argument seems to be that literature seeks to reveal its own essence, which is nevertheless not literary, hence not to be found in literature—and that this essence, which determines literature without being of literature, is ethical. The essence of literature is ethical, but this ethics is not to be found in literature, but

in the world. It is the secret of the world. But Moreiras never says what the world is, that we might find in it the essence of literature. Further, it is entirely unclear how a universal ethics *qua* the essence of literature might be found in the world (which is not found in literature, but rather literature is found in it), which is not, as far as anyone can see, universally ethical.

6. Derrida writes: "It is because there would be telepathy that a postcard can always not arrive at its destination. The ultimate naïveté would be to allow oneself to think that telepathy guarantees a destination that 'posts and telecommunications' fail to assure. On the contrary, everything I said about the postcarded structure (*la structure cartepostalée*) of the mark (interference, parasiting, divisibility, iterability, and so on) is found in the network. This goes for any telesystem—whatever its content, form, or medium" (1987b, 1:249–250/2007, 239).
7. Aristotle proposed the idea that the highest form of thought was *noesis noeseos*, or thought thinking itself. In *Politiques de l'amitié*, however, Derrida argues that thought thinking nothing but itself amounts to thinking nothing at all: "But one then thinks of someone who cannot think or who thinks nothing other than self, who does not think to the extent that he thinks nothing but self" (1994a, 252/1997, 223).
8. It first appears in the testimony of Amadeo Salvatierra when he recounts the names of the "Directorio de Vanguardia" published in *Actual, No.1*: "The directory began with the names of Rafael Cansinos-Assens and Ramón Gómez de la Serna. Strange, isn't it? Cansinos-Assens and Gómez de la Serna, as if Borges y Manuel [Maples Arce] had been in telepathic communication, wouldn't you say?" (1998, 218/2007, 225). But given that Salvatierra acknowledges that Borges knew Maples Arce's work, having reviewed it in 1922 (218/225), the idea that Borges and Maples Arce would be on the same page with respect to who constituted the vanguard of modern art and poetics can be explained without recourse to telepathy. The second reference occurs in his testimony of the same long, drunken night in January 1976, in response to either Ulises Lima's or Arturo Belano's question concerning what happened to Encarnación Guzmán; Salvatierra reports, "I took my time answering. Or maybe first I answered telepathically, as drunk old men often do, and then, in the face of the obvious, I opened my big mouth and said . . ." (458/485–486). The third instance appears in Barbara Patterson's testimony, dated March 1981, of her life in San Diego with Rafael and of their encounter with a Cuban poet, "the great lyric poet of the Revolution." She remarks: "I tried to tell Rafael telepathically: don't blow it now, don't fuck this up"; but she didn't try to communicate with him by telepathy only, because she adds parenthetically, "(before we went in I told him I'd kill him if he did it)" (323/341), that is, if he mentioned the *vicerealistas*.
9. And it may not have been. Or rather, there was not one cadaver, but many, and Gregorio's may or may not have been among the bones found in the clandestine common grave: "With respect to Gregorio, no news was conclusive. According to some forensic experts, his body could be among the pile of bones exhumed from that clandestine cemetery, but to be sure, a DNA test should be done, but the

government didn't have the resources or didn't have the interest to do the test and so every day the test gets put off a little farther" (Bolaño 1997, 27/2006, 16). We have read this story before.

10. On the double demands of temporal dislocation, see Sussman 2009, 1035–1036.
11. See Schmid 2005, especially 68–72. Schmid quotes from the first US edition of John Brophy, *The Meaning of Murder* (New York: Thomas Y. Crowell, 1967), 166. Although he acknowledges that Brophy established the concept or category of serial murder, he also notes that in the United States, it was not until an FBI news conference on 26 October 1983 that "the concept of 'serial murder' came to the attention of the American public for the first time" (77).
12. In the bibliography to *The Killing Fields*, Washington Valdez lists an interview (undated) with Ressler as the source for this statement. She does, however, claim that Ressler "coined the term 'serial killer'" (2006, 349).
13. See Kant 1998, 273–274; A141–142/B180–181. On transcendental schematism and its signature, see Johnson 2011, 106–112.
14. See chapter three, note 38; and Johnson 2011.
15. First published in *Caras* (Santiago, Chile), 20 February 1998. Bolaño seems almost immediately to retract this statement: "Did I say that one comes to literature by chance? No, no, no, to literature one never comes by chance. Never, never. You need to understand this. It is, let's say, destiny, yes? An obscure destiny, a series of circumstances that make you choose. And you always knew that that was your path. And I have always known it; I've always been very fanciful" (2006, 99). How to read this? In fact, it follows the logic already outlined. If one's destiny is obscure, it means one cannot see it, one cannot know it, except posthumously, after the fact; one always sees one's destiny in the rearview mirror. If literature—understood as one's destiny—always arrives in the rearview mirror, that is, if one knows that literature has arrived (or that one has arrived at literature) only after the fact, then the experience of literature, of its event or happening, is marked by jet lag, delay. The circumstances of literature's event can only be explained—known—posthumously, after the fact. The decisions we make to arrive at literature can be said to have led us to literature only once literature is already behind us.
16. Uranga writes: "The Mexican's behaviors or conducts are the 'modes' of accidentalization of its originary accidentality. When we say that the ontological origin of the Mexican is found in the accident, one must not think that in order to obtain the Mexican in its concretion, in 'flesh and bone,' one would have to add something to that accident. The concrete is the accident itself" (2013, 54).
17. Leopoldo Zea begins *El occidente y la conciencia de México* by observing that

> the concern of Mexican being, that is, for its humanity, as a philosophical problem has provoked, among other things, the critique of this question. Never, it is objected, has a Plato, a Descartes, a Hume, or a Kant wondered about the being of the Greek, the French, the English or the German. When they speak of man they refer to man in general, to Man with majuscule. Their philosophy is authentic philosophical philosophizing because they refer to the universal: to Man, not

> to the man of this or that place, of this or that time. They refer simply to Man, such that the Greek, the French, the English or the German is something purely accidental. (1952, 77)

CHAPTER 5: SUSPENDING SUR/RENDER

Epigraph translations:
"Who is the stranger?, we ask. . . . The one in whom walks the word in a language foreign to these lands to name the things that man's labor puts in the world? The one who rejects the dark color of his skin, who is ashamed of his past and uses the word 'Indian' as an insult and disqualification?" (EZLN, 2 October 1994).

"The Mexican flag, the supreme law of the nation, the Mexican hymn, and the national crest are now under the care of the forces of the Resistance until legality, legitimacy, and sovereignty are restored throughout the national territory. . . . The EZLN will support the civilian population in the work of restoring national legality, order, legitimacy, and sovereignty, and in the struggle for the formation and installation of a national government of transition to democracy" (EZLN, "Third Declaration," 2 January 1995).

1. Nicol writes:

> No one currently doubts that the notion of the body is in effect a notion derived from immediate experience, and not derived from an abstract philosophical conception. To affirm that in man there is no body, or that what is perceived immediately is not a body, would seem to be a paradox. Nevertheless, the differential characteristics of the human body, as human, are precisely those that determine a peculiar modality of attentional disposition, and some peculiar modalities of existential relation with the foreign body, very different from the modalities that the subject adopts when it relates with those beings that are properly pure bodies. The presence of the body is indubitable in the cadaver, because the cadaver is precisely body without spirit; but neither is the cadaver for us an indifferent body, but rather, on the contrary: our attitude before the cadaver still accentuates the human character of that dead body. (2009, 500)

2. To be sure, this line begins with the Ateneo de la Juventud (Alfonso Reyes, Pedro Henríquez Ureña, Antonio Caso, and Vasconcelos, among others) and moves through Ramos and the Spanish expatriate José Gaos to the Grupo Hiperión (which included, among others, Leopoldo Zea, Emilio Uranga, Luis Villoro, and Jorge Portilla), which proposed to develop a "*filosofía de lo mexicano*." Paz published *El laberinto de la soledad* in Jesús Silva Herzog's *Cuadernos americanos* in 1949, with a second edition appearing in Fondo de la Cultura Económica in 1959. Although *El laberinto* responds to Ramos's *El perfil del hombre y la cultura en México* (1934), Paz recalled in *Postdata* that in *El laberinto* he was not interested in the question of *lo mexicano*. There are, of course, others whose works might

easily—if somewhat more problematically—be ranked among those concerned with *lo mexicano*: Carlos Fuentes, Rosario Castellanos, Carlos Monsívais, Elena Poniatowska, Roger Bartra, to name some of the most prominent.

3. In the twentieth century this line begins with the figure of Emiliano Zapata, but it would also include—again, problematically—Miguel León-Portilla, whose *La filosofía náhuatl estudiada en sus fuentes* (1959) is influenced by European existentialism while also instancing one of the first attempts (following but also extending Ángel María Garibay's work) to take seriously Náhuatl traditions, literature, and ritual practices as thought, as philosophy. This effort, along with León-Portilla's translations of Náhuatl literature and his rediscovery of the work of Bernardino de Sáhagun, opened the door toward a new and profound engagement with Amerindian thought and culture. The revolutionary and agrarian reformist Rubén Jaramillo, who was assassinated by government agents in 1962, would also find a place in this trajectory.
4. Vasconcelos singles out the Argentine paleontologist Florentino Ameghino (1854–1991), who contended that all the mammals of the world—humans included—had their origin in Argentine Patagonia and South America.
5. See, for instance, Stephens 1841 and 1843; and Johnson 1995.
6. "Imitation," Kant writes, "becomes **aping** if the student copies everything, even down to that which the genius had to leave in, as a deformity, only because it could not easily have been removed without weakening the idea" (2001, §49: 196). For Kant genius names a specific relation of the faculties of imagination and understanding. Unlike cognitive decisions, where the imagination "is under the constraint of the understanding and is subject to the limitation of being adequate to its concept" (§49:194), in aesthetic judgments

> the imagination is free to provide, beyond that concord with the concept, unsought extensive undeveloped material for the understanding, of which the latter took no regard in its concept, but which it applies, not so much objectively, for cognition, as subjectively, for the animation of the cognitive powers, and thus also indirectly to cognitions; thus genius really consists in the happy relation, which no science can teach and no diligence can learn, of finding ideas for a given concept on the one hand and on the other hitting upon the **expression** for these, through which the subjective disposition of the mind that is thereby produced, as an accompaniment of a concept, can be communicated to others. (§49:194–195)

Finally, genius names the possibility of communicating the incommunicable, of sharing that which cannot be shared, and thus opening the possibility of community, that is, of bringing the human being out of itself in relation to others. It is the free play of the imagination that makes community possible in the absence of law, of normativity. Before the law, there is the imagination and with it the promise of universal communicability or expression. At stake, then, although Kant does not say so, is perhaps what Vasconcelos calls the "law of sympathy."

> The latter talent is really that which is called spirit, for to express what is unnameable in the mental state in the case of a certain representation and to make it universally communicable, whether the expression consist in language, or painting, or in plastic art—that requires a faculty for apprehending the rapidly passing play of the imagination and unifying it into a concept (which for that very reason is original and at the same time discloses a new rule, which could not have been deduced from any antecedent principles or examples), which can be communicated without the constraint of rules. (§49:195)

7. Despite Vasconcelos's and Ramos's agreement that Amerindians lack (the) imagination, the faculty performs different operations in their respective philosophies. In Vasconcelos, the imagination—as the supreme faculty and the operator of the law of sympathy—makes possible immediate judgments or decisions. In the epoch of its superiority, it is that which takes the place of reflection or reflexivity. In Ramos, the imagination provides for the possibility of self-critique and self-reflection.
8. "For lack of certain information about our soul, we have lacked our points of reference for ordering the vision of European things from a Mexican perspective. It has never been thought according to a conscious and methodical selection of the forms of European culture capable of acclimatizing themselves to our land. Doubtless such a system is possible, taking as it ground certain instinctive affinities that incline our race to prefer some aspects of the culture more than others" (Ramos 1990, 1:146).
9. In *L'intuition philosophique* (first presented as a lecture on 10 April 1911), Bergson remarked,

   > Can we grasp again that intuition itself? We have only two means of expression, the concept and the image. It is in concepts that the system develops; it is in an image that it narrows itself when we push it back toward the intuition from which it descends: that if one wants to leave behind the image in going higher than it, one necessarily falls back upon concepts, and on vaguer, still more general concepts than those from which one departed in the search for the image and the intuition. (2011c, 15–16)

   The gap (*l'écart*) between *l'image médiatrice* and *l'intuition* cannot be crossed, cannot be closed. Of *l'image médiatrice*, which neither is the intuition nor represents it, but which nonetheless is the source of all concepts and ideas of or about (hence that represent) the intuition, Bergson writes that it is "an image that is almost matter in that it still lets itself be seen, and is almost mind in that it no longer lets itself be touched—a phantom that haunts us while we turn around the doctrine and to which must be addressed in order to obtain the decisive sign, the indication of the attitude to take and of the point from which to look" (2011c, 14).
10. Letter to Harald Höffding, 15 March 1915.

11. Ramos writes: "As by magical influence, the indigenous 'Egyptianism' seems to have been communicated to all the men and things of Mexico" (1990, 1:108).
12. All inheritance is divided: the Pontifical University of Mexico, founded in 1982 by the Vatican, might also be considered the heir to the Royal and Pontifical University of Mexico.
13. Also, according to Ramos: "All thought should part from the acceptance that we are Mexicans and that we have to see the world from a unique perspective, [as the] outcome of our position in it" (1990, 1:176).
14. On Spain's missing the Enlightenment, see Paz 1979, 44; on the absence of *la crítica*, see Paz 1999, 114.
15. Paz lists them as "bureaucratic party regimes, monopolies of information, corruption, etc." (1999, 246).
16. The list of examples is Paz's; see 1967, 98.
17. Has there ever been such a primitive person? Perhaps the Greek who thought a portrait was a living man. The first sentence of Aristotle's *Categories* reads: "When things have only a name in common and the definition of being which corresponds to the name is different, they are called *homonymous*" (1a1).
18. See also Paz 1967, 112–113.
19. Critique (*crítica*) comes from the Greek *kritikós* and *krísis*, meaning "able to discern, critical" and "a power of distinguishing, choice, selection" (Liddell and Scott 2006).
20. Paz claims, "When a society becomes corrupt, the first thing that becomes gangrenous is the language" (1999, 274). The resuscitation of political life begins, therefore, with the critique of language:

> The critique of society, consequently, begins with the grammar and with the re-establishment of meanings. This is what has happened in Mexico. The critique of the status quo was not initiated either by the moralists or the radical revolutionaries but by the writers (a few from the older generations and the majority of the younger). Their critique has not been directly political—although they have not avoided treating political themes in their work—but rather verbal: the exercise of critique as exploration of language and the exercise of language as critique of reality. (1999, 274/1985, 263)

According to Paz,

> Criticism of the language is an active operation that means digging into the language to discover what is hidden there: the worm-eaten foundations of institutions, the mire of the subsoil, the slimy creatures therein, the endless underground galleries like prisons, those Mexican prisons in which so many of the young are now locked up. . . . The appearance of this critical and passionate art, obsessed with the double images of daily marvels and banalities, of humor and passion, surprised and disturbed the new class in power. (1999, 275/1985, 265)

21. See Kant 1998, A137–147/B176–187, 271–277.

22. We should note that Fuentes believed that during the administration of Luis Echeverría (who succeeded Gustavo Díaz Ordaz as president), "many Mexicans felt free to criticize, to express themselves, to organize without fear of repression" (1994, 166). Despite this, Fuentes nonetheless acknowledges that "Echeverría did not fulfill one basic condition for political democratization to triumph: he did not dismantle the repressive apparatus created in 1968" (166). And on 10 June 1971 this apparatus once again violently repressed demonstrations.
23. In the early twenty-first century, after the PRI's removal from (2000, 2006) and return to (2012) the presidency, Mexico continues to call for democracy and democratization. There can never be enough democracy, although there appears to be some debate over what constitutes democracy or what kind of democracy Mexico needs; see, for example, Villoro 1997, 329–381, and 2007, 117–129; and Hurtado 2011, 50–69.
24. The best recent attempt to account for this haunting is Samuel Steinberg, *Photopoetics at Tlatelolco: Afterimages of Mexico, 1968* (Austin: University of Texas Press, 2016).
25. Steinberg suggests that the MEP ended abruptly after Tlatelolco, not having the time to betray itself or to wither away. Of course, this is, strictly speaking, impossible. As Derrida puts it in *Specters of Marx*, "As soon as one identifies a revolution, it begins to imitate, it enters into a death agony" (1993b, 188/1994b, 115). Such autoimitation, which is the condition of possibility of the revolution, of resistance, ineluctably falsifies the revolution. To be sure, 2 October 1968 can be read as the "end" of the movement, both in the sense that so many died there and in the sense that the movement seemed to lose its direction, but it is no less possible to read December 1968, some two months later, as another possible ending:

> The resistance lasted one more month. Hundreds of rallies, debates, brigade activity. . . . But we were in the stage of no return. We needed to find new forms of struggle, and we couldn't. In the end, on 4 December, the last schools accepted the resumption of classes. I voted to end the strike, thinking that we had to bring the repression to an end and reorganize. The National Strike Council disbanded. Everyone swore in their particular way that there could be no forgetting, that something would have to be done, that one day we would return. (Taibo II 2008, 107/2004, 117)

Two months after Tlatelolco, the movement voted to retire, to surrender or to cease resistance, in anticipation of its return at a later date. What does this decision mean? Does it amount to the self-betrayal, the democratic destruction of the movement in the name of the movement? And if so, is this not a necessary possibility of any—of every—democracy?
26. See Rancière 1995, 51–52/1999, 28–29; see also A. Acosta 2014, 13.
27. See also the communiqué dated 12 October 1995, marking the 503rd anniversary of Columbus's arrival, which recalls the Zapatistas' heritage as stemming from "our greatest grandfathers, those who initiated the long struggle of resistance

against the pride of power and the violence of money" and which claims that the indigenous citizens are the "fundamental part of a country whose governors have a foreign vocation and look with contempt and repugnance on our past" (EZLN 1997, 3:37–38). This communiqué is instructive not least for its discussion of the word (which is indigenous and which is life) and of silence (which is imposed on the original inhabitants by the conquerors—and by neoliberalism—and which is death), but also for its determination of the "indigenous heart [by which] we call ourselves Mexicans" (3:38).

28. This double inheritance is invoked in the Zapatista message on the seventy-fifth anniversary (10 April 1995) of Zapata's assassination: "In us, in our weapons, in our covered face, in our true word, Zapata is united to the wisdom and struggle of our most ancient ancestors" (EZLN 1995, 2:307).
29. Quoted in Volpi 2004, 283.
30. See also EZLN 1994, 1:163, and 1995, 2:99.
31. See, for example, EZLN 1995, 2:58; see also EZLN 1995, 2:135, 2:138, 2:145.
32. On the federal government's identification of Marcos, see Guillermoprieto 2002; Stavans 2002; Volpi 2004, 137–139. In an announcement on 25 May 2014, Marcos officially "retired" from his position as the "voice" through which the EZLN and its CCRI-CG speaks. He claimed in the announcement that Marcos was always only a "hologram"—thus a ghost or specter—and his new *nom de guerre* was "Galeano"; "Mexico's Zapatista Leader Subcomandante Marcos Steps Down," 26 May 2014, www.bbc.com/news/world-latin-america-27569695. In a gesture that replicates the Mexican government's insistence on denying Marcos his name, the BBC report insists on quoting not Marcos but Rafael Guillén Vicente.
33. Marcos himself offers a different reason why the Zapatistas hide their faces. When asked if the Zapatistas would wear the *pasamontañas* during the 2001 Marcha del Color de la Tierra (the so-called "Zapatour"), he responded, "Yes, they will go with ski masks. Because the ski mask is already a symbol of Zapatismo. The ski mask signals that the government didn't see the Indians when they showed themselves, and now that they hide themselves, yes, they see them. It's also an invitation to everyone to feel a part of this struggle" (2003, 5:84). See also EZLN 1994, 1:98–99, and 1:167. For Marcos's and the EZLN's recognition of the problem of the media focus on "Marcos," see 1995, 2:136, and 2003, 5:347.
34. Signatories include Subcomandante Insurgente Marcos, El Sup, and El Sup Marcos but also the CCRI-CG del EZLN; comandantes David, Tacho, Bulmaro, Mister, Abel, Moisés, Zebedeo, Omar, Abraham, and Alejandro; and comandantas Ana, Esther, Yolanda, Susana, and Fidelia.
35. This is the autoimmunity of language, of symbolization. In *La vérité en peinture*, Derrida remarks that the bridge is not one analogy among others:

> The bridge is not *an* analogy. The recourse to analogy, the concept and effect of analogy are or make *the bridge* itself. . . . The analogy of the abyss and of the bridge over the abyss is an analogy which says that there must surely be an analogy between two absolutely heterogeneous worlds, a third term to cross the

> abyss, to heal over the gaping wound and think the gap. In a word, a *symbol*. The bridge is a symbol, it passes from one bank to the other, and the symbol is a bridge. (Derrida 1978c, 43/1987c, 36)

36. For Marcos's understanding that the missive or communiqué is necessarily cut off from sender (*remitente*) and receiver (*destinatario*), see 2003, 5:82–83.
37. On 11 January 1994, as the fifth and final item in a communiqué addressed "To the people of Mexico/To the peoples and governments of the world," the CCRI-CG declared, "The only valid documents as emitted by the EZLN and recognized by all the Zapatista combatants are those that have the signature of comrade insurgent Subcommander Marcos" (1994, 1:80). Yet on 16 February 1994, Marcos is unsure if he will be included in the delegation that will participate in the peace talks with the Salinas administration's commissioner for peace, Manuel Camacho Solís, and, in any event, he has been ordered to maintain media silence: "However it may turn out, go or not, the CCRI-CG has ordered me to maintain written silence, thus I will put away my powerful machine for 'making communications' (a pen) upon finishing this" (1:154). There follow nine brief postscripts under the general title "The Mercantilist Postscript," and Marcos's signature: "The *sup* in ostracism" (1:154–155). The strategic failures of the EZLN are routinely blamed on Marcos's "protagonism": "Our word has not been, many times, the most successful or the most timely. Who has the voice and the ears of the Zapatista National Liberation Army has been mistaken on not a few occasions, in his word and in his interloctors" (1995, 2:136).
38. The "Fifth Declaration from the Lacandon Jungle" asserts, "There will be no transition to democracy, nor reform of the state, nor real solution of the principal problems of the national agenda, without the Indian peoples. With the indigenous a better and new country is necessary and possible. Without them, there is no future as a nation" (2003, 4:234).
39. In fact, in Náhuatl there are at least two words that mean "to surrender" or *rendirse*: *mactia* and *temaca* (and *temachtia*); see Karttunen 1992. In Mayan there is at least one: *kubulte*; see Restall 1998.
40. Bonfil Batalla insists, no doubt correctly, that there was constant contact among the diverse cultures of precolonial Mexico and that the relations between the various cultures and even between Mesoamerican civilization and non-Mesoamerican civilization (to the north, for example) "were not in every case violent" (1987, 30/1996, 9).
41. See Kwasi Wiredu 1999, "Democracy and Consensus in African Traditional Politics," *Polylog* no. 1: 131, https://them.polylog.org/2/fwk-en.htm.
42. Yet isn't this the definition of all democracy, that is, of democracy? Doesn't democracy instance the institution of a State of Revolution that necessarily and continuously ruins itself? Isn't this the logic of democracy?
43. On this matter, see Kant 1996, §§18–19:57–58.

POSTSCRIPT

1. Poniatowska cites the former French president Valéry Giscard d'Estaing as an exemplary politician who, like her, was personally opposed to abortion but believed that, as the president of a secular state, he could not impose his personal, religious convictions on his fellow citizens; rather, he thought he should procure for women their civil rights; see Poniatowska 2007, 60–61. The then-effective French law denied women the right to an abortion and subjected them to criminal prosecution for pursuing the voluntary interruption of pregnancy (*interruption volontaire de grossesse*, or IVG). Poniatowska claims this occurred in 1982 and gives the impression that the change in the law is largely attributable to Giscard d'Estaing. Giscard d'Estaing, however, was in office only from 1974 to 1981. In France, the law granting women the right to an abortion is generally referred to as "*la loi Veil*," in honor of the woman largely responsible for its passage, Simone Veil (whom Poniatowska does not mention and who served as the minister of health during the Giscard d'Estaing administration), who was a proponent of a woman's right to abortion long before she joined Giscard d'Estaing's administration. The law became effective on 17 January 1975, perhaps in part as the result of the *affaire Bobigny* (1972), in which a sixteen-year-old girl, Marie-Claire Chevalier, was raped and impregnated by a classmate, Daniel P. She sought to have an abortion, which was prohibited under French law. Marie-Claire and her mother, Michèle Chevalier, along with three other women (Lucette D., Renée S., and Madame B., the "*faiseuse d'anges*") were prosecuted for either pursuing or performing an abortion. In France, in the decade prior to the *affaire Bobigny*, women seeking or performing abortions were rather aggressively prosecuted, more so, in fact, than at any time other than the period of the Vichy government. In 1965, for instance, some 588 women were condemned for practicing (or pursuing) abortions. In the three years immediately preceding the prosecution of the Bobigny affair (1970–1972), 1,241 women were condemned, but in 1973 the number of guilty verdicts fell to 67. In 1974 there were only 13, and 1975 only 10. The drop in prosecutions and guilty verdicts is largely attributable to the anticipation of the change of law in the wake of the Bobigny case. In Mexico the opposite has happened. In the aftermath of the Paulina case, Mexican states have become more conservative and have more aggressively prosecuted women seeking and performing abortions. I thank Andrea Garrido for pointing out Poniatowska's error and for alerting me to the Bobigny case.
2. As reported in Alyn Gaestel and Allison Shelley's 1 October 2014 article, "Mexican Women Pay High Price for Country's Abortion Laws," www.theguardian.com/global-development/2014/oct/01/mexican-women-high-price-abortion-laws.

REFERENCES

Acosta, Abraham. 2014. *Thresholds of Illiteracy: Theory, Latin America, and the Crisis of Resistance*. New York: Fordham University Press.

Acosta, María del Rosario. 2012. "Variaciones sobre el perdón: Una sugerencia sobre política y transición a partir de Hegel." *Universitas philosophica* 59: 33–50.

Aguilar Camín, Héctor. 2012. *La modernidad fugitiva: México 1988–2012*. Mexico, DF: Editorial Planeta Mexicana.

Aguilar Camín, Héctor, and Jorge G. Castañeda. 2009. *Un futuro para México*. Mexico, DF: Santillana Ediciones Generales.

Alter, Robert. 2004. *The Five Books of Moses: A Translation with Commentary*. New York: W. W. Norton.

Arasse, Daniel. 1987. *La guillotine et l'imaginaire de la Terreur*. Paris: Flammarion.

Aristotle. 1984. *The Complete Works of Aristotle: The Revised Oxford Translation*. Edited by Jonathan Barnes. 2 vols. Princeton, NJ: Princeton University Press.

Arriola, Elvia R. 2010. "Accountability for Murder in the *Maquiladoras*: Linking Corporate Indifference to Gender Violence at the U.S.-Mexico Border." In *Making a Killing: Femicide, Free Trade, and La Frontera*, edited by Alicia Gaspar de Alba with Georgina Guzmán, 25–61. Austin: University of Texas Press.

Artaud, Antonin. 1984. *México y viaje al país de los tarahumaras*. Mexico, DF: Fondo de Cultura Económica.

Aubenque, Pierre. 2013. *Le problème de l'être chez Aristote*. Paris: Presses Universitaires de France.

Bartra, Roger. 1987. *La jaula de la melancolía: Identidad y metamorfosis del mexicano*. Mexico, DF: Editorial Grijalbo.

———. 2006. *Antropología del cerebro: La conciencia y los sistemas simbólicos*. Mexico, DF: Fondo de Cultura Económica.

———. 2012. *La sombra del futuro: Reflexiones sobre la transición mexicana*. Mexico, DF: Fondo de Cultura Económica.

Bergson, Henri. 2011a. *Écrits philosophiques*. Paris: Presses Universitaires de France.

———. 2011b. *L'âme et le corps*. Paris: Presses Universitaires de France.

———. 2011c. *L'intuition philosophique*. Paris: Presses Universitaires de France.

Bernet, Rudolf. 1991. "Le concept husserlien du noème." Translated by Gérard Granel. *Les études philosophiques* 1: 79–100.

Bolaño, Roberto. 1996. *Estrella distante*. Barcelona: Editorial Anagrama.

———. 1997. *Llamadas telefónicas*. Barcelona: Editorial Anagrama.

———. 1998. *Los detectives salvajes*. Barcelona: Editorial Anagrama.

———. 2004. *2666*. Barcelona: Editorial Anagrama.

———. 2006. *Last Evenings on Earth*. Translated by Chris Andrews. New York: New Directions.

———. 2007. *The Savage Detectives*. Translated by Natasha Wimmer. New York: Farrar, Straus, Giroux.

———. 2008. *2666*. Translated by Natasha Wimmer. New York: Farrar, Straus, Giroux.

———. 2011a [2006]. *Bolaño por sí mismo: Entrevistas escogidas*. Edited by Andrés Braithwaite. Santiago: Universidad Diego Portales.

———. 2011b. *Los sinsabores del verdadero policía*. Barcelona: Editorial Anagrama.

———. 2012. *Woes of the True Policeman: A Novel*. Translated by Natasha Wimmer. New York: Farrar, Straus, Giroux.

Bonfil Batalla, Guillermo. 1990. *México profundo: Una civilización negada*. Mexico, DF: Editorial Grijalbo.

———. 1996. *Mexico Profundo: Reclaiming a Civilization*. Translated by Philip A. Dennis. Austin: University of Texas Press.

Borges, Jorge Luis. 1996. *Obras completas*. 4 volumes. Buenos Aires: Emecé Editores.

———. 2000. *Selected Non-Fictions*. Edited by Eliot Weinberger. New York: Penguin.

Bueno-Hansen, Pascha. 2010. "*Feminicidio*: Making the Most of an 'Empowered Term.'" In *Terrorizing Women: Feminicide in the Américas*, edited by Rosa-Linda Fregoso and Cynthia Bejarano, 290–311. Durham, NC: Duke University Press.

Caso, Antonio. 1922. *Discursos a la nación*. Mexico, DF: Porrúa.

———. 1972. *Obras completas*. Vol. 7, *El acto ideatorio, La filosofía de Husserl, Positivismo, neopositivismo y fenomenología*. Mexico, DF: Universidad Nacional Autónoma de México.

Caso, Antonio, Alfonso Reyes, Pedro Henríquez Ureña, Carlos González Peña, José Escofet, José Vasconcelos. 2000. *Conferencias del Ateneo de la Juventud*. Edited by Juan Hernández Luna. Mexico, DF: Universidad Nacional Autónoma de México.

Cassin, Barbara. 1995. *L'effet sophistique*. Paris: Gallimard.

Colón, Cristóbal. 1989. *The Diario of Christopher Columbus's First Voyage to America, 1492–1493*. Translated by Oliver Dunn and James E Kelley Jr. Norman: University of Oklahoma Press.

———. 1992. *Textos y documentos completos*. Edited by Consuelo Varela and Juan Gil. Madrid: Alianza Editorial.

Cortés, Hernán. 1986. *Letters from Mexico*. Translated by Anthony Pagden. New Haven, CT: Yale University Press.

———. 1990–1992. *Documentos cortesianos*. 4 vols. Edited by José Luis Martínez. Mexico, DF: Fondo de Cultura Económica.

———. 1993. *Cartas de relación*. Edited by Ángel Delgado Gómez. Madrid: Editorial Castalia.

Courtine, Jean-François. 2005. *Inventio analogiae: Métaphysique et ontothéologie*. Paris: Librairie Philosophique J. Vrin.

———. 2007. *La cause de la phénoménologie*. Paris: Presses Universitaires de France.

Crépon, Marc. 2005. *Langues sans demeure*. Paris: Éditions Galilée.

———. 2008. *La culture de la peur*. Vol. 1, *Démocratie, Identité, Sécurité*. Paris: Éditions Galilée.

———. 2014. *La vocation de l'écriture: La littérature et la philosophie à l'épreuve de la violence*. Paris: Odile Jacob.

Cypess, Sandra Messinger. 1991. *La Malinche in Mexican Literature: From History to Myth*. Austin: University of Texas Press.

De Man, Paul. 1996. *Aesthetic Ideology*. Edited by Andrzej Warminski. Minneapolis: University of Minnesota Press.

Derrida, Jacques. 1962. Introduction to *L'Origine de la géométrie*, by Edmund Husserl, 3–171. Translated by Jacques Derrida. Paris: Presses Universitaires de France.

———. 1967a. *De la grammatologie*. Paris: Les Éditions de Minuit.

———. 1967b. *L'écriture et la différence*. Paris: Éditions du Seuil.

———. 1972a. *La dissémination*. Paris: Éditions du Seuil.

———. 1972b. *Marges de la philosophie*. Paris: Les Éditions de Minuit.

———. 1974. *Of Grammatology*. Translated by Gayatri Chakravorty Spivak. Baltimore: Johns Hopkins University Press.

———. 1978a. *Husserl's Origin of Geometry: An Introduction*. Translated by John P. Leavey. Lincoln: University of Nebraska Press.

———. 1978b. *Writing and Difference*. Translated by Alan Bass. Chicago: University of Chicago Press.

———. 1978c. *La vérité en peinture*. Paris: Flammarion.

———. 1980. *La carte postale: De Socrate à Freud et au-delà*. Paris: Flammarion.

———. 1981. *Dissemination*. Translated by Barbara Johnson. Chicago: University of Chicago Press.

———. 1982. *Margins of Philosophy*. Translated by Alan Bass. Chicago: University of Chicago Press.

———. 1987a. *The Postcard: From Socrates to Freud and Beyond*. Translated Alan Bass. Chicago: University of Chicago Press.

———. 1987b. *Psyché: L'invention de l'autre*. 2 vols. Paris: Éditions Galilée.

———. 1987c. *Truth in Painting*. Translated by Geoffrey Bennington and Ian McCleod. Chicago: University of Chicago Press.
———. 1988. *Limited Inc*. Translated by Samuel Weber. Evanston, IL: Northwestern University Press.
———. 1990a. *Le problème de la genèse dans la philosophie de Husserl*. Paris: Presses Universitaires de France.
———. 1990b. *Limited Inc*. Edited by Elizabeth Rottenberg. Paris: Éditions Galilée.
———. 1992. "'This Strange Institution Called Literature.'" In *Acts of Literature*. Edited by Derek Attridge. London: Routledge.
———. 1993a. *Aporias*. Translated by Thomas Dutoit. Stanford, CA: Stanford University Press.
———. 1993b. *Spectres de Marx: L'État de la dette, le travail du deuil, et la nouvelle Internationale*. Paris: Éditions Galilée.
———. 1993c. *Passions*. Paris: Éditions Galilée.
———. 1994a. *Politiques de l'amitié*. Paris: Éditions Galilée.
———. 1994b. *Specters of Marx: The State of the Debt, the Work of Mourning, and the New International*. Translated by Peggy Kamuf. London: Routledge.
———. 1995a. *Mal d'archive: Une impression freudienne*. Paris: Éditions Galilée.
———. 1995b. *On the Name*. Edited by Thomas Dutoit. Translated by David Wood, John P. Leavy Jr., and Ian McLeod. Stanford, CA: Stanford University Press.
———. 1996a. *Apories: Mourir—s'attendre aux "limites de la vérité."* Paris: Éditions Galilée.
———. 1996b. *Le monolinguisme de l'autre ou la prothèse de l'origine*. Paris: Éditions Galilée.
———. 1996c. *Archive Fever: A Freudian Impression*. Translated by Eric Prenowitz. Chicago: University of Chicago Press.
———. 1997. *Politics of Friendship*. Translated by George Collins. London: Verso.
———. 1998a. *Demeure: Maurice Blanchot*. Paris: Éditions Galilée.
———. 1998b. *Monolingualism of the Other, or the Prosthesis of the Origin*. Translated by Patrick Mensah. Stanford, CA: Stanford University Press.
———. 1999. *Donner la mort*. Paris: Éditions Galilée.
———. 2000. *Demeure: Fiction and Testimony*. Translated by Elizabeth Rottenberg. Stanford, CA: Stanford University Press.
———. 2001. *L'Université sans condition*. Paris: Éditions Galilée.
———. 2002a. "Force of Law: 'The Mystical Foundation of Authority.'" In *Acts of Religion*, edited by Gil Anidjar. London: Routledge.
———. 2002b. "The University without Condition." In *Without Alibi*, edited and translated by Peggy Kamuf, 202–237, 300–302. Stanford, CA: Stanford University Press.
———. 2003a. *Béliers: Le dialogue ininterrompu: Entre deux infinis, le poème*. Paris: Éditions Galilée.
———. 2003b. *Chaque fois unique, la fin du monde*. Edited by Pascale-Anne Brault and Michael Naas. Paris: Éditions Galilée.
———. 2003c. *Voyous: Deux essais sur la raison*. Paris: Éditions Galilée.

———. 2003d. *The Problem of Genesis in Husserl's Philosophy.* Translated by Marian Hobson. Chicago: University of Chicago Press.

———. 2003e. "Autoimmunity: Real and Symbolic Suicides: A Dialogue with Jacques Derrida." In *Philosophy in a Time of Terror: Dialogues with Jacques Derrida and Jürgen Habermas*, edited by Giovanna Borradori, 85–136. Chicago: University of Chicago Press.

———. 2004. "*Et cetera* . . . (and so on, und so weiter, and so forth, et ainsi de suite, und so überall, *etc.*)." In *L'Herne Derrida*, edited by Marie-Louise Mallet and Ginette Michaud, 21–34. Paris: Éditions de l'Herne.

———. 2005a. *Rogues: Two Essays on Reason.* Translated by Pascale-Anne Brault and Michael Naas. Stanford, CA: Stanford University Press.

———. 2005b. "Rams: Uninterrupted Dialogue—Between Two Infinities, the Poem." In *Sovereignties in Question: The Poetics of Paul Celan*, edited by Thomas Dutoit and Outi Pasanen, 135–163. New York: Fordham University Press.

———. 2007. "Telepathy." Translated by Nicholas Royle. In *Psyche: Inventions of the Other*, vol. 1. Edited by Peggy Kamuf and Elizabeth Rottenberg. Stanford, CA: Stanford University Press.

———. 2008a. "Aphorism Countertime." Translated by Nicholas Royle. In *Psyché: Inventions of the Other*, vol. 2. Edited by Peggy Kamuf and Elizabeth Rottenberg, 127–142, 304. Stanford, CA: Stanford University Press.

———. 2008b. *The Gift of Death, second edition, and Literature in Secret.* Translated by David Wills. Chicago: University of Chicago Press.

———. 2010. *Séminaire La bête et le souverain.* Vol. 2, 2002–2003. Edited by Michel Lisse, Marie-Louise Mallet, and Ginette Michaud. Paris: Éditions Galilée.

———. 2011. *The Beast and the Sovereign.* Vol. 2, 2002–2003. Edited by Michel Lisse, Marie-Louise Mallet, and Ginette Michaud. Translated by Geoffry Bennington. Chicago: University of Chicago Press.

———. 2012. *Séminaire La peine de mort.* Vol. 1, 1999–2000. Edited by Geoffrey Bennington, Marc Crépon, and Thomas Dutoit. Paris: Éditions Galilée.

———. 2014. *The Death Penalty.* Vol. 1. Edited by Geoffrey Bennington, Marc Crépon, and Thomas Dutoit. Translated by Peggy Kamuf. Chicago: University of Chicago Press.

Díaz del Castillo, Bernal. 1991 [1576]. *Historia verdadera de la conquista de la Nueva España.* Edited by Carmelo Sáenz de Santa María. Mexico, DF: Alianza Editorial.

Dove, Patrick. 2014. "Ayotzinapa: Antes y después." *Horizontal 19: n.p.* Accessed 25 Jan. 2018. https://horizontal.mx/ayotzinapa-antes-y-despues.

———. 2016. *Literature and "Interregnum": Globalization, War, and the Crisis of Sovereignty in Latin America.* Albany, NY: SUNY Press.

Dreyfus, Hubert L. 1982. "Husserl's Perceptual Noema." In *Husserl, Intentionality and Cognitive Science*, edited by Hubert L. Dreyfus with Harrison Hall, 97–123. Cambridge, MA: MIT Press.

Drummond, J. J. 1992. "An Abstract Consideration: De-Ontologizing the Noema." In *The Phenomenology of the Noema*, edited by J. J. Drummond and L. Embree, 89–109. Dordrecht, Netherlands: Kluwer Academic Publishers.

Ejército Zapatista de Liberación Nacional (EZLN). 1994–2003. *EZLN: Documentos y comunicados*. 5 vols. Foreword by Antonio García de León. Mexico, DF: Ediciones Era.

Espinosa H., Patricia. 2006. "Secreto y simulacro en *2666* de Roberto Bolaño." *Estudios filológicos* 41:71–79. Accessed 6 March 2018. https://scielo.conicyt.cl/scielo.php?script=sci_arttext&pid=S0071-17132006000100006.

Farred, Grant. 2010. "The Impossible Closing: Death, Neoliberalism, and the Postcolonial in Bolaño's *2666*." *Modern Fiction Studies* 56, no. 4: 689–708.

Føllesdal, Dagfinn. 1969. "Husserl's Notion of Noema." *Journal of Philosophy* 66, no. 20: 680–687.

Foucault, Michel. 1975. *Surveiller et punir*. Paris: Gallimard.

———. 2015. *Qu'est-ce que la critique? Suivi par La Culture de Soi*. Paris: J. Vrin.

Franco, Jean. 2013. *Cruel Modernity*. Durham, NC: Duke University Press.

Fregoso, Rosa-Linda, and Cynthia Bejarano, eds. 2010a. *Terrorizing Women: Feminicide in the Américas*. Durham, NC: Duke University Press.

———. 2010b. "A Cartography of Feminicide in the Américas." Introduction to *Terrorizing Women: Feminicide in the Américas*, edited by Fregoso and Bejarano, 1–42.

Fuentes, Carlos. 1971. *Tiempo mexicano*. Mexico, DF: Joaquín Mortiz.

———. 1994. *Nuevo tiempo mexicano*. Mexico, DF: Aguilar.

Gasché, Rodolphe. 1986. *The Tain of the Mirror: Derrida and the Philosophy of Reflection*. Cambridge, MA: Harvard University Press.

———. 2012. *Georges Bataille: Phenomenology and Phantasmology*. Translated by Roland Vegso. Stanford, CA: Stanford University Press.

Gaspar de Álba, Alicia. 2005. *Desert Blood: The Juárez Murders*. Houston: Arte Público.

Gaspar de Alba, Alicia, ed., with Georgina Guzmán. 2010a. *Making a Killing: Femicide, Free Trade, and La Frontera*. Austin: University of Texas Press.

———. 2010b. "*Feminicidio*: The 'Black Legend' of the Border." Introduction to *Making a Killing: Femicide, Free Trade, and La Frontera*, edited by Gaspar de Alba, with Guzmán, 1–21.

Gaston, Sean. 2011. "Derrida and the End of the World." *New Literary History* 42, no. 3: 499–517.

Gibson, John. 2007. *Fiction and the Weave of the World*. Oxford: Oxford University Press.

Giletti Benso, Silvia. 2014. "Los crímenes de género y sus huellas: Aproximación al femigenocidio." *Deportate, esuli, profughe: Rivista telematica di studi sulla memoria femminile* 24: 1–17.

González Rodríguez, Sergio. 2006 [2002]. *Huesos en el desierto*. Mexico, DF: Editorial Anagrama.

———. 2009. *El hombre sin cabeza*. Mexico, DF: Editorial Anagrama.

———. 2012. *The Femicide Machine*. Los Angeles: Semiotext(e).

———. 2014. *Campo de guerra*. Mexico, DF: Editorial Anagrama.

———. 2015. *Los 43 de Iguala: México: Verdad y reto de los estudiantes desaparecidos*. Mexico, DF: Editorial Anagrama.

Gracia, Jorge J. E. 2002. "Borges's 'Pierre Menard': Philosophy or Literature?" In *Literary Philosophers: Borges, Calvino, Eco*, edited by Jorge J. E. Gracia, Carolyn Korsmeyer, and Rodolphe Gasché, 85–107. New York: Routledge.

Graff Zivin, Erin, ed. 2018. *The Marrano Spirit: Derrida and Hispanism*. New York: Fordham University Press.

Guillermoprieto, Alma. 2002. "The Unmasking." In *The Zapatista Reader*, edited by Tom Hayden, 33–45. New York: Nation Books.

Guzmán, Patricio, dir. 2010. *Nostalgia de la luz*. Paris: Atacama Productions.

Hägglund, Martin. 2008. *Radical Atheism: Derrida and the Time of Life*. Stanford, CA: Stanford University Press.

———. 2012. *Dying for Time: Proust, Woolf, Nabokov*. Cambridge, MA: Harvard University Press.

Hayden, Tom, ed. 2002. *The Zapatista Reader*. New York: Nation Books.

Hegel, G. W. F. 1971. *The Philosophy of Mind*. Translated by William Wallace. Oxford: Oxford University Press.

———. 1975. *Hegel's Aesthetics: Lectures on Fine Art*. 2 vols. Translated by T. M. Knox. Oxford: Oxford University Press.

———. 1991. *Elements of the Philosophy of Right*. Edited by Allen W. Wood. Translated by H. B. Nisbet. Cambridge: Cambridge University Press.

Heidegger, Martin. 1995. *Aristotle's Metaphysics θ 1–3: On the Essence and Actuality of Force*. Translated by Walter Brogan and Peter Warnek. Bloomington: Indiana University Press.

Hénaff, Marcel. 2012. *Le don des philosophes: Repenser la réciprocité*. Paris: Éditions du Seuil.

Holmes, Richard H. 1975. "An Explication of Husserl's Theory of the Noema." *Research in Phenomenology* 5, no. 1: 143–153.

Hurtado, Guillermo. 2011. *México sin sentido*. Mexico, DF: Siglo XXI Editores.

Husserl, Edmund. 1962. *L'Origine de la géométrie*. Translated by Jacques Derrida. Paris: Presses Universitaires de France.

———. 1978. "The Origin of Geometry." Translated by David Carr. In *Husserl's Origin of Geometry: An Introduction*, by Jacques Derrida, translated by John P. Leavey, 157–180. Lincoln: University of Nebraska Press.

———. 1983 [1913]. *Ideas Pertaining to a Pure Phenomenology and to a Phenomenological Philosophy*. Vol. 1, *General Introduction to a Pure Phenomenology*. Translated by F. Kersten. Boston: Kluwer Academic Publishers.

———. 1999. *Cartesian Meditations: An Introduction to Phenomenology*. Translated by Dorion Cairns. Boston: Kluwer Academic Publishers.

———. 2001. *The Shorter Logical Investigations*. Translated by J. N. Findlay. London: Routledge.

Irlam, Shaun. 2009. "*Antigone in Africa*: Perpétue Nshimirimana's *Lettre à Isidore* and the Right to Last Rites." *Textus* 22: 483–504.

Jaén, Didier T. 1997. Introduction to *The Cosmic Race/La raza cósmica*, by José Vasconcelos, translated by Didier T. Jaén, ix–xxxiii. Baltimore: Johns Hopkins University Press.

Johnson, David E. 1992. "The Place of the Translator in the Discourses of Conquest:

On Hernán Cortés's *Cartas de relación* and Roland Joffé's 'The Mission.'" In *Amerindian Images and the Legacy of Columbus*, edited by Nicholas Spadaccini and René Jara, 401–424. Minneapolis: University of Minnesota Press.

———. 1995. "'Writing in the Dark': The Political Fictions of American Travel Writing." *American Literary History* 7, no. 1: 1–27.

———. 2001. "Mexico's Gas, Mexico's Tears: Expositions of Identity." In *What Happens to History: The Renewal of Ethics in Contemporary Thought*, edited by Howard Marchitello, 149–188. New York: Routledge.

———. 2007. "How (Not) to Do Latin American Studies." *South Atlantic Quarterly* 106, no. 1: 1–19.

———. 2011. *Kant's Dog: On Borges, Philosophy, and the Time of Translation*. Albany, NY: SUNY Press.

———. 2014. "Wartime: Foucault, Hobbes, and the Promise of Peace." *Revista pléyade* 13: 61–85.

———. 2015. "Touching the Imagination: Aristotle, Derrida, and the Homonymy of Life." In "Derrida Matters," special issue, *theory@buffalo* 18: 48–77.

———. 2018. *El mundo en llamas*. Translated by Paula Cucurella. Santiago, Chile: Pólvora Editorial.

Jones, Philip B. N.d. *The* Secreto de los secretos, *a Castilian Version: A Critical Edition*. Baltimore: Scripta Humanistica.

Jörgensen, Beth E. 1994. *The Writing of Elena Poniatowska: Engaging Dialogues*. Austin: University of Texas Press.

———. 2011. *Documents in Crisis: Nonfiction Literatures in Twentieth-Century Mexico*. Albany, NY: SUNY Press.

Kant, Immanuel. 1996. *The Metaphysics of Morals*. Edited and Translated by Mary Gregor. Cambridge: Cambridge University Press.

———. 1998. *Critique of Pure Reason*. Translated by Paul Guyer and Allen Wood. Cambridge: Cambridge University Press.

———. 2001. *Critique of the Power of Judgment*. Translated by Paul Guyer and Eric Matthews. Cambridge: Cambridge University Press.

Karttunen, Frances. 1992. *An Analytical Dictionary of Nahuatl*. Norman: University of Oklahoma Press.

Kelman, David. 2018. "Spectral Comparisons: Cortázar and Derrida." In *The Marrano Spirit: Derrida and Hispanism*, edited by Erin Graff Zivin, 31–48. New York: Fordham University Press.

Kohut, Karl. 2002. "Política, violencia y literatura." *Anuario de estudios americanos* 59: 193–222.

Kosowski, Lukasz. 2012. "The Structure of the Noema in the Process of Objectivation." *Husserl Studies* 28: 143–160.

Las Casas, Bartolomé de. 1986 [1561]. *Historia de las Indias*. 3 vols. Edited by Agustín Millares Carlo. Mexico, DF: Fondo de Cultura Económica.

Levinson, Brett. 2018. "The Jew or Patriarchy (or Worse)." In *The Marrano Spirit: Derrida and Hispanism*, edited by Erin Graff Zivin, 67–80. New York: Fordham University Press.

Liddell, George Henry, and Robert Scott. 2006. *A Greek-English Lexicon*. 9th ed. New York: Oxford University Press.

Lomnitz, Claudio. 2005. *Death and the Idea of Mexico*. New York: Zone Books.

Lyotard, Jean-François. 1954. *La phénoménologie*. Paris: Presses Universitaires de France.

Marcos, Subcomandante, and the Zapatistas. 2006. *The Other Campaign/La otra campaña*. San Francisco: City Lights.

Marrati, Paola. 2005. *Genesis and Trace: Derrida's Reading of Husserl and Heidegger*. Translated by Simon Sparks. Stanford, CA: Stanford University Press.

Mendoza, Élmer. 2008. *Balas de plata*. Mexico City: Tusquets Editores.

Michaelsen, Scott, and Scott Cutler Shershow. 2005. "Is Nothing Secret?" *Discourse* 27, nos. 2–3: 124–154.

———. 2007. "Rethinking Border Thinking." *South Atlantic Quarterly* 106 no. 1: 39–60.

Monárrez Fragoso, Julia Estela. 2009. *Trama de una injusticia: Feminicidio sexual sistémico en Ciudad Juárez*. Tijuana: El Colegio de la Frontera Norte; and Mexico, DF: Miguel Ángel Porrúa.

———. 2010a. "The Suffering of the Other." Translated by Georgina Guzmán. In *Making a Killing: Femicide, Free Trade, and La Frontera*, edited by Alicia Gaspar de Alba, with Georgina Guzmán, 183–199. Austin: University of Texas Press.

———. 2010b. "The Victims of Ciudad Juárez Feminicide: Sexually Fetishized Commodities." In *Terrorizing Women: Feminicide in the Américas*, edited by Rosa-Linda Fregoso and Cynthia Bejarano, 59–69. Durham, NC: Duke University Press.

Monárrez Fragoso, Julia E., and Cynthia Bejarano. 2010. "The Disarticulation of Justice: Precarious Life and Cross-Border Feminicides in the Paso del Norte Region." In *Cities and Citizenship at the U.S.-Mexico Border: The Paso del Norte Metropolitan Region*, edited by Kathleen Staudt, César M. Fuentes, and Julia E. Monárrez Fragoso, 43–70. New York: Palgrave Macmillan.

Monsiváis, Carlos. 1971. *Días de guardar*. Mexico, DF: Ediciones Era.

Montaigne, Michel de. 1965. *Essais*. 3 vols. Edited by Pierre Michel. Paris: Éditions Gallimard.

Moreiras, Alberto. 2007. "Infrapolitics and the Thriller: A Prolegomenon to Every Possible Form of Anti-Moralist Literary Criticism: On Héctor Aguilar Camín's *La guerra de Galio* and *Morir en el golfo*." In *The Ethics of Latin American Literary Criticism: Reading Otherwise*, edited by Erin Graff Zivin, 137–189. New York: Palgrave Macmillan.

Morison, Samuel Eliot. 1942. *Admiral of the Ocean Sea: A Life of Christopher Columbus*. Boston: Little, Brown.

Naas, Michael. 2008. *Derrida from Now On*. New York: Fordham University Press.

The New Oxford Annotated Bible. 2004. Oxford: Oxford University Press.

Nicol, Eduardo. 2009 [1958]. "El falso problema de la intercomunicación." In *La fenomenología en México: Historia y antología*, edited by Antonio Zirión Quijano, 487–506. Mexico, DF: Universidad Nacional Autónoma de México.

O'Gorman, Edmundo. 1998 [1958]. *La invención de América: Investigación acerca de la estructura histórica del Nuevo Mundo y del sentido de su devenir*. Mexico, DF: Fondo de Cultura Económica.

Ortigues, Edmond. 1962. *Le discours et le symbole*. Paris: Éditions Aubier-Montaigne.

Osorno, Diego Enrique. 2012. *La guerra de los Zetas: Viaje por la frontera de la necropolítica*. Mexico, DF: Grijalbo.

Oyarzún, Pablo. 2009. *La letra volada: Ensayos sobre literatura*. Santiago, Chile: Universidad Diego Portales.

Paz, Octavio. 1967 [1956]. *El arco y la lira*. Mexico, DF: Fondo de Cultura Económica.

———. 1979. *El ogro filantrópico: Historia y política, 1971–1978*. Mexico, DF: Joaquín Mortiz.

———. 1985. *The Labyrinth of Solitude and The Other Mexico; Return to the Labyrinth of Solitude; Mexico and the United States; The Philanthropic Ogre*. Translated by Lysander Kemp, Yara Milos, and Rachel Phillips Belash. New York: Grove Press.

———. 1990. *Pequeña crónica de grandes días*. Mexico, DF: Fondo de Cultura Económica.

———. 1999. *El laberinto de la soledad, Postdata, Vuelta a El labertino de la soledad*. 3rd ed. Mexico, DF: Fondo de Cultura Económica.

Poniatowska, Elena. 1971. *La noche de Tlatelolco: Testimonios de historia oral*. Mexico, DF: Ediciones Era.

———. 2007. *La herida de Paulina*. Barcelona: Seix Barral.

Rabanaque, Luis Roman. 2005. "Hyle, Genesis, and Noema." *Husserl Studies* 19: 205–215.

Ramos, Samuel. 1990. *Obras completas*. 3 vols. Mexico, DF: Universidad Nacional Autónoma de México.

Rancière, Jacques. 1995. *La mésentente: Politique et philosophie*. Paris: Éditions Galilée.

———. 1999. *Disagreement: Politics and Philosophy*. Translated by Julie Rose. Minneapolis, MN: University of Minnesota Press.

Reguillo, Rossana. 2011. "La narcomáquina y el trabajo de la violencia: Apuntes para su decodificación." *E-misférica* 8, no. 2. Accessed 29 July 2016. http://hemispheric institute.org/hemi/es/e-misferica-82/reguillo.

Restall, Matthew. 1998. *Maya Conquistador*. Boston: Beacon.

Reyes, Alfonso. 1960a. *Vision de Anáhuac 1519*. In *Obras completas*, 2:10–35. Mexico, DF: Fondo de Cultura Económica.

———. 1960b. "Pasado inmediato." In *Obras completas*, 12:182–216. Mexico, DF: Fondo de Cultura Económica.

———. 1962. *La experiencia literaria*. In *Obras completas*, 14:19–233. Mexico, DF: Fondo de Cultura Económica.

———. 1963a. *El deslinde*. In *Obras completas*, 15:17–422. Mexico, DF: Fondo de Cultura Económica.

———. 1963b. "Algo de Semántica." In *Obras completas*, 21:214–234. Mexico, DF: Fondo de Cultura Económica.

———. 2009 [1942]. "El espejo de Husserl." In *La fenomenología en México: Historia y antología*, edited by Antonio Zirión Quijano, 327–331. Mexico, DF: Universidad Nacional Autónoma de México.

Rodríguez, Ileana. 2009. *Liberalism at Its Limits: Crime and Terror in the Latin American Cultural Text*. Pittsburg: University of Pittsburg Press.

Rogozinski, Jacob. 2017. *Djihadisme: Le retour du sacrifice*. Paris: Éditions Desclée de Brouwer.

Sahagún, Bernardino de. 1999 [c. 1585]. *Historia general de las cosas de Nueva España*. Edited by Ángel María Garibay K. Mexico, DF: Porrúa.

Santos-Herceg, José. 2011. *Conflicto de representaciones: América Latina como lugar para la filosofía*. Santiago: Fondo de Cultura Económica.

Schmid, David. 2005. *Natural Born Celebrities: Serial Killers in American Culture*. Chicago: University of Chicago Press.

Schmidt Camacho, Alicia R. 2005. "Ciudadanía X: Gender Violence and the Denationalization of Women's Rights in Ciudad Juárez, Mexico." *CR: The New Centennial Review* 5, no. 1: 255–292.

Segato, Rita Laura. 2010. "Territory, Sovereignty, and Crimes of the Second State: The Writing on the Body of Murdered Women." Translated by Sara Koopman. In *Terrorizing Women: Feminicide in the Américas*, edited by Rosa-Linda Fregoso and Cynthia Bejarano, 70–92. Durham, NC: Duke University Press.

Shell, Marc. 1993. *Money, Language, and Thought*. Baltimore: Johns Hopkins University Press.

Shershow, Scott Cutler. 2014. *Deconstructing Dignity: A Critique of the Right-to-Die Debate*. Chicago: University of Chicago Press.

Smith, David Woodruff, and Ronald McIntyre. 1975. "Husserl's Identification of Meaning and Noema," *The Monist* 59, no. 1: 115–132.

Staudt, Kathleen, César M. Fuentes, and Julia E. Monárrez Fragoso, eds. 2010. *Cities and Citizenship at the U.S.-Mexico Border: The Paso del Norte Metropolitan Region*. New York: Palgrave Macmillan.

Stavans, Ilan. 2002. "Unmasking Marcos." In *The Zapatista Reader*, edited by Tom Hayden, 386–395. New York: Nation Books.

Steinberg, Samuel. 2016. *Photopoetics of Tlatelolco: Afterimages of 1968*. Austin: University of Texas Press.

Stephens, John Lloyd. 1963 [1843]. *Incidents of Travel in Yucatán*. 2 vols. New York: Dover.

———. 1969 [1841]. *Incidents of Travel in Central America, Chiapas, and Yucatán*. 2 vols. New York: Dover.

Sussman, Henry. 2009. "The Phenomenology of Jetlag." *MLN* 124: 1031–1047.

Tabuenca Córdova, María Socorro. 2010. "Ghost Dance in Ciudad Juárez at the End/Beginning of the Millennium." Translated by Georgina Guzmán. In *Making a Killing: Femicide, Free Trade, and La Frontera*, edited by Alicia Gaspar de Alba, with Georgina Guzmán, 95–119. Austin: University of Texas Press.

Taibo, Paco Ignacio, II. 2004. *'68*. Translated by Donald Nicholson-Smith. New York: Seven Stories Press.

———. 2008. *68*. Mexico, DF: Editorial Planeta Mexicana.

Taussig, Michael. 1999. *Defacement: Public Secrecy and the Labor of the Negative*. Stanford, CA: Stanford University Press.

Todorov, Tzvetan. 1982. *La conquête de l'Amerique: La question de l'autre*. Paris: Éditions Seuil.

———. 1984. *The Conquest of America: The Question of the Other*. Translated by Richard Howard. New York: Harper and Row.

———. 1995. *The Morals of History*. Translated by Alyson Waters. Minneapolis: University of Minnesota Press.

Uranga, Emilio. 2013 [1952]. *Análisis del ser del mexicano*. Mexico, DF: Porrúa y Obregón.

Uslar Pietri, Arturo. 1996. *La invención de América Mestiza*. Edited by Gustavo Luis Carrera. Mexico, DF: Fondo de Cultura Económica.

Valadés, Diego de. 1989 [1579]. *Retórica cristiana*. Translated by Tarsicio Herrera Zapión. Mexico City: Universidad Nacional Autónoma de México/Fondo de Cultura Económica.

Vasconcelos, José. 1997. *The Cosmic Race/La raza cósmica*. Translated by Didier T. Jaén. Baltimore: Johns Hopkins University Press.

Villalobos-Ruminott, Sergio. 2013. *Soberanías en suspenso: Imaginación y violencia en América Latina*. Buenos Aires: Ediciones la Cebra.

Villoro, Luis. 1996 [1950]. *Los grandes momentos del indigenismo en México*. Mexico, DF: Fondo de Cultura Económica.

———. 1997. *El poder y el valor: Fundamentos de una ética política*. Mexico, DF: Fondo de Cultura Económica.

———. 2007. *Los retos de la sociedad por venir: Ensayos sobre justicia, democracia y multiculturalismo*. Mexico, DF: Fondo de Cultura Económica.

Volpi, Jorge. 1998. *La imaginación y el poder: Una historia intellectual de 1968*. Mexico, DF: Ediciones Era.

———. 2004. *La guerra y las palabras: Una historia intelectual*. Mexico, DF: Ediciones Era.

———. 2008. *Mentiras contagiosas: Ensayos*. Madrid: Editorial Páginas de Espuma.

———. 2011. *Leer la mente: El cerebro y el arte de la ficción*. Mexico, DF: Santillana Ediciones Generales.

Washington Valdez, Diana. 2006. *The Killing Fields: Harvest of Women—The Truth about Mexico's Bloody Border Legacy*. Los Angeles: Peace at the Border Publications.

Williams, Gareth. 2011. *The Mexican Exception: Sovereignty, Police, and Democracy*. New York: Palgrave Macmillan.

Zahavi, Dan. 2004. "Husserl's Noema and the Internalism-Externalism Debate." *Inquiry* 47, no. 1: 42–66.

Zamora, Margarita. 1993. *Reading Columbus*. Berkeley: University of California Press.

¡Zapatistas! Documents of the New Mexican Revolution (December 31, 1993–June 12, 1994). 1994. Brooklyn, NY: Autonomedia.

Zea, Leopoldo. 1952. *Conciencia y posibilidad del mexicano y El occidente y la conciencia de México: Dos ensayos sobre México y lo mexicano*. Mexico, DF: Editorial Porrúa.

Zirión Quijano, Antonio, ed. 2009. *La fenomenología en México: Historia y antología*. Mexico, DF: Universidad Nacional Autónoma de México.

INDEX